The I-Series

Microsoft® Office
Access 2003

Brief

The I-Series

Microsoft® Office Access 2003

Brief

Stephen Haag
University of Denver

James Perry
University of San Diego

Merrill Wells
University of Denver

McGraw Hill **Technology Education**

Boston   Burr Ridge, IL   Dubuque, IA   Madison, WI   New York   San Francisco   St. Louis
Bangkok   Bogotá   Caracas   Kuala Lumpur   Lisbon   London   Madrid   Mexico City
Milan   Montreal   New Delhi   Santiago   Seoul   Singapore   Sydney   Taipei   Toronto

 Technology Education

THE I-SERIES: MICROSOFT OFFICE ACCESS 2003, BRIEF

Published by McGraw-Hill/Technology Education, a business unit of The McGraw-Hill Companies, Inc., 1221 Avenue of the Americas, New York, NY, 10020. Copyright © 2004 by The McGraw-Hill Companies, Inc. All rights reserved. No part of this publication may be reproduced or distributed in any form or by any means, or stored in a database or retrieval system, without the prior written consent of The McGraw-Hill Companies, Inc., including, but not limited to, in any network or other electronic storage or transmission, or broadcast for distance learning.
Some ancillaries, including electronic and print components, may not be available to customers outside the United States.

This book is printed on acid-free paper.

1 2 3 4 5 6 7 8 9 0 WEB/WEB 0 9 8 7 6 5 4 3

ISBN 0-07-283058-1

Editor-in-chief: *Bob Woodbury*
Publisher: *Brandon Nordin*
Senior sponsoring editor: *Donald J. Hull*
Associate sponsoring editor: *Craig S. Leonard*
Editorial assistant: *Veronica Vergoth*
Marketing manager: *Andy Bernier*
Senior producer, Media technology: *David Barrick*
Lead project manager: *Mary Conzachi*
Senior production supervisor: *Rose Hepburn*
Lead designer: *Pam Verros*
Senior supplement producer: *Rose M. Range*
Senior digital content specialist: *Brian Nacik*
Cover design: *Asylum Studios*
Interior design: *Mary Christianson*
Typeface: *10.5/12 Minion*
Compositor: *GAC Indianapolis*
Printer: *Webcrafters, Inc.*

Library of Congress Cataloging-in-Publication Data
Haag, Stephen.
    Microsoft Office Access 2003 : brief / Stephen Haag, James Perry, Merrill Wells.—1st ed.
        p. cm.—(The I-series)
    Includes Index
    ISBN 0-07-283058-1 (alk. paper)
    1. Database management. 2. Microsoft Access. I. Perry, James T. II. Wells, Merrill.
III. Title. IV. Series
QA76.9.D3H328 2004
005.75'65—dc22

www.mhhe.com

MCGRAW-HILL TECHNOLOGY EDUCATION

At McGraw-Hill Technology Education, we publish instructional materials for the technology education market, in particular computer instruction in post-secondary education—from introductory courses in traditional 4-year universities to continuing education and proprietary schools. McGraw-Hill Technology Education presents a broad range of innovative products—texts, lab manuals, study guides, testing materials, and technology-based training and assessment tools.

We realize that technology has created and will continue to create new mediums for professors and students to use in managing resources and communicating information to one another. McGraw-Hill Technology Education provides the most flexible and complete teaching and learning tools available, and offers solutions to the changing world of teaching and learning. McGraw-Hill Technology Education is dedicated to providing the tools for today's instructors and students that will enable them to successfully navigate the world of Information Technology.

- McGraw-Hill/Osborne—This division of The McGraw-Hill Companies is known for its best-selling Internet titles, Harley Hahn's *Internet & Web Yellow Pages*, and the *Internet Complete Reference*. For more information, visit Osborne at www.osborne.com.

- Digital Solutions—Whether you want to teach a class online or just post your "bricks-n-mortar" class syllabus, McGraw-Hill Technology Education is committed to publishing digital solutions. Taking your course online doesn't have to be a solitary adventure, nor does it have to be a difficult one. We offer several solutions that will allow you to enjoy all the benefits of having your course material online.

- Packaging Options—For more information about our discount options, contact your McGraw-Hill sales representative at 1-800-338-3987 or visit our Web site at www.mhhe.com/it.

McGraw-Hill Technology Education is dedicated to providing the tools for today's instructors and students

THE I-SERIES PAGE

By using the I-Series, students will be able to learn and master applications skills by being actively engaged—by *doing*. The "I" in I-Series demonstrates Insightful tasks that will not only Inform students, but also Involve them while learning the applications.

How Will the I-Series Accomplish This for You?

Through relevant, real-world chapter opening cases.

Tasks throughout each chapter incorporating steps and tips for easy reference.

Alternative methods and styles of learning to keep the student involved.

Rich, end-of-chapter materials that support what the student has learned.

I-Series Titles Include:

Computer Concepts

Computing Concepts, 2e, Introductory

Computing Concepts, 2e, Complete

Microsoft Office Applications

Microsoft Office 2003, Volume I

Microsoft Office 2003, Volume II

Microsoft Office Word 2003 (Brief, Introductory, Complete Versions) 11 Total Chapters

Microsoft Office Excel 2003 (Brief, Introductory, Complete Versions) 12 Total Chapters

Microsoft Office Access 2003 (Brief, Introductory, Complete Versions) 12 Total Chapters

Microsoft Office PowerPoint 2003 (Brief, Introductory Versions) 8 Total Chapters

Microsoft Office Outlook 2003 (Brief, Introductory Versions) 8 Total Chapters

Microsoft Office FrontPage 2003 (Brief Version) 4 Total Chapters

Microsoft Office XP, Volume I

Microsoft Office XP, Volume I Expanded (with Internet Essentials bonus chapters)

Microsoft Office XP, Volume II

Microsoft Word 2002 (Brief, Introductory, Complete Versions) 12 Total Chapters

Microsoft Excel 2002 (Brief, Introductory, Complete Versions) 12 Total Chapters

Microsoft Access 2002 (Brief, Introductory, Complete Versions) 12 Total Chapters

Microsoft PowerPoint 2002 (Brief, Introductory Versions) 8 Total Chapters

Microsoft Internet Explorer 6.0 (Brief Version) 5 Total Chapters

Microsoft Windows

Microsoft Windows 2000 (Brief, Introductory, Complete Versions) 12 Total Chapters

Microsoft Windows XP (Brief, Introductory, Complete Versions) 12 Total Chapters

For additional resources, visit The I-Series Online Learning Center at www.mhhe.com/i-series

GOALS/PHILOSOPHY

The I-Series applications textbooks strongly emphasize that students learn and master applications skills by being actively engaged—by *doing*. We made the decision that teaching how to accomplish tasks is not enough for complete understanding and mastery. Students must understand the importance of each of the tasks that lead to a finished product at the end of each chapter.

Approach

The I-Series chapters are subdivided into sessions that contain related groups of tasks with active, hands-on components. The session tasks containing numbered steps collectively result in a completed project at the end of each session. Prior to introducing numbered steps that show how to accomplish a particular task, we discuss why the steps are important. We discuss the role that the collective steps play in the overall plan for creating or modifying a document or object, answering students' often-heard questions, "Why are we doing these steps? Why are these steps important?" Without an explanation of why an activity is important and what it accomplishes, students can easily find themselves following the steps but not registering the big picture of what the steps accomplish and why they are executing them.

I-Series Applications for 2003

The I-Series offers three levels of instruction. Each level builds upon knowledge from the previous level. With the exception of the running project that is the last exercise of every chapter, chapter cases and end-of-chapter exercises are independent from one chapter to the next, with the exception of Access. The three levels available are

Brief Covers the basics of the Microsoft application and contains Chapters 1 through 4. The Brief textbooks are typically 200 pages long.

Introductory Includes chapters in the Brief textbook plus Chapters 5 through 8. Introductory textbooks typically are 400 pages long and prepare students for the Microsoft Office Specialist (MOS) Core Exam.

Complete Includes the Introductory textbook plus Chapters 9 through 12. The four additional chapters cover advanced-level content and the textbooks are typically 600 pages long. Complete textbooks prepare students for the Microsoft Office Specialist (MOS) Expert Exam. The Microsoft Office User Specialist program is recognized around the world as the standard for demonstrating proficiency using Microsoft Office applications.

In addition, there are two compilation volumes available.

Office I Includes introductory chapters on Windows and Computing Concepts followed by Chapters 1 through 4 (Brief textbook) of Word, Excel, Access, and PowerPoint. In addition, material from the companion Computing Concepts book is integrated into the first few chapters to provide students with an understanding of the relationship between Microsoft Office applications and computer information systems.

Office II Includes introductory chapters on Windows and Computing Concepts followed by Chapters 5 through 8 from each of the Introductory-level textbooks including Word, Excel, Access, and PowerPoint. In addition, material from the companion Computing Concepts book is integrated into the introductory chapters to provide students with a deeper understanding of the relationship between Microsoft Office applications and computer information systems. An introduction to Visual Basic for Applications (VBA) completes the Office II textbook.

STEPHEN HAAG

Stephen Haag is a professor and Chair of Information Technology and Electronic Commerce and the Director of Technology in the University of Denver's Daniels College of Business. Stephen holds a B.B.A. and M.B.A. from West Texas State University and a Ph.D. from the University of Texas at Arlington. He has published numerous articles appearing in such journals as *Communications of the ACM, The International Journal of Systems Science, Applied Economics, Managerial and Decision Economics, Socio-Economic Planning Sciences,* and the *Australian Journal of Management.*

Stephen is also the author of 20 other books including *Interactions: Teaching English as a Second Language* (with his mother and father), *Case Studies in Information Technology, Information Technology: Tomorrow's Advantage Today* (with Peter Keen), and *Excelling in Finance.* He is also the lead author of the accompanying I-Series *Computing Concepts* text, released in both an Introductory and a Complete version. Stephen lives with his wife, Pam, and their four sons—Indiana, Darian, Trevor, and Elvis—in Highlands Ranch, Colorado.

JAMES PERRY

James Perry is a professor of Management Information Systems in the University of San Diego's School of Business. He holds a B.S. in mathematics from Purdue University and a Ph.D. in computer science from The Pennsylvania State University. Jim has published several journal and conference papers. He is the co-author of 60 other textbooks and trade books including *Using Access with Accounting Systems, Building Accounting Systems, Understanding Oracle, The Internet,* and *Electronic Commerce.* His books have been translated into Chinese, Dutch, French, and Korean. Jim teaches both undergraduate and graduate courses at the University of San Diego and has worked as a computer security consultant to various private and governmental organizations including the Jet Propulsion Laboratory. He was a consultant on the Strategic Defense Initiative ("Star Wars") project and served as a member of the computer security oversight committee. Jim lives with his wife, Nancy, in San Diego, California. He has three grown children: Jessica, Stirling, and Kelly.

PAIGE BALTZAN

Paige Baltzan is a professor of Information Technology and Electronic Commerce in the University of Denver's Daniels College of Business. Paige holds a B.S.B.A. from Bowling Green State University and an M.B.A. from the University of Denver. Paige's primary concentration focuses on object-oriented technologies and systems development methodologies. She has been teaching Systems Analysis and Design, Telecommunications and Networking, Software Engineering, and The Global Information Economy at the University of Denver for the past three years. Paige has contributed materials for several McGraw-Hill publications including *Using Information Technology* and *Management Information Systems for the Information Age.*

Prior to joining the University of Denver Paige spent three years working at Level(3) Communications as a Technical Architect and four years working at Andersen Consulting as a Technology Consultant in the telecommunications industry. Paige lives in Lakewood, Colorado, with her husband, Tony, and her daughter, Hannah.

AMY PHILLIPS

Amy Phillips is a professor of Information Technology and Electronic Commerce in the University of Denver's Daniels College of Business. She holds a B.S. degree in environmental biology and an M.S. degree in education from Plymouth State College. Amy has been teaching for more than 18 years: 5 years in public secondary education and 13 years in higher education. She has also been an integral part of both the academic and administrative functions within the higher educational system.

Amy's main concentration revolves around database driven Web sites focusing on dynamic Web content, specifically ASP and XML technologies. Some of the main core course selections that Amy teaches at the University of Denver include Analysis and Design, Database Management Systems, Using Technology to Communicate, and Using Technology to Manage Information. Her first book, *Internet Explorer 6.0,* written with Stephen Haag and James Perry, was published in September 2002.

MERRILL WELLS

Merrill Wells is a professor of Information Technology and Electronic Commerce in the University of Denver's Daniels College of Business. Merrill holds a B.A. and M.B.A. from Indiana University. Although her goal was to teach and write, she followed the advice of her professors and set out to gain business experience before becoming a professor herself.

Merrill began her nonacademic career as a business systems programmer developing manufacturing, accounting, and payroll software using relational databases. Throughout her first career Merrill worked in the aerospace, manufacturing, construction, and oil and gas industries. After years of writing technical manuals and training end users, Merrill honored her original goal and returned to academia to become an active instructor of both graduate and undergraduate technology courses.

Merrill is the author of several online books including *An Introduction to Computers, Introduction to Visual Basic,* and *Programming Logic and Design.* Merrill lives with her husband, Rick, in Denver, Colorado. They have four children—Daniel, Dusty, Victoria (Tori), and Evan—and foster twins Connor and Gage.

Each textbook features the following:

Did You Know   Each chapter has six or seven interesting facts—about both high-tech and other topics.

Sessions   Each chapter is divided into two or three sessions.

Chapter Outline   Provides students with a quick map of the major headings in the chapter.

Chapter and Microsoft Office Specialist Objectives   At the beginning of each chapter is a list of 5 to 10 action-oriented objectives. Any chapter objectives that are also Microsoft Office Specialist objectives indicate the Microsoft Office Specialist objective number.

Chapter Opening Case   Each chapter begins with a case. Cases describe a mixture of fictitious and real people and companies and the needs of the people and companies. Throughout the chapter, the student gains the skills and knowledge to solve the problem stated in the case.

Introduction   The chapter introduction establishes the overview of the chapter's activities in the context of the case problem.

Another Way and Another Word   Another Way is a highlighted feature providing a bulleted list of steps to accomplish a task, or best practices—that is, a better or faster way to accomplish a task such as pasting a format onto an Excel cell. Another Word, another highlighted box, briefly explains more about a topic or highlights a potential pitfall.

Step-by-Step Instructions   Numbered step-by-step instructions for all hands-on activities appear in a distinctive color. Keyboard characters and menu selections appear in a **special format** to emphasize what the user should press or type. Steps make clear to the student the exact sequence of keystrokes and mouse clicks needed to complete a task such as formatting a Word paragraph.

Tips   Tips appear within a numbered sequence of steps and warn the student of possible missteps or provide alternatives to the step that precedes the tip.

Task Reference and Task Reference Summary   Task References appear throughout the textbook. Set in a distinctive design, each Task Reference contains a bulleted list of steps showing a generic way to accomplish activities that are especially important or significant. A Task Reference Summary at the end of each chapter summarizes a chapter's Task References.

Microsoft Office Specialist Objectives Summary   A list of Microsoft Office Specialist objectives covered in a chapter appears in the chapter objectives and the chapter summary.

Making the Grade   Short answer questions appear at the end of each chapter's sessions. They test a student's grasp of each session's contents, and Making the Grade answers appear at the end of each chapter so students can check their answers.

Rich End-of-Chapter Materials   End-of-chapter materials incorporating a three-level approach reinforce learning and help students take ownership of the chapter. Level One, Review of Terminology, contains fill in the blank, true/false, and multiple choice questions that enforce review of a chapter's key terms. Level Two, Review of Concepts, contains review questions and a Jeopardy-style create-a-question exercise. Level Three contains Hands-On Projects (see the paragraph following this one). Level Four, Analysis, contains short questions that require students to step back from the details of what they learned and think about higher level concepts covered in the chapter.

Hands-On Projects   Extensive hands-on projects engage the student in a problem-solving exercise from start to finish. There are seven clearly labeled categories that each contain one or two questions. Categories are Practice, Challenge!, E-Business, On the Web, Around the World, Analysis, and a Running Project that carries throughout all the chapters.

We understand that, in today's teaching environment, offering a textbook alone is not sufficient to meet the needs of the many instructors who use our books. To teach effectively, instructors must have a full complement of supplemental resources to assist them in every facet of teaching, from preparing for class to conducting a lecture to assessing students' comprehension. The **I-Series** offers a complete supplements package and Web site that is briefly described below.

INSTRUCTOR'S RESOURCE KIT

The Instructor's Resource Kit is a CD-ROM containing the Instructor's Manual in both MS Word and .pdf formats, PowerPoint Slides with Presentation Software, Brownstone test-generating software, and accompanying test item files in both MS Word and .pdf formats for each chapter. The CD also contains figure files from the text, student data files, and solutions files. The features of each of the three main components of the Instructor's Resource Kit are highlighted below.

Instructor's Manual Featuring:

- Chapter learning objectives
- Chapter key terms
- Chapter outline and lecture notes
  - Teaching suggestions
  - Classroom tips, tricks, and traps
  - Page number references
- Additional end-of-chapter practice projects
- Answers to all Making the Grade and end-of-chapter questions
- Text figures

PowerPoint Presentation

The PowerPoint presentation is designed to provide instructors with comprehensive lecture and teaching resources that will include

- Chapter learning objectives followed by source content that illustrates key terms and key facts per chapter
- FAQ (frequently asked questions) to show key concepts throughout the chapter; also lecture notes, to illustrate these key concepts and ideas

- End-of-chapter exercises and activities per chapter, as taken from the end-of-chapter materials in the text
- Speaker's Notes, to be incorporated throughout the slides per chapter
- Figures/screen shots, to be incorporated throughout the slides per chapter

Test Bank

The I-Series Test Bank, using Diploma Network Testing Software by Brownstone, contains over 3,000 questions (both objective and interactive) categorized by topic, page reference to the text, and difficulty level of learning. Each question is assigned a learning category:

- Level 1: Key Terms and Facts
- Level 2: Key Concepts
- Level 3: Application and Problem-Solving

The types of questions consist of 20 percent Multiple Choice, 50 percent True/False, and 30 percent Fill-in-the-Blank Questions.

ONLINE LEARNING CENTER/ WEB SITE

To locate the I-Series OLC/Web site directly, go to www.mhhe.com/i-series. The site is divided into three key areas:

- **Information Center** Contains core information about the text, the authors, and a guide to our additional features and benefits of the series, including the supplements.
- **Instructor Center** Offers instructional materials, downloads, additional activities and answers to additional projects, answers to chapter troubleshooting exercises, answers to chapter preparation/post exercises posed to students, relevant links for professors, and more.
- **Student Center** Contains chapter objectives and outlines, self-quizzes, chapter troubleshooting exercises, chapter preparation/post exercises, additional projects, simulations, student data files and solutions files, Web links, and more.

RESOURCES FOR STUDENTS

SimNet

SimNet is a simulated assessment and learning tool for either Microsoft® Office XP or Microsoft® Office 2003. SimNet allows students to study MS Office skills and computer concepts, and professors to test and evaluate students' proficiency, within MS Office applications and concepts. Students can practice and study their skills at home or in the school lab using SimNet, which does not require the purchase or installation of Office software. SimNet includes:

Structured Computer-Based Learning **SimNet** offers a complete computer-based learning side that presents each skill or topic in several different modes. *Teach Me* presents the skill or topic using text, graphics, and interactivity. *Show Me* presents the skill using an animation with audio narration to show how the skill is used or implemented. *Let Me Try* allows you to practice the skill in SimNet's robust simulated interface.

Computer Concepts Coverage! **SimNet** includes coverage of 60 computer concepts in both the Learning and the Assessment side.

The Basics and More! **SimNet** includes modules of content on:

Word	Windows 2000
Excel	Computer Concepts
Access	Windows XP Professional
PowerPoint	Internet Explorer 6
Office XP Integration	FrontPage
Outlook	

More Assessment Questions! **SimNet** includes over *1,400* assessment questions.

Practice or Pre-Tests Questions! **SimNet** has a separate pool of over *600* questions for Practice Tests or Pre-Tests.

Comprehensive Exercises! **SimNet** offers comprehensive exercises for each application. These exercises require the student to use multiple skills to solve one exercise in the simulated environment.

Simulated Interface! The simulated environment in **SimNet** has been substantially deepened to more realistically simulate the real applications. Now students are not graded incorrect just because they chose the wrong submenu or dialog box. The student is not graded until he or she does something that immediately invokes an action—just like the real applications!

DIGITAL SOLUTIONS FOR INSTRUCTORS AND STUDENTS

PageOut PageOut is our Course Web Site Development Center that offers a syllabus page, URL, McGraw-Hill Online Learning Center content, online exercises and quizzes, gradebook, discussion board, and an area for student Web pages. For more information, visit the PageOut Web site at www.pageout.net.

Online Courses Available OLCs are your perfect solutions for Internet-based content. Simply put, these Centers are "digital cartridges" that contain a book's pedagogy and supplements. As students read the book, they can go online and take self-grading quizzes or work through interactive exercises.

Online Learning Centers can be delivered through any of these platforms:

McGraw-Hill Learning Architecture (TopClass)

Blackboard.com

College.com (formerly Real Education)

WebCT (a product of Universal Learning Technology)

Did You Know?

A unique presentation of text and graphics introduce interesting and little-known facts.

CHAPTER

one

1

Creating Worksheets for Decision Makers

did you

know?

one-third *of online shoppers abandon their electronic shopping carts before completing the checkout process.*

goldfish *lose their color if they are kept in a dim light or if they are placed in a body of running water such as a stream.*

electric *eels are not really eels but a type of fish.*

in *1963, baseball pitcher Gaylord Perry said, "They'll put a man on the moon before I hit a home run." Only a few hours after Neil Armstrong set foot on the moon on July 20, 1969, Perry hit the first and only home run of his career.*

Chapter Objectives

- Start Excel and open a workbook
- Move around a worksheet using the mouse and arrow keys
- Locate supporting information (help)—MOS XL03S-1-3
- Select a block of cells
- Type into worksheet cells text, values, formulas, and functions—MOS XL03S-2-3
- Edit and clear cell entries—MOS XL03S-1-1
- Save a workbook
- Add a header and a footer—MOS XL03S-5-7
- Preview output—MOS XL03S-5-5
- Print a worksheet and print a worksheet's formulas—MOS XL03S-5-8
- Exit Excel

Chapter Objectives

Each chapter begins with a list of competencies covered in the chapter.

Task Reference

Provides steps to accomplish an especially important task.

task reference   Opening an Excel Workbook

- Click **File** and then click **Open**
- Ensure that the Look in list box displays the name of the folder containing your workbook
- Click the workbook's name
- Click the **Open** button

SESSION 1.1

Making the Grade

Short-answer questions appear at the end of each session, and answers appear at the end of each chapter.

making the grade

1. A popular program used to analyze numeric information and help make meaningful business decisions is called a _____ program.

2. _____ analysis is observing changes to spreadsheets and reviewing their effect on other values in the spreadsheet.

3. An Excel spreadsheet is called a(n) _____ and consists of individual pages called _____.

4. Beneath Excel's menu bar is the _____ toolbar, which contains button shortcuts for commands such as Print, and the _____ toolbar containing button shortcuts to alter the appearance of worksheets and their cells.

5. The _____ cell is the cell in which you are currently entering data.

Modifying the left and right margins:

1. With the Print Preview window still open, click the **Setup** button. The Page Setup dialog box opens

2. Click the **Margins** tab and double-click the **Left spin control box** to highlight the current left margin number

3. Type **0.5** to set the left margin to one-half inch

4. Double-click the **Right spin control box** to highlight the current right margin number

5. Type **0.5** to set the right margin to one-half inch

6. Click **OK** to close the Page Setup dialog box

tip: If you still cannot see the entire worksheet on one page, you can force the worksheet to fit by clicking the **Page** tab in the Page Setup dialog box and then click the **Fit to** option button in the Scaling section of [...] it fits on a single page

7. Click the **Close** butto[n...] and return to the wo[...]

Step-by-Step Instruction

Numbered steps guide you through the exact sequence of keystrokes to accomplish the task.

Tips

Tips appear within steps and either indicate possible missteps or provide alternatives to a step.

---

hands-on projects

practice

LEVEL **THREE**

CHAPTER ONE

1. Creating an Income Statement

Carroll's Fabricating, a machine shop providing custom metal fabricating, is preparing an income statement for its shareholders. Betty Carroll, the company's president, wants to know exactly how much net income the company has earned this year. Although Betty has prepared a preliminary worksheet with labels in place, she wants you to enter the values and a few formulas to compute cost of goods sold, gross profit, selling and advertising expenses, and net income. Figure 1.26 shows an example of a completed worksheet.

1. Open the workbook **ex01Income.xls** in your student disk in the folder Ch01

2. Click **File** and then click **Save As** to save the workbook as **Income2.xls** in the folder Ch01

3. Scan the Income Statement worksheet and type the following values in the listed cells: Cell C5, **987453**; cell B8, **64677**; cell B9, **564778**; cell B10, **-43500**; cell B15, **53223**; cell B16, **23500**; cell B17, **12560**; cell B18, **123466**; cell B19, **87672**

4. In cell C10, write the formula =SUM(B8:B10) to sum cost of goods sold

5. In cell C12, type the formula for Gross Profit: **=C5-C10**

6. In cell C19, type the formula to sum selling and advertising expenses: **=SUM(B15:B19)**

7. In cell C21, type the formula **=C122C19** to compute net income (gross profit minus total selling and advertising expenses)

8. In cell A4, type **Prepared by** <your name>

9. Click the Save button on the Standard toolbar to save your modified worksheet

10. Print the worksheet and print the worksheet formulas

FIGURE 1.26
Income statement

EX 1.41
EXCEL

www.mhhe.com/i-series

Screen Shots

Screen shots show you what to expect at critical points.

End-of-Chapter Hands-On Projects

A rich variety of projects introduced by a case lets you put into practice what you have learned. Categories include Practice, Challenge, On the Web, E-Business, Around the World, and a running case project.

---

another word   . . . on Cell Ranges

A SUM function can contain more than one cell range. For example, the function =SUM(A1:A5,B42:B51) totals two cell ranges. Place commas between distinct cell ranges within the SUM function. The collection of cells, cell ranges, and values in the comma-separated list between a function's parentheses is its **argument list**

Another Way/ Another Word

Another Way highlights an alternative way to accomplish a task; Another Word explains more about a topic.

---

task reference summary

Task	Location	Preferred Method
Opening an Excel workbook	EX 1.00	• Click **File**, click **Open**, click workbook's name, click the **Open** button
[Writing] a formula	EX 1.00	• Select cell, type =, type formula, press **Enter**
Entering the SUM function	EX 1.00	• Select cell, type =**SUM(**, type cell range, type **)**, and press **Enter**
Editing a cell	EX 1.00	• Select cell, click formula bar, make changes, press **Enter**
Saving a workbook with a new name	EX 1.00	• Click **File**, click **Save As**, type filename, click **Save** button
Obtaining help	EX 1.00	Obtaining help

Task Reference Summary

Provides a quick reference and summary of a chapter's task references.

brief *brief* contents

table of contents

The I-Series

Microsoft® Office Access 2003

Brief

1

Understanding Relational Databases

did you know?

a *NUKE InterNETWORK poll found that 52 percent of Internet users have cut back on watching TV in order to spend more time online; 12 percent have cut back on seeing friends.*

Time *magazine named the computer its "Man of the Year" in 1982.*

dating *back to the 1600s, thermometers were filled with brandy instead of mercury.*

Bill Gates *formed a company to sell a computerized traffic counting system to cities, which made $20,000 its first year. Business dropped sharply when customers learned Gates was only 14 years old.*

a *1999 survey of 25,500 standard English-language dictionary words found that _____ percent of them have been registered as .coms.*

to *find out how many English-language words had been registered as .coms by the middle of 1999, visit www.mhhe.com/i-series.*

Chapter Objectives

- Learn what relational databases are and how they function
- Define the terms *field, record, table,* and *database*
- Understand the use of primary keys, aggregate keys, and foreign keys
- Navigate Access records—MOS AC03S-2-2
- Create an Access database using a Wizard—MOS AC03S-1-1
- Create a query with the Simple Query Wizard—MOS AC03S-1-7
- Build a table with the Table Wizard—MOS AC03S-1-2
- Create an AutoForm—MOS AC03S-1-8
- Print table design—MOS AC03S-4-3
- Print data in a form and datasheet—MOS AC03S-4-3

KoryoKicks: Starting a Personal Business

Missy and Micah Hampton are twins who have been practicing martial arts for as long as they can remember. Their parents are both master instructors who participated in international competitions representing the United States when they were in college and now coach international competitors. Missy and Micah have been leading youth classes at their parents' martial arts studio and entering competitions since they were eight years old. Both are second-degree black belts.

The twins are away from home in college and are members of their college's martial arts team. Both have also made the national team. Although their course and workout schedules are very full, they need more spending money and want to go into business for themselves. Since they can no longer work for their parents but are familiar with martial arts, they have decided to offer self-defense classes to their fellow college students.

To begin, they contacted each fraternity and sorority on campus and secured permission to offer self-defense classes in the house. They then conducted demonstrations at each house willing to participate. The exhibitions consisted of forms, sparring, and board breaking emphasizing that these skills are designed to help individuals defend themselves. Students were recruited and payment accepted at the demonstrations. Classes were scheduled for two nights a week in any house with 10 or more committed students.

FIGURE 1.1
Martial arts supplies

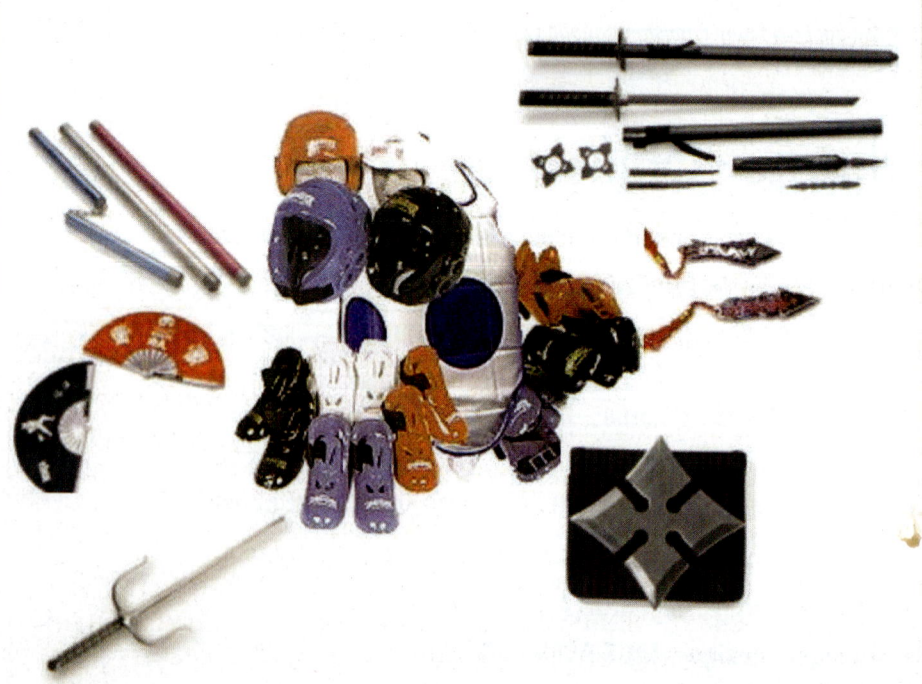

For the first classes, Micah accepted payments and handwrote the receipts while Missy collected contact information such as name, phone number, and previous self-defense experience. Unfortunately, over time this methodology proved inadequate. They were unable to keep track of when a student started, when they could test for a belt, or when they needed to pay for additional sessions.

To project a more professional image and aid in student tracking, they decided to automate by using Word for receipts and invoices and Excel to track profits and expenses. After six months the partially automated business was a success, but data were still inadequate to meet business reporting and scheduling requirements.

What had started out as a way to earn a little extra cash had grown into a complex organization with a need to collect and track multifaceted data.

They had stacks of paper relating to students, classes attended, payments, invoices, locations, customers, demonstration schedules, house contacts, and supplies (see Figure 4.1). The problem was that finding information needed to make a business decision was onerous. Something as simple as determining how many people owed money or who to contact to extend classes required a frustrating manual search.

It is obvious that the data organization and reporting capabilities of a database could help, but the twins have no experience in this area. They ask you to help them determine how best to automate data gathering and evaluation. KoryoKicks will be used throughout this book to demonstrate the data needs of an entrepreneurial business and the use of Access to develop effective data applications.

SESSION 1.1 INTRODUCING RELATIONAL DATABASES

Before evaluating the specific needs of KoryoKicks, you decide to review your knowledge of databases. Because relational databases are the most efficient way to store and manipulate data, you will focus your research on those concepts.

Uses and Benefits of Relational Databases

All organizations maintain and use data for day-to-day business operations, history, and performance analysis. Data are stored about members of the organization (employees, customers), products of the organization (services, goods), suppliers (vendors, consultants), and transactions (sales, purchases). The data maintained are determined by the needs of the organization. Schools keep data on employees, students, and business operations such as ordering products and paying for products and services.

Data are a valuable organizational resource. Good data and information retrieval technology can improve the organization's ability to compete in an industry, deliver products to consumers, and evaluate opportunities. The loss or contamination of an organization's data can contribute to failure.

A *database management system (DBMS)* is the software that is used to store data, maintain those data, and provide easy access to stored data. Good DBMSs provide users with

- Common interfaces to share data
- Software tools needed to design the storage area for data
- Facilities to maintain stored data
- Tools to create screens (forms) used to view and update data
- Query services to obtain fast answers to questions about the data
- Report generation capabilities
- Utilities to secure, back up, and restore data

Relational database management systems (RDBMSs) are a type of DBMS that store data in interrelated tables. Tables are related by sharing a common field as shown in Figure 1.2. The tblVendor and tblSoftware tables share the common field VendorCode. If you select a product like Math Tester from tblSoftware, the VendorCode from that table can be matched to the VendorCode in tblVendor to retrieve data about Academic Software, the Math Tester vendor.

RDBMSs are flexible, reliable, and efficient because they use data storage and retrieval methodology based on mathematics. *Data integrity* is the term used to describe

FIGURE   1.2

Using related tables

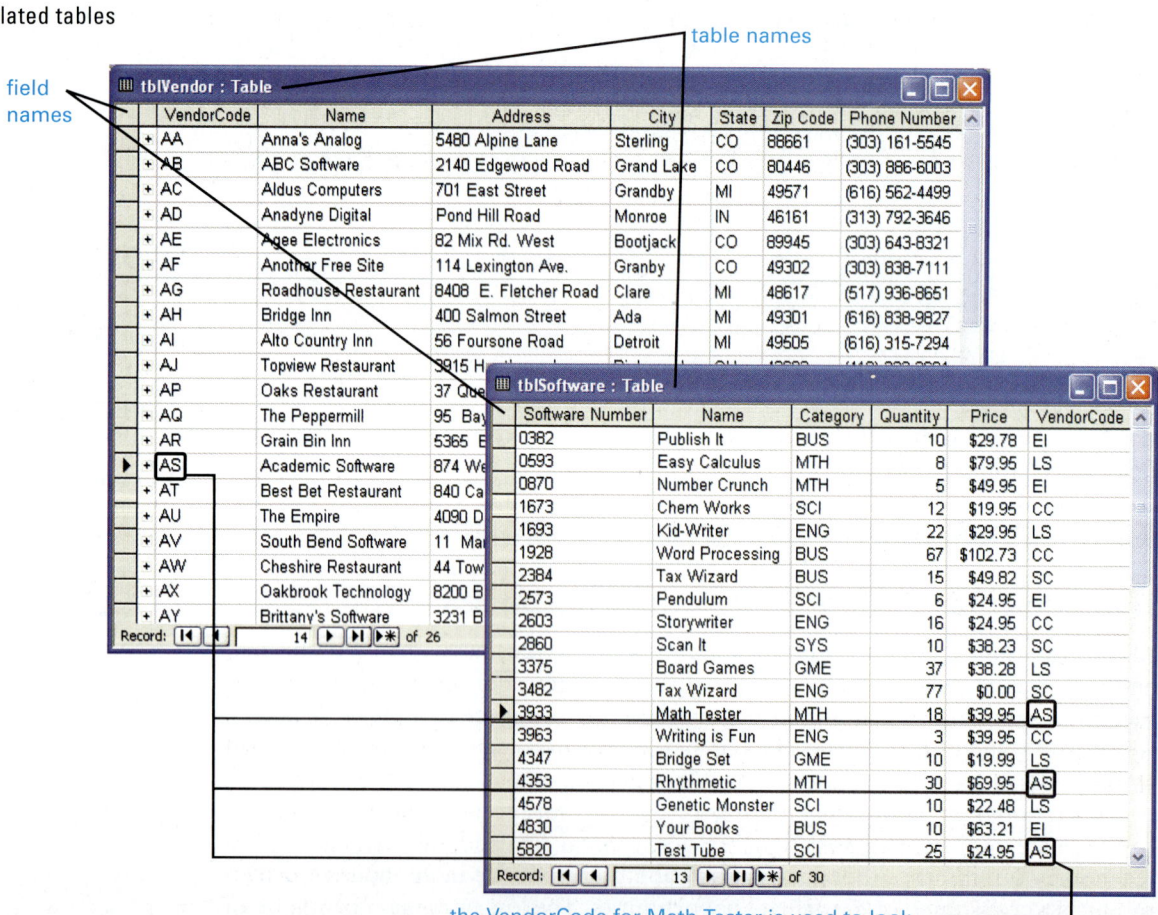

field names

table names

VendorCode	Name	Address	City	State	Zip Code	Phone Number
+ AA	Anna's Analog	5480 Alpine Lane	Sterling	CO	88661	(303) 161-5545
+ AB	ABC Software	2140 Edgewood Road	Grand Lake	CO	80446	(303) 886-6003
+ AC	Aldus Computers	701 East Street	Grandby	MI	49571	(616) 562-4499
+ AD	Anadyne Digital	Pond Hill Road	Monroe	IN	46161	(313) 792-3646
+ AE	Agee Electronics	82 Mix Rd. West	Bootjack	CO	89945	(303) 643-8321
+ AF	Another Free Site	114 Lexington Ave.	Granby	CO	49302	(303) 838-7111
+ AG	Roadhouse Restaurant	8408 E. Fletcher Road	Clare	MI	48617	(517) 936-8651
+ AH	Bridge Inn	400 Salmon Street	Ada	MI	49301	(616) 838-9827
+ AI	Alto Country Inn	56 Foursome Road	Detroit	MI	49505	(616) 315-7294
+ AJ	Topview Restaurant	3915 H				
+ AP	Oaks Restaurant	37 Que				
+ AQ	The Peppermill	95 Bay				
+ AR	Grain Bin Inn	5365 E				
+ AS	Academic Software	874 We				
+ AT	Best Bet Restaurant	840 Ca				
+ AU	The Empire	4090 D				
+ AV	South Bend Software	11 Mai				
+ AW	Cheshire Restaurant	44 Tow				
+ AX	Oakbrook Technology	8200 B				
+ AY	Brittany's Software	3231 B				

Record: 14 of 26

tblVendor : Table

tblSoftware : Table

Software Number	Name	Category	Quantity	Price	VendorCode
0382	Publish It	BUS	10	$29.78	EI
0593	Easy Calculus	MTH	8	$79.95	LS
0870	Number Crunch	MTH	5	$49.95	EI
1673	Chem Works	SCI	12	$19.95	CC
1693	Kid-Writer	ENG	22	$29.95	LS
1928	Word Processing	BUS	67	$102.73	CC
2384	Tax Wizard	BUS	15	$49.82	SC
2573	Pendulum	SCI	6	$24.95	EI
2603	Storywriter	ENG	16	$24.95	CC
2860	Scan It	SYS	10	$38.23	SC
3375	Board Games	GME	37	$38.28	LS
3482	Tax Wizard	ENG	77	$0.00	SC
3933	Math Tester	MTH	18	$39.95	AS
3963	Writing is Fun	ENG	3	$39.95	CC
4347	Bridge Set	GME	10	$19.99	LS
4353	Rhythmetic	MTH	30	$69.95	AS
4578	Genetic Monster	SCI	10	$22.48	LS
4830	Your Books	BUS	10	$63.21	EI
5820	Test Tube	SCI	25	$24.95	AS

Record: 13 of 30

the VendorCode for Math Tester is used to look up the vendor in tblVendor

the reliability of data. Data stored in a relational database are more likely to be correct because

- They are validated as they are entered using *data validation rules* to ensure that entries are within appropriate bounds
- A specific piece of data such as customer name is stored only once—thereby avoiding the errors that could be introduced by making the same update to several files. Having one update point is said to reduce *data redundancy*
- Database security ensures that only authorized people can access and update data

Relational Database Concepts

In the computing world where software becomes obsolete almost before it can be implemented, relational database technology is relatively old and stable. Relational database theory was developed by E. F. Codd, a researcher at IBM in the 1960s. The first RDBMS was released in the mid-1970s for IBM mainframes. Since then RDBMS software has been developed for every size computer and operating system. Better implementations and graphical user interfaces (GUIs) have been produced, but the basic technology remains the same.

RDBMSs provide a *data definition language (DDL)* for structuring the data tables and their relationships and a *data access language (DAL)* for rapidly retrieving and organizing stored data. Questions or queries are posed to a relational database using *Structured Query Language (SQL)*. Most database management software, including Access, provide graphical interfaces that allow users to create tables, queries, forms, and reports without knowing the underlying language.

Relations

As previously demonstrated, relational databases store data in tables. The formal name for a table is a relation. A relation (table) consists of rows and columns of related data. Each row represents the unique data for one *entity* (person, place, object, idea, or event) and also can be referred to as a *record* or tuple. Each column represents a unique property of an entity such as LastName, BirthDate, or Quantity and also can be referred to as a *field* or attribute. The intersection of a row and column contains data pertaining to one attribute of one entity and is called a *data value*. For example, $39.95 is the Price (attribute) associated with SoftwareNum 3963 (entity identifier) in Figure 1.3. A *relational database* is a collection of such relations.

All entries in the table for one attribute belong to the same *domain*. The domain is the list of all possible values of an attribute. For example, the list of all Software Names is the domain for the Name attribute in tblSoftware.

Since each cell in a table represents the value for one entity and one attribute, the order in which the columns and rows are stored is irrelevant. You can view columns and rows in any order without impacting the validity of the data. The only restriction is that a column contains data values for only one attribute and a row represents the data for one entity.

Keys

Keys are table attributes that perform a special function in the relation. The *primary key* uniquely and minimally identifies an entity with one and only one row of data. In tblSoftware above, the field Software Number holds a unique value for each software company, identifying each as a distinct entity in the table. A primary key can identify one and only one row in the table. An error message will be generated and the update aborted by the RDBMS if a duplicate primary key is entered. To meet the minimal requirement of the primary key definition, the key must contain no unnecessary data. For example, the Software Number and Name fields could be used in combination to

F I G U R E   1.3

Example of a relation (table)

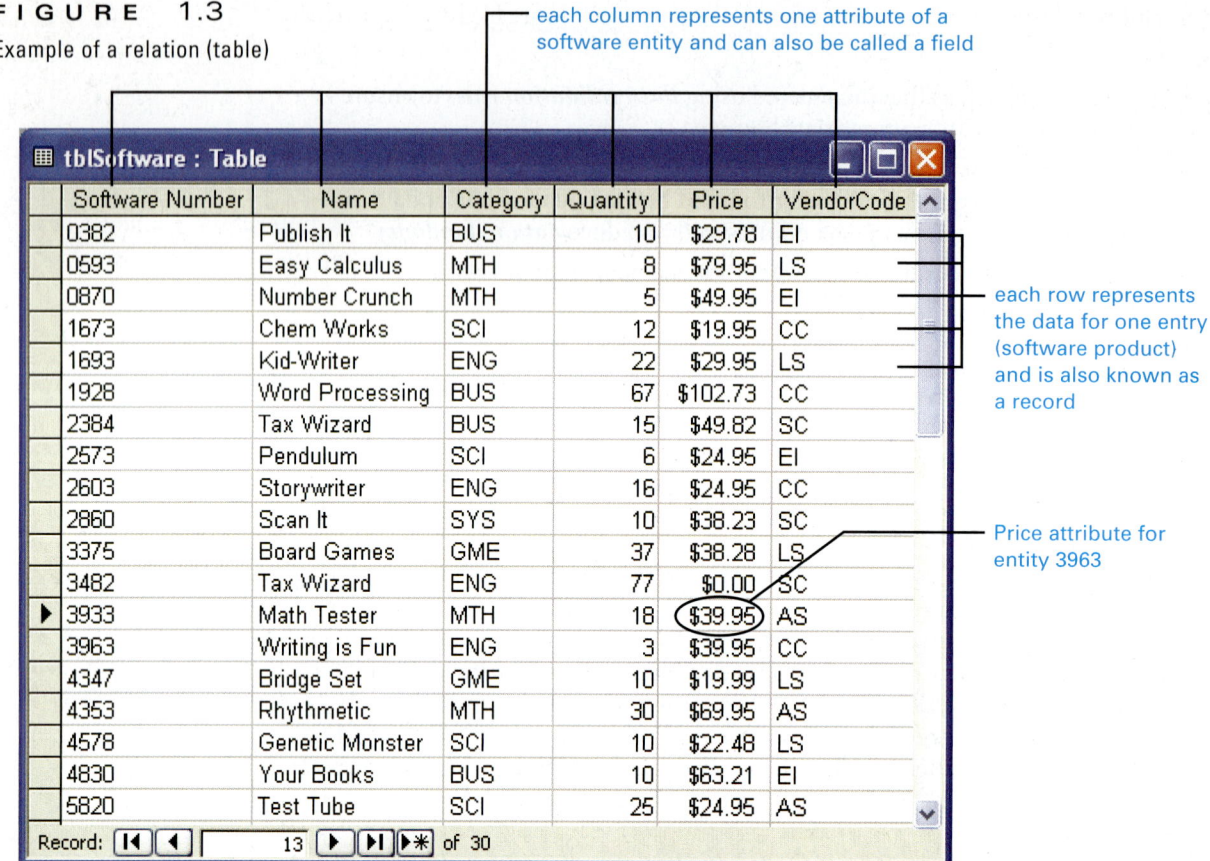

each column represents one attribute of a
software entity and can also be called a field

each row represents
the data for one entry
(software product)
and is also known as
a record

Price attribute for
entity 3963

uniquely identify each row of data in tblSoftware; however, the combination does not meet the minimal test because Software Number alone is a unique identifier.

Sometimes there is no one attribute (column) in a table with values that can uniquely identify each row of data. In such cases the designer looks for a combination of attributes that can act as the table primary key. When multiple columns of data are used for the primary key, the result is a **composite key**. As an example, a composite key is advisable when storing data about U.S. cities. The city name alone is not sufficient since multiple U.S. cities carry the same name (for example, Bloomington, IN, and Bloomington, IL). In this case, both the city and state columns would be required for a unique key.

In many instances, there are multiple attributes in the table that each could serve as the primary key of that table. Each attribute that could be defined as the primary key is called a **candidate key**. One of the candidate keys is assigned as the primary key and the others are called **alternate keys**. In tblSoftware Software Number and Name each uniquely and minimally identifies one row in the table and is therefore a candidate key. Software Number was named the primary key, so Name remains an alternate key.

A **foreign key** (see Figure 1.4) is used to match the values from one table to those in another table. VendorCode in tblSoftware is a foreign key that matches values in the tblVendor VendorCode attribute. In tblVendor VendorCode is the primary key. Most designers will give the same name to attributes stored in multiple tables so it is obvious that they are really the same attribute.

FIGURE 1.4

Software database demonstrating one-to-many relationship

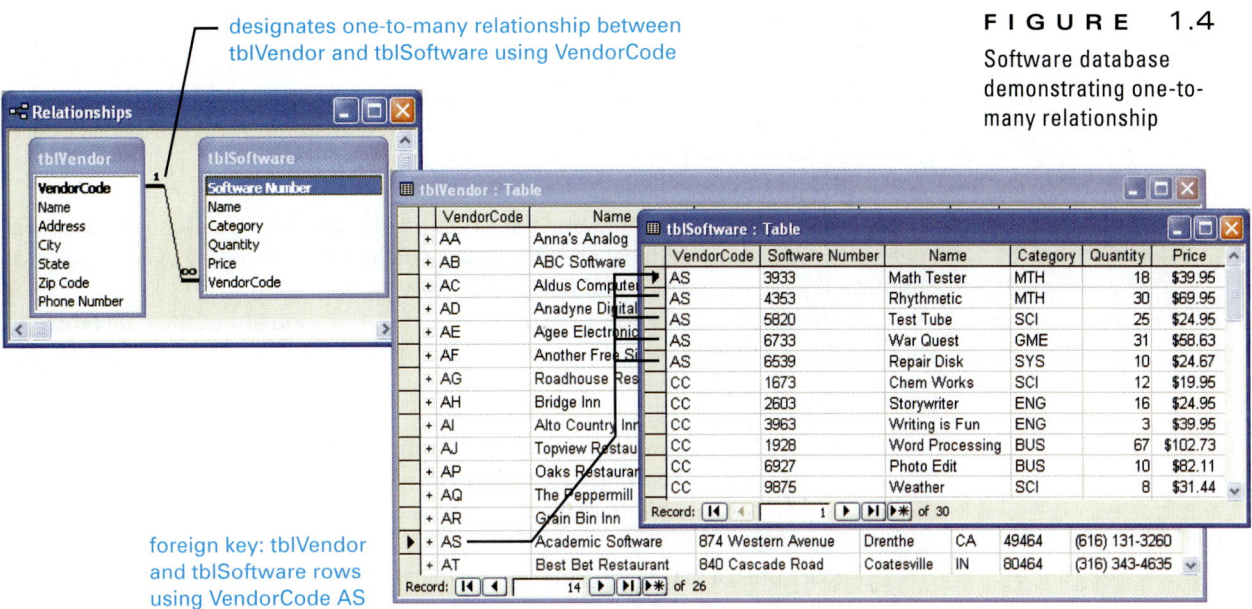

designates one-to-many relationship between tblVendor and tblSoftware using VendorCode

foreign key: tblVendor and tblSoftware rows using VendorCode AS

Because there are so many types of keys, the word *key* used alone can seem ambiguous, but it is not. When the word *key* is used without identifying the type of key (i.e., foreign key), it always means the primary key.

Relationships

When a foreign key from a table is used to link to the data in another table, it is called **joining**. Join relationships take one of the three forms discussed in the following paragraphs.

One-to-one (abbreviated 1:1) relationships exist when one row of the first table matches to one and only one row of the second table and both tables have the same primary key. One-to-one relationships are unusual because such closely related data would normally be stored in a single table. When table requirements exceed Access's limit of 255 columns per table, two tables with a one-to-one relationship are created to hold all of the data. Security and privacy issues also can cause closely related data to be stored in multiple tables. For example, in the medical community some patient data must be reported and some must be held private. Even though all of the data are for patients, it makes sense to store the private data in a separate table and use a one-to-one relationship to join it with the more public data.

One-to-many (abbreviated 1:M or 1:∞) relationships exist when one row of the first table matches to multiple rows in the second table. One-to-many relationships are the most common. Figure 1.4 shows the tables needed to keep inventory information for a small business like KoryoKicks. The tblSoftware table is used to store inventory information while tblVendor stores data about vendors who provide the software.

Many-to-many (abbreviated M:N or ∞:∞) relationships exist when one row in the first table matches with multiple rows in the second table and one row in the second table matches with multiple rows in the first table. Many-to-many relationships can't be directly modeled in relational databases but are broken into multiple one-to-many relationships.

Relational Database Objects

In general an object is a reusable template or structure that will speed development. Relational database objects assist in developing the components for the database. All RDBMSs support table, query, report, form, index, and stored procedure objects. The *database* file is a container that organizes the tables, queries, forms, reports, and other objects.

The *Table* object is the fundamental structure of a relational database management system. The function of a table object is to store data about a category of things such as employees in records (rows) and fields (columns).

The *Query* object will allow you to formulate a question about the data stored in your tables, or a request to perform an action on the data and store it as a reusable object. A query can bring together data from multiple tables to serve as the source of data for a form, report, or data access page.

The *Form* object allows you to create a custom interface for taking actions or for entering, displaying, and editing data in fields. A typical form, like the one in Figure 1.5, displays one row of data from a table in contrast to the default table grid that displays several rows of data.

A *Report* object prints information formatted and organized according to your specifications. Examples of reports are sales summaries, phone lists, and mailing labels.

Indexing

When storing more than a few records in a table, it is important to optimize the table so that data can be efficiently retrieved. Conceptually, storing and accessing data in tables are straightforward, but scanning tables for values or sorting the rows for output can be very inefficient. Consider looking for a specific topic in this book like *Saving Access as HTML*. One approach would be to scan the pages of this book until you found the topic. A second approach would be to find the topic in the index and then proceed to the correct page(s). In the vast majority of searches, the index approach would provide the fastest and most complete results.

FIGURE   1.5

Tabbed form from the Northwind sample database

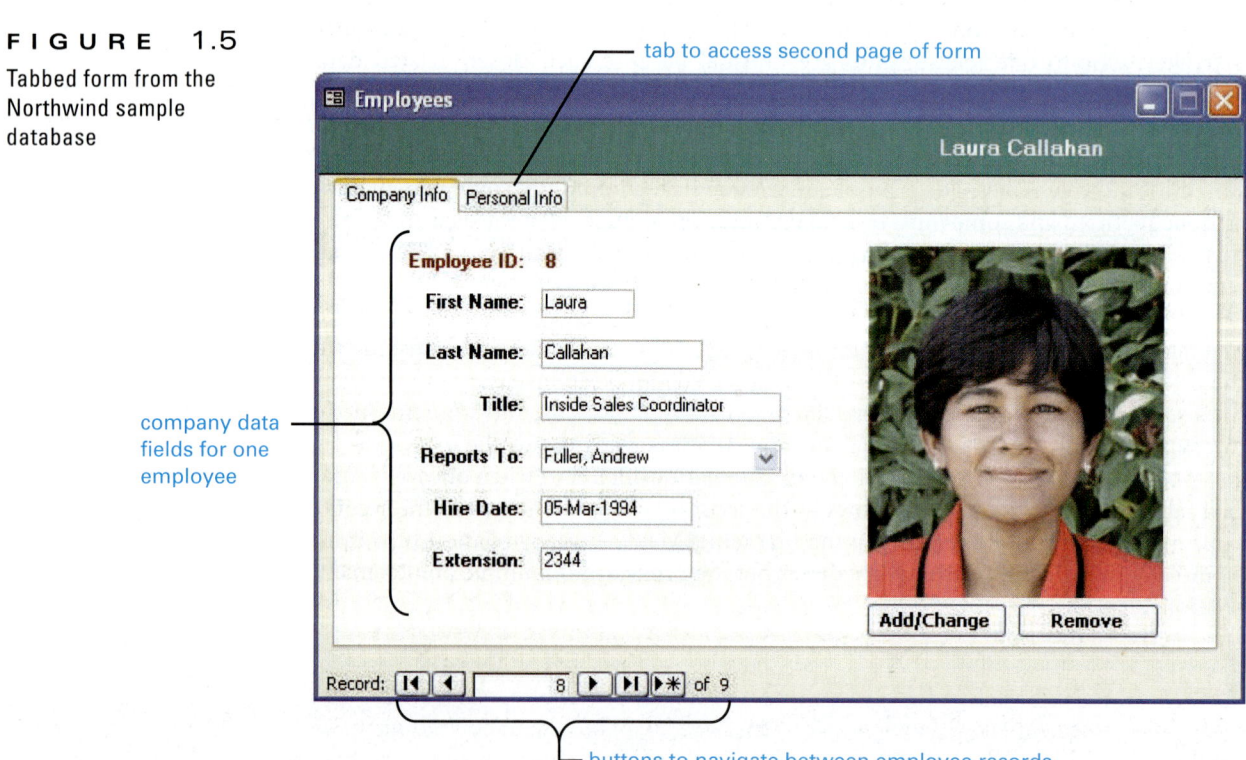

tab to access second page of form

company data fields for one employee

buttons to navigate between employee records

FIGURE 1.6

Indexes for the Customers table

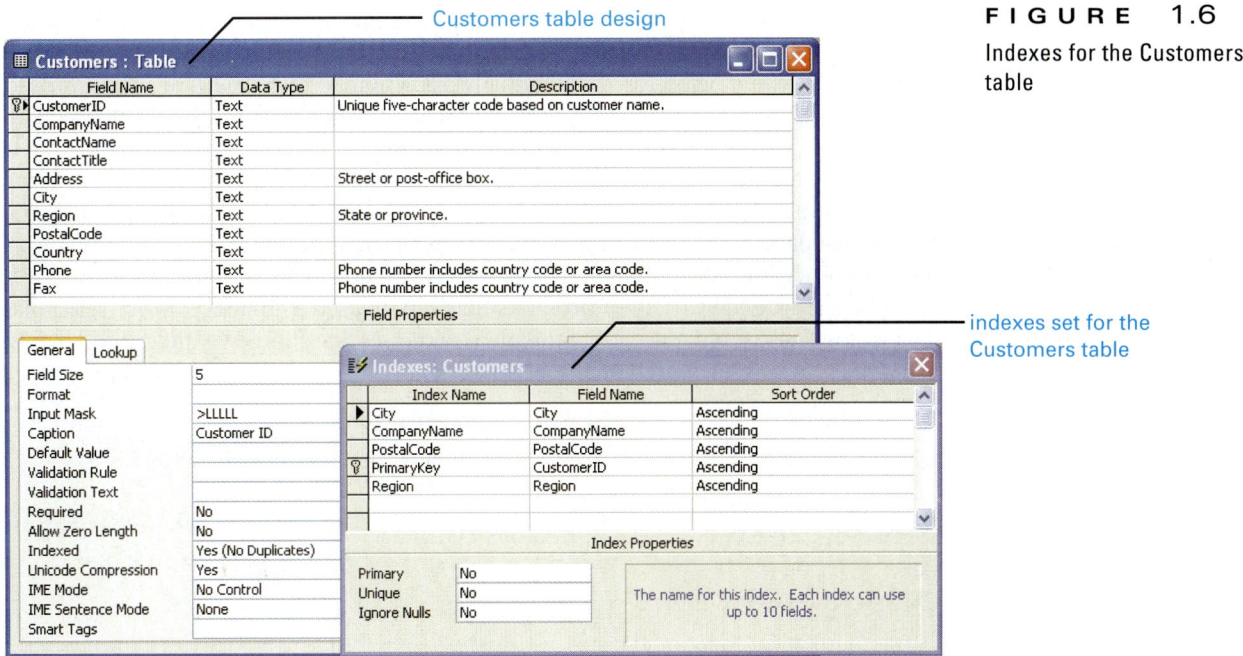

Customers table design

indexes set for the Customers table

Table *indexes* can be applied to improve table search performance and are similar in function to the index of a book. A table index tracks where the rows for a particular value are stored in the table so that the values can be accessed without scanning through the entire table. When you have a primary key, a unique index is automatically defined for the key values. Any other fields that are frequently used to search for values or sort data are also candidates for indexing. Figure 1.6 shows the fields and indexes for a Customer table. Notice that indexes have been set for the PrimaryKey (CustomerID) and PostalCode because both fields are frequently used to sort and retrieve data.

Indexes are automatically updated as table data are added or changed. There are no restrictions on the number of indexes applied to a table. Indexes can be added and deleted as they are needed using table Design View.

Database Management Systems

Database management systems are the various software products that allow organizations to store data in a central location using a standard format. While we are concentrating on the relational database model that stores data in tables, it is important to understand where the relational model fits in the overall data storage scheme. There are also hierarchical, network, and object-oriented models for database management systems.

DBMS Models

Hierarchical and network database management system models are older and more restricted than the relational model. Both the hierarchical and network models depend on predefined data relationships, while the relational database model allows new relationships to be defined at any time. There are, however, situations where users have fixed storage and reporting requirements where the older models will outperform relational databases.

Evolving user needs and emerging technologies have given rise to object-oriented DBMS models. In addition to handling conventional rows and columns of data, an object-oriented database will store documents, diagrams, graphics, multimedia, and more. In an object-oriented database, each item stored is an *object*. An object is virtually anything—traditional data, a moving image, people talking, a photograph, narrative, text, music, or any combination. Objects can be accessed individually or in combination. For example a graphic and a voice recording each could be a stored object in a database. These objects could be accessed individually or combined into a new object comprised of both the graphic and sound. Regardless of what is stored and how it will be used, the idea is to have a natural-looking way to interact with all types of data.

No leader has emerged in object-oriented database technology, and most current implementations are actually object-relational databases. An object-relational DBMS is a relational database that can store other objects such as graphics, video, audio, methods, and procedures describing how the objects will behave.

There are a wide variety of products that can be used to manage object-relational data access. Each product has strengths and weaknesses that should be understood before using the product. A few RDBMSs that, to one extent or another, can store objects are

- Microsoft Access—widely used on personal computers
- Microsoft SQL Server—used to share data on Microsoft NT networks
- Oracle—popular Web-commerce database
- DB2—IBM mini and mainframe data storage software

Client/Server DBMS

Besides looking at the model used to store the data, DBMSs can be divided into two basic categories: *personal databases* and *client/server databases*. Many of the same concepts apply to both DBMS categories. The differences lie largely in the amount of data that can be stored, the number of concurrent users supported, networking capabilities, and the level of data security provided.

Personal database management systems like Microsoft Office Access 2003 work best in single-user environments. The ideal environment is one user updating and reporting on the data from one PC. Although personal database management systems can be networked and shared, the general rule-of-thumb is that there should be no more than 10 concurrent users. If security, network traffic, or the ability to recover from system failures is important, a client/server DBMS would be a better choice.

Client/server DBMSs are designed to support multiple users in a networked environment. Powerful servers store and process large quantities of organizational data, while client PCs can request data from the server and then query, update, and report on it locally. A typical client/server application has a front end like Microsoft Office Access 2003 that runs on the local client workstation and a back end like Microsoft SQL Server that runs on the server. In these implementations, the front end provides the local user interface on a PC, while the back end has the power to store and process data from multiple users on a network server.

For example, the client (you at your PC) could request a listing of August computer sales. The server database holds the information for all organizational sales and must run a query to retrieve August computer sales, which it then passes to the requesting client (your computer). You now have a local copy of August computer sales that you can use your local client software to manipulate. Depending on the application, you might make changes to the local data and then the client could send updates to the server that are then applied to the organizational database.

Client/server applications are cost effective and scalable. They also can take advantage of common PC software like Microsoft Office Access 2003 on the client, making them easy for users to learn and use. On the down side, shared data are never as secure as centralized data stored on a mainframe.

Opening an Access Database

Access 2003 software can be opened from the Start menu or by opening an Access document directly. When an Access database file is double-clicked, Access is launched and then the database is loaded in one step.

Starting Access and opening a blank database:

1. Verify that Windows has loaded and is ready to launch programs

2. Click the **Start** button on the Windows Taskbar and then pause over **All Programs** to list the programs available on your computer

3. Pause over **Microsoft Office 2003** and then select **Microsoft Office Access 2003** to launch Access

FIGURE 1.7

Launching Access from the Start menu

tip: *Your screen may differ from what is depicted due to the settings on your computer, the operating system parameters, and what software has been installed*
   If Microsoft Access is not listed in your Programs menu, you will need to either install Access or seek technical assistance

4. After a short pause, the Microsoft Access 2003 copyright information is displayed on the screen and then the Microsoft Access 2003 window displays

F I G U R E   1.8

The Microsoft Access window

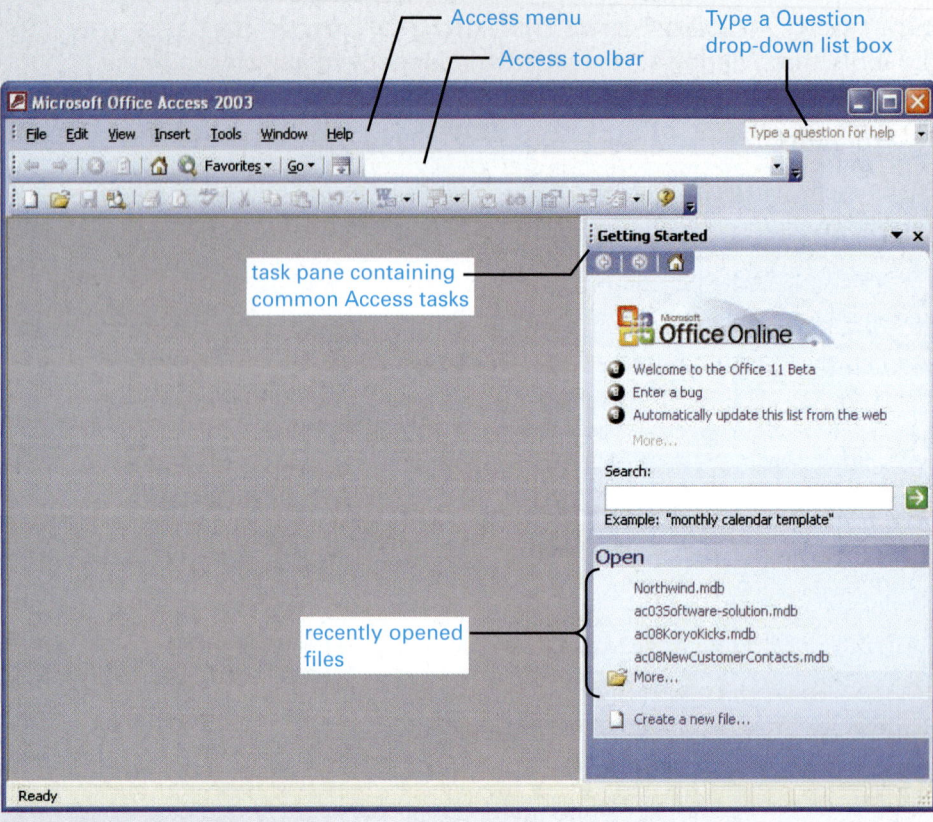

tip: *The specific files listed in the Open a file list will reflect database files loaded on your system. If the task pane is not displayed, use the Toolbars option of the view menu to display it*

5. In the task pane, click **Create a new file** and then click **Blank Database**
   a. Use the Save in drop-down list to select a location for your database
   b. Change the default filename to **ac01Blank.mdb**
   c. Click **Create**

The Access database, ac01Blank.mdb, created in the previous steps is an empty container ready to store objects. The only object that can be built in an empty database is a table. After at least one table is added, query, form, and report objects to manipulate table data can be created and stored.

Database Window

Like all Microsoft Office System applications, the Access 2003 opening page contains a menu, a toolbar, an edit pane, and a task pane. Once the Access program has been initiated, the task pane displays on the right-hand side of the screen. The initial file options in the task pane are to open an existing file, create a new database file, use an existing database file to create a new database, or use one of Microsoft's templates to create a new database. The last option in the task pane is a check box that will turn off the task pane so that it does not show each time Access loads. If you don't need the task pane, it can be closed using the Close button in its Title bar.

Remember that a database file is used to organize related tables, queries, forms, and reports. A prototype of the Customer database for KoryoKicks has been created using the customer information Missy and Micah provided.

Opening the Customers database:

1. Verify that Access is running and make sure that the data files for this course are in the proper drive

2. If the task pane is not displayed, click **View**, pause over **Toolbars**, and click **Task Pane**

FIGURE 1.9

Microsoft Access Open dialog box

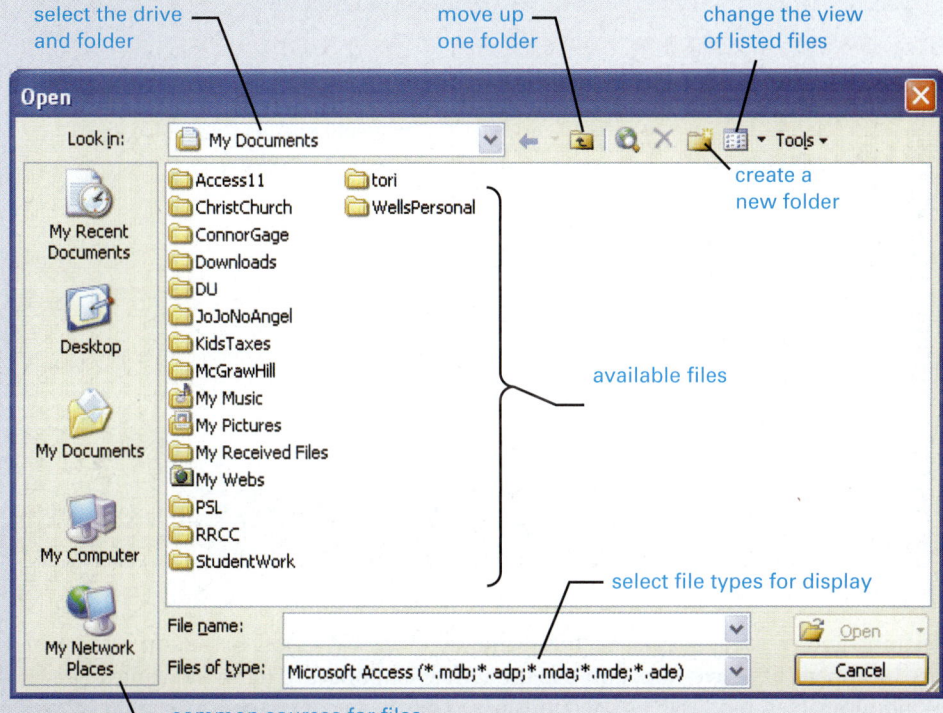

3. If the **ac01Customers.mdb** database displays in the task pane, select it and *skip to step 5*

4. If the ac01Customers.mdb database does not display, click the **More files** option in the task pane to display a standard Open file dialog box

tip: *The Open dialog box will display the files from My Documents on your computer, so the files and folders displayed will be different on each computer*

5. Click the **Look in** drop-down arrow and select the drive and folder containing your data. Open the folder for Chapter 1 and select the **ac01Customers.mdb** file

6. Once the file is selected, click **Open** to load the database into Access

Windows and Toolbars

The Access 2003 user interface consists of a series of windows that display inside the main *Access Window*. As you can see in Figure 1.10, when a database is open, it displays in its own window called the *Database Window*. Tasks that are common to all Access operations reside on the Access Window, while those specific to a database are accomplished from the Database Window. Other windows will be discussed as we explore more features of Access.

Each open window has a toolbar with operations that are relevant to the functions of that window. For example, the toolbar in the Database Window contains options for

FIGURE 1.10

The Customers database

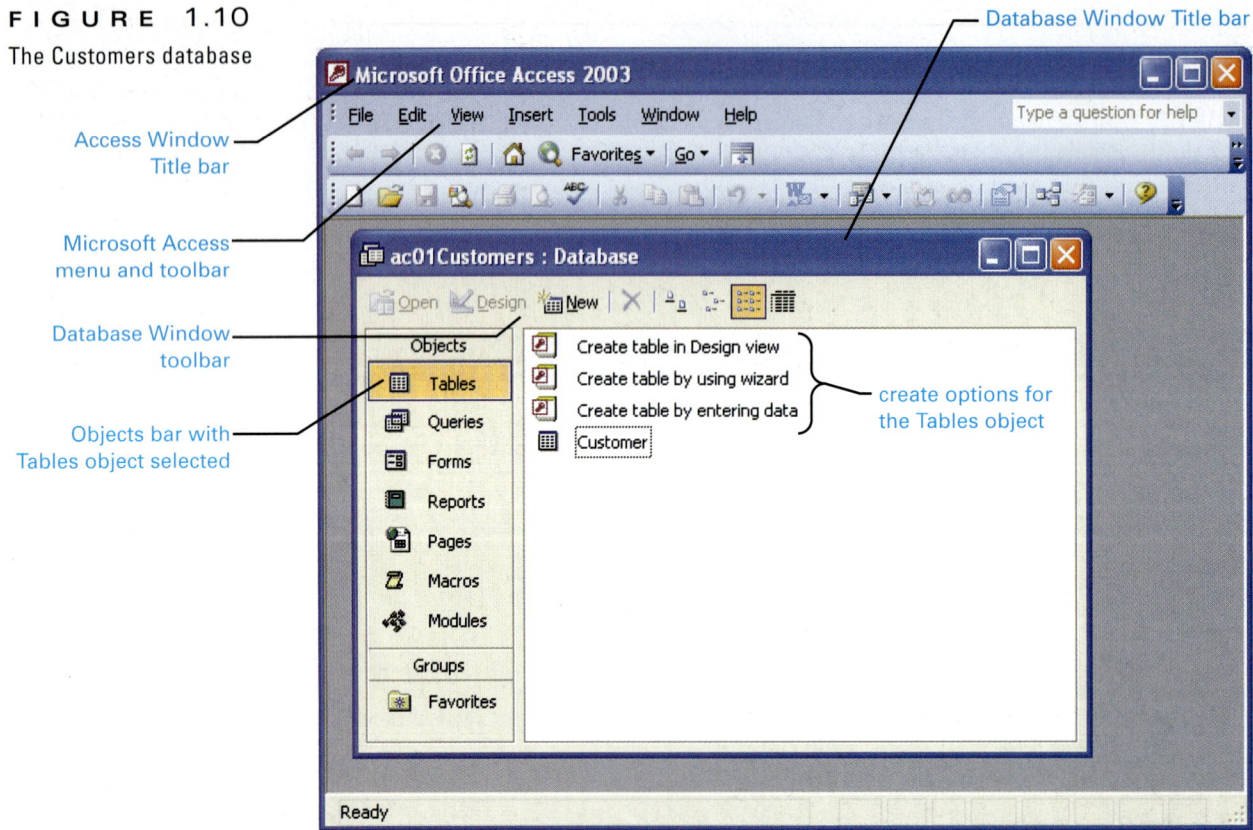

Database Window Title bar

Access Window Title bar

Microsoft Access menu and toolbar

Database Window toolbar

Objects bar with Tables object selected

create options for the Tables object

opening and creating database tables while the Access Window has common features used to open files, save files, and use the Office Clipboard. The toolbar in the Access Window enables and disables selections based on the needs of the active window.

Identifying Access Database Objects

The Database Window is made up of panes. The left pane holds the Objects bar and the Groups bar. The right pane displays the selections made from the left pane. The **Objects bar** displays icons for each of the objects that can be created for the open database. Clicking one of the Objects bar selections displays options for that object in the main pane of the Database Window. The **Groups bar** allows the user to group database objects for easier manipulation.

Tables

Clicking Tables in the Objects bar will display a list of tables for the open database. The Tables object is the backbone of a database, meaning that if there are no tables in the database, none of the other database objects can function. It should make sense that to query (ask questions of) a table, the table and its data must already exist.

For relational databases, tables are designed using a process called normalization, their structures are defined during the table creation process, and then data are entered. Notice in Figure 1.10 that the first three options presented when the Tables object is selected are tools used to create new tables in the database. Each table that has already been built is listed below the Create table tools.

Queries

Selecting Queries from the Objects bar will display valid query options for the open database. Queries are used to view, change, and analyze data in different ways. They also

FIGURE 1.11

Selecting the Queries
object

Queries object

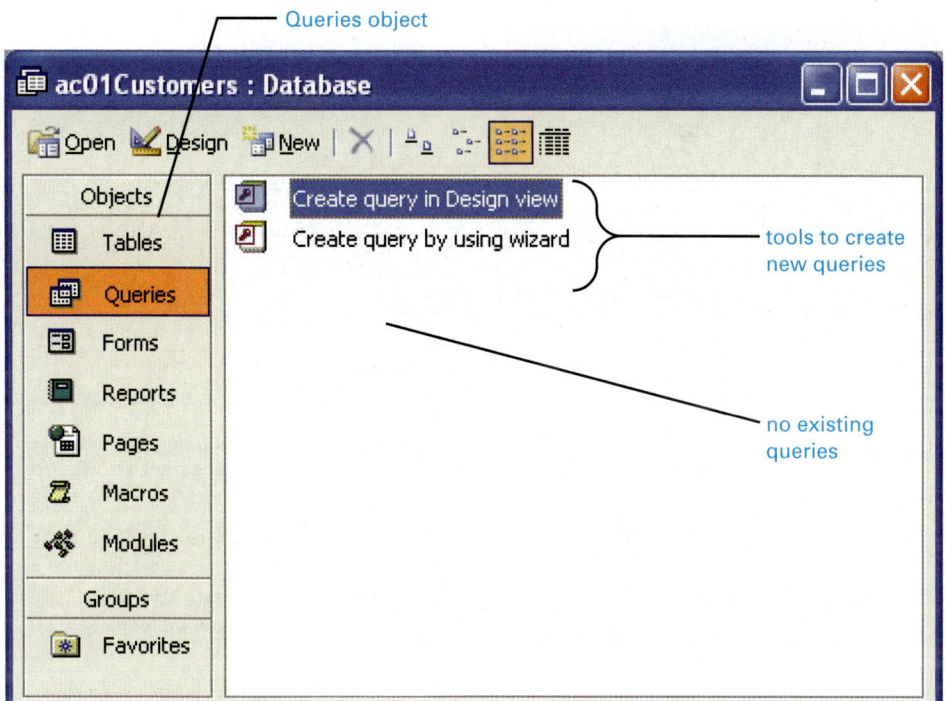

tools to create
new queries

no existing
queries

can be used to select and sort data for forms, reports, and data access pages. Access 2003
provides both QBE (Query by Example) and SQL (Structured Query Language) interfaces. Several types of queries are available in Microsoft Access 2003.

Select queries are the most common and are used to retrieve data from one or
more tables. Select queries also can perform simple calculations and organize the data.
Selected data can be updated or used for other processes like reporting.

Parameter queries are select queries that prompt the user for criteria that will be
used in selecting data from the database. For example, the user might be prompted
for two dates and then the query would display sales that occurred between the dates
entered.

Crosstab queries are used to analyze data. They group data and calculate values for
each group. If you have worked with Excel, it is very similar to crosstab reporting in that
application.

Action queries update the data in a database in some fashion. Action queries can
be used to delete a group of records that meet a criterion, to update a group of records,
to add records to an existing table, or to add records to a new table. Action queries are
very powerful and are most effective when used to update or move large quantities of
data. For example, suppose that your database was very large. To improve performance,
you decide to move data for customers who have not purchased anything in the last
year to an inactive table. You could review and move records manually or use an action
query with criteria for inactive accounts to select the records and move them to the inactive table in a single operation.

Forms

A form is a database object used primarily to enter and display database data. Forms
also can be used to create a user interface for a database. Forms that create a user interface are called switchboards. A switchboard would contain options to open the tables,
queries, forms, reports, and other objects of the database (see Figure 1.12). A dialog box
is also a form that accepts user input and carries out an action based on the input. All
forms are used to make it easier for a user to interact with the database.

F I G U R E   1.12

Examples of forms—
switchboard, input, and
dialog box

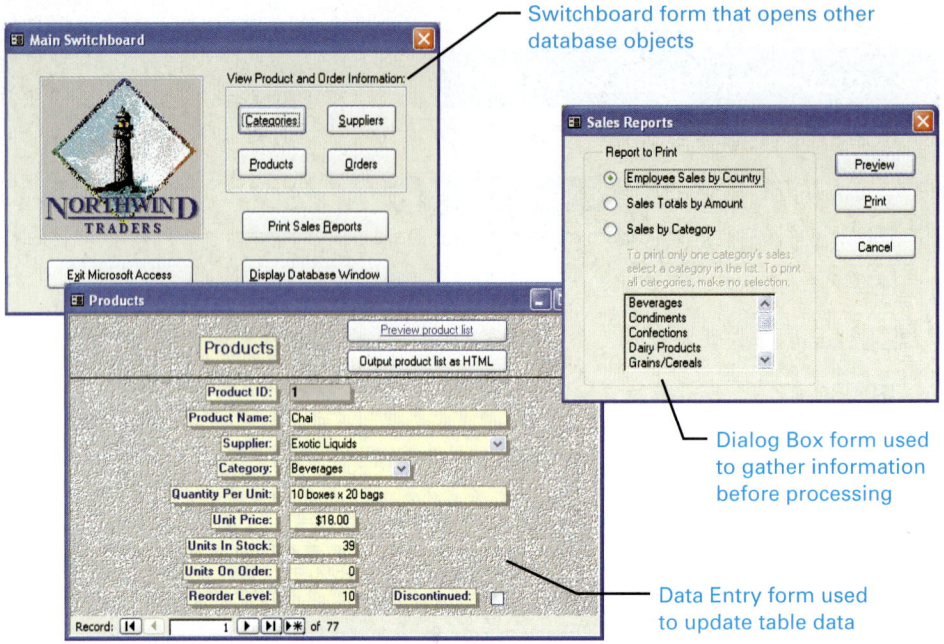

Switchboard form that opens other database objects

Dialog Box form used to gather information before processing

Data Entry form used to update table data

Reports

The Reports object is used to display database data in print. Reports can be as simple as mailing labels or contain complex formatting and graphics. Normally a report is based on the result of a query. Using a query to select the data ensures that the report contains only the desired rows and columns.

Once the data are selected, the report design specifies how those data will be displayed. The design includes specifications for the report title, sort order, and grouping and summarizing of data. Expressions can be used to create calculations based on data values. For example, if you were creating a sales report, you might want subtotals for the sales by month or by department.

Locating database objects:

1. From the Objects bar of the Database Window select **Tables**

tip: *It may already be selected. The Customer table object should display*

2. Click **Queries** in the Objects bar. No queries have been created so there are no objects to view

3. Explore the remaining database objects (which are all empty) and then return to **Tables**

help yourself *Use the Type a Question combo box to view the Help topics by typing* **tables**. *Review the contents of About Tables. Close the Help window when you are finished*

Pages

The Access 2003 Pages object supports the creation and deployment of Web pages. There are three types of Web pages that are related to data in a database. How the data will be used determines which type of page should be created.

FIGURE 1.13

The Macro window

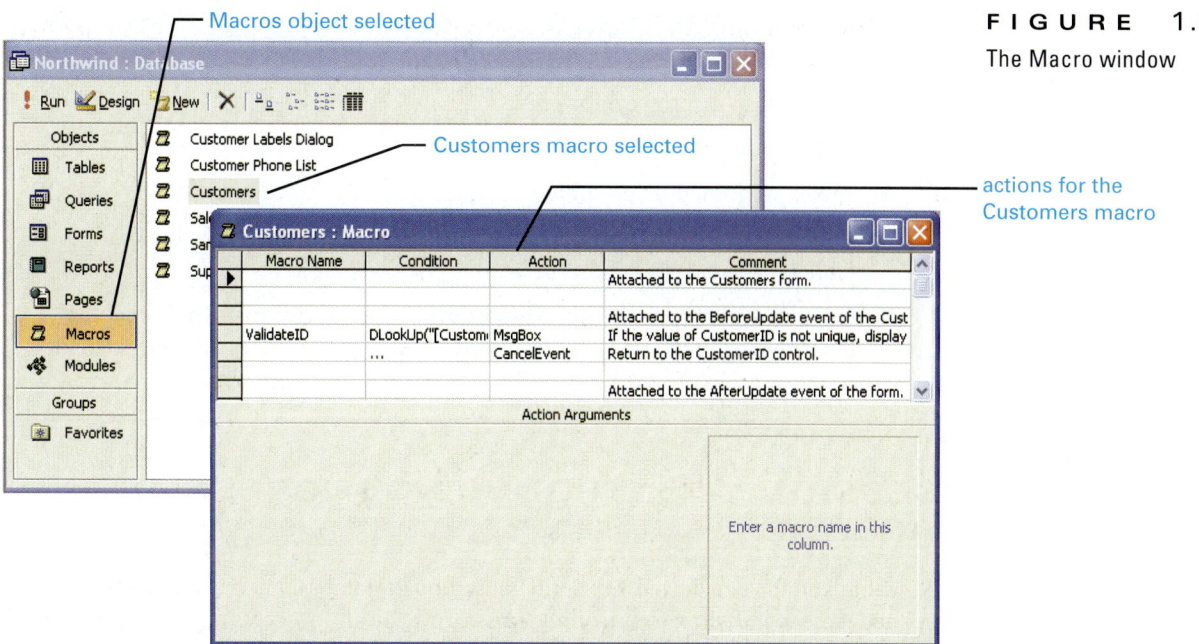

Data Access Pages allow a Web browser to be used to view and update table data. A Data Access Page has a live connection to the data in your database. It can be used on an intranet or published to the Internet using DHTML (Dynamic HTML) technology.

An **Active Server Page (ASP)** is designed to display up-to-date read-only data. The data are selected by the server and displayed in a table format. Opening or refreshing an ASP file from a Web browser causes the page to be dynamically created from current values and sent to the browser.

Finally, **static HTML** pages can be used to publish a snapshot of the data. Static pages can be based on tables, queries, forms, or reports. Each object will display in a format consistent with its on-screen appearance. No user action can cause a static page to update. If the data change, you must update the HTML pages and post them to the Web again. HTML template files can be used to create a consistent publishing format for static pages.

Macros

Macros are used to automate repetitive database tasks. The basic building block of a macro is an action: a self-contained instruction or command like Open Table. Actions are selected from a drop-down list box (see Figure 1.13) and include options for manipulating tables, queries, reports, and forms.

Modules

Modules are used to customize the way tables, forms, reports, and queries in your database look and function. Modules are written in Visual Basic (VB), a programming language used to develop Windows applications. A **module** is a collection of Visual Basic statements and procedures that are organized and stored together to be accessed as a unit. You can create simple event procedures that are initiated by a user action such as clicking or double-clicking. Complex custom functionality also can be added with a solid understanding of programming concepts.

SESSION 1.1

making *the grade*

1. RDBMS is an acronym for _____.

2. SQL (Structured Query Language) is _____.

3. Tables are joined using shared _____.

4. A table attribute that uniquely and minimally identifies each row in the table is called a(n) _____.

5. Go back and review the KoryoKicks case at the beginning of this chapter. Considering the twins' business needs, create a list of data attributes (fields) the KoryoKicks database would need to store about its customers.

SESSION 1.2 INTRODUCING MICROSOFT ACCESS

Now that you have reviewed your understanding of database management systems and opened Access, it is time to introduce Missy and Micah to Access and begin to formulate a plan for KoryoKicks. Since KoryoKicks has some standard business needs like storing customer data, it makes sense to look at customer tables first.

Opening an Existing Table

Tables are the central objects of a database. They store the data on which all other Access objects operate. To view or update table data, the table must be opened.

Viewing Table Data

Since relational databases store data in tables, the default layout used to display Access data is a table or *Datasheet View*. In the datasheet, you can move to a new row by clicking the *record selector* button to the left of a record. An entire column of data can be selected using the *field selector* button above the column. The record selector is also called a row selector and the field selector can be called the column selector.

TRADITIONAL NAVIGATION. The Tab key can be used to advance from cell to cell in the datasheet. Arrow keys also will move from cell to cell and have the added advantage of moving up and down between rows. When using keyboard navigation, the default is for the entire contents of a cell to be selected. This can be effective if you want to type and replace existing contents. If, however, you want to move character by character in a cell, you will need to choose Options from the Tools menu and change the Keyboard options to either Go to start of field or Go to end of field. You also can click in any cell using a pointing device or use the navigation buttons below the datasheet. Navigation buttons are outlined in Figure 1.14.

VOICE NAVIGATION. Access 2003 is enabled to use speech for both dictation and command control. This feature is only effective if speech recognition training has been completed (covered in general Office Topics) and you own a good microphone headset. Activate speech recognition by selecting Speech from the Tools menu. The Language Bar—shown in Figure 1.15—will float over the Access Title bar, allowing you to control language options.

FIGURE   1.14

Datasheet navigation buttons

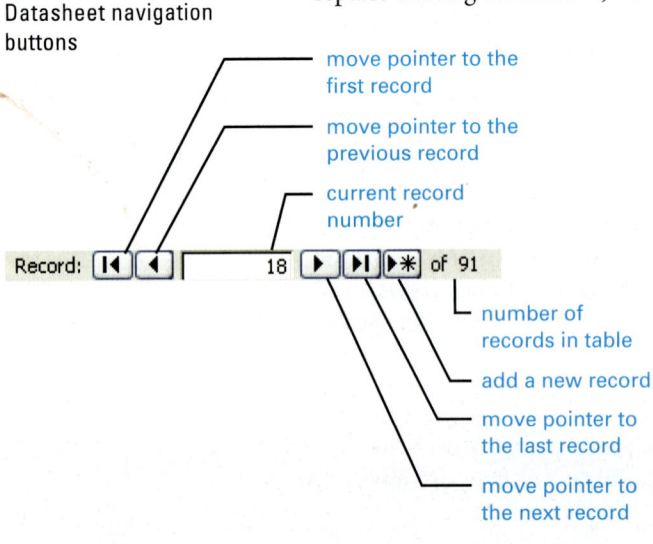

move pointer to the first record

move pointer to the previous record

current record number

number of records in table

add a new record

move pointer to the last record

move pointer to the next record

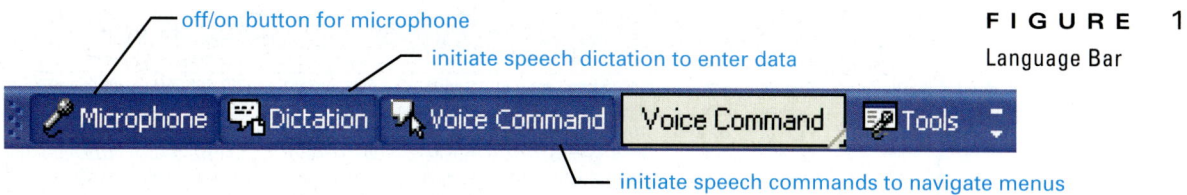

Voice commands can be issued by choosing Voice Command from the Language Bar and speaking menu options such as File Print. Because of the complexity of the Access interface, dictation is time consuming to learn and of limited functionality. Speaking keywords such as Tab moves from cell to cell in a datasheet, but dictating data values is challenging. For example, speaking "CustmrNmbr 048" (zero four eight) results in "zer" being stored in the field because speech recognition tried to write out zero but the field only allows 3 characters. Speaking "forty-eight" places 48 in the cell when 048 is the correct value. Similar problems arise when speaking dates and phone numbers.

---

task reference   Opening an Access Object

- Click the type of object that you would like to open in the Database Window's Objects bar

- Select the object that you would like to open

- Click the **Open** button

Opening the Customer table:

1. If you are not continuing from the previous session, start Access and open the ac01Customers.mdb database. Verify that the **Tables** object is selected in the Database Window

tip: *Refer to Figure 1.10 to find the Tables object*

2. Double-click the **Customer** table. The contents of the table will display in Datasheet view

3. Navigate the table data by clicking in several cells

4. Select the record for Ben Katz by clicking the record selector (the gray button before the record)

5. Select the State column by clicking the column selector (the gray button above the data labeled State)

6. Click in any cell and use the Tab and Shift+Tab keys to navigate forward and backward through the cells

anotherway
. . . to Open Database Objects

Select the object and use the **Open** button of the Database Window toolbar.

OR

Right-click an object and select the **Open** option from the shortcut menu

Adjusting Column Widths and Row Heights

Besides navigating table data, you can adjust the appearance of datasheet contents. When the datasheet loads, default sizes for rows and columns are used. Often the column is larger or smaller than the data it contains. Resizing the columns and rows will make the data more readable.

F I G U R E   1.16

The Customer table

current record indicator

navigation bar

	CstmrNmbr	LastName	FirstName	Street	City	State	ZipCode	Phone	FirstContact
▶	01	Wagoner	Sam	5480 Alpine Lane	Sterling	CO	88661	(303)161-5545	05/25/1999
	02	Calahan	Eliza	2140 Edgewood Road	Grand Lake	CO	80446	(303)886-6003	05/25/2001
	03	Lake	James	701 East Street	Grandby	MI	49571	(616)562-4499	08/25/1999
	04	Meadows	Sara	Pond Hill Road	Monroe	IN	46161	(313)792-3646	02/28/1999
	07	Calahan	Casey	82 Mix Rd. West	Bootjack	CO	89945	(303)643-8321	04/03/1999
	21	Smith	Alto	114 Lexington Ave.	Granby	CO	49302	(303)838-7111	06/02/1996
	22	Lewis	Ronnie	8408 E. Fletcher Road	Clare	MI	48617	(517)936-8651	04/12/1999
	23	Chinn	Bridgett	400 Salmon Street	Ada	MI	49301	(616)838-9827	04/17/2001
	25	Katz	Ben	56 Foursone Road	Detroit	MI	49505	(616)315-7294	06/12/2001
	27	Gray	Monica	3915 Hawthorne Lane	Richmond	OH	43603	(419)332-3681	07/29/2001
	28	Rivers	Ramona	37 Queue Highway	Lacota	MI	49063	(313)329-5364	04/20/2002
	29	Amstont	Sandy	95 Bay Boulevard	Jenison	CO	80428	(616)131-9148	04/27/2000
	31	Hill	James	5365 Bedford Trail	Eagle Point	CO	80031	(906)395-2041	05/01/2000
	33	Florentine	Haven	874 Western Avenue	Drenthe	CA	49464	(616)131-3260	05/03/2001
	35	Calahan	Thomas	840 Cascade Road	Coatesville	IN	80464	(316)343-4635	05/11/2001
	36	Benton	Cleo	4090 Division St.	Borculo	OH	49464	(616)838-2046	05/11/2002
	43	Pointe	Bryson	11 Marsh Rd	Shelbyville	IN	46344	(616)379-5681	10/24/1999
	47	Krizner	Jean	44 Tower Lane	Mattawan	MI	49071	(517)630-4431	09/18/2000

Record: |◀ ◀   1   ▶ ▶| ▶✱ of 26

Changing Customer table column widths and row heights:

1. Verify that the Customer table is open in Datasheet View

2. Place the pointer on the right edge of the State field selector until the pointer has left- and right-pointing arrows, as demonstrated in Figure 1.17

F I G U R E   1.17

Adjusting column widths and row heights

adjust State column width

adjusting the height of one row changes all rows

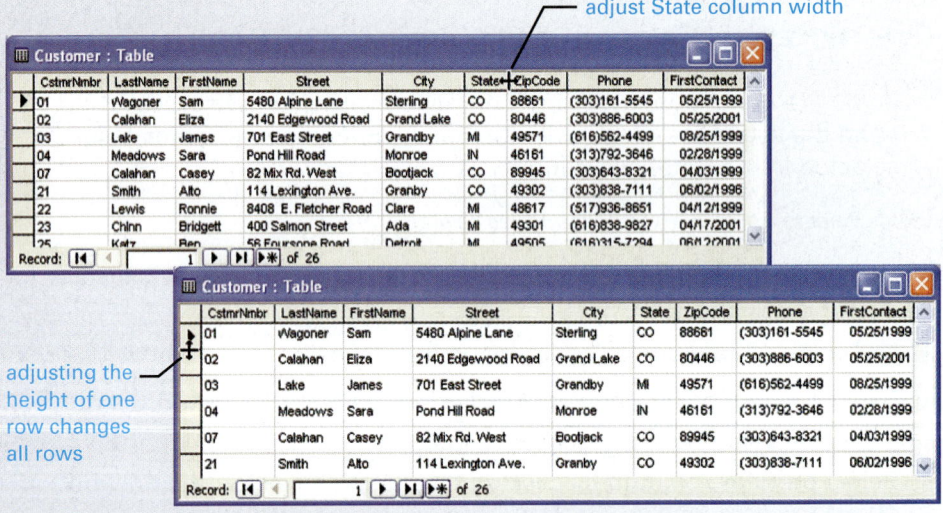

3. Click and drag the State column until it is just wide enough to display the data

4. To allow Access to automatically size a column based on the data it contains, double-click the right edge of the field selector. Use this method to adjust the width of the Street column

5. Place the pointer between any two record selectors and drag the rows to the desired height. Notice that all rows are adjusted to the same height

Changes to the column and row dimensions cannot be reversed with the Undo command from the toolbar or the Edit menu. When you close the datasheet, you will be prompted to save the changes to the layout of the table. Select Yes to retain the size adjustments, No to discard them, and Cancel to return to the datasheet.

Printing Table Data

Access print features are very similar to those of other Office products. There are two common methods for printing Access objects:

- Click the Print 🖨 button on the toolbar to print an open datasheet or other open object. If there is no datasheet open, the Print button will cause the selected object to print

- Alternatively, you can use the Print option of the File menu, which will open the Print dialog box. The Print dialog box provides options for setting up your output page, changing the printer, controlling printer properties, and printing multiple copies

The toolbar's Print Preview button is an excellent way to verify the content and format of output before printing. The Print Preview toolbar contains options to control the zoom (magnification) of the output and the number of pages that display for review and to change the printer setup. If you have made and saved formatting changes such as column widths or fonts to the datasheet, they will be reflected in the printed output.

Viewing Table Design

The *Design View* for a table displays the attributes of each field in the table called the table structure. Design View can be used to build tables from scratch or make changes to the design of existing tables. You and the twins will take a look at the design of the KoryoKicks Customer table prototype.

Displaying the Customer table's design:

1. If the Customer table is open, close it. From the Database Window, select **Table** from the Object bar and **Customer** from the main pane

2. Click the **Design View** 🔲▾ button from the Database Window toolbar

3. Review the attributes of the CstmrNmbr field

4. Close the Customer table Design View

In table Design View, the key icon in the CstmrNmbr selector (see Figure 1.18) indicates that it is the primary key. The Text data type means that it will accept any text entered (letters, numbers, or punctuation), a Field Size of 3 denotes that a maximum of three characters can be stored, and an Indexed value of Yes indicates that the field has been indexed.

F I G U R E   1.18
Customer table Design
View

key field indicator

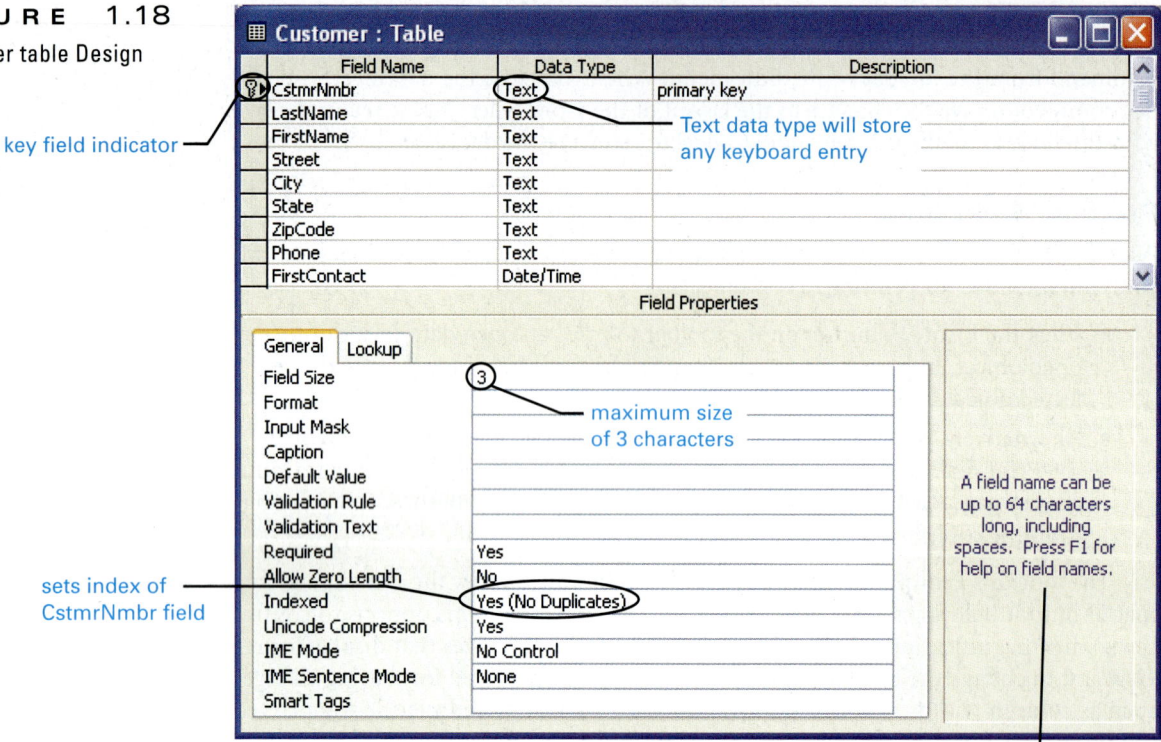

Text data type will store
any keyboard entry

maximum size
of 3 characters

A field name can be
up to 64 characters
long, including
spaces. Press F1 for
help on field names.

sets index of
CstmrNmbr field

tips about current action

anotherword   . . . **on Changing Views**

Many Access objects support multiple views like the table object. The Design
View allows you to see and update the table design while the Datasheet View allows you to see and update the stored data. You can move easily from one object view to another using the View button on the toolbar. The View button is a
drop-down button that will display the valid views for the open or selected object. The two most common views are Datasheet 📊 ▾ and Design 📐

Printing Table Design

It is a good idea to keep paper documentation outlining the design of your tables.
Printing table design *cannot* be accomplished using the Print option of the File menu,
as you would expect. Special tools are used to analyze and document the design of
Access objects. The documentation feature of the Database Analyzer includes the ability to print table designs.

Printing the Customer table's design:

1. From the **Tools** menu, select **Analyze** and then **Documenter**

tip: *No particular object or view is necessary for this operation*

2. The Documenter dialog box will display to allow you to select the object
to be documented and the options for the documentation

3. Verify that the **Tables** tab is selected and **check** the Customer table check
box

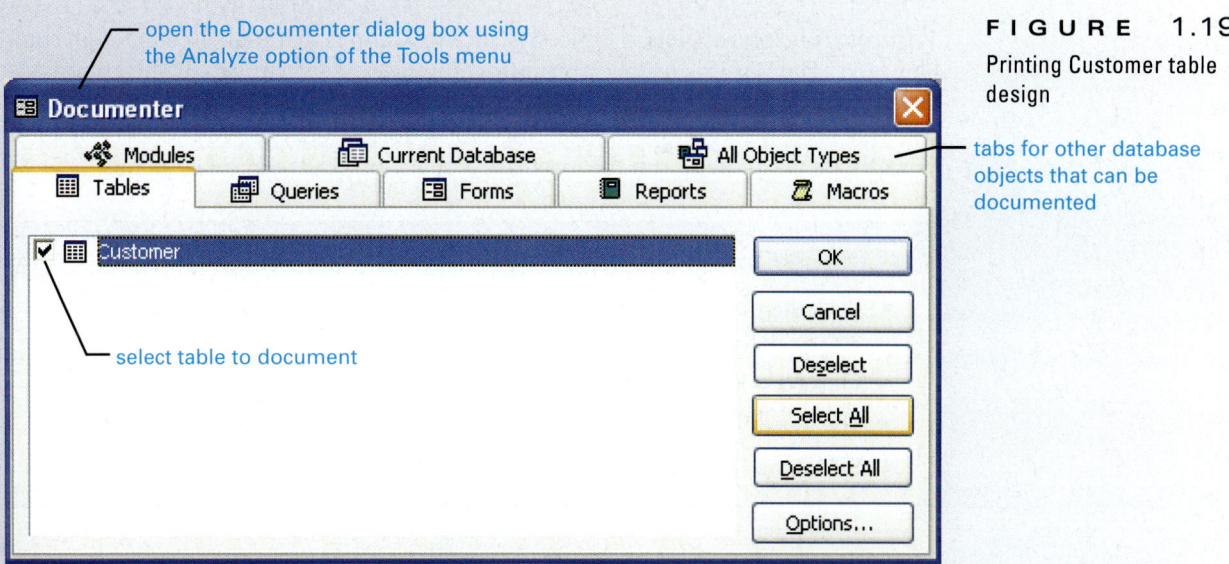

tabs for other database objects that can be documented

tip: *The table to be documented must be checked; highlighting is not sufficient*

4. Click the **Options** button to display the Print Table Definition dialog box. The options selected here determine what documentation will print for the Customer table. The default values are shown in Figure 1.20

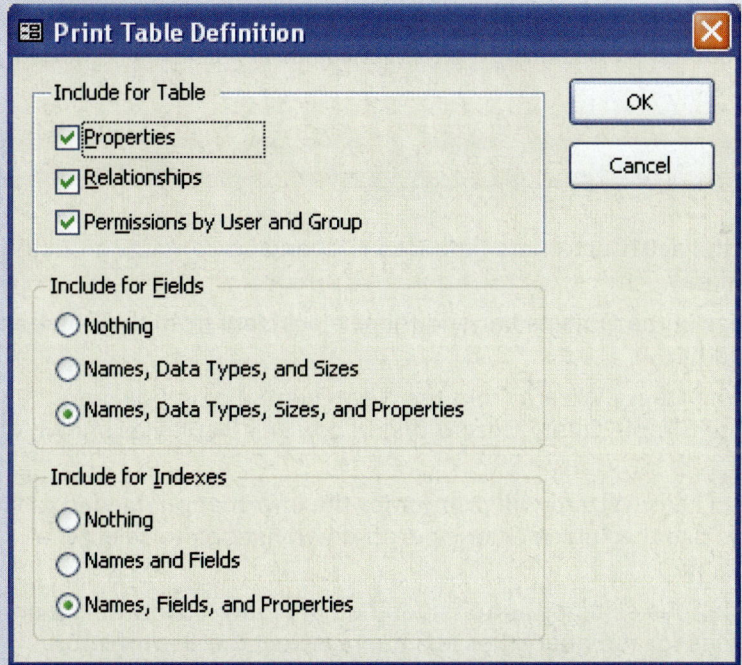

5. Click **OK** to exit the Print Table Definition dialog box

6. Click **OK** in the Documenter dialog box to generate a preview copy of the documentation

7. Select the **Printer** button from the toolbar to complete the Table Design. Print as you would print any other document

Using Access Wizards

Wizards are helpful applets in Office System Applications that walk users through complex tasks. The Wizards installed on your computer are determined by the options selected when Access was installed. To work along with the instructions in the section, you will need the Wizards for creating tables, forms, queries, and reports. If these Wizards are not present, run the installation again or seek technical assistance.

---

task reference   **Activating Access Wizards**

- Click the object (Queries, Forms, Reports) whose Wizard you would like to access in the Database Window's Objects bar
- Click **New** in the Database Window's toolbar
- The available Wizards will be listed
- Select the Wizard and respond to its questions

The Simple Query Wizard

The Simple Query Wizard allows columns (fields) to be specified for retrieval from one or more tables in a database. Simple calculations such as COUNT, SUM, or AVERAGE can be added to the results. This Wizard does not allow criteria for selecting specific rows of data, so all rows of the table(s) are included in the return set.

The Simple Query Wizard displays a series of dialog boxes requesting the information needed to complete the query. Each Wizard dialog box contains navigation buttons that will allow you to move to the previous dialog box (Previous), move to the next dialog box (Next), cancel the operation (Cancel), or complete the task with the data entered so far (Finish).

Querying the Customer table:

anotherway
. . . to Initiate the Simple Query Wizard

Once the Queries object is selected, double-click on Create query by using Wizard. The Simple Query Wizard dialog box will open in one step

1. Verify that the ac01Customers database is open and contains a Customer table with data

2. Click **Queries** in the Objects bar and then select **New** from the Database Window toolbar

3. Select **Simple Query Wizard** from the New Query dialog box, and then click **OK**. The Simple Query Wizard dialog box will display as shown in Figure 1.21

4. The Simple Query Wizard will prompt for the information needed to create a query. Use the Tables/Queries drop-down list box to select the **Customer** table

5. Practice using the selector buttons outlined in Figure 1.22 to select and unselect fields for the query. For this query, select the **CstmrNmbr**, **LastName**, **FirstName**, and **Phone** columns and then click **Next**

6. The Next dialog box allows the creation of a custom title for your query output. The default of Customer Query does not need to be changed. Click **Finish**

7. The query results are displayed in Datasheet View and can be manipulated, formatted, updated, or printed using the same techniques as when reviewing an entire table in Datasheet View

8. Close the datasheet and notice that Customer Query has been added to the list of Queries as shown in Figure 1.23

select the Queries object

click New

pick Simple
Query Wizard

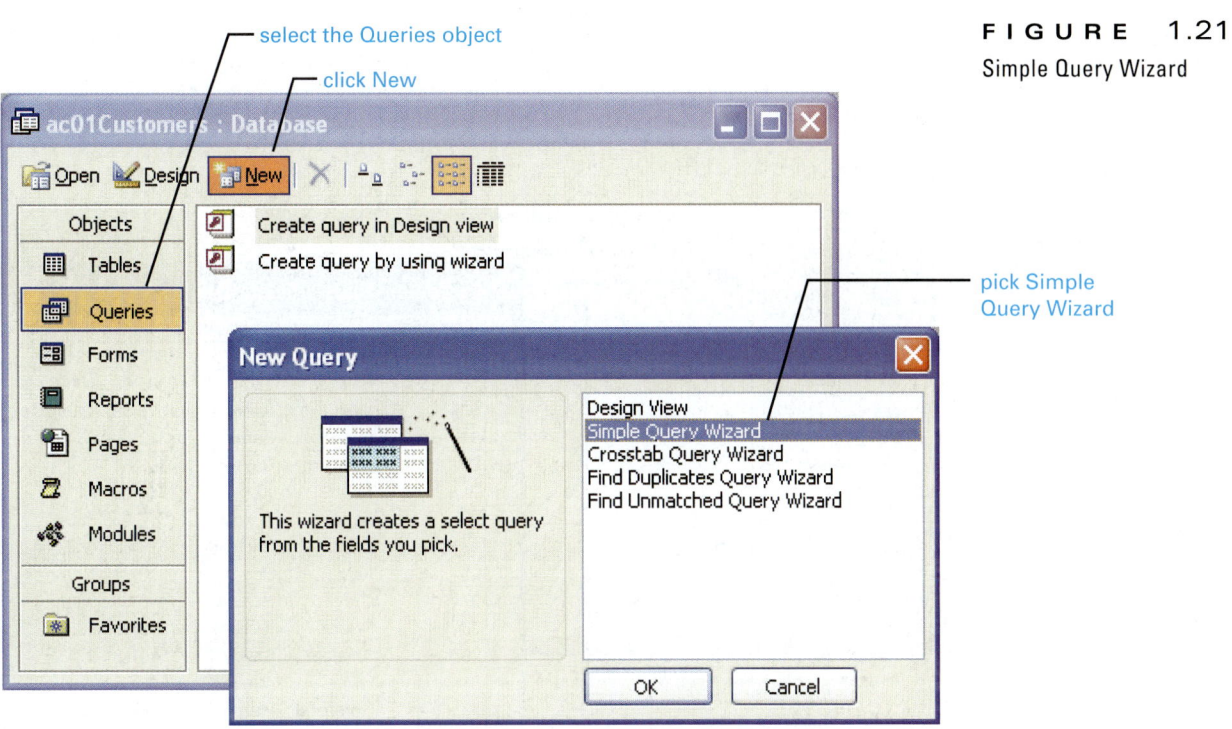

select table to be queried

move all Available Fields to
Selected Fields

move highlighted Available
Fields to Selected Fields

remove highlighted
Selected Fields

remove all Selected Fields

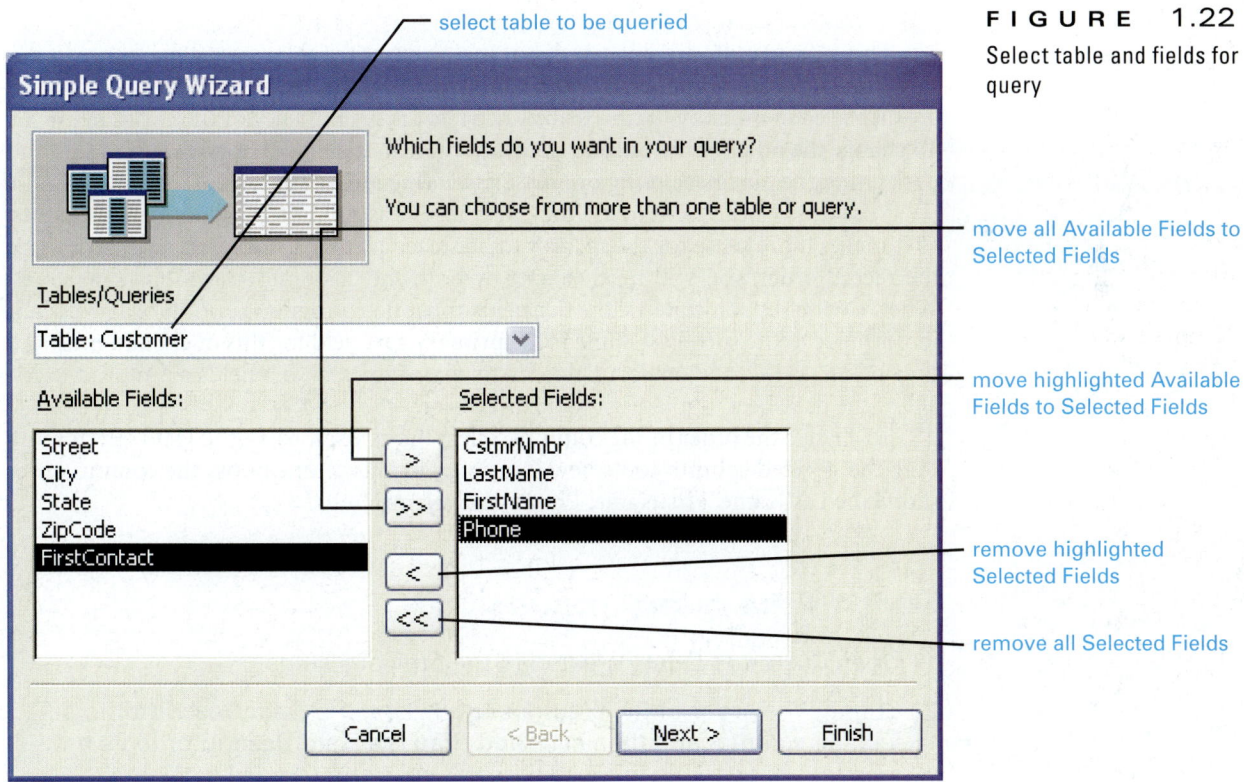

FIGURE 1.23

Customer query results

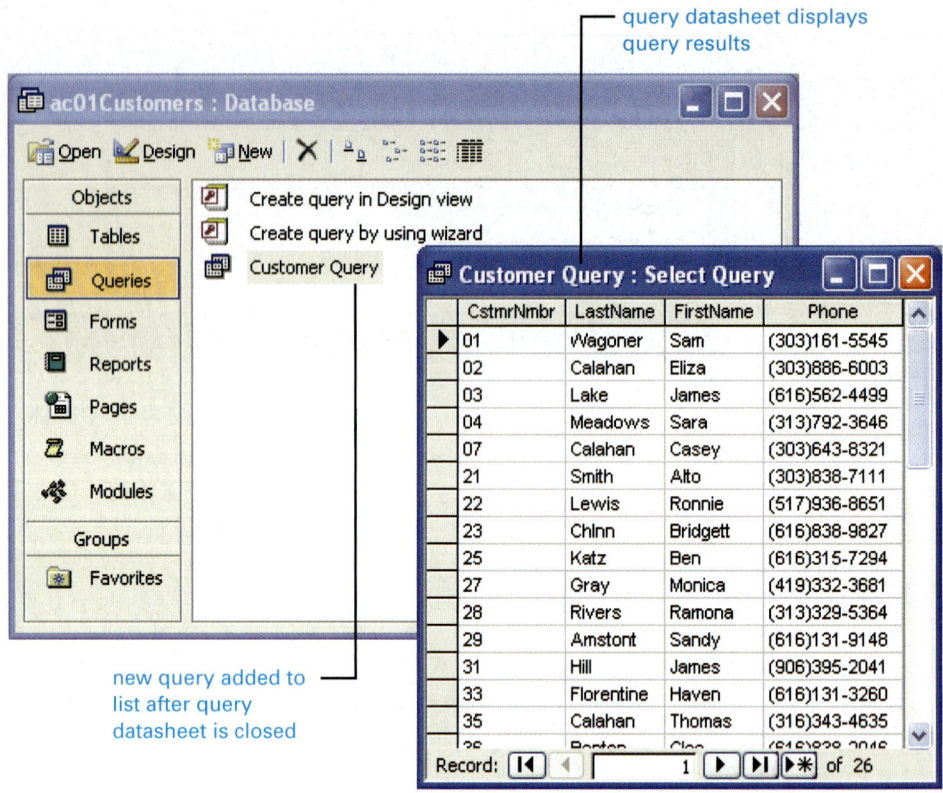

query datasheet displays
query results

new query added to
list after query
datasheet is closed

The query results are not saved, but the query criteria are stored for future use. A saved query can be reopened by double-clicking the title. By default, the query results are displayed in order by CstmrNmbr since it is the primary key of the Customer table. To change the order of the output, click anywhere in the field that you want to sort and click either the *Sort Ascending* or *Sort Descending* toolbar button.

Missy and Micah want to use the query results as a phone book of their customers, so it makes more sense for the records to be sorted by the customer's name. To change the record order, you will need to sort by both the customer's last and first names. When sorting by multiple fields, the fields must be contiguous and in order of their importance to the sort. LastName is the primary sort field for this query and must appear before the secondary sort field, FirstName. Typically sort fields are moved to the left of the datasheet to make using the list easier.

To change the order of the columns, select the column using the Field selector and drag the selected column to its new location. For this phone book, the column order should be LastName, FirstName, Phone, and CstmrNmbr.

Sorting the query results:

1. **Open** Customer Query created in the previous steps

2. Change the order of the columns by clicking the **Field Descriptor** to select the column, and then click and drag the Field Descriptor to its new location. Repeat this process until the column order is LastName, FirstName, Phone, and CstmrNmbr

tip: *The Field Descriptor is the box with the field name above each column of data*

3. Place the cursor in the LastName field and click the **Sort Descending** button on the toolbar

FIGURE 1.24

Reordering Customer
Query results

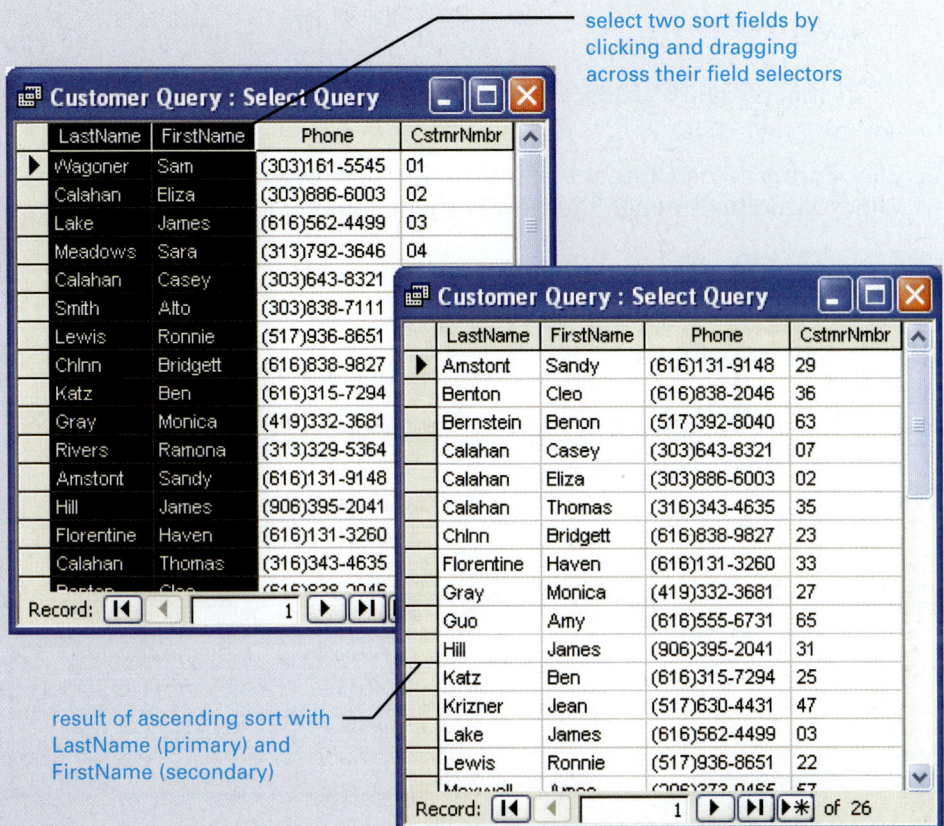

select two sort fields by
clicking and dragging
across their field selectors

result of ascending sort with
LastName (primary) and
FirstName (secondary)

4. Notice that while the data are sorted correctly by last name, the first names are not correctly ordered. The Calahans are not sorted by their first names. If you click in FirstName and sort, the data are no longer sorted by LastName

5. To sort both fields simultaneously, use the Field Selectors to select both the FirstName and LastName columns by clicking and dragging across both Field Selectors

6. When both the FirstName and LastName columns are selected, click the **Sort Ascending** button on the toolbar (see Figure 1.24)

7. Now that the data are arranged, the datasheet can be printed using the **Print** button of the Access toolbar

8. When you close the sorted query results, you will be prompted to save the layout changes that you have made. Choose **Yes** so that the next run of the Customer Query will be sorted by customer name

The Form Wizard

Forms are primarily used to display or update database data on a computer screen. There are two ways to create simple forms. AutoForm is the fastest and most efficient when you want a form displaying all fields from a single table. The Form Wizard will create more complex forms involving multiple tables and formatting.

Using AutoForm:

1. Verify that the ac01Customers database is open and that the Customer table contains data

2. Click **Forms** in the Objects bar, and then select **New** from the Database Window toolbar to open the New Form dialog box

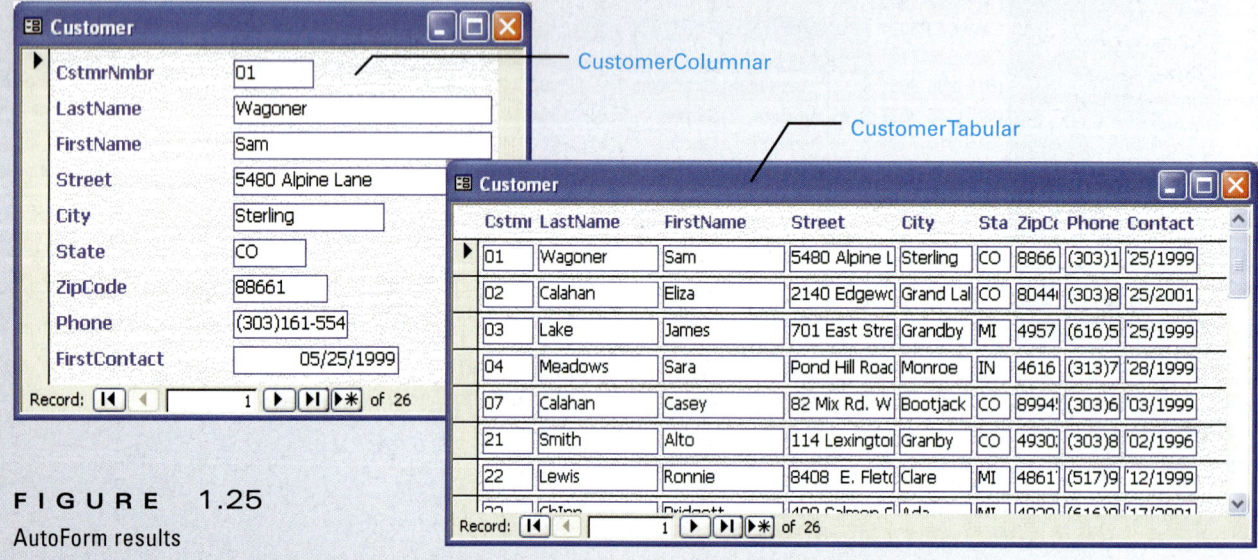

FIGURE 1.25
AutoForm results

3. Each of the five AutoForm Wizards produces the form in a different layout. Datasheet is the default form with which you have already worked. Select **AutoForm: Columnar** to produce a single-column form

4. Select the **Customer** table from the drop-down list and click **OK**

5. Close the Form saving it as **CustomerColumnar**

6. Repeat the process for **AutoForm: Tabular**. Compare the results of the two types of AutoForms

7. Use the Close button in the Form toolbar to close the tabular AutoForm, naming it **CustomerTabular**

Save any form specifications that will be used in the future. Forms also can be printed. Clicking the Printer button on the toolbar will print out all records in the table. Choosing Print from the File menu provides options to print all or a subset of the records.

Printing forms with data:

1. Open the **CustomerColumnar** form created in the previous steps

2. Use the navigation bar to move to the fourth record

3. From the Access menu select **File** and then **Print** to open the Print dialog box

4. The Print Range options determine what records print. All will print all
table records. Pages From will print the specified range and Selected
Record(s) will print the current selection. Choose **Selected Record(s)** to
print the fourth record

FIGURE 1.26
Printing forms with data

1. display record to print

2. click the Printer button
   on the toolbar

3. print only the current
   record

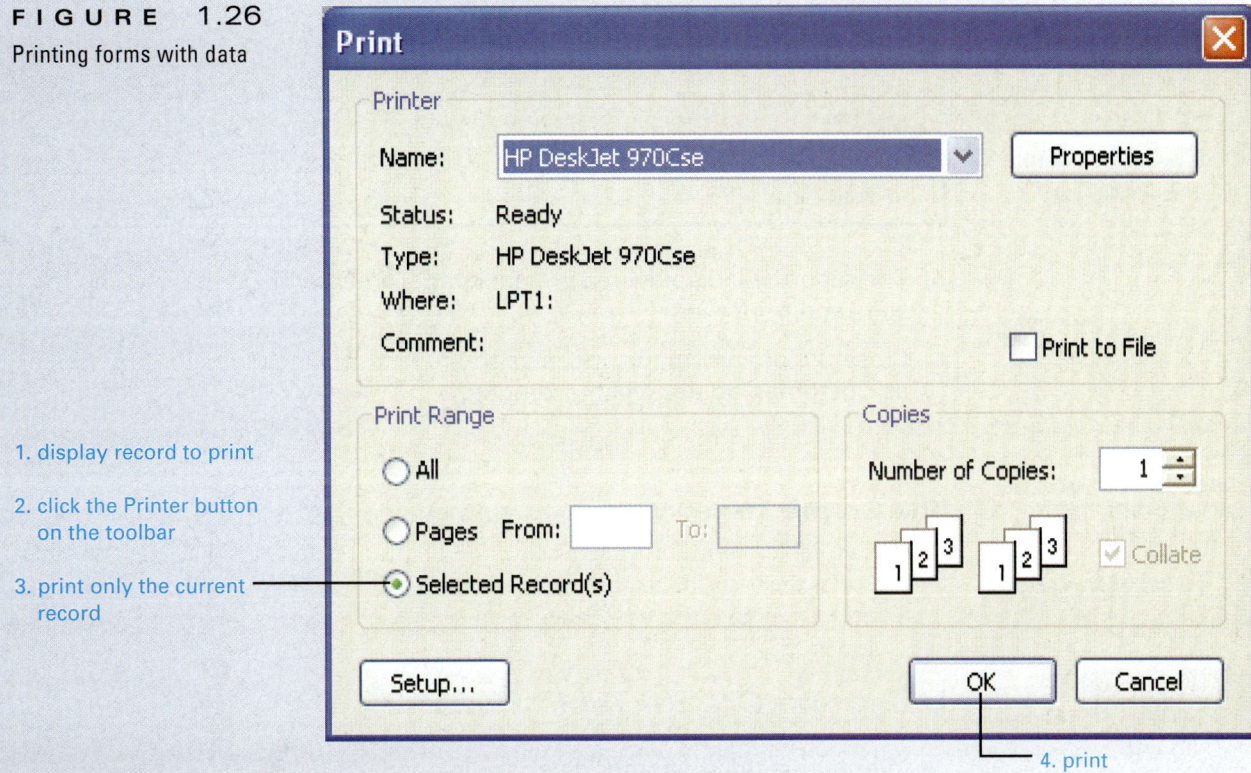

4. print

5. Click **OK** to print the record

6. Close the form

The Report Wizard

Reports are primarily used to consolidate and format data for printing. There are two
types of report Wizards available. The AutoReport Wizard creates default reports from
one table or query. The Report Wizard will create multitable reports with calculations
and custom formatting.

Using the Report Wizard:

1. Verify that the Customer database is open and that the Customer table
contains data

2. Click **Reports** in the Objects bar and then select **New** from the Database
Window toolbar. The New Report dialog box will open

3. Click **AutoReport: Tabular** to create a report in rows and columns

4. Select the **Customer** table from the drop-down list and click **OK**

F I G U R E   1.27

Report Wizard results

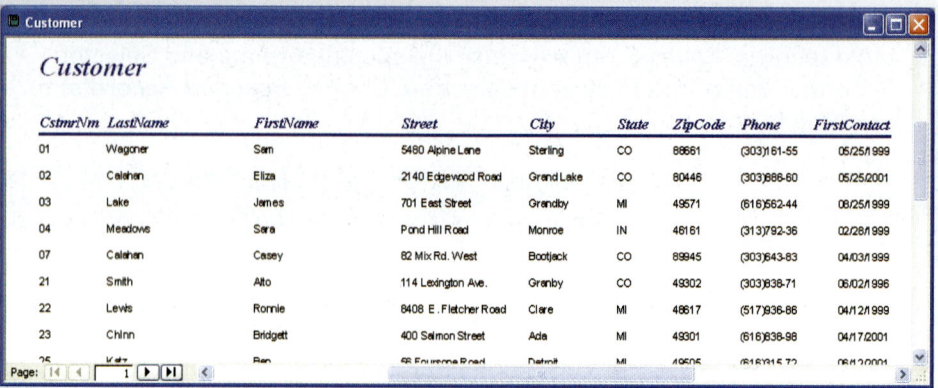

5. The report will display in a preview pane, where you can review the results and print them

6. Close the preview pane and save the report specifications for future use as **CustomerTabular** when prompted

The Create Table Wizard

The Create Table Wizard provides a collection of business and personal database tables to be used as the basis for creating your table.

Using the Create Table Wizard:

1. Verify that the Customer database is open

2. Click **Tables** in the Objects bar, double-click **Create table by using Wizard** to open it without viewing the intermediate dialog boxes (see Figure 1.28)

3. Review the Business table samples provided by the Wizard

4. Click the **Personal** table category

5. Select the **Household Inventory** from the list of Sample Tables. Move **HouseholdInvID**, **RoomID**, **ItemName**, **Description**, **Manufacturer**, **PurchasePrice**, and **AppraisedValue** from the Sample Fields list to the Fields in my new table list. Click **Next**

6. Name the table **Household Inventory**, choose to set a primary key, and click **Next** (see Figure 1.29)

7. Ensure that your new table is not related to other tables in the database

8. Click **Finish**

9. Enter at least five of your possessions into the Household Inventory table

10. Print table data using the Standard toolbar's Print button

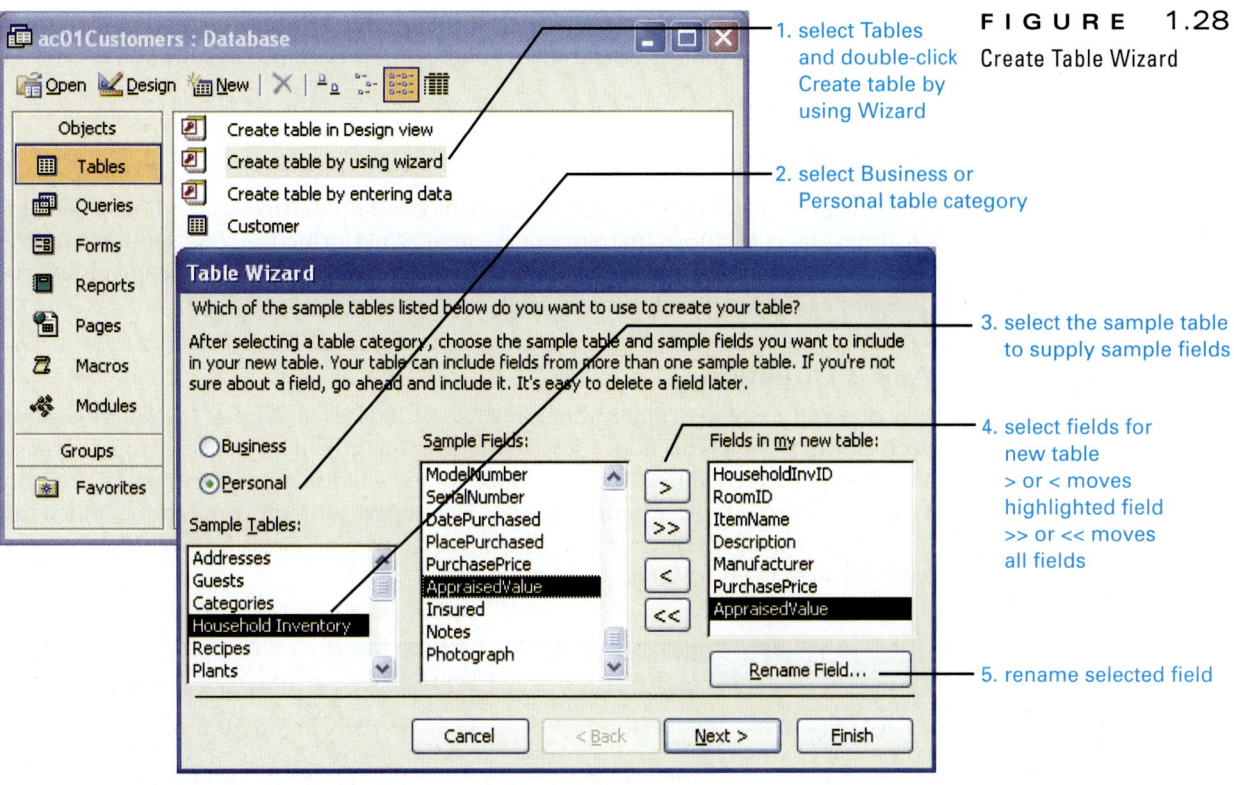

1. select Tables
   and double-click
   Create table by
   using Wizard

2. select Business or
   Personal table category

3. select the sample table
   to supply sample fields

4. select fields for
   new table
   > or < moves
   highlighted field
   >> or << moves
   all fields

5. rename selected field

F I G U R E   1.28
Create Table Wizard

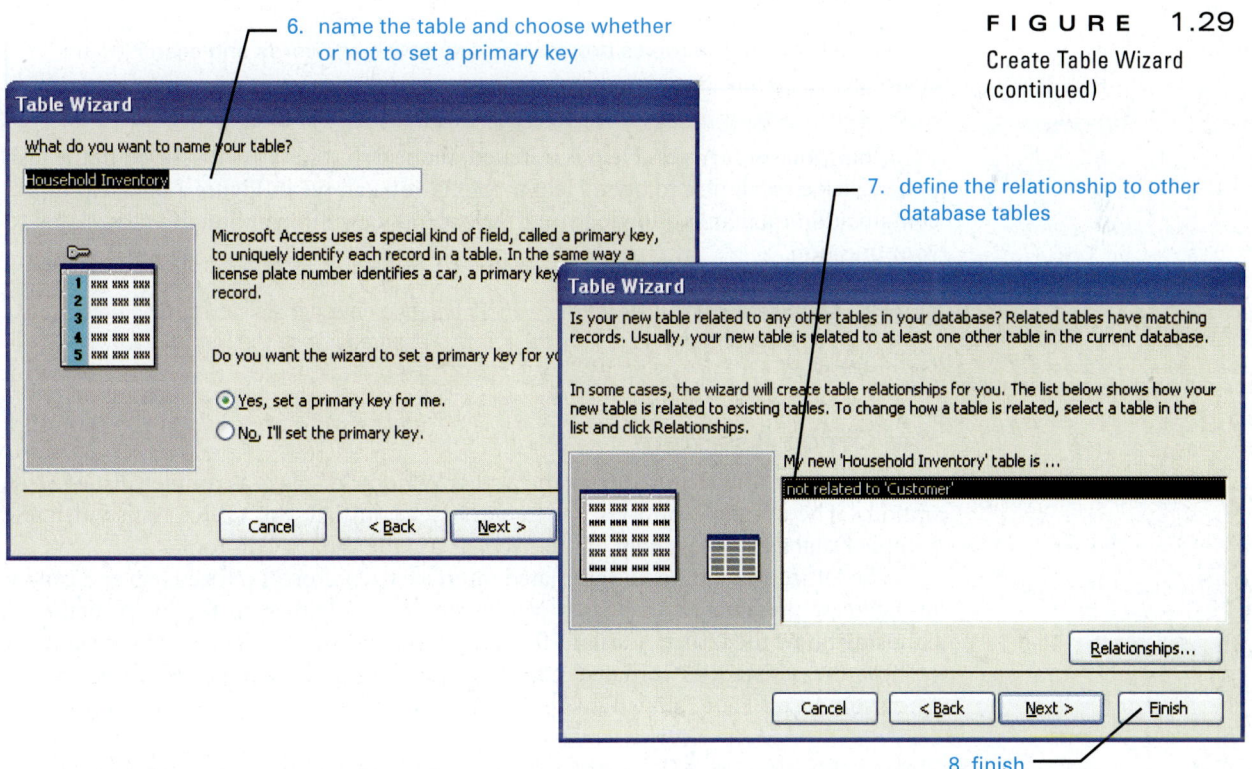

6. name the table and choose whether
   or not to set a primary key

7. define the relationship to other
   database tables

8. finish

F I G U R E   1.29
Create Table Wizard
(continued)

ACCESS

It is important to remember that the Create Table Wizard uses templates to build the fields of a new table. All field names and properties can be customized to suit the current use.

Getting Help

Even people who work with Access on a daily basis need direction on how to accomplish new tasks or those that are not frequently performed. Access supports several methods of obtaining help. The technique selected for getting help depends on the question being posed and the work style.

Ask a Question

Like other Office System applications, the Access 2003 menu bar has the Ask a Question drop-down list box. This is an effective way to request help on a specific topic. Type in a question and press Enter. A list of related topics will display, as shown in Figure 1.30. When you select a topic, Microsoft Access Help opens with more selections, which can be clicked to bring up instructions. The instructions can display on your screen as you work through them in Access.

---

task reference   Getting Help

- Click in the Type a Question drop-down text box in the Access menu

- Type in keywords relevant to your topic. Full sentences are not necessary and do not improve the performance of the search

- Press **Enter**

- Select from the topics provided or adjust the keywords and search again

---

Once Microsoft Access Help is initiated, the search results are displayed in the task pane. Click a result link to open Help topic. As you can see in Figure 1.30, Help topics contain additional links allowing you to select and view information directly related to your question.

help yourself *To learn more about creating new Access tables, type **new table** in the Type a Question box and review the topics presented. Close the Help window when you are finished*

The Office Assistant

Dropping down the Help menu in the Access Window displays a complete list of Help options. The available options are to start Help, initiate the Office Assistant, view Sample Databases, access help on the Web, or use the What's This tool.

The Office Assistant is the animated interface to Microsoft Office Help and can be initiated by pressing F1, choosing Microsoft Access Help from the Help menu, or choosing Show the Office Assistant from the Help menu (see Figure 1.31). Regardless of how the assistant is initiated, typing a question and clicking Search will open Microsoft Access Help (shown in Figure 1.30) with topics related to your search.

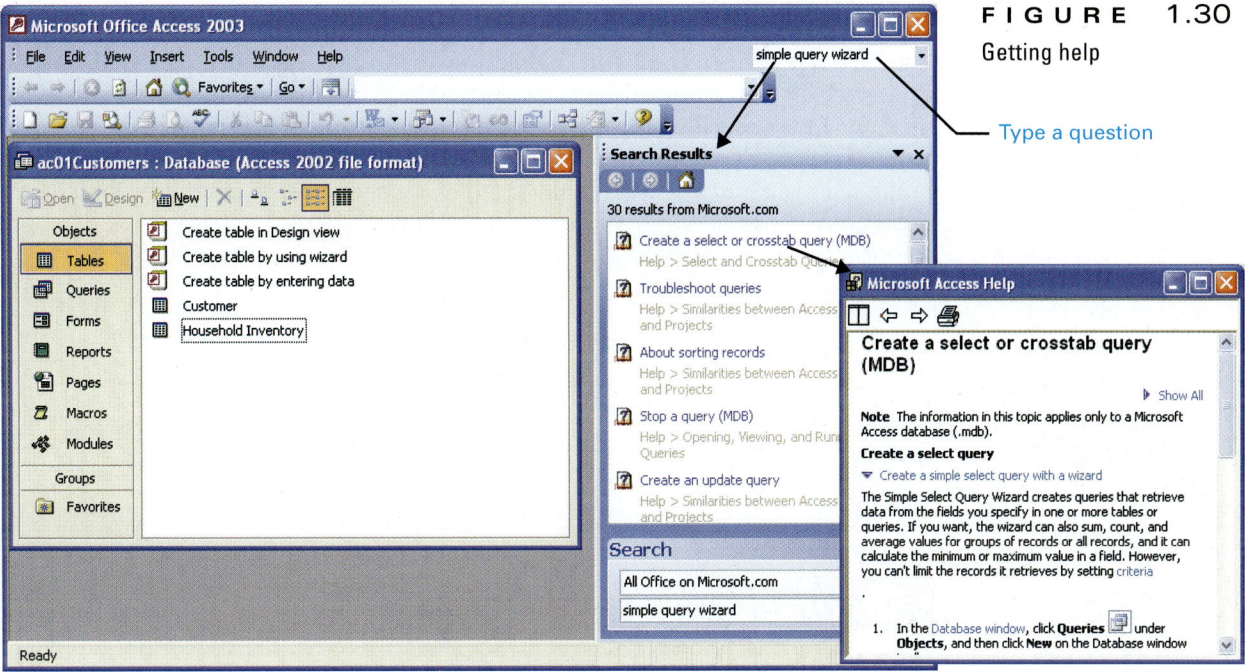

F I G U R E   1.30

Getting help

Type a question

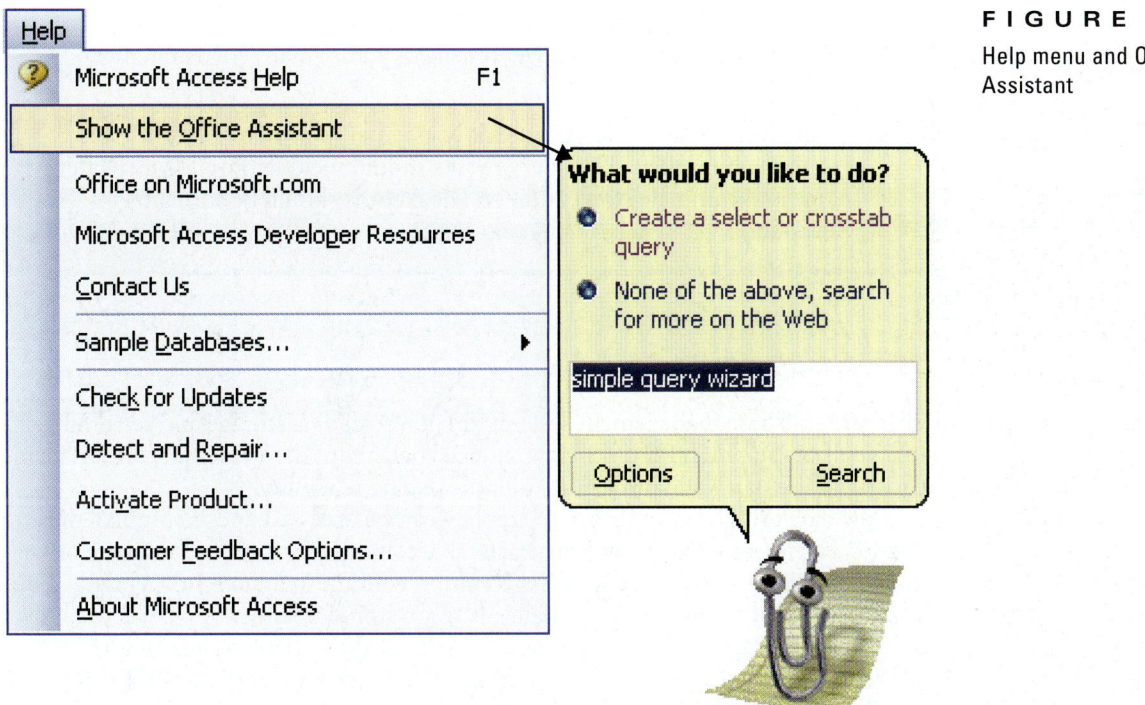

F I G U R E   1.31

Help menu and Office
Assistant

Right-clicking the Office Assistant displays options that control how the assistant
works. The visual presentation gallery includes Merlin the magician, a robot, a cat, and
a dog. If he is left active and set to do so, the assistant will provide tips as you work. He
can also be hidden or disabled.

Exiting Access

Exiting Access is accomplished by choosing the Close button of the main Access Window. The Exit option of the File menu also will close Access. Regardless of the exit method employed, all open objects will be closed before Access is closed. If you have made unsaved changes to open objects such as a table or datasheet, you will be prompted to save or abandon changes. When all open objects have been successfully closed, Access will close.

Exiting Access:

1. Select **File** and then **Exit** from the menu
2. If prompted to save changes, do so

SESSION 1.2

making the grade

1. Access database objects include _____, _____, and _____.

2. T F   Changes made in the Datasheet View such as widening columns are automatically saved when the view is closed.

3. Describe the purpose of the Documenter (Tools|Analyze|Documenter) menu option.

4. Create a query from the KoryoKicks Customer table that will be used to create mailing labels. The query results should include the customer's full name and complete street address. The records should be sorted by ZipCode.

SESSION 1.3 SUMMARY

Relational database management systems are powerful data storage and retrieval technologies. Data stored in RDBMSs have reduced data redundancy and increased data integrity and use data validation rules to improve data reliability.

Raw data are stored in tables where they can be accessed and manipulated using Queries, Forms, and Reports objects. Each table column represents an attribute or field of an entity. For example, Gender is a common column in a table storing data about employees. All of the attributes for one entity are stored in a row or record, so all data stored for one employee are in the same row. All of the possible values of an attribute are called its domain. Indexes are used to speed data retrieval and output sorting.

Ideally each table should have a primary key that uniquely and minimally identifies each row of data. Social Security Number is one likely primary key when storing data about people. Tables are joined to each other using shared fields. A field that can be used to join to another table is called a foreign key. When tables are joined, they have definable relationships such as one-to-one or one-to-many.

Wizards are an easy way to create simple queries, forms, and reports. Queries are a way to ask questions of the database data by specifying what data to retrieve and how to organize them. Queries also can be used to update multiple rows of data in one step. Forms are a user-friendly way to view and update data on a computer screen. Reports allow you to format data for printing.

Database objects support multiple views. Personal preference and the operation to be performed determine the view to be used. For example, a table's Datasheet View is used to view, navigate, and maintain data while the Design View is used to change the structure of the table.

Visit www.mhhe.com/i-series/ to explore related topics.

MICROSOFT OFFICE SPECIALIST OBJECTIVES SUMMARY

- Create Access databases using the Wizard—MOS AC03S-1-1
- Find and move among records—MOS AC03S-2-2
- Create tables using Table Wizard—MOS AC03S-1-2
- Create Select Queries using the Simple Query Wizard—MOS AC03S-1-7
- Create forms using the Form Wizard—MOS AC03S-1-8
- Print database objects and data—MOS AC03S-4-3

making the grade answers

SESSION 1.1

1. relational database management system.

2. the standardized language used to ask questions of data stored in relational databases.

3. columns, attributes, fields, or foreign keys. Each is an acceptable answer.

4. primary key.

5. A wide range of answers can be considered appropriate for this. There are some key components that all acceptable answers should contain. At a minimum, the answer should contain fields for FirstName, LastName, StreetAddress, City, State, and ZipCode. Better answers would also contain fields for OrderDate, Product, and OrderQuantity and address the need to find a unique key to identify each customer.

SESSION 1.2

1. Any answers from the following list are correct: Tables, Queries, Forms, Reports, Pages, Macros, or Modules.

2. False. The user is prompted to save them when they close the view.

3. One of the features of the Documenter is the ability to create printed documentation about an Access object such as a table. The chapter example used the Documenter to print the Customer table design.

4. The query results should include the customer's full name and complete street address. The records should be sorted by ZipCode.

ACCESS

task reference *summary*

Task	Page #	Preferred Method
Opening an Access object	AC 1.19	• Click the type of object that you would like to open in the Database Window's Objects bar • Select the object that you would like to open • Click the **Open** button
Activating Access Wizards	AC 1.24	• Click the object (Queries, Forms, Reports) whose Wizard you would like to access in the Database Window's Objects bar • Click **New** in the Database Window's toolbar • The available Wizards will be listed • Select the Wizard and respond to its questions
Getting help	AC 1.32	• Click in the Type a Question drop-down text box in the Access menu • Type in keywords relevant to your topic. Full sentences are not necessary and do not improve the performance of the search • Press **Enter** • Select from the topics provided or adjust the keywords and search again

TRUE/FALSE

1. Reports are designed to be viewed on a computer screen.

2. Wizards are helpful applets that walk you through complex operations like creating a table.

3. A table must be open in Design View to print the design of the table.

4. Tables, forms, reports, and queries are examples of Access database objects.

5. Access database indexes are similar to an index of a book and are used to speed looking up data values.

6. Relationships allow data from multiple tables to be used together in queries, forms, and reports.

7. The data in one cell of a table are called a data value.

FILL-IN

1. The Access object used to create printed output is the _____ object.

2. Database _____ ensures that only authorized people can access and update database data.

3. _____ is the language used to define the structure of a database table.

4. When using the Simple Query Wizard, the _____ button will add the current field to those that will appear in the query results.

5. The _____ is one way to obtain help in Access.

6. A(n) _____ key is a field that could have been defined as the primary key but was not.

MULTIPLE CHOICE

1. A database management system (DBMS) provides
   a. facilities to maintain data.
   b. the ability to store data.
   c. tools to build reports and forms.
   d. all of the above.

2. A relational database
   a. stores data in tables.
   b. stores data in a hierarchical structure.
   c. stores data in a dominion.
   d. stores data in a networked structure.

3. The primary key is important to data stored in a database because it
   a. is used to define many-to-many relationships.
   b. allows data from other tables to be retrieved.
   c. uniquely identifies each row of data stored.
   d. is a required database object.

4. In the relational database environment an object is
   a. the foreign key.
   b. an item that can be stored like a table or form.
   c. a client/server database.
   d. an Access Window.

5. A query
   a. creates a formatted printout of data.
   b. can select and calculate based on criteria.
   c. is a member of the Groups bar.
   d. is initiated using the field selector.

review of concepts

REVIEW QUESTIONS

Each of the following topics should be addressed in one to three paragraphs.

1. Discuss at least two ways to open an Access database.

2. Discuss the benefits and difficulties of using database management systems.

3. How does reduced data redundancy decrease errors in database data?

4. Outline at least two Customer data queries that might benefit KoryoKicks.

5. Discuss the various types of keys introduced in the chapter and how they are used in relational databases.

6. What are the benefits of storing data in a relational database? Are there any negative issues that must be dealt with?

7. Describe the various ways that data in relational database tables can be joined.

CREATE THE QUESTION

For each of the following answers, create the question.

ANSWER	QUESTION
1. They are specific to each Access object and appear at the top of a window	_____
2. Setting a primary key automatically creates the first one for a table	_____
3. The object that allows you to create a custom user interface to display and manipulate data	_____
4. A reusable template that will speed the development of Access database components such as tables and queries	_____
5. The Table view used to change the Table structure	_____

FACT OR FICTION

For each of the following, determine whether the statement is fact, fiction, or both and present your arguments for that conclusion.

1. Relational databases are the only databases in use by today's businesses.

2. The Office Assistant is the only way to obtain Access help.

3. The Query Datasheet toolbar can be displayed while viewing a form.

4. A query is another way to store data.

5. The Print button can be used to print the design of a table.

6. The Simple Query Wizard allows you to select columns that will be returned by a query, but not the rows.

1. Working with a Database for Curbside Recycling

Curbside Recycling is a Muncie, Indiana, recycling organization that picks up recyclables from homeowners. Neighborhoods subscribe to the service so that pickup is cost effective. Curbside provides special containers to subscribers for sorting recyclables: a blue container for paper products and a purple container for aluminum, plastic, and glass products.

Subscribers place their recycling containers on the curb for biweekly pickup. Each recycling container is weighed before being emptied. Curbside drivers carry handheld recording devices used to track each pickup. Subscribers receive quarterly profit-sharing checks based on their contributions. If Curbside does not make a profit, subscribers don't get paid for their recyclables. If Curbside makes a profit, subscribers share in that profit. Curbside has asked you to help develop a database that will effectively track subscribers using the data downloaded from the drivers' devices. Eventually, there will be multiple tables in the database. The Customers table will hold static customer information such as name, address, and phone. The CustomerRecords table holds data about each recyclable pickup. It currently contains test data and is the one with which you will be working.

1. Make sure that you have access to the data from your data disk

2. Start Access and open the **ac01CurbsideRecycling.mdb** database from your Chapter 1 files

FIGURE 1.32
Customer table update form

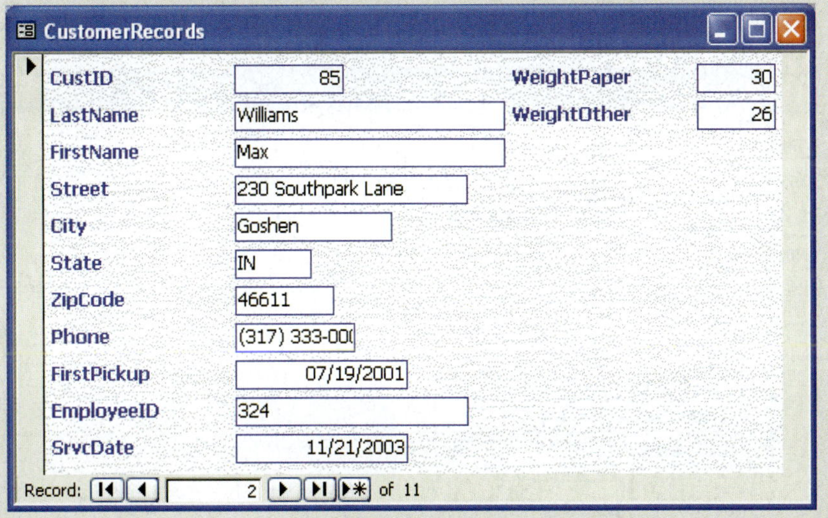

3. Open the **CustomerRecords** table, add records for yourself and a friend with CustID 30 and 31, today's date as both the SrvcDate and FirstPickup, and EmployeeID 902

4. Sort the datasheet rows by EmployeeID, SrvcDate, and CustID. Print the result

5. Make the following updates to existing data:

   CustId 2, SvcDate 11/22/2003 WeightOther should be updated to **17**

   CustID 20, SvcDate 11/22/2003 WeightOther should be updated to **26**

6. Sort the CustomerRecords datasheet. Use EmployeeId as the primary sort and WeightOther as the secondary sort. Print the results and save the format changes to the table. Make the sort fields the leftmost columns

7. Use the Simple Query Wizard to create a query containing EmployeeID, WeightPaper, and WeightOther. When prompted, choose Summary and set the Summary Options to Sum WeightPaper and WeightOther. The query should be named **EmployeeTotals** and display one row of totals for each employee

8. Use AutoForm: Columnar to create a data entry form with all fields from the Customer table. Display the Max Williams record for Svc Date 11/21/2003 and print it. Close the form saving it as **CustomerUpdate**

9. Use the Report Wizard to create a tabular report. Print the result. Close the report saving it as **CustomerReport**

10. If your work is complete, exit Access; otherwise, continue to the next assignment

2. Working with a Database for Lalier Construction

Lalier Construction Inc. (LCI) is a Colorado company started by Mike and Niki Lalier. LCI's primary business is commercial roofing, but also includes residential roofing and small remodeling jobs. During the off-season LCI provides work for only eight full-time employees, while at the height of a construction season it can employ over 300 people on 25 or more projects. Mike manages initial client contact, project bids, and the various construction crews. Niki recruits and hires crew employees, handles customer follow-up, and keeps all of the company books.

LCI uses bookkeeping software for billing, receivables, and financial statements but has been tracking employee contact and effectiveness data on 3 × 5 cards. Because the business is seasonal and the workforce is temporary, a better way to recruit and manage employees is needed. Niki has started creating a Microsoft Access database to track employees who have already worked for LCI and any potential employees that come to her attention. The goal is to have a ready resource for rapidly staffing any project that Mike contracts.

1. Make sure that you have access to the data from your data disk

2. Start Access and open the **ac01LalierConstruction.mdb** database from your Chapter 1 files

3. Open the **Employees** table and add records for yourself and at least three of your friends. Each new record should be for a JobSkill of **Roofing**, BillingRate of **$70**, and an HourlyRate of **$40**

4. Sort the datasheet rows by City. Make City the leftmost field and print the result

5. Sort the datasheet rows by FirstName within LastName (first sort field). Make the following updates to existing data and then print the result

   - Justin Modahl's *Home Phone* should be updated to **3039285729**

   - Evan Navaro's *Billing Rate* should be updated to **$75**

   - Garrett Stiefler's JobSkills should be updated to **Texture**

6. Use the Simple Query Wizard to create a query containing EmployeeID, LastName, FirstName, and HomePhone. Save the query as **PhoneList** and print the resulting datasheet

7. Use AutoForm: Columnar to create a data entry form. Display the Adam Kiernes record and print it. Save the form as **EmployeeUpdate**

8. Use the Report Wizard to create the default tabular report. Print the result. Close the report saving it as **EmployeeReport**

9. If your work is complete, exit Access; otherwise, continue to the next assignment

FIGURE 1.33

EmployeeUpdate and EmployeeReport

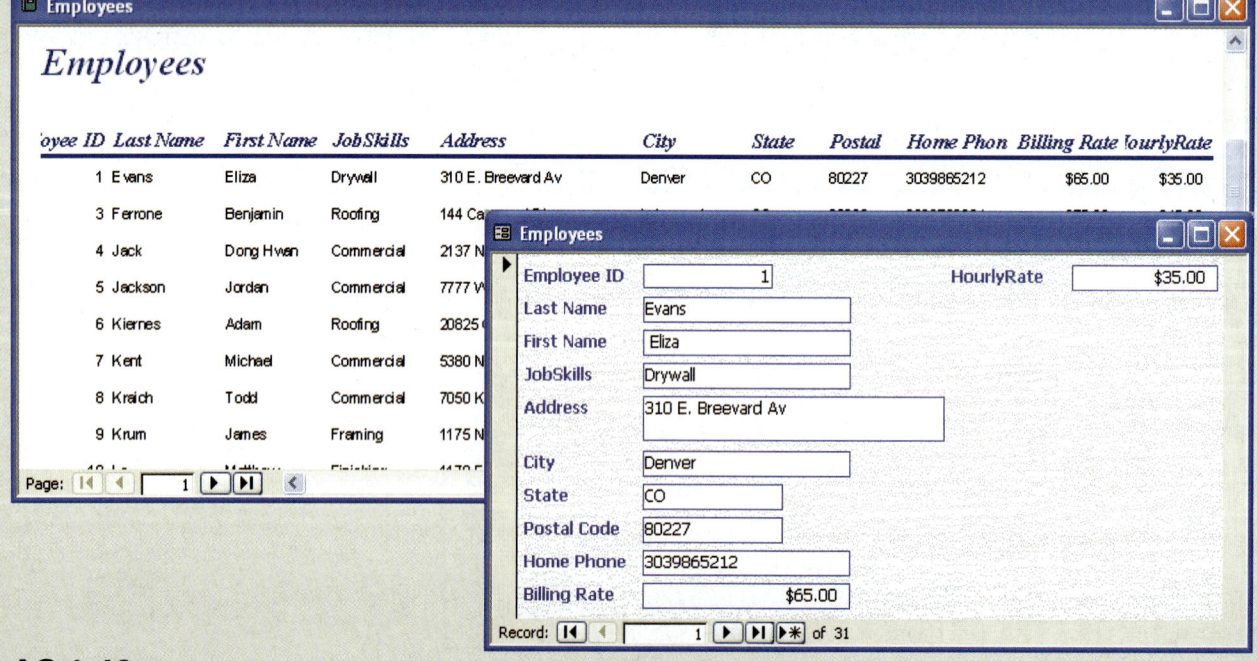

challenge!

1. Tracking Employees at Little White School House

Samuel Mink is the director of the Little White School House, a small private mountain community school. There are 142 students from preschool through grade 6. The staff consists of eight teachers, the director, a secretary, and community volunteers. Current records for the school are kept manually or in an Excel spreadsheet. Samuel would like more automation, consistency in record keeping, and reporting capabilities. You have met with Samuel and he has provided you with sample forms and a copy of the current data.

Your plan is to begin by putting employee tracking into an Access database according to the criteria listed below.

1. Use Microsoft Word to create a list of employee attributes that should be contained in the Little White School House Employee table

2. Open Access, create a new database (select Blank Database from the New category of the task pane), and name it **ac01LittleWhiteSchoolHouse**

3. Use the Table Wizard to create an Employee table with a primary key. Remember that while you need to store personal data, payroll data, and contact information, this is a small organization, so all of the suggested fields are not needed

4. Enter the following data:

<your name>	Secretary	22,400
Samuel Mink	Director	58,929
Margaret Frost	Preschool teacher	31,211
Rachael Dawson	1st grade teacher	28,452
Robert Gibbs	2nd grade teacher	36,283
Randi Evans	3rd grade teacher	45,879
Asayah Muhammad	4th grade teacher	44,962
David Mackall	5th grade teacher	30,980
Kasey Johnson	Music teacher	30,281
Ennis Johnson	Art teacher	30,486

5. Add two of your friends as volunteers (0 salary) and make up the remaining data so there are no blank cells in the table

6. Update Margaret Frost's salary to **31,311**

7. Sort the table by employee first and last name. Make the name fields leftmost fields and print

8. Sort the table by decreasing salary. Make Salary the leftmost field and print

9. Print the table design

10. Use the AutoForm: Columnar Wizard to create a form for this table. Print the form with the data for Asayah Muhammad showing (Figure 1.34). Name the form **Employees**

11. Use AutoReport: Tabular to create the default report from this data. Name the report **Employees**

12. Close the database and exit Access if your work is complete

FIGURE 1.34

Employee table form

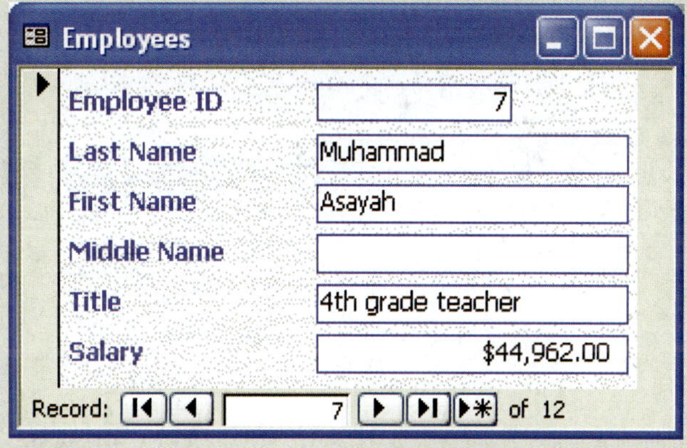

2. Tracking Your Recordings

Personal databases can be used to track and report on your personal assets, possessions, and plans. Sometimes this tracking can simply catalog a collection or collections. Other times, a database is an effective way to produce reports needed for taxes, other government reporting, banking, or personal business uses. To experience the simplicity of building and populating a database of a personal collection, you will create a database and table to hold information about your personal recording collection.

1. Open Access, create a new database (select Blank Database from the New category of the task pane), and name it **ac01<yourname>Recordings.mdb**

2. Use the Table Wizard to create a new table. Use the **Recordings** sample table in the **Personal** Table Category to add the following fields to your table

   - RecordingId
   - RecordingTitle
   - RecordingArtistID renamed to **RecordingArtist**
   - MusicCategoryID renamed to **MusicCategory**
   - RecordingLabel
   - YearReleased

3. Name the table **MyMusic**

4. Open the table in Design View. Modify the table design by setting the Data Type of both RecordingArtist and MusicCategory to **Text**

5. Switch to Datasheet View saving the table when prompted. Remember that RecordingID is automatically generated as you enter the data shown in Figure 1.35

6. Enter the data for at least 15 of your own recordings (use your friends' if you do not have 15 of your own). Be sure to add music in at least two different MusicCategory values

7. Use the Simple Query Wizard to produce a list containing MusicCategory, RecordingArtist, and RecordingTitle. Save the query as **MusicCategory**

8. Use AutoForm: Columnar to create a data entry form from the **MyMusic** table. Display the John Coltrane record and print it. Save the form as **MyMusicUpdate**

9. Use the Report Wizard to create the default tabular report for the MyMusic table. Print the result. Close the report saving it as **MyMusicReport**

10. If your work is complete, exit Access; otherwise, continue to the next assignment

FIGURE 1.35

MyMusic data and
MyMusicUpdate form

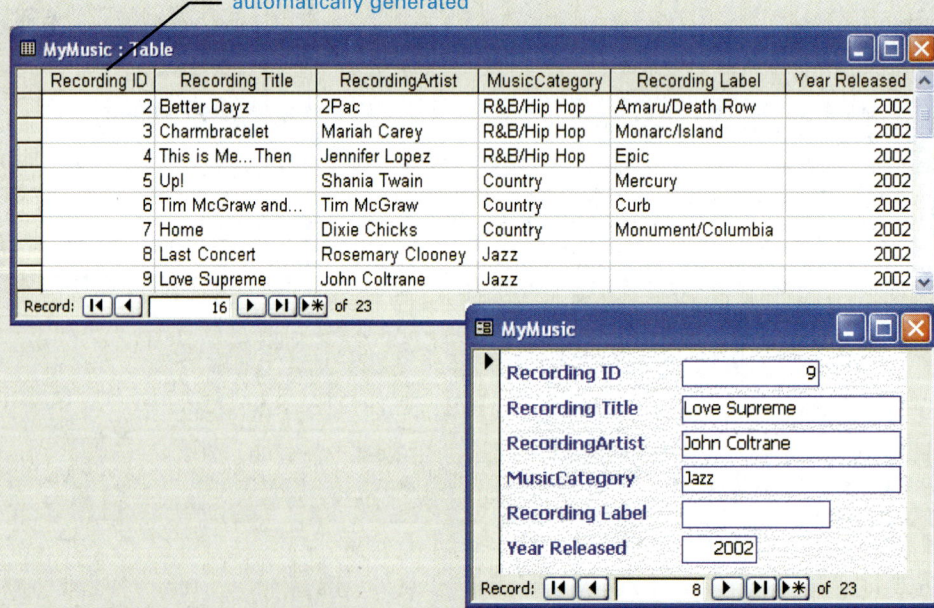

1. Exotic Flora Price List

Exotic Flora is a worldwide consortium of small florists who provide unique fresh flower arrangements for every occasion. Each florist pays a membership fee and agrees to deliver ordered arrangements within 24 hours of payment verification. All arrangements are guaranteed to match the order and to last for at least 10 days.

The bulk of flower orders is generated through an e-storefront that accepts orders, verifies payment, and forwards the order to the appropriate florist. Forty-two percent of the profit for each order goes to the e-store-front management organization, 10 percent goes to the Exotic Flora association, and the florist who delivers the flowers keeps the remainder.

For the e-storefront to work effectively, the member florists must provide product data to the storefront managers in a convenient format. After some trial and error, the florists have settled on Access as the tool that best suits their needs. Each member florist provides a weekly table of available arrangements with the arrangement name, price, picture, availability dates, and maximum quantity that can be delivered. The e-storefront manager consolidates the Access tables provided by the various florists into a large Oracle database that is used to generate the e-storefront site.

Gabriella Juarez is a small florist in Pahoa, Hawaii, who has decided to join Exotic Flora to increase her business. She has no experience with computers and has asked you to build the database that she needs.

1. Open Access, create a new database (select Blank Database from the New category of the task pane), and name it **ac01ExoticFlora**

2. Use the Table Wizard to create a Products table:

   a. From the Products sample table select ProductID, ProductName, ProductDescription, and UnitPrice

   b. From the Employees sample table select Photograph

   c. Set ProductId as the primary key that is automatically generated

3. Enter the data from Figure 1.36 into the table. Instructions for adding the jpg image are in the Tip

tip: *Click the Photograph cell, choose Object from the Insert menu, click Create from File, and browse to find this chapter's pictures. The actual photograph is not visible in this view. You can change the photograph by deleting the current cell contents and inserting a new photo*

4. Sort the data by product name and print

5. Print the table design

6. Use the AutoForm: Columnar Wizard to create a form for this table

tip: *Later chapters will teach you to customize forms to fully display labels and pictures*

Print the form with the data for Kea Mix showing

7. Close the ExoticFlora database and exit Access if your work is complete

FIGURE 1.36

ExoticFlora data and form

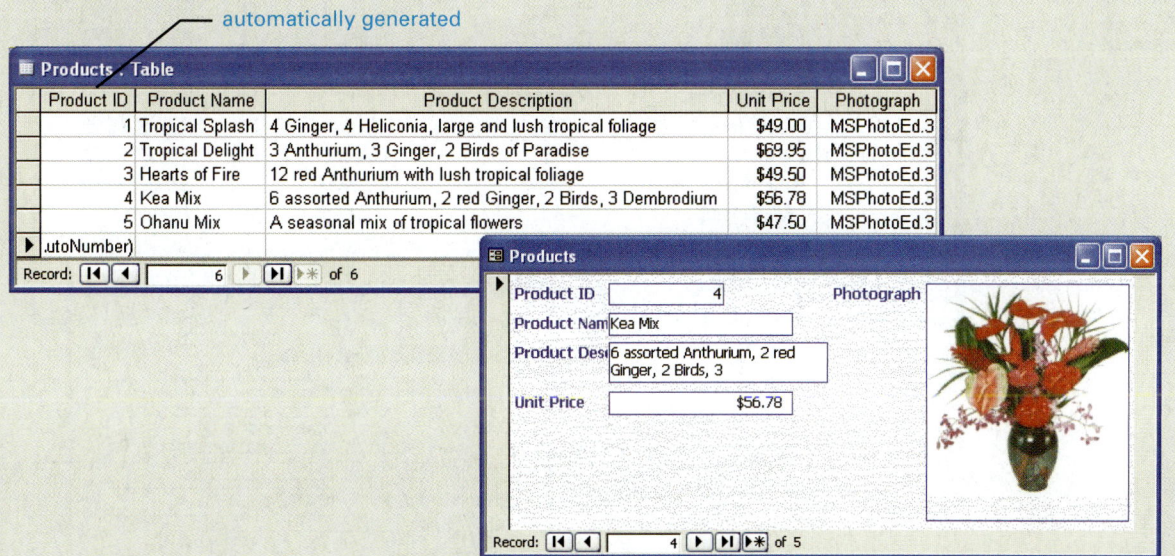

2. Tracking Customers at Delroy Ocean Travel

Rolfe Delroy is the owner of Delroy Ocean Travel (DOT), a small private travel agency specializing in ocean-related adventures. The DOT staff consists of eight agents, a promotions manager, a secretary, and Rolfe. Current customer and cruise records are kept manually or in an Excel spreadsheet. Rolfe would like more automation, consistency in record keeping, the ability to use customer lists from other businesses, and the enhanced reporting capabilities available from a database. You have met with Rolfe and he has provided you with sample forms and examples of how the current data are stored. Your plan is to begin by putting customer tracking into an Access database.

1. Open Access, create a new database (select Blank Database from the New category of the task pane), and name it **ac01DelroyTravel.mdb**

2. Use the Table Wizard to create a new table. Use the **Customers** sample table in the **Business** Table Category to add the following fields to your table design

   - CustomerID
   - ContactLastName renamed to **CustomerLastName** using the Wizard's Rename Field button
   - ContactFirstName renamed to **CustomerFirstName** using the Wizard's Rename Field button
   - City

   - StateorProvince renamed to **State** using the Wizard's Rename Field button
   - PhoneNumber

3. Set CustomerID as the automatically generated primary key and save the table naming it **DOTCustomer**

4. Remember that CustomerID is automatically generated as you enter the data shown in Figure 1.37

5. Add two of your friends with their correct data. There should be no blank cells in the table

6. Sort the table by CustomerFirstName within CustomerLastName (first sort field) and print

7. Sort the table by descending state and print

8. Print the table design

9. Use the Simple Query Wizard to produce a list containing CustomerLastName, CustomerFirstName, and PhoneNumber. Save the query as **CustomerList**

10. Use the AutoForm: Columnar Wizard to create a form for this table. Print the form with the data for yourself showing. Save the form as **CustomerUpdate**

11. Use the Report Wizard to create the default tabular report. Print the result. Close the report saving it as **CustomerReport**

12. Close the database and exit Access if your work is complete

FIGURE 1.37

CustomerUpdate data and form

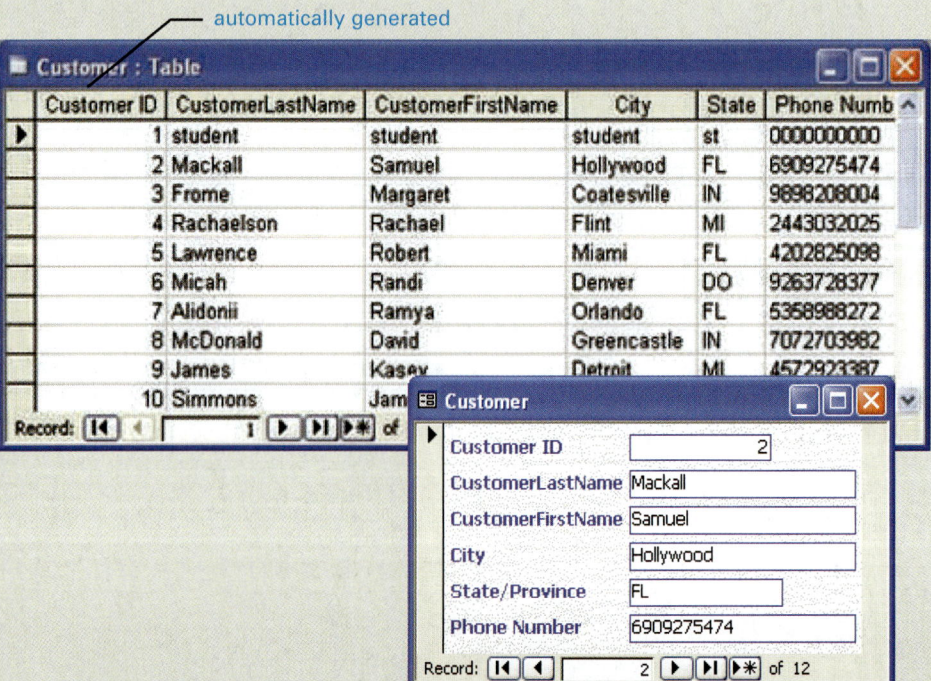

1. Searching for Service Organizations

The Wheeler Helping Hand Association (WHHA) is an alliance of missions, food banks, and service organizations supporting central Indiana. The goal of the group is to provide assistance to people who need food, shelter, clothing, job training, and counseling. The organization has two full-time staff to organize and coordinate hundreds of volunteers. Volunteers are the backbone of the organization, doing everything from cooking to counseling.

All supplies are donated through charitable contributions. Most of the contributions are received through churches, but there is also an annual Thanksgiving phone drive and a new Internet contributions site. The Internet contributions site has two purposes. The first is to let people know what the current needs of the organization are by posting a list of the most needed food, clothing, and services. The second is to promote the Wheeler Helping Hand vision and accept monetary contributions.

You have volunteered and have been asked to use your computer expertise to support the services being provided. You know that the Internet is a great resource and have decided to look for better ways to promote the association and support the volunteers. One of your ideas is to provide a database of Web sites that have useful services for WHHA clients. Although the clients are unlikely to have computer access, volunteers who need to be able to provide support without much training would find the information useful.

1. Use your favorite search engine to find organizations and services that could benefit the WHHA clientele

2. Record the information from at least six sites to be entered into the volunteer database

3. Open Access, create a new database (select Blank Database from the New category of the task pane), and name it **ac01WHHA.mdb**

4. Use the Table Wizard to create a **Services** table
   a. From the Suppliers Sample Table select SupplierID, SupplierName, ContactName, ContactTitle, PhoneNumber, EmailAddress, and Notes
   b. Rename (click the Rename Field button with the field selected) SupplierID to **ServicesID**, SupplierName to **ServicesName**, and EmailAddress to **WebAddress**
   c. Set ServicesId as the automatically generated primary key

5. Enter the data from your Web search in the Services table. Make up the contact data if needed and include your comments about the services and the Web site in notes. Do not leave any blank cells

6. Print the table design

7. Use the AutoForm: Columnar Wizard to create a form for the Services table named **WHHA**. Print the form with the data for your third record showing (see Figure 1.38)

8. Close the WHHA database and exit Access if your work is complete

FIGURE 1.38

WHHA form

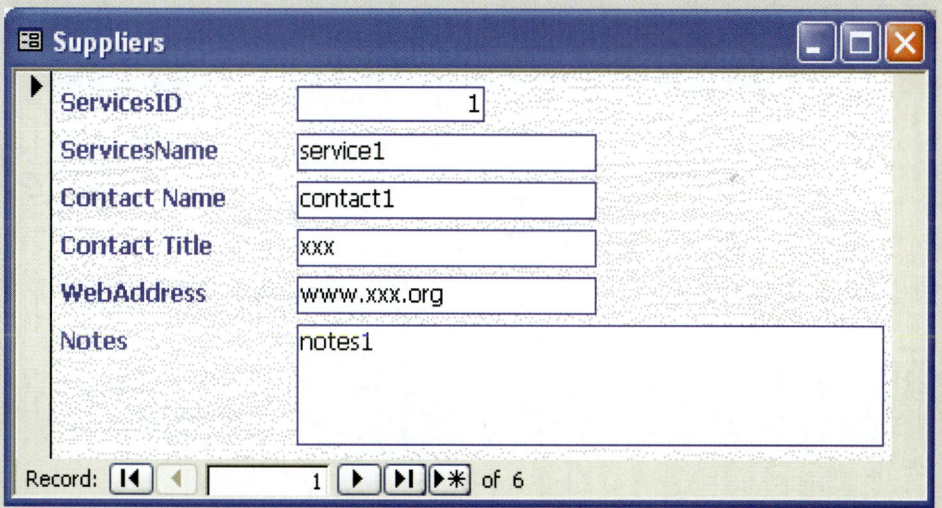

around the world

1. Tracking International Trade Consultants

The Alliance for Global Commerce (AGC) is an organization that tracks and rates businesses participating in international trade. The three businessmen who founded AGC were able to navigate the various cultures and rituals participating in trades, but had a persistent problem with knowing which other traders were reliable. Since trial and error had proved costly, they started AGC.

The AGC vision was to create something like the Better Business Bureau on an international scale. Initially the three men gathered data on trade incidents necessary to support their own trade activities and then published the data in a newsletter distributed to trade, retail, and wholesale organizations. After that, the newsletter recipients reported trade incidents that were tracked and published in the newsletter. Incidents are any behavior of a trade organization that negatively impacts the viability of the trade pact. The most common incidents are failure to pay and shipments over one week late. Initially there was a concern that false incident reports would be a problem, but they proved not to be.

The founders now believe that as international commerce increases, the problems with unreliable and unscrupulous traders will become more prevalent, increasing the need for tracking and analysis. They have hired you to spearhead the data gathering and analysis. You have begun by building a table of traders and searching for new trade organizations.

1. Start Access and open the **ac01AGC.mdb** database

2. Open the Traders table and become familiar with its contents

3. Add the following data for TraderNmbrs 80, 81, and 82

   South Side Imports, 3850 S. Emerson Ave., Indianapolis, IN, 46121, (317)786-8188, Automobiles, 0

   Titan International, 4515 W 16th St., Dayton, OH, 48378, (383)484-9195, Automobiles, 2

   Auto Network, 8441 Castleton Corner Dr., Atlanta, GA, 30301, (290)748-2070, Clothing, 0

   tip: *Commas are used to separate the fields and should not be entered*

4. Look in your local phone book and find four international trade businesses. Enter the data into the Traders table. Use TraderNmbrs 83 through 86

5. Sort by TraderNmbr and print

6. Make TradeArea the first column, sort by it, and then print

7. Make BusinessName the first column, sort by it, and then print

8. Make Incidents and Business Name the first columns. Sort the table by descending Incidents and Business Name and print

9. Print the table design

10. Use the AutoForm: Columnar Wizard to create a form for this table. Print the form with the data for AutoNetwork showing

11. Use the AutoReport: Tabular Wizard to create and print a report

12. Close the AGC database and exit Access if your work is complete

FIGURE 1.39

AGC form and report

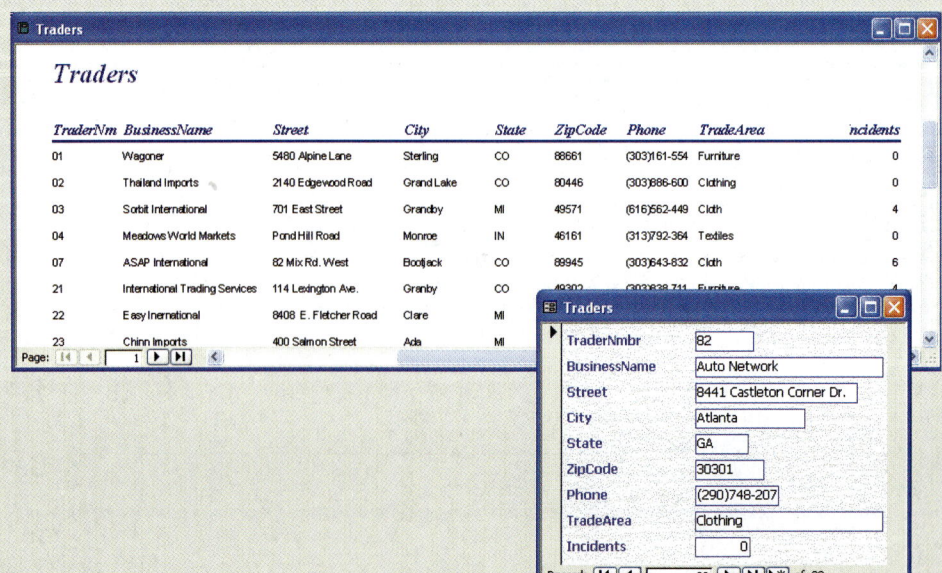

running project: tnt web page design

Beginning the TnT Database

TnT is a custom Web page development company founded by Victoria (Tori) Salazar and her college roommate Tonya O'Dowd. Tonya was an art major learning graphic design and Tori was a computer science major studying programming languages. The company was born when both had final projects due at the end of their second semester. Tonya was creating custom graphics and Tori was using Java to automate a Web site when they decided that they could create a killer site if they combined their talents.

Their first project was to put the college newspaper online. As a result of this project, both were hired as interns at the local newspaper.

After college, Tonya was hired as a graphic artist at a Web design company and Tori was hired as a Web software developer by a Fortune 500 company. They lived in different parts of the country but maintained contact via e-mail. After a few years Tori began picking up some extra work doing e-commerce development for fun and contracted with Tonya to create the graphics. The women liked working together and having control of what they worked on and decided to pick up more contracts. As business grew, both women quit their other jobs to concentrate on Web development.

They are frequently asked for customer references and samples of their work, and it has become tedious to maintain the Web site that provides this information. Tori and Tanya ask you to develop a database that will support their business. At some point they would like to store links to their customers and the sites that they have developed and update their Web site automatically. The first step is to create the Customer table.

1. Make sure that you have access to the data disk
2. Start Access and open the **ac01TnT.mdb** database
3. Open the **tblCustomers** table in Datasheet View
4. Sort the table by CusCountry and CusName. Make the sort field the leftmost column. Print the results
5. Print the table design
6. Use the Simple Query Wizard to create a query displaying the customer name, city, state, country, and phone. Sort by customer name. Print and save
7. Add yourself and two of your friends as customers
8. Create a columnar form and print your record
9. Create a tabular report. Save and print
10. Close the database and exit Access if your work is complete

FIGURE 1.40
TnT form

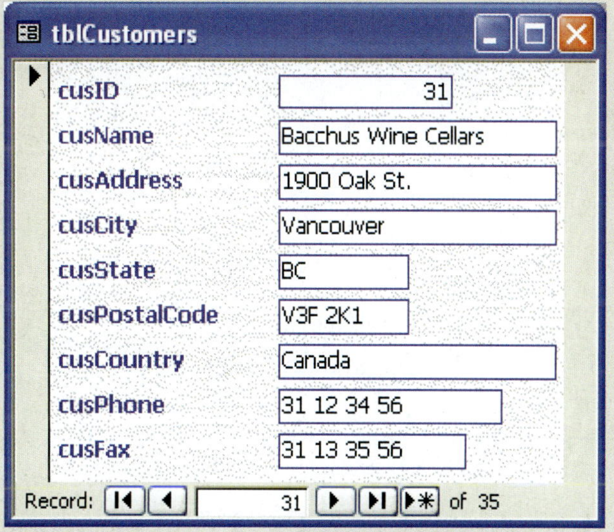

tblCustomers	
cusID	31
cusName	Bacchus Wine Cellars
cusAddress	1900 Oak St.
cusCity	Vancouver
cusState	BC
cusPostalCode	V3F 2K1
cusCountry	Canada
cusPhone	31 12 34 56
cusFax	31 13 35 56

Record: 31 of 35

1. Create a Personal Database

Evaluate your personal needs and select an area such as classes, grades, or belongings that could benefit from a database. Describe how the database will be used, being sure to document your database needs and the benefits that you expect to gain by creating the database.

Create a new blank database named **ac01<your-name>.mdb**. Use the Wizards introduced in this chapter to create table(s) in the database. Populate at least one table with 10 or more records. Use the Wizards to create an update form, simple query, and simple report for the populated table. Print the design of each table. Print each object created.

2. Start a Personal Business

Assume that you are starting a personal services business such as mowing lawns or tutoring. Document the type of data that you would need to track in order to effectively run your business. Describe how a database could be used to improve storage and access to the data needed for your business. Are there valid reasons to create a database? Not to create a database?

Create a new blank database named **ac01<your-name>Business.mdb**. Use the Wizards introduced in this chapter to create table(s) in the database. Populate at least one table with 10 or more records. Use the Wizards to create an update form, simple query, and simple report for the populated table. Print the design of each table. Print each object created.

Maintaining Your Database

know? did you

according *to Dennis Changon, spokesman for the International Civil Aviation Organization in Montreal, Canada, if all of the commercial planes in the world were grounded at the same time, there wouldn't be space to park them all at the gates.*

Colonel *Waring, New York City Street Cleaning Commissioner, was responsible for organizing the first rubbish-sorting plant for recycling in the United States in 1898.*

early *models of vacuum cleaners were powered by gasoline.*

honey *is used as a center for golf balls and in antifreeze mixtures.*

the *first commercial passenger airplane began flying in 1914.*

focus *group information compiled by CalComp revealed that _____ percent of computer users do not like using a mouse.*

to *find out how many computer users don't like using a mouse, visit* www.mhhe.com/i-series.

Chapter Objectives

- **Maintain table data using various methods to add records, delete records, and update field data—MOS AC03S-2-1**

- **Learn to organize and find table data using Datasheet View**

- **Understand how to design relational database tables**

- **Create and save Access table definitions using table Design View**

- **Use the Clipboard to copy records between tables**

- **Format datasheets—MOS AC03S-3-4**

- **Sort records in Datasheet View—MOS AC03S-3-5**

KoryoKicks: Starting a Personal Business

Missy and Micah are pleased with the progress that has been made in evaluating the database needs of KoryoKicks. The twins have significantly improved their understanding of databases and are happy with what they have learned by manipulating the Customer table prototype. Now they understand enough to help you design and develop a database to support the full data requirements of their business.

You know that education for database users is critical to the success of any database development project. If you build a wonderful database but the customer doesn't know how to use it, the result is an ineffective product. To avoid this situation, the process of familiarizing Missy and Micah with Access needs to continue. You want to ensure that they are comfortable organizing, maintaining, and using the stored data. Additionally, both are interested in learning how to design and develop databases so that they have a better understanding of potential applications for their data. They understand that Access can help them to market their martial arts classes and supplies using e-commerce.

Missy and Micah have provided you with paper copies of the Excel spreadsheets and manual reports that are currently being used. You have evaluated these documents to understand their business and get a better idea of how to design a database to support it. The preliminary assessment of the organization's database requirements indicates that tables are needed for customers (both students and people who purchase products are customers), orders, products, and suppliers. The Customer table prototype was built in Chapter 1 and is already in use. The Orders table would hold data about each order including order number, product ordered, and quantity ordered. The Products table would list products with their availability such as supplier, quantity on hand, and lead time needed to order. The Suppliers table would contain contact information and performance history for vendors who supply products to KoryoKicks.

Although you have a good idea of the tables Missy and Micah need, it is always a good idea to spend some time using a formal design process before developing tables. You will proceed with a more detailed analysis of data requirements and then develop a prototype for each table specified in the design process. You have decided to begin by looking at the data necessary to bill customers using the sample invoice from Figure 2.1. Missy and Micah will be involved throughout the analysis, design, development, and implementation steps of this process.

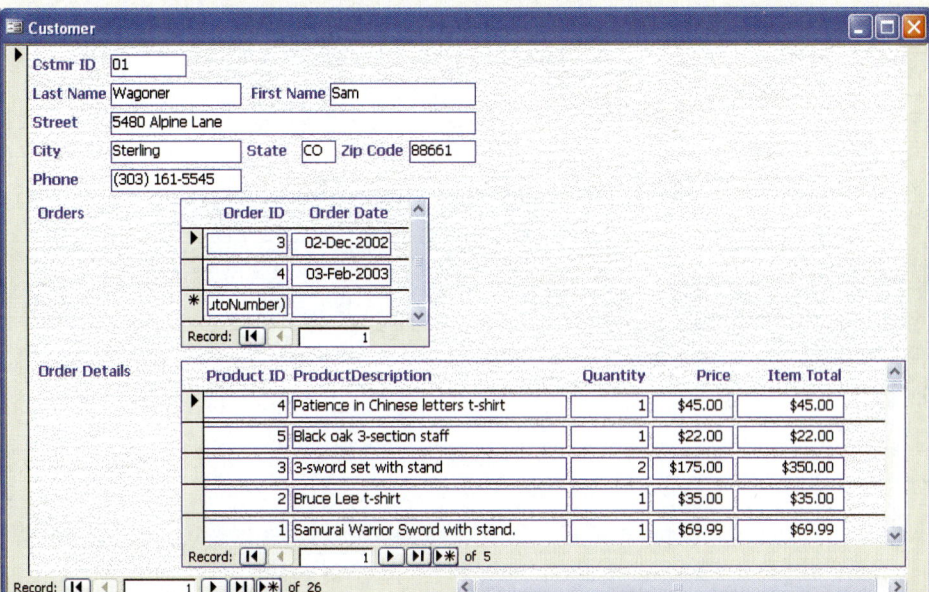

FIGURE 2.1

KoryoKicks customer invoice form

SESSION 2.1 MAINTAINING ACCESS DATA

To be effective, data stored in a database must be kept current. The process of keeping data current is called maintenance. Maintenance tasks include adding new records, removing old records, and changing values in existing records. Missy and Micah will both use KoryoKicks data, but there will be only one copy of the database and one user at a time. It is critical that they each understand how to sort, find, and update table data. They also need to develop a methodology for sharing maintenance tasks.

Ordering, Finding, and Entering Data

Access table data can be maintained many ways. The best way to maintain data will depend on the size of the tables, the frequency of updates, the design features that have been applied, and personal preferences. Because all Access objects support updates from the Datasheet View, you will review that method with Missy and Micah first.

Recall from the previous chapter that the Datasheet View displays stored values in a tabular format. Each row of data is a record and each column is a field. You can use the record selector to select an entire record, the field selector to select a column, and the Tab key to move from cell to cell. While this might be all the navigation that you need in a small database, the deficiencies of these methods should be obvious when contemplating the maintenance of tables containing hundreds or thousands of records.

Sorting Records

Database data are physically stored in what is called natural order, or the sequence the records were added to the table. By default the datasheet shows data in order by the primary key if there is one. Many times the primary key is wonderful for uniquely identifying records, but not an effective tool for humans to use in finding records. For example when you are looking for data on a specific person, you would have a hard time finding him or her by Social Security Number, the most likely primary key. However, it would be relatively easy to find him or her using the last and first names.

FIGURE 2.2

Various sorts of the
Customer table

sorted by LastName
and FirstName

sorted by State

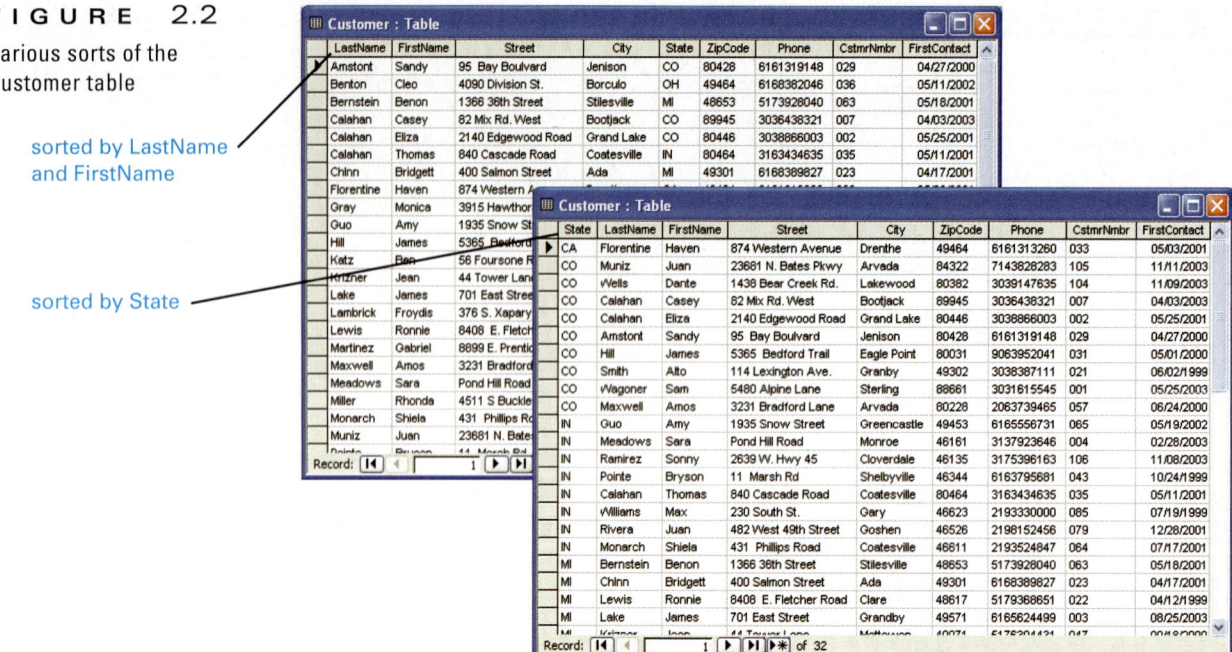

Finding and updating the correct row and column of data are critical to the integrity of database data. A simple way to improve your ability to find specific records in a large table of data is to sort the records in a manner related to the way they are being used. The same table data can be displayed in various sort orders that match the assorted ways that the data are used (see Figure 2.2). Normally the sort fields are placed to the left of the data to simplify visual searches of the list.

Moving Table Columns

Sorting table data in Datasheet View works in much the same way as sorting query output, which was introduced in the previous chapter. The first step in changing the order of the records is typically to move the sort column(s) to the left of the datasheet to visually indicate which field has been used to order. Most users expect data to be sorted by the first column(s) displayed for a table.

Changing the column order significantly improves the usability of a datasheet and has no impact on how the data are actually stored. When the column order reflects how the data are sorted (leftmost fields) and matches the way it is used (source documents like drivers licenses), updates are much more likely to be valid.

Micah lets you know that when he takes orders for martial arts supplies or signs up a student, he asks for the customers' name, address, city, state, zip, and then phone number. He would like the Customer table data to display in that order.

Reorganizing datasheet columns:

1. Open the Customer table of the **ac02Customers.mdb** database in Datasheet View

2. Use the field selector to select the CstmrNmbr column

3. Click and drag the column until it is between Phone and FirstContact

help yourself *Use the Type a Question combo box to improve your understanding of reorganizing table columns in the datasheet by typing* **move table column***. Review the contents of* Move a column*. The contents of* Tutorial: Formatting and Printing a Table *are also helpful. Close the Help window when you are finished*

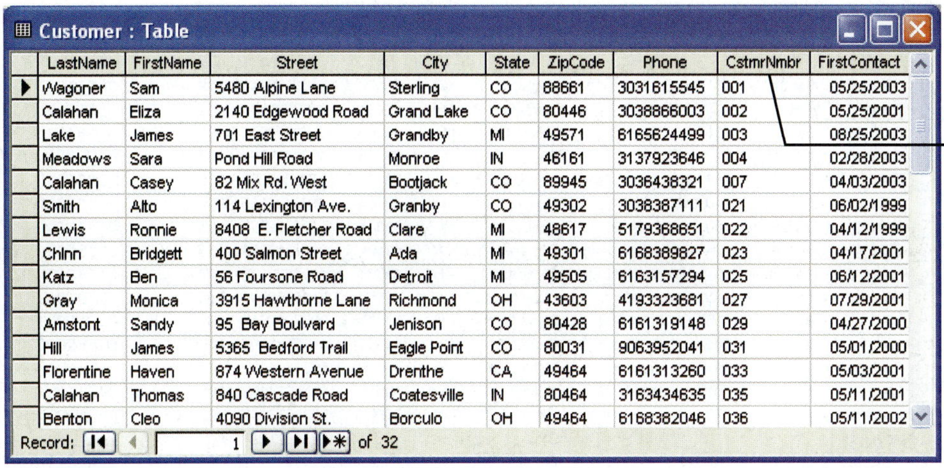

LastName	FirstName	Street	City	State	ZipCode	Phone	CstmrNmbr	FirstContact
Wagoner	Sam	5480 Alpine Lane	Sterling	CO	88661	3031615545	001	05/25/2003
Calahan	Eliza	2140 Edgewood Road	Grand Lake	CO	80446	3038866003	002	05/25/2001
Lake	James	701 East Street	Grandby	MI	49571	6165624499	003	08/25/2003
Meadows	Sara	Pond Hill Road	Monroe	IN	46161	3137923646	004	02/28/2003
Calahan	Casey	82 Mix Rd. West	Bootjack	CO	89945	3036438321	007	04/03/2003
Smith	Alto	114 Lexington Ave.	Granby	CO	49302	3038387111	021	06/02/1999
Lewis	Ronnie	8408 E. Fletcher Road	Clare	MI	48617	5179368651	022	04/12/1999
Chinn	Bridgett	400 Salmon Street	Ada	MI	49301	6168389827	023	04/17/2001
Katz	Ben	56 Foursone Road	Detroit	MI	49505	6163157294	025	06/12/2001
Gray	Monica	3915 Hawthorne Lane	Richmond	OH	43603	4193323681	027	07/29/2001
Amstont	Sandy	95 Bay Boulvard	Jenison	CO	80428	6161319148	029	04/27/2000
Hill	James	5365 Bedford Trail	Eagle Point	CO	80031	9063952041	031	05/01/2000
Florentine	Haven	874 Western Avenue	Drenthe	CA	49464	6161313260	033	05/03/2001
Calahan	Thomas	840 Cascade Road	Coatesville	IN	80464	3163434635	035	05/11/2001
Benton	Cleo	4090 Division St.	Borculo	OH	49464	6168382046	036	05/11/2002

Record: |◄ ◄ | 1 | ► ►| ►* | of 32

FIGURE 2.3

Customer table with new column order

repositioned CustmrNmber column

Organizing Records

Sorting by one field is as simple as clicking anywhere in the column and selecting the Sort Ascending or Sort Descending key from the toolbar. Unless a sort field contains unique values for each row in the table, multiple sort fields are needed to completely organize the data. For example, LastName is a nonunique field that can contain multiple rows with the value, Hampton for instance. When a sort field has multiple rows with the same value in the *primary sort* field, a *secondary sort* field like FirstName is needed to organize records. Access will allow you to select two or more adjacent columns for a sort. The order of the columns determines the importance of the field to the sort. Access will sort by the leftmost column first and then continue sorting with each of the other selected columns moving from left to right.

To achieve the desired order for the Customer table, you will show Missy and Micah how to sort by both the customer's last and first names. LastName is the primary sort field and must appear in the table before the secondary sort field, FirstName. To sort the data, select both the LastName and FirstName columns and then select the appropriate sort key button from the Access toolbar.

Sorting the Customer table:

1. Verify that ac02Customers.mdb is open

2. Open the Datasheet View of the Customer table

3. Verify that the column order is set so that LastName is the primary sort field and FirstName is the secondary sort field

4. Select both the LastName and FirstName columns and click the **Sort Ascending** ▲↓ button on the toolbar (see Figure 2.4)

5. When you close the datasheet, you will be prompted to save the layout changes that you have made. Choose **Yes** so that the next time you open the Customer table it will still be sorted

The impact of ascending and descending sorts on various types of data is represented in Figure 2.5. If you need to sort nonadjacent columns or use an ascending sort on some fields and descending sort on others, this can be accomplished in a query.

FIGURE 2.4

Reordering Customer table
data

sorted by FirstName
within LastName

FIGURE 2.5

Sort behaviors

Type of Data	Ascending Sort Behavior	Descending Sort Behavior
Number	Sorts from lowest to highest value	Sorts from highest to lowest value
Text	Sorts from A to Z	Sorts from Z to A
Date	Sorts from oldest to newest date	Sorts from newest to oldest date
Time	Sorts from oldest to newest time	Sorts from newest to oldest time
Yes/No	Sorts Yes or checked first	Sorts No or unchecked first

Finding Records

Access provides a Find tool for locating specific records. It can be used in many of the
views of a database including the Datasheet View. Click in the column whose values will
be searched and then click the Find button on the toolbar or select the Find option of
the Edit menu.

The Find and Replace dialog box is used to set the criteria for a search. Valid criteria are outlined in Figure 2.6.

The Find and Replace dialog box can be used to find and replace values. It is best
to test the Find criteria and then add the Replace value so that data are not accidentally
destroyed. In the next exercise you will replace the word "Road" with the abbreviation
"Rd." in the Customer table's Street addresses column.

anotherway

. . . to Initiate
**Access Operations
for the Current
Column**

Pressing **Ctrl+F** will
initiate the Find and
Replace dialog box
for the active column

task reference   Finding Specific Data Values

- Click in the column to search
- Click the **Find** 🔍 button
- Enter the Find What criteria using data values and wildcards to create a
  search pattern. Remember that a question mark (?) can be used as a
  wildcard for one character and an asterisk (*) is a wildcard for multiple
  characters
- Click the **Find Next** button. If multiple rows match the Find What criteria,
  repeat this step until the desired row is found

Find and Replace Dialog Box		
Criteria	**Action**	
Find What	Sets the value that will be matched in the search	
Look In	Determines what will be searched. The default is the active column, but you also can choose to search the entire table.	
Match	Any Part of Field	Matches if the *Find What* value is anywhere in the field
	Whole Field	Matches if the *Find What* value is all that is in the field
	Start of Field	Matches if the *Find What* value is at the start of the field
Search	All	Searches for a match in the entire *Look In* area
	Up	Searches for a match above the cursor in the *Look In* area
	Down	Searches for a match below the cursor in the *Look In* area
Match Case	Matches the case of *Find What* when clicked on	

Finding and replacing values in the Customer table:

1. Verify that the Customer table of ac02Customers.mdb database is open in Datasheet View

2. Click in the **LastName** column and activate the Find and Replace dialog box using the **Find** [icon] button on the toolbar

3. Enter **Calahan** in the Find What text box and click **Find Next**. The first Calahan occurrence should highlight. Click **Find Next** again to display the second occurrence and again to find the third occurrence

tip: *When Find Next is clicked after all occurrences of a value have been found, a dialog box displays stating "Microsoft Access finished searching the records. The search item was not found"*

click cursor in LastName field to search that column

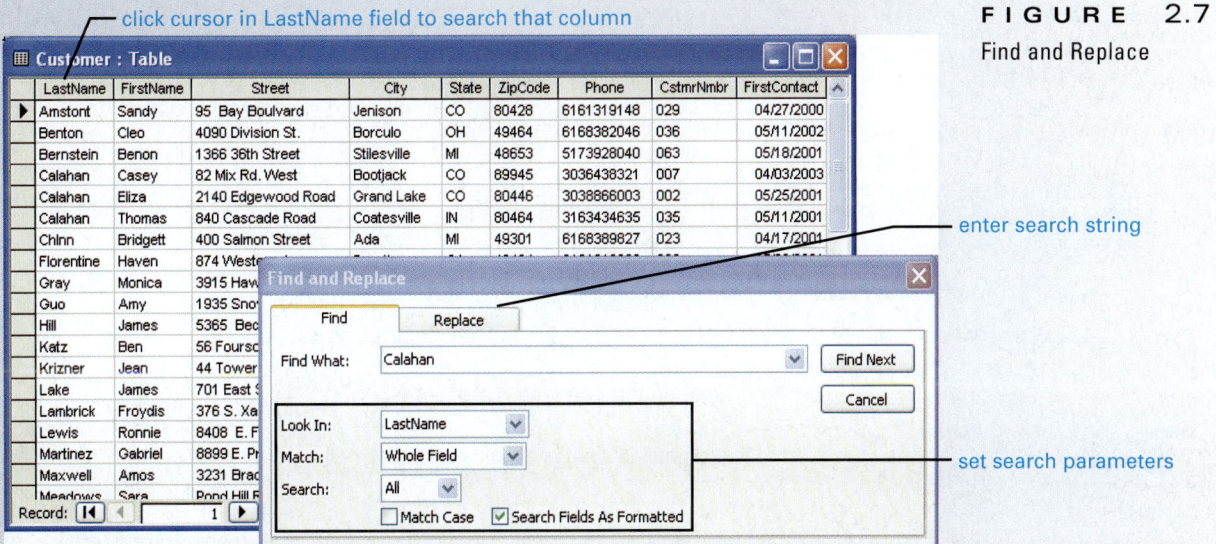

enter search string

set search parameters

4. Click in the Street column and enter a Find What value of **Road** and set Match to **Any Part of Field**. Click **Find Next** repeatedly to step through all of the values

tip: *Be sure that only the word "Road" is being selected from the street address. When the replace is applied in the next step, it will replace everything selected—not just the Find What value. If the entire contents of the Street are being selected, double-check the Match setting*

5. Now that the Find works, lets replace "Road" with the abbreviation "Rd." in all of the addresses. Click the **Replace** tab of the Find and Replace dialog box. Enter **Rd**. in the Replace With text box

6. Click **Replace All** to update all of the records at once

7. Verify that the replace worked correctly

Wildcards

When entering the Find What criteria, wildcards are used to create a pattern match (see Figure 2.8). A question mark (?) can be used to represent any single character in a pattern. Let's say, for example, that you were looking for a female Tony, but are not sure of the spelling. A search for Ton? would return both Toni and Tony. It would also return Tone, Tong, and Tons if they were stored in the field. The asterisk (*) wildcard will replace any number of characters so that searching for Ton* would return Tonaba, Toni, Tony, Tons, Tonka, Tonanbaum, and so on.

It is important to note that wildcards are not meant to be used with date, time, and numeric data types. Using wildcards with these data types can cause incomplete or erroneous data retrieval. Confusion arises because wildcards on numeric fields often appear to work and sometimes produce the correct results. Ideally wildcards are used on text data when you only know part of the value or want to find data that match a pattern.

FIGURE 2.8

Access wildcards

	Access Wildcards	
Character	Description	Example
*	Matches any number of characters; it can be used as the first or last character of a search value	wh* Finds what, who, whale, and wham
?	Matches any single alphabetic character	b?ll Finds bill, bell, ball, and bull
#	Matches any single numeric character	b#98 Finds b098, b98, and b998
[]	Matches any one of the characters contained in the brackets	b[ae]ll Finds ball and bell
	! Negates a condition	b[!ae]ll Finds bill, and bull because they do not contain *a* or *e*
	- Specifies a range of conditions	B[a-g]ll Finds ball, bbll, bcll, bdll, bell, bfll, and bgll

Using wildcards to find Customer table data:

1. Verify that the Customer table of ac02Customers.mdb database is open in Datasheet View

2. Click in the **Street** column and activate the Find and Replace dialog box using the **Find** button on the toolbar

3. Enter ***hill*** in the Find What area

tip: *This Find What criterion will find any street addresses containing the characters "hill"*

4. Repeatedly click **Find Next**, evaluating each found address until there are no more matches

5. Click in the **FirstName** column and activate the Find and Replace dialog box by clicking it

6. For this exercise we would like to retrieve first names with three letters. Type **???** in the Find What text box. Set the Match to **Whole Field**

7. Repeatedly click **Find Next**, evaluating each name found until there are no more matches

8. Click in the **State** column and activate the Find and Replace dialog box by clicking it

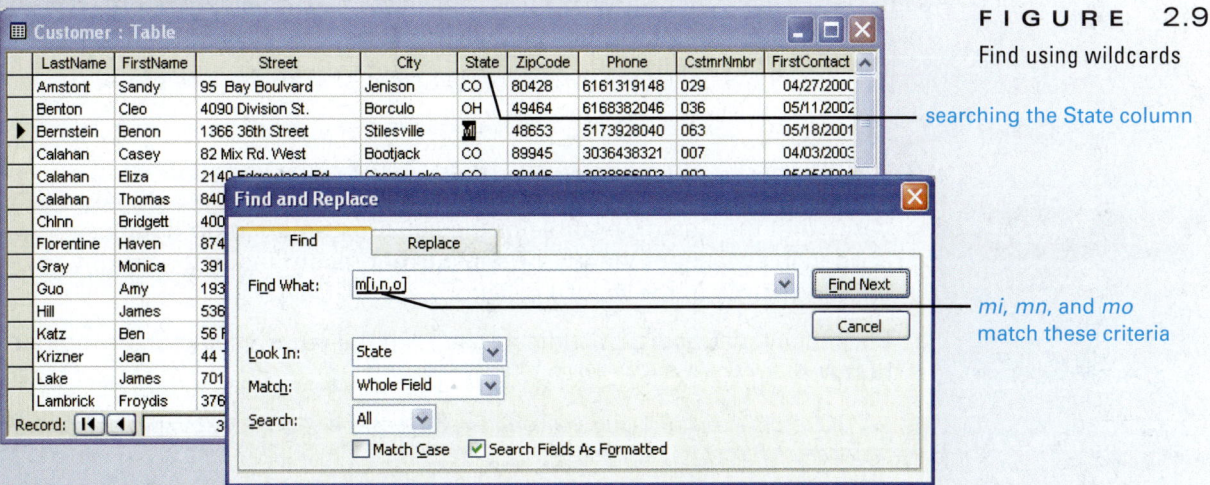

FIGURE 2.9

Find using wildcards

searching the State column

mi, mn, and *mo* match these criteria

9. For this exercise we would like to retrieve data for the states of Michigan (MI), Missouri (MO), and Minnesota (MN), so you will need to enter **m[i,n,o]** in the Find What text box and click **Find Next**. The first matching occurrence should highlight. Click **Find Next** until you have reviewed all selected records (see Figure 2.9)

Adding Table Records

The order of table data display has nothing to do with the order in which it is stored. It is therefore *not* important to view table columns in a consistent order to insert new records in any particular order. The primary key or a user-defined sort criterion will determine the order of records displayed for a user.

Whether a table simply needs some new records added or is empty because it has just been built, the datasheet is a simple place to create new records. When you open a table, the default is to display the data in Datasheet View. Unless the field order has been changed, the columns display in the order they were defined when the table was built.

FIGURE 2.10

Customer table in
Datasheet View

current record indicator —

new record indicator —

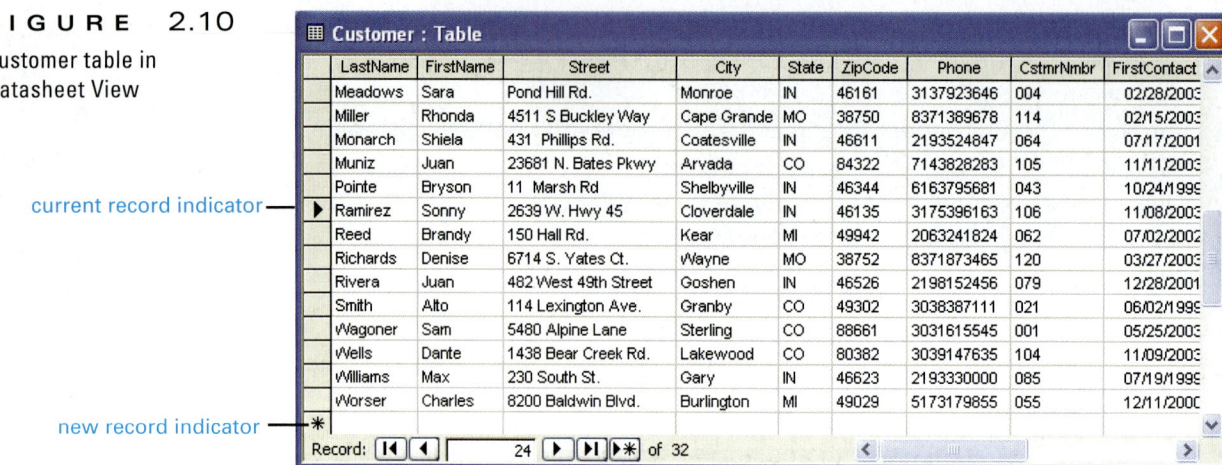

FIGURE 2.10

Customer table in
Datasheet View

current record indicator —

new record indicator —

The last row displayed in the datasheet is blank with an asterisk in the record indicator, as shown in Figure 2.10.

Clicking in the new record row will change the record indicator to an arrow, meaning that it is the current record. As you begin to enter data in the row, the record indicator changes to a pencil to point out that the record is being edited. Once the record is in edit mode, you can key in field data using the Tab key to advance to the next field and Shift+Tab to move to the previous field. Moving to the next empty record or to any other row of the datasheet will automatically save newly entered data. If a required field such as the primary key has been left blank, an error message will display.

Adding new records to the Customer table:

1. Verify that the Customer table of the ac02Customers.mdb database is open in Datasheet View. Find the current record indicator, a right-pointing arrow in the record selector

2. Click the **New Record** ▶* indicator, an * in the record selector, or toolbar button

tip: *The record indicator should convert to a pencil as you begin making modifications to indicate that the record is in edit mode*

3. Verify that the empty record is the current record and then enter the data in Figure 2.11 using the Tab key to move from cell to cell

FIGURE 2.11

New data for the
Customer table

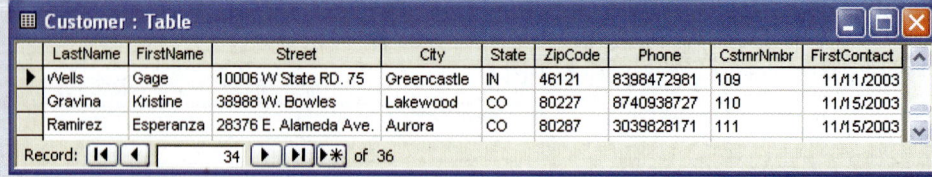

tip: *Correct typing errors by using the Backspace key to delete characters to the left of the insertion point or the Delete key to remove characters to the right of the insertion point, or by double-clicking a data value to select the entire value and overtype it*

4. Add yourself as customer 108

5. Re-sort the table contents by LastName and FirstName and then print the table using the Print button from the toolbar

Updating Data

Besides adding new records to database tables, existing data must be updated to keep them current. Customers move, changing their address information; get married or divorced, changing their name; or sometimes the original data were entered erroneously and must be corrected. Whatever the cause, deleting old data and updating existing data are critical to the integrity of a database.

Deleting Data

Database data need to be removed from tables when they are no longer useful. Unnecessary rows of data slow processing and confuse users. Most businesses do not simply delete old data because they could be useful as history or may need to be retained for legal reasons (tax and personnel data must be retained for periods specified by laws). In such cases, the data are backed up or stored to an alternate location before they are deleted from the active table.

Actually deleting a single record is a simple process. Use the record selector to highlight the record to be deleted and then press the Del key on the keyboard. There is also a Delete button on the toolbar, a Delete Record option in the Edit menu, and a Delete Record option in the pop-up menu. Once completed, the delete process *cannot* be reversed, so be careful to verify that you are deleting the correct record.

Deleting a record from the Customer table:

1. Verify that the Customer table of the ac02Customers.mdb database is open in Datasheet View

2. Use the record selector to choose the record for Monica Gray

3. Press the **delete** button on the toolbar or the **Del** key on your keyboard

4. Answer **Yes** to the warning that the delete can't be undone

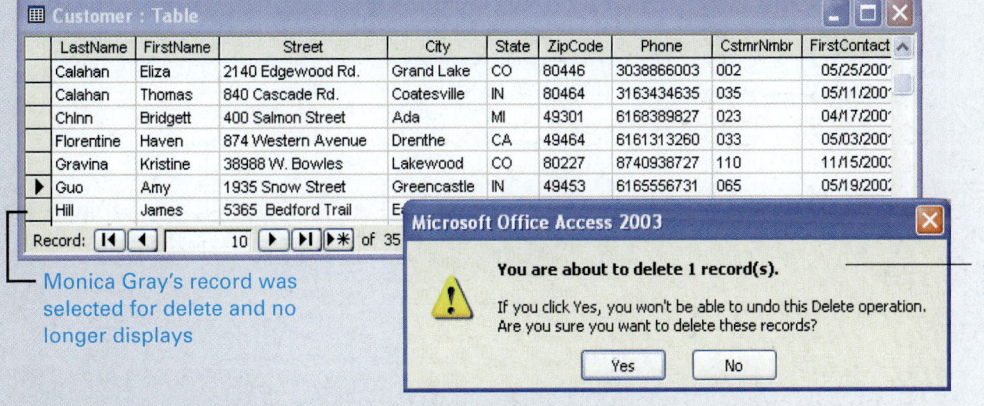

FIGURE 2.12

Deleting a Customer table record

Monica Gray's record was selected for delete and no longer displays

dialog box warning that the delete cannot be recovered

5. Make CstmrNmbr the first column and sort the data by it

6. Close the Customer table saving your changes

Using Find to locate records for deletion is an effective way to ensure that the correct record is selected. It is also possible to delete a group of records. Use click and drag across multiple record selectors to highlight several contiguous records. Any of the previously mentioned delete methods will remove all selected records. The warning dialog box will list the number of records selected for deletion.

Modifying Data

Modifying data is the process of changing specific values in a record or records. Access navigation can be customized to simplify the editing process. When using *keyboard navigation* (Tab and arrow keys), Access's default navigation settings cause the entire contents of a cell to be selected when the cell is entered. Typing while all contents of a cell are selected will replace the entire data value. If, however, the goal is to move character by character in a cell, choose Options from the Tools menu and change the Keyboard options to either Go to start of field or Go to end of field.

In *navigation mode* (Tab selects the entire cell contents), using the Home and End keys will move the cursor to the first and last cell in a record, respectively. The arrow keys move the cursor from cell to cell. In edit mode (Go to start or end of field), the Home and End keys move the cursor to the beginning and end of a field. The left and right arrow keys move the cursor character by character within the cell.

The mouse also can be used to navigate during editing operations. Clicking an insertion point in the text of a field will allow new characters to be added to the existing data. Click and drag to select multiple characters of a data value for typeover. When editing with the mouse, each table cell is edited like a word-processing document.

Using Undo

When editing records in Datasheet View, the Undo feature of Access 2003 will allow changes to be reversed. Undo can be accessed from the Edit menu or via the toolbar button. As edits are completed, Undo stores each action. Before they are saved, actions on a single record can be undone one at a time or from a point backward using the Undo button.

Once the cursor moves to another record or the view is exited, any changes made to a record are saved to the database and Undo is cleared. At that point selecting Undo Saved Record from the Edit menu will restore the original record (see Figure 2.13).

Updating with the Microsoft Office Clipboard

The Windows Clipboard is a temporary storage area that will hold cut or copied information from any Windows program. Stored information can be pasted into any open

FIGURE 2.13

Undo saved record

text changes to match the action that can be undone

Can't Undo indicates that nothing can be undone

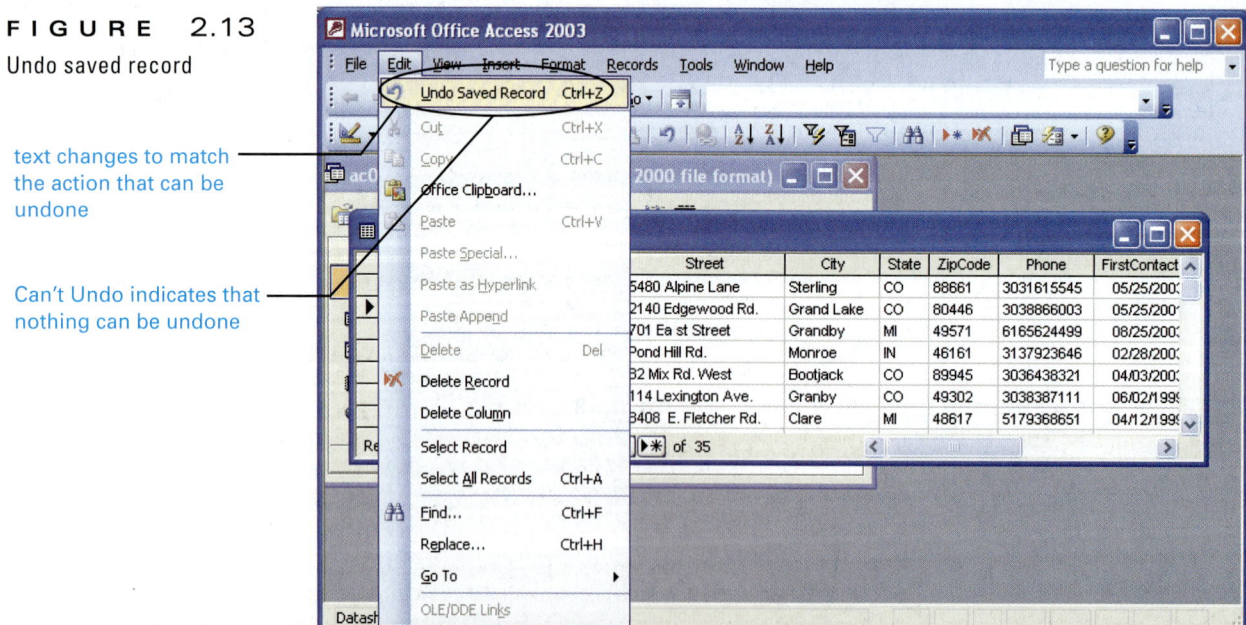

Windows program. The Windows Clipboard holds only one item. By contrast, the Microsoft Office Clipboard allows multiple text and graphic items from any number of *Office* programs to be collected and then pasted into any open *Office* document. For example, some text from a Microsoft Word document, some data from a Microsoft Excel spreadsheet, a bulleted list from Microsoft PowerPoint, and some text from Microsoft FrontPage or Microsoft Internet Explorer could all be copied to the MS Office Clipboard and then pasted into a Microsoft Access datasheet.

Like the Windows Clipboard, the Office Clipboard works with the Cut and Copy buttons on the toolbar. The Office Clipboard, however, will hold up to 24 items. Items remain on the Office Clipboard until all Office applications are closed or the Clipboard is cleared. The Paste button on the toolbar pastes the contents of the *Windows* Clipboard, which is also the last entry from the Office Clipboard. The Office Clipboard opens as soon as two items are cut or copied from the same application. The contents of the Office Clipboard are viewed in the task pane by selecting Office Clipboard from the Edit menu or pressing Ctrl+C twice.

The Office Clipboard can be used to copy values from one row of a database table to another row or rows to speed repetitive data entry and reduce errors. The Clipboard can also be used to copy entire records and move data from other Office System applications. Each Clipboard item carries the icon of the originating Office System product (see Figure 2.14). Items can be selected and pasted individually or the Paste All button can be used to paste the entire Clipboard contents at once.

Notice in Figure 2.14 that when multiple fields are copied, Access data are placed on the Clipboard with the field name as well as the copied contents. The field name is informational and will not be pasted. The selection can be any part of a field, an entire column, multiple fields of a record, an entire record, or multiple rows of a table to be placed on the Clipboard. When pasting data from multiple fields to a datasheet, make sure the columns match the order of the data you want to copy or move.

In the next series of steps, the Office Clipboard will be used to copy the records of customers with billing problems to a new table.

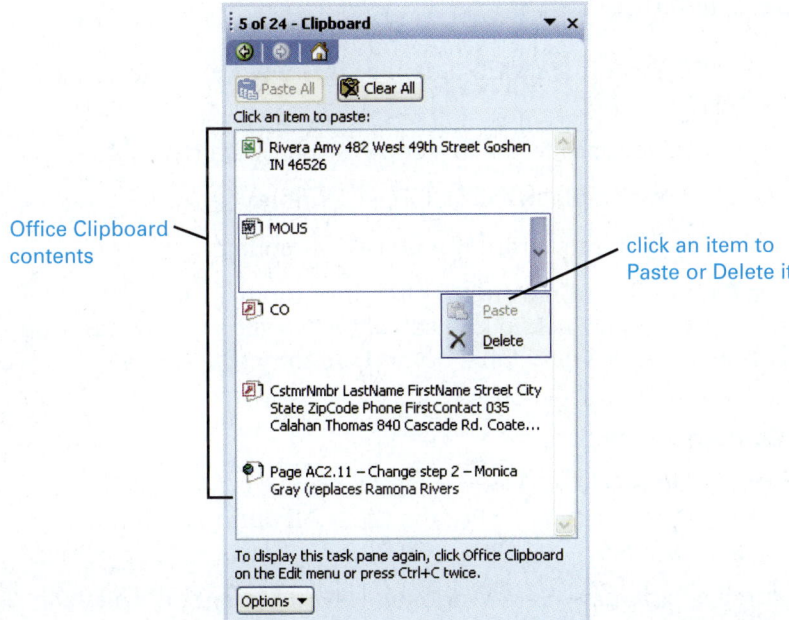

Office Clipboard contents

click an item to Paste or Delete it

FIGURE   2.14
The Office Clipboard

task reference — Using the Office Clipboard

- Collect items to paste
  - Display the Office Clipboard by selecting **Office Clipboard** from the **Edit** menu
  - Select the item to be copied
  - Click the **Copy** or **Cut** button in the Standard toolbar
  - Continue placing items on the clipboard (up to 24) until you have collected everything that you need
- Paste collected items
  - Display the Office Clipboard if it is not already present. If the Office Clipboard option of the Edit menu is not available, you are in an application or view that does not support the Office Clipboard
  - Click or select the area where you want to place items
  - Do one of the following:
    - Select the **Paste All** button to paste the entire contents of the Office Clipboard
    - Select a Clipboard item and choose **Paste** from its drop-down menu
- Remove Office Clipboard items when it is open
  - To clear one item, click the arrow next to the item you want to delete and then click **Delete**
  - To clear all Clipboard contents, click the **Clear All** button
  - Placing more than 24 items on the Clipboard will replace existing items beginning with the oldest item

Using the Office Clipboard with the Customer table:

1. Verify that the ac02Customers.mdb database is open. Close the Customer table if it is open

2. Use the Windows Clipboard to make a copy of the Customer table

   a. Select the **Customer** table in the Database Window

   b. Select the **Copy** button from the Standard toolbar

   c. Select the **Paste** button from the Standard toolbar. Name the copied table **CustomerBackup** and select the **Structure Only** paste options. This will create a new table named CustomerBackup with no data

3. Open the **Customer** table

4. Select the **Office Clipboard** option of the **Edit** menu to view current Clipboard contents. If necessary, click the **Clear All** button to remove existing Clipboard contents

5. There are three customers—Sam Wagoner, Haven Florentine, and Jean Krizner—with billing problems whose data need to be put in the new table. Select each record and copy it to the Clipboard using the Copy button

6. Close the Customer table

7. Open the **CustomerBackup** table, which should contain no records

FIGURE 2.15

Pasting records from the Office Clipboard

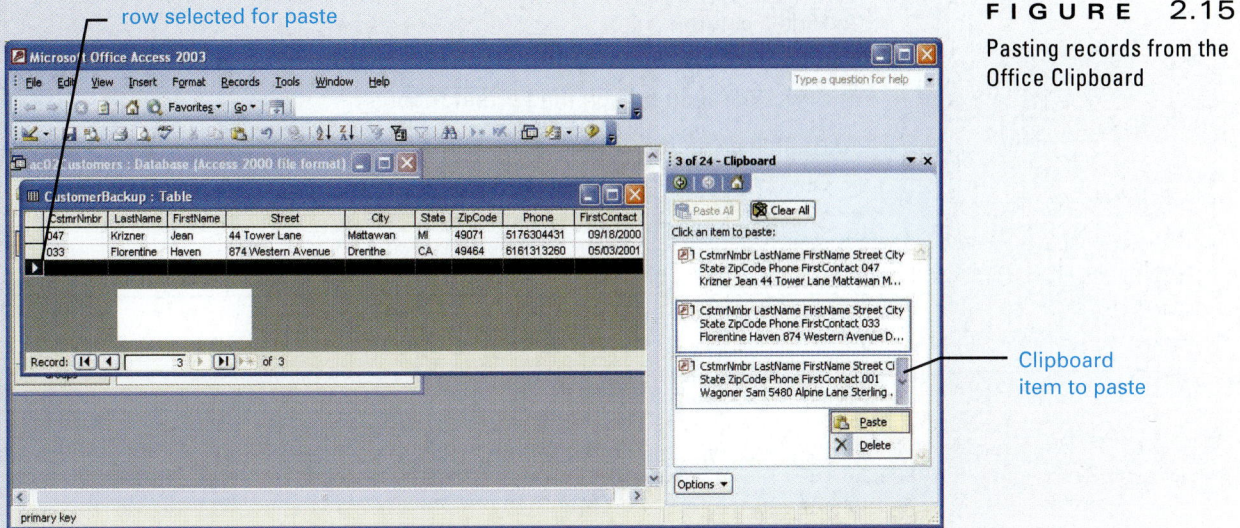

row selected for paste

Clipboard item to paste

8. Select the new record row of CustomerBackup and select the **Paste** option for the first item on the Office Clipboard. Repeat this process for the other two items on the Office Clipboard

tip: *If you get a paste error, verify that the entire row of CustomerBackup is selected before trying to paste a record from the Office Clipboard*

9. Close CustomerBackup

When pasting multiple fields, it is important for the paste area to match the size and shape of the copy area (same number of cells). When pasting multiple cells or entire rows of data, it is important for the field names of the paste area to match the field names of the copy area.

In Access only one database can be open at a time. Using the Office Clipboard it is possible to move or copy data between databases by opening the first database, placing data on the Clipboard, opening another database, and then pasting the Office Clipboard contents.

Organizing a Datasheet

Datasheets are often bigger than your computer screen, making data updates difficult. Hiding and freezing columns can improve your ability to enter data in the correct rows and columns.

Hiding and Unhiding Columns

When there are columns in a datasheet that are not relevant to the task at hand, they can be hidden. Hiding removes columns from display but does not remove the stored data. When only the needed columns are displayed, more of the table will fit on the screen, you do not have to tab through unwanted data, and only the displayed columns will print.

---

task reference　　　　Hiding and Unhiding Datasheet Columns

- Open a table, query, or form in Datasheet View
- To Hide a column
  - Click the field selector of the column to be hidden
  - Click **Hide Columns** on the **Format** menu
- To Unhide a column
  - On the **Format** menu, click **Unhide Columns**
  - Select the names of the columns to show from the Unhide Columns dialog box

---

another word　　　　. . . on Hiding and Unhiding Columns

The Unhide Columns dialog box can be activated when no columns are hidden. It is a convenient way to hide multiple columns by unchecking them. The shortcut menu containing the Unhide Columns option can be activated by right-clicking the datasheet window outside the data area (for example, in the Title bar)

Hiding and unhiding columns of the Customer table:

1. Open the Customer table of the ac02Customers.mdb database in Datasheet View
2. Click the column selector for State
3. Select the **Format** menu and then select **Hide Columns**. The column will remain hidden until it is unhidden or until you close the datasheet without saving the formatting changes
4. To unhide columns, select **Unhide Columns** from the **Format** menu
5. Check the **State** checkbox in the Unhide Columns dialog box and click **Close**

Freezing and Unfreezing Columns

Freezing columns is useful when the datasheet is wider than the viewing area of your screen. As you move to the far-right columns, the leftmost columns scroll off the screen, making it difficult to determine what entity's record is being edited. Freezing the column containing entity identification information causes that column or columns to stay on the screen while scrolling through the remaining columns.

- Open a table, query, or form in Datasheet View
- Select the column(s) to freeze or unfreeze
- To Freeze column(s), select **Freeze Columns** on the **Format** menu
- To Unfreeze column(s), select **Unfreeze All Columns** on the **Format** menu

Freezing and unfreezing columns of the Customer table:

1. Verify that the Customer table of ac02Customers.mdb database is open in Datasheet View

2. Narrow the datasheet window to display only five columns of data by dragging its right corner to the left. Use the Tab key to navigate through a record to demonstrate that the identifying values (CstmrNmbr, LastName, FirstName) scroll out of the viewing area

3. Select both the **LastName** and **FirstName** columns by clicking and dragging across their field selectors

4. Select the **Format** menu and then select **Freeze Columns**. The LastName and FirstName columns will be moved to the first columns of the datasheet

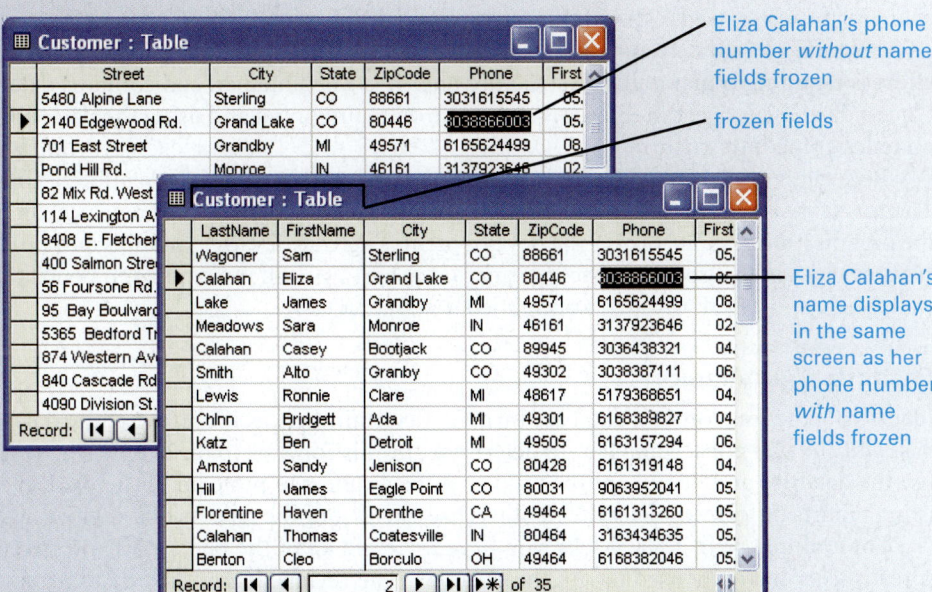

Eliza Calahan's phone number *without* name fields frozen

frozen fields

Eliza Calahan's name displays in the same screen as her phone number *with* name fields frozen

FIGURE 2.16

Unfrozen and frozen Customer table columns

5. Tab through the columns of a record. Notice that the frozen fields stay visible while the remaining fields scroll

6. To unfreeze columns, select **Unfreeze All Columns** from the **Format** menu

7. Close ac02Customers.mdb

making *the grade*

1. What is the significance of an asterisk in the row selector of a table?

2. Discuss the use of wildcards when finding data in a table.

3. When/how are changes made to a record stored in the table?

4. Discuss the importance of column order when sorting by multiple fields.

5. T F   Rows deleted from a table can be restored.

6. T F   The Windows Clipboard and the Office Clipboard are the same thing.

SESSION 2.2 DESIGNING AND BUILDING A DATABASE

Now that Missy and Micah are comfortable with the Customer table, it is time to assess the remaining data requirements for KoryoKicks. The twins are interested in learning how to design and develop databases and have asked to work through this process with you. Involving users in the design process helps to ensure that their needs will be met by the completed database.

Assessing Information Needs

The longevity and effectiveness of a database are rooted in the quality of its design. Poorly designed databases are tedious to work with and do not effectively adapt to changing business needs. The 90/10 rule is often cited. It states that 90 percent of your effort should go into designing the database structure so that only 10 percent of your effort is required to maintain the structure after it is implemented and contains data. Once a database is live, the emphasis should be on maintaining and using the data, not on redesigning the structure.

Regardless of the size of the project, the first step is to assess the information needs. The formality and duration of this process are governed by the size of the project and the organization responsible for the development. There are a variety of tools and procedures that can be used to define information needs. You will use paper and pencil to walk Missy and Micah through a simplified design process.

Outline the Mission

Identifying the mission of a database involves determining specifically what the database will and will not accomplish. To determine the mission, talk to the people who will use the database and document the tasks that they want it to perform. If there are existing reports or forms, collect them; otherwise, sketch out the reports that users want.

For example, with KoryoKicks, you have reviewed all of the paper files and Excel spreadsheets currently used to run the business. The review determined that current tracking fits generally into one of the following areas:

- Tracking customer orders
- Determining product availability
- Tracking suppliers
- Tracking payments
- Tracking class schedules

The next step is to find out what the current system won't do that the new system needs to do. A simple way of determining requirements is to write down the business questions the database should be able to answer. Missy and Micah tell you they are generally happy with the data they have, but it is taking too much time to find and consolidate.

The business questions they consider most important are

- What are the total sales for each month?
- What do my customers owe me?
- How many multiple-order customers do I have?
- Which suppliers provide the best service?
- What do I owe suppliers?
- How much of each product do I have available?

These questions define the outputs that are required of the KoryoKicks database and are used to determine what fields (inputs) need to be stored in database tables. The questions are also a very good start at outlining the forms, queries, and reports needed to provide answers.

Establish Table Subjects

Each table in a database contains data about only one subject (one type of entity). Determining table subjects is not always as easy as it sounds. The business questions that establish the results needed from the database correspond nicely to queries, reports, and forms but *do not* dictate table structure. Categorizing the information into tables is done by evaluating the impacts of various table configurations on the effectiveness of the database. A formal set of steps called normalization often is used to help ensure effective table design. This session will demonstrate an informal application of normalization rules. Common sense and good judgment help in this process.

Let's consider an invoice for a KoryoKicks customer (see Figure 2.17). The invoice would contain information such as the invoice number, invoice date, customer's name and address, product identification, product description, product price, quantity ordered, item total, tax, shipping, and invoice total. While all of these appear on one invoice, it would be problematic to store everything in one table. A customer can order multiple products at a time, which would mean that there would be a row of data for each product ordered. If a customer ordered three products, everything would be entered in the table three times. That is great for the data that change each time, but static data such as the customer's name and address would also be entered three times, significantly multiplying the chance of data entry errors. Duplication also increases maintenance by requiring multiple records to be updated if the customer moves.

To reduce the storage of duplicate data, put the data that do not change often in one table and the changing data in another. The data that do not change often are referred to as *static data* while frequently changing data are called *transaction data*. The Customer table will hold the static data about the customer. It is also apparent that a table holding data about products would be beneficial. Common shorthand used to describe tables is to list the table name with its attributes (fields) in parentheses after it. In this notation, the primary key is underlined. Using this notation with the invoice data, we can demonstrate the tables currently being evaluated as shown in Figure 2.18.

The next step is to review the unassigned attributes to be certain that they do not belong in either the Customer or Product table. The question to ask to determine whether the field belongs in the Customer table is "Does this attribute belong to the customer?" Similarly, ask if the attribute belongs to the Product table. For all of the unassigned values shown in Figure 2.18, the answer to both questions is no, meaning that at least one more table is needed.

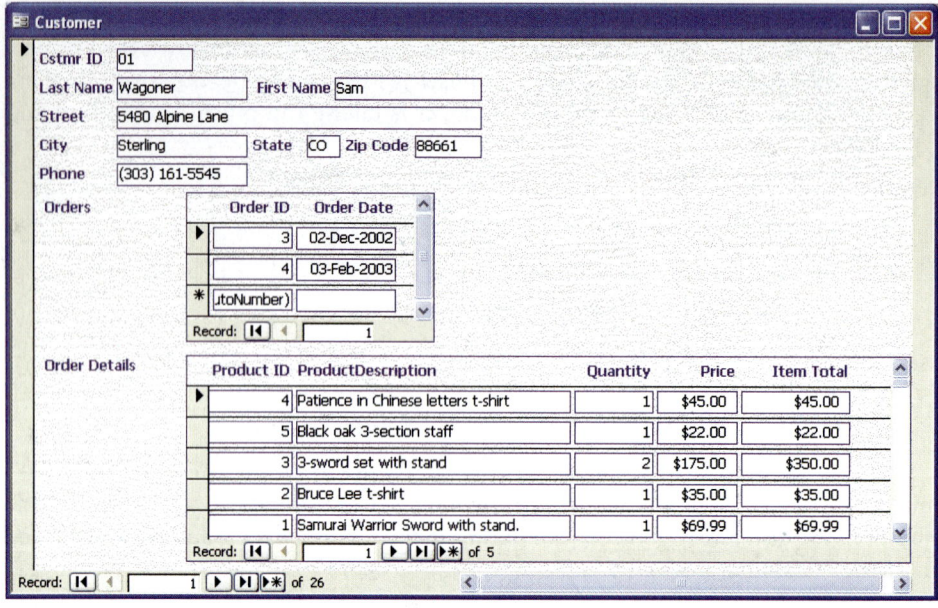

While the formal rules of normalization have not been presented, this informal process is achieving the same result. One further rule holds that derived or calculated data should not be stored in tables. Following that axiom, tax, shipping, and invoice total should be calculated when the invoice is created, not stored in a table, so they can be removed from consideration. The remaining unassigned attributes of invoice number, invoice date, and quantity ordered could all be considered to be order data. Each of these fields is frequently updated with information generated by customer orders. This design stage is shown in Figure 2.19.

help yourself *Use the Type a Question combo box to solidify your understanding of database design by typing* **database design**. *Review the contents of* About designing a database. *Be sure to click to expand all topics. Close the Help window when you are finished*

This evaluation process needs to be completed for each output defined in the mission statement. The result will be a list of tables and possible attributes covering most of the user's requirements.

F I G U R E   2.18

First table design break out

Customer (name, address)

Product (product identification, product description, product price)

Unassigned (invoice number, invoice date, quantity ordered, item total, tax, shipping, and invoice total)

F I G U R E   2.19

Table design after removing calculated values

Customer (name, address)

Product (product identification, product description, product price)

Order (invoice number, invoice date, quantity ordered)

Establish Table Fields

Now that the table entities (subjects) and what they should store are established, it is time to determine exactly what attributes need to be stored in each table and how they will be named. In general, field names should be descriptive and not contain spaces or special characters. Here are some tips for defining fields:

- Each field must directly describe the subject of the table. A field that does not describe the subject belongs in another table

- Store data in their smallest logical part. It is easy to merge attributes in queries, forms, and reports, but very difficult to access part of a data value. Combined data values also make it difficult to retrieve and analyze the data. Create separate fields for each part of a person's name and address. Consider breaking up any field that you might want to access part of, such as a part number with embedded information. For easy reporting, such a part number could be broken into PartCategory and PartID, which combine to make a unique part number

- Assign a primary key field to each table. The primary key field(s) should uniquely and minimally identify a specific entity or row of data in the table. If there is no naturally occurring primary key, one should be generated. For example, because names can be duplicated in the data, use either Social Security Number or a sequential number to uniquely identify each person

Applying these tips to the previous design results in creating multiple fields for the customer's name and address and adding CstmrID as the key to the customer table (see Figure 2.20). ProductID is added as the key for the Product table and OrderID is made the key of the Orders table.

At this point it is wise to return to the information gathered while creating the mission statement. Be sure that all of the data to create the defined outputs are assigned to a table. Further ensure that all of the questions documented for the design can be answered from the data assigned to tables.

Defining Relationships

The power of relational databases is their ability to rapidly locate and organize data stored in multiple tables. For example, the current design stores the data to create a customer invoice in three tables. Data from multiple tables are joined by matching values in a shared field. Those relationships have to be identified and foreign key fields added to the tables so this joining can take place.

Decide what tables are related and then how they are related. Remember that table relationships are classified by how many records in the first table are related to how many records in the second table. One-to-many relationships are the most common and occur when one record in Table A relates to many records in Table B. For example, one customer can have many orders. In a one-to-one relationship, one record from the first table can be related to one record of the second table. One-to-one relationships are created when there are too many fields for one Access table, or there are fields that are blank for most of the rows.

Customer (*CstmrID*, LastName, FirstName, Street, City, State, Zip)

Product (*ProductID*, ProductDescription, ProductPrice)

Order (*OrderID*, OrderDate, QuantityOrdered)

FIGURE 2.20

Table design with field names and primary keys assigned

Many-to-many relationships are the most complex because many records from one table are related to many rows in another table. For example, one customer can buy many products and one product can be purchased by many customers. Since relational databases can't directly model many-to-many relationships, a new table is added that has a one-to-many relationship with each table in the many-to-many relationship.

One way to determine relationships is to diagram them. There are usually multiple ways to set the relations in a database; choosing the best fit takes practice. Begin by drawing a rounded box for each table and placing the table name in it. Connect tables that are related with a line and label the line with a brief description of the relationship.

Figure 2.21 presents one possible model of the Customer, Product, and Order relationships. These diagrams are read from entity to entity as shown in the relationships figure notes.

Notice that the relationship between products and orders is many-to-many. To model this relationship, an intermediate table having a one-to-many relationship with each table in the many-to-many relationship must be added to the design. In this case, OrderDetail has been added as the intermediate table (see Figure 2.22). It has one-to-many relationships to both the Order and Product tables. Each row in OrderDetail represents one invoice line item (the order for one product). To complete the design, the primary key from the table on the one side of the relationship is added to the table on the many side as a foreign key, enabling the tables to be joined. The final design is described in Figure 2.22.

FIGURE 2.21

Preliminary entity diagrams for invoicing design

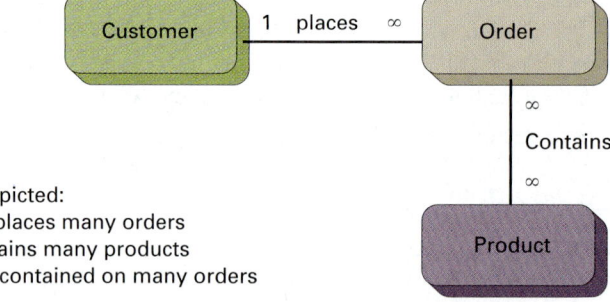

Relationships depicted:
• One customer places many orders
• One order contains many products
• One product is contained on many orders

FIGURE 2.22

Invoicing design with two one-to-many relationships replacing a many-to-many relationship

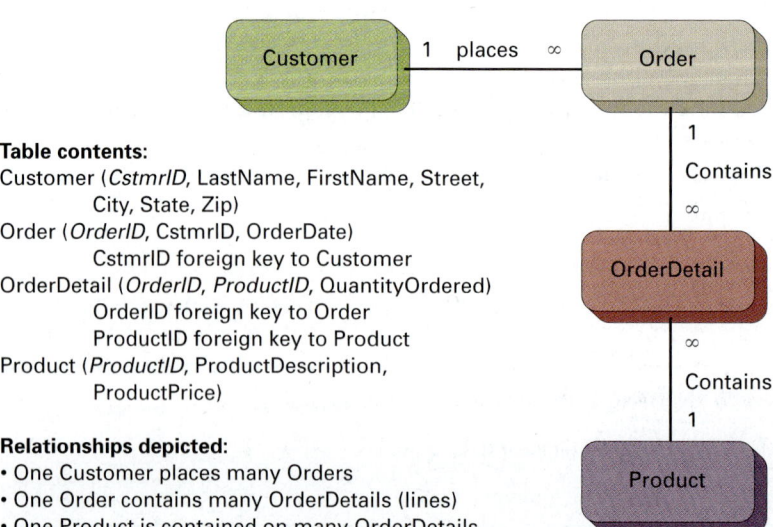

Table contents:
Customer (*CstmrID*, LastName, FirstName, Street,
        City, State, Zip)
Order (*OrderID*, CstmrID, OrderDate)
        CstmrID foreign key to Customer
OrderDetail (*OrderID*, *ProductID*, QuantityOrdered)
        OrderID foreign key to Order
        ProductID foreign key to Product
Product (*ProductID*, ProductDescription,
        ProductPrice)

Relationships depicted:
• One Customer places many Orders
• One Order contains many OrderDetails (lines)
• One Product is contained on many OrderDetails

Designing a Prototype

Once the tables, fields, and relationships are designed, it is time to build a prototype for testing. Create the tables, specify the relationships, and enter some test data. The test data should be representative of the data the table will actually hold in order to successfully evaluate the design. Create rough drafts of the queries, forms, and reports to see if they contain the data needed to answer the questions outlined in the mission statement.

As you work with the prototype, note where the design can be improved. Are any data missing? Are data repeated? Are the primary keys working correctly? Can tables be joined effectively? Update the prototype and continue testing until it is ready for production.

Building Access Tables Using Design View

In Session 1.2 a table was built using the Table Wizard. Now it's time to take a look at what is going on behind the Wizard. There are many table attributes automatically set by the Table Wizard. The attributes of a table determine how data will be stored, displayed, and processed. Field attributes include a field's name, data type, size, and key. Building tables in Design View allows control over all table attributes.

Field Names

The *Field Name* property is used to retrieve data from a column in queries, forms, and reports. Although the design already specifies field names, it is important to understand the rules that govern name selection. In Microsoft Access field names must be unique within a table and can

- Be up to 64 characters long
- Include any combination of letters, numbers, spaces, and special characters except a period (.), an exclamation point (!), an accent grave (`), and brackets ([ ])
- *Not* start with a space
- *Not* contain control characters

Although Access allows spaces within field names, it is best to capitalize the first letter of each word and not use spaces. So while both Customer number and CustomerNumber are valid field names, CustomerNumber is the better choice. Finally, short but descriptive names are best since the assigned names will be used frequently.

Data Types

The *Data Type* property of a field establishes what data values it can store and what other properties can be set for the field. For example, setting the OrderDate field to a Date data type ensures that only valid dates and/or times can be stored. Figure 2.23 outlines Access data types. Notice that numbers not used in calculations are best stored in Text fields.

In addition to determining what data can be stored in a field, the Number, Date/Time, Currency, and Yes/No data types have display formats. Display formats define what the user sees as output from these fields.

You, Missy, and Micah add data types to the table design as outlined in Figure 2.24. CstmrID is a field that contains numbers that won't be used in calculations and will not be automatically generated. Such numbers are faster to search, sort, and process when they are stored in a Text field.

FIGURE 2.23

Microsoft Access data type overview

Data Type	Use for	Size
Text	Text or combinations of text and numbers, such as addresses. Also numbers that do not require calculations, such as phone numbers, part numbers, or postal codes	Up to 255 characters
Memo	Lengthy text and numbers, such as notes or descriptions	Up to 64,000 characters
Number	Numeric data to be used for mathematical calculations, except calculations involving money. Set the FieldSize property to define the specific Number type	Dependent on the field size chosen
Date/Time	Dates and times	8 bytes
Currency	Currency or other values with 4 or fewer decimals. Accurate to 15 digits to the left of the decimal point and 4 digits to the right. Calculations do not round	8 bytes
AutoNumber	Unique sequential (incrementing by 1) or random numbers automatically inserted when a record is added	4 bytes
Yes/No	Fields that will contain only one of two values, such as Yes/No, True/False, On/Off	1 bit
OLE Object	Objects (such as Microsoft Word documents, Microsoft Excel spreadsheets, pictures, sounds, or other binary data), created in other programs using the OLE protocol, that can be linked to or embedded	Up to 1 gigabyte (limited by disk space)
Hyperlink	Field that will store hyperlinks. A hyperlink can be a UNC path or a URL	Up to 64,000 characters
Lookup Wizard	A field that allows you to choose a list of values from another table using a combo box. Choosing this option initiates a Wizard to define this for you	The same size as the primary key field that is also the Lookup field; typically 4 bytes

Field Sizes

The *Field Size* property is available for Text, Number, and AutoNumber data types. The other data types either have a fixed field size or adjust to fit the data entered. Field size determines the maximum value a field can store, how much storage space it requires, and how fast it processes. In general, use the smallest field size that will meet your needs.

For fields with a Text data type, the field size can be set from 0 to 255 characters. The default text field size is 50 characters. Text fields only store the data entered without any trailing spaces, so setting a smaller field size does not reduce storage requirements. Smaller text field sizes do improve the validity of stored data. For example, if a company has 15-character part numbers, setting the field size to 15 stops the user from entering more than 15 characters. The valid field sizes for Number data types are outlined in Figure 2.25.

If the DataType property is set to AutoNumber, the FieldSize property can be set to Long Integer or Replication ID, as outlined in Figure 2.25. AutoNumber fields are frequently used to generate unique primary keys for records without a natural primary key. It is important to note that the currency field size is not just for tracking dollars and cents. The currency field size will provide faster fixed-point calculations than either Single or Double and should be used for all noncurrency data of one to four decimal places.

FIGURE 2.24

Table design with data types

Table	Field Name	Data Type
Customer	CstmrID	Text
	LastName	Text
	FirstName	Text
	Street	Text
	City	Text
	State	Text
	Zip	Text
Order	OrderID	AutoNumber
	CstmrID	Text
	OrderDate	Date/Time
OrderDetail	OrderID	Number
	ProductID	Number
	QuantityOrdered	Number
Product	ProductID	AutoNumber
	ProductDescription	Text
	ProductPrice	Currency

FIGURE 2.25

Microsoft Access field sizes for number data type

Field Size	Description	Decimal Precision	Storage Size
Byte	Stores numbers from 0 to 255 (no fractions)	None	1 byte
Decimal	Stores numbers from $-10^{28} - 1$ through $10^{28} - 1$	28	12 bytes
Integer	Stores numbers from $-32,768$ to $32,767$ (no fractions)	None	2 bytes
Long Integer	(Access Default) Stores numbers from $-2,147,483,648$ to $2,147,483,647$ (no fractions)	None	4 bytes
Single	Stores numbers from 3.402823E38 to 1.401298E$-$45 for negative values and from 1.401298E$-$45 to 3.402823E38 for positive values	7	4 bytes
Double	Stores numbers from $-1.79769313486231E308$ to $-4.94065645841247E-324$ for negative values and from 1.79769313486231E308 to 4.94065645841247E$-$324 for positive values	15	8 bytes
Replication ID	Globally unique identifier	N/A	16 bytes

FIGURE 2.26
Database design with field sizes

Table	Field Name	Data Type	Field Size
Customer	*CstmrID*	Text	5
	LastName	Text	30
	FirstName	Text	30
	Street	Text	30
	City	Text	30
	State	Text	2
	Zip	Text	5
Order	*OrderID*	AutoNumber	LongInteger
	CstmrID	Text	5
	OrderDate	Date/Time	N/A
OrderDetail	*OrderID*	Number	LongInteger
	ProductID	Number	LongInteger
	QuantityOrdered	Number	Integer
Product	*ProductID*	AutoNumber	LongInteger
	ProductDescription	Text	30
	ProductPrice	Currency	N/A

The database design with field sizes added is shown in Figure 2.26.

Building a Table Definition

It's finally time to build the KoryoKicks table definitions in Access using Design View and set all of the attributes that have been outlined. Before you begin, review the Order table design in Figure 2.27.

FIGURE 2.27
Order table design

Order Table Design			
Table	Field Name	Data Type	Field Size
Order	OrderID	AutoNumber	LongInteger
	CstmrID	Text	5
	OrderDate	Date/Time	N/A

---

task reference   Defining a Table Field

- Click **Tables** in the Options bar
- Click the **Design View** [icon] button on the toolbar
- Enter a field name
- Select a data type
- Define other field attributes as needed

Building the Order table:

1. Open the ac02KoryoKicks.mdb file. The Customer and Products tables have already been built. Use both Design and Datasheet Views to review the existing tables

2. Click the **Tables** object in the Database Window and select the **New** button on the toolbar

3. Select **Design View** from the New Table dialog box and click **OK**

4. Review the Design View grid. Note the default table name, Table1. Find the columns for Field Name, Data Type, and Description. As you create fields, the General tab at the bottom of the page will display other attributes such as Field Size

5. The first field of the Order table is OrderID. To create that field, type **OrderID** in the Field Name column of the first row. Tab to or click in Data Type to activate the drop-down list. Select **AutoNumber** as the Data Type and leave the Field Size as **LongInteger**

tip: *The Description attribute is for the developer's notes about the design and contents of a field. The value can be up to 255 characters and will display in the Access status bar when the field is active in Datasheet View*

6. Repeat step 5 for the CstmrID field using Figure 2.27. Be sure to set the Field Size for CstmrID on the General tab

7. Repeat step 5 for the OrderDate field using Figure 2.27

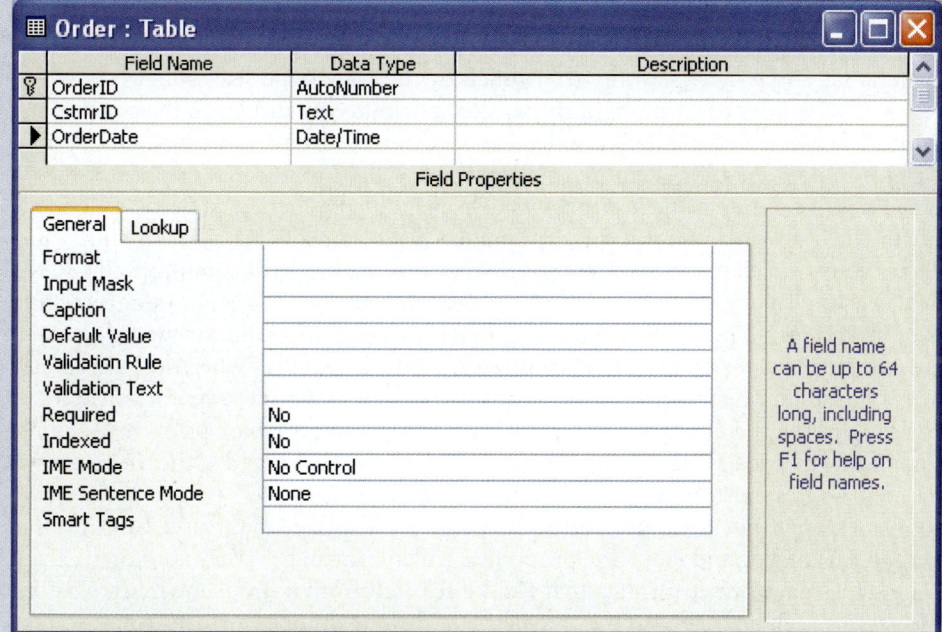

FIGURE 2.28

Field definitions for the Order table

8. Set the table primary key by clicking the record indicator for the OrderID field and then selecting the **Key** button from the Access toolbar

9. Close the Design View window and answer **Yes** to Do you want to save changes to the design of table 'Table1'?

10. Enter **Order** in the Save As dialog box and click **OK**

F I G U R E   2.29

Order table listed in the
Database Window

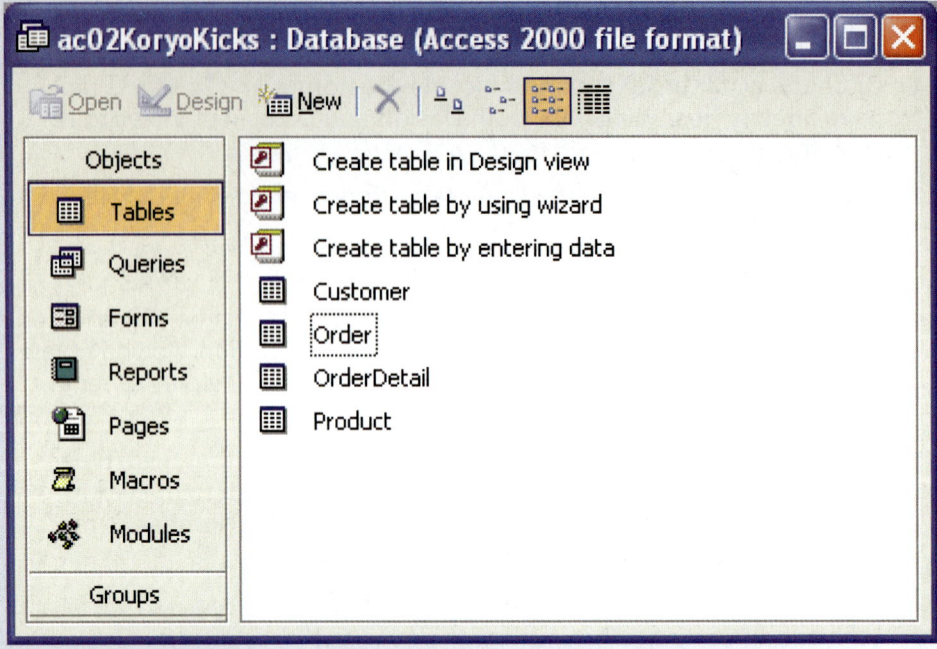

11. Verify that your new Order table is listed in the Database Window
(see Figure 2.29)

General Tab Attributes

Let's take a look at some of the other table attributes. The attributes that display on the General tab in Design View are determined by the Data Type selection, as shown in Figure 2.30. A brief description of the selected attribute will display in the panel to the right of the General tab. Attributes that are common to all data types include Caption, Default Value, Validation, Required, and Indexed.

A field's *Caption* is the text that will display in forms, queries, and reports to identify the field. If you do not set the Caption, the Field Name will display. *Default Value* allows you to speed data entry by automatically placing the most common value in the field each time a new record is added. The user can override the default value by typing over it. *Validation* holds the rules that govern what data are valid for the field, which are covered in a later chapter. The *Required* attribute is set to yes when the field cannot be blank and no when blank entries are acceptable. *Indexed* is set to yes for a field when indexing by that field will improve database performance. A table's primary key is automatically indexed. In general, foreign keys also should be indexed. Other fields are indexed to address performance issues when the database is in use.

A field's *Format* attribute controls how data are displayed to the user. Contrast this with the Data Type and Field Size properties, which control how they are stored. Many Data Types have preset formats that can be selected from a drop-down list. Custom formats also can be created as they are needed. Custom Number formats use a # to represent each number in the output. For example, ###.### would cause all number values to display with three decimal places.

Custom date formats are more complex, using the symbols outlined in Figure 2.31. A Date/Time field is capable of storing both the date and time in the same field. If both are stored, the format can be set to display either one or both. Custom time formats are not covered here.

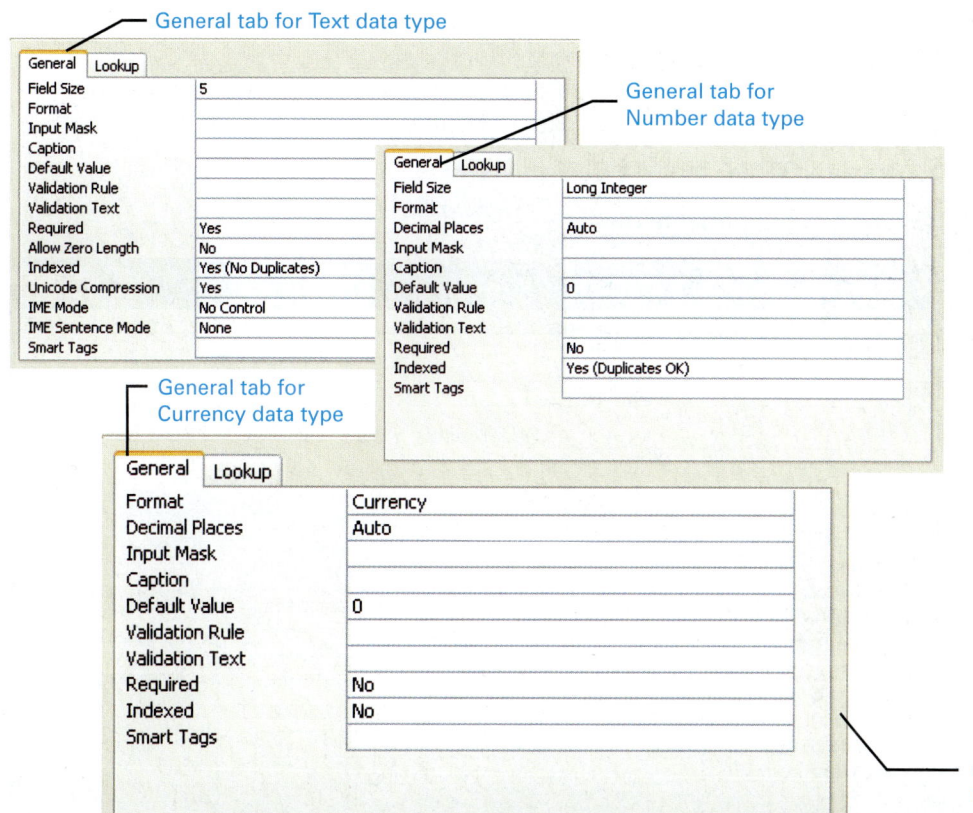

General tab for Text data type

General tab for Number data type

General tab for Currency data type

description of selected General tab attributes

FIGURE 2.30

General tab attributes for Text, Number, and Currency

FIGURE 2.31

Custom date format symbols

Symbol	Uses
/	Date separator
d	Formats the day of the month
	d—day of the month without leading zeroes (1–31)
	dd—day of the month in two digits (01–31)
	ddd—weekday abbreviations (Sun–Sat)
	ddddd—full weekday (Sunday–Saturday)
w	Sets week formats
	w—day of the week (1–7)
	ww—week of the year (1–53)
m	Formats the month
	m—month without leading zeroes (1–12)
	mm—two-digit month (01–12)
	mmm—month abbreviations (Jan–Dec)
	mmmm—full month name (January–December)
y	Formats the year
	yy—two-digit year (01–99)
	yyyy—full year (0100–9999)

Setting General tab attributes:

1. Verify that the ac02KoryoKicks.mdb file is open

2. Open the **Order** table in Design View

3. Select the **OrderDate** field

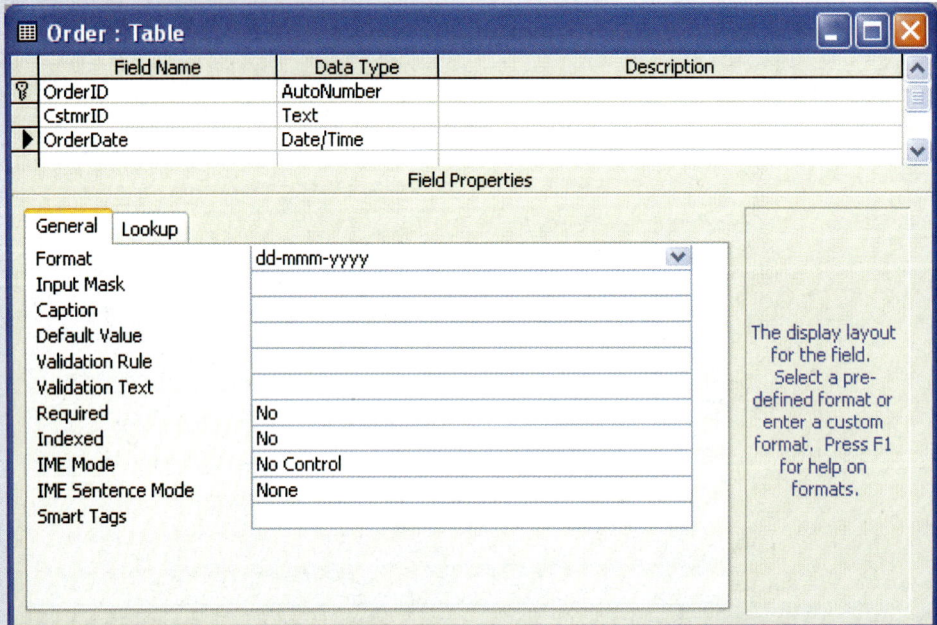

4. Enter the custom format **dd-mmm-yyyy**. Dates entered in this field will display with a two-digit day, a three-character month abbreviation, and a four-digit year (15-Jul-2002)

5. Verify your custom format and close the Design window

6. Answer **Yes** to save the design changes that you have made

If a Number field is set to Currency format (not the same as Currency field size), it will display values based on the regional settings in the Windows Control Panel. Changes made to the regional settings in the Windows Control Panel will be automatically reflected in table fields set to currency format.

To complete the database prototype, the OrderDetail table must be built and table relationships defined. You will build OrderDetail in the next series of steps. Setting relationships is covered later.

Building the OrderDetail table:

1. Verify that the ac02KoryoKicks.mdb file is open

2. Open a new table by selecting **Tables** from the Object bar and clicking **New** on the toolbar

3. Use what you have learned to build the table fields outlined in Figure 2.33

Table	Field Name	Data Type	Field Size	Other Attributes
OrderDetail	OrderID	Number	LongInteger	
	ProductID	Number	LongInteger	
	QuantityOrdered	Number	Integer	Required, Default value 1

F I G U R E   2.33
OrderDetail fields and attributes

4. Click and drag over the record indicators for OrderID and ProductID to select them both. Use the key icon in the Access toolbar to set them as the composite primary key

tip: *If you are successful, both fields should have a key icon in their record selector*

5. Verify your fields and field attributes

6. Close the Design window and save the table as **OrderDetail**

7. Open the **OrderDetail** table in Datasheet View. The table is now ready to hold data

8. Close OrderDetail

9. Close the ac02KoryoKicks.mdb database

Using Undo and Redo when Defining Tables

The Microsoft Access Undo feature has more options in Design View than it does in Datasheet View. The difference stems from the way the two views save data. Design View saves data on exit. The Datasheet View updates the database as soon as the cursor moves to a new record.

In Design View Access keeps a list of the 20 most recent actions that can be undone. The Undo button on the Access toolbar has a drop-down list that displays those actions. Clicking an action to undo will also undo all actions above the selection on the list. One action at a time can be undone by repeatedly typing Ctrl+Z.

The Redo button stores the 20 most recent undone actions. Like the Undo button, when redoing an action, the Redo button reinstates all actions above it on the list. Both the Undo and Redo lists are cleared when the view is changed.

> *another***word** . . . on Saving Table Designs
>
> You will be prompted to save your changes when you access another view, but you can save them at any point by clicking the Save button on the Access toolbar

Working with New Tables

New tables have now been created using both the New Table Wizard and Table Design View. Table Design View provides the developer with much more control than using a Wizard. Many developers use the Wizard to create the first draft of a table and then use Design View to customize the table generated by the Wizard. Regardless of how you choose to build tables, the ability to move comfortably between table views and add data are critical.

Navigate between Views

When working with Access objects, it is tedious to close an object to use a different view. Fortunately Access provides an easy way to move between views using the View

View button of the Access
toolbar

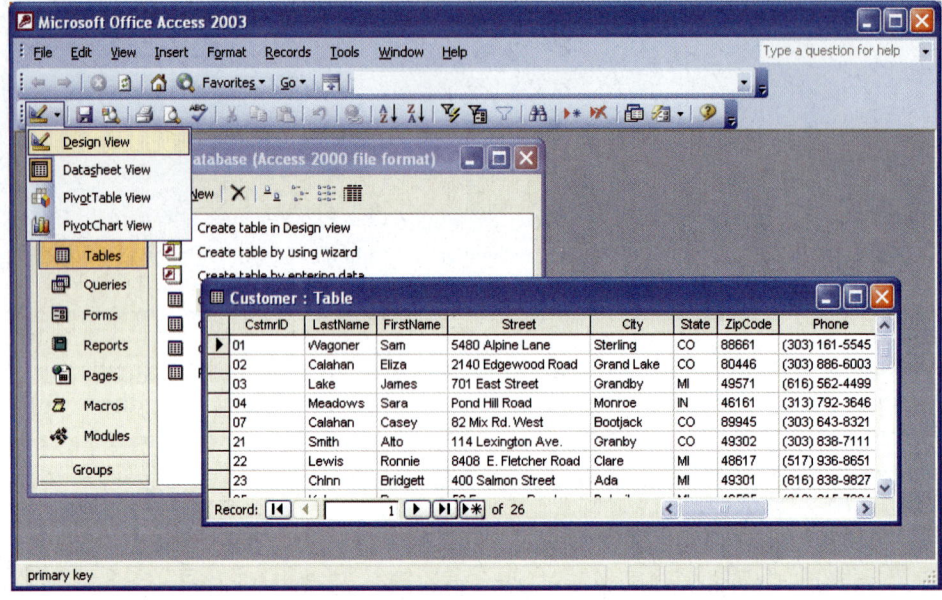

button on the Access toolbar. The View button is a drop-down list box that displays
valid options for the current or open object (see Figure 2.34).

Remember that the undo and redo buffers are cleared when you change views, but
the Clipboard is not cleared. Changes made in one view can impact data in another
view. Be especially careful when changing the design of an object. The impacts of table
design changes are discussed in a later chapter.

Populate New Tables

Session 2.1 covered adding, deleting, and updating records in a table. As has been
noted, table Datasheet View is a simple way to enter and maintain data. Forms and
queries also can be used to add and maintain table data. The Clipboard can copy data
that exist elsewhere and paste them into the table. Finally, data can be imported from
existing documents maintained by other Office products like Excel.

Regardless of how tables are being populated, there are dangers in entering data before the entire database has been built and table relationships set. The defined relationships between tables enforce integrity of the data that are entered. With the
independent tables that are in the KoryoKicks database now, an order could be entered
for a customer who is not in the Customer table. Similarly an order could be entered for
a product that is not in the Product table. Because building table relationships is outside the scope of this presentation, a copy of KoryoKicks.mdb has been created with the
table relationships set. The relationships will keep you from entering orders for nonexistent customers and products.

The ac02KoryoKicks2.mdb prototype will be used in the remaining steps. Table relationships have been set and the Customer and Product tables have already been populated. You will be entering orders.

Populating the Order table:

1. Open the **ac02KoryoKicks2.mdb** database

2. Explore the table designs using Design View—they are the same as what
   you built earlier in this session

3. Explore the data in the Customer and Product tables

4. Select **Relationships** from the **Tools** menu to view the table relationships that have been set up (see Figure 2.35)

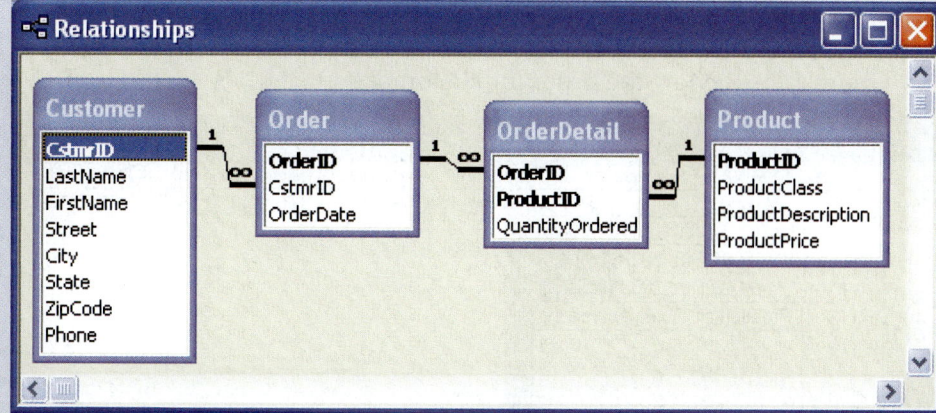

FIGURE 2.35
KoryoKicks table relationships

5. Open the **Order** table in Datasheet View and add a record for customer **5** on **12/15/03**. You will receive the error shown in Figure 2.36 because customer 5 is not in the Customer table

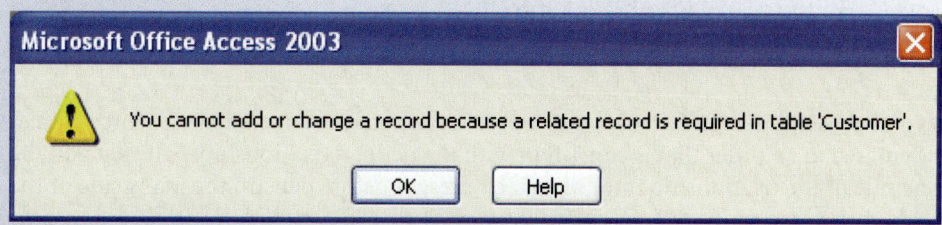

FIGURE 2.36
Table relationships being enforced

tip: *The ESC key is used to abandon the update*

6. Enter the records shown in Figure 2.37 for customers 01 and 02 who have already been added to the Customer table

7. Close the Order table

8. Open the **OrderDetail** table. The one-to-many relationship between Order and OrderDetail means that Order must be entered before OrderDetail (line items) can be added for that order. If you try to add a nonexistent OrderDetail, you will receive the error shown in Figure 2.36

9. Enter the records shown in Figure 2.38. These data represent the product and quantity (invoice detail lines) for orders 03 and 05

FIGURE 2.38
Records for the OrderDetail table

OrderDetail : Table

OrderID	ProductID	QuantityOrdered
2	4	1
2	8	1
2	38	4
3	1	1
3	10	1
4	11	10
4	29	2
4	37	3
5	15	8
5	19	2
5	20	35
5	21	4
0	0	1

Record: 1 of

FIGURE 2.37
Records for the Order table

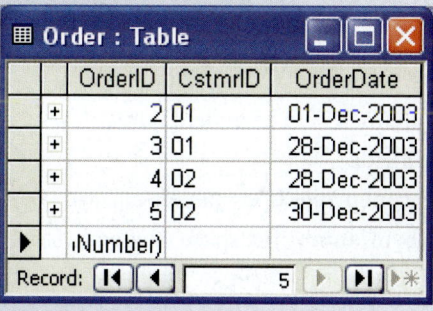

Order : Table

	OrderID	CstmrID	OrderDate
+	2	01	01-Dec-2003
+	3	01	28-Dec-2003
+	4	02	28-Dec-2003
+	5	02	30-Dec-2003
▶	(Number)		

Record: 5

10. Close the OrderDetail table

11. Open the **Customer** table. You can view all of the linked table data in a subdatasheet by clicking the plus sign in front of the customer record. The Order and OrderDetail records for Customer 01 are shown in Figure 2.39. Review the order for customer 2

FIGURE 2.39

Order and OrderDetail rows for Customer 01 shown in subdatsheets

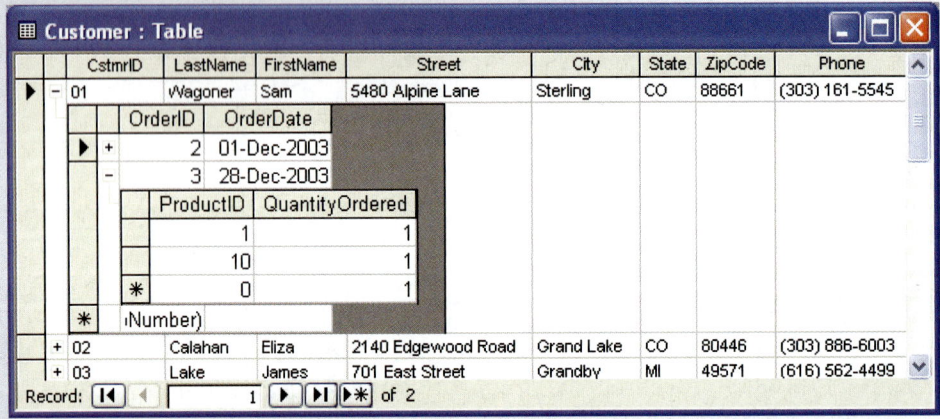

12. Close the ac02KoryoKicks2.mdb file

These steps demonstrated how properly designed relational databases force data to be entered in an order that is consistent with the defined relationships. The data on the one side of the relationship must always be present before data on the many side of the relationship can be added. Conversely a parent record (one side of the relationship) cannot be deleted when there are child records. You entered two orders for customer 01. The Customer record for customer 01 could not be deleted unless the Order and associated OrderDetail were deleted first.

When relationships are built between tables, Access uses *subdatasheets* to display data from related tables. When viewing data from the parent or primary table in Datasheet View, a plus sign indicates that a subdatasheet can be displayed. To view the related data, click the plus sign. To remove the subdatasheet, click the minus sign.

Access Limitations

The general specifications for Microsoft Access are very broad and reflect optimal implementations. The model of computer, available memory, and use of the database can reduce the maximums significantly. An Access database can

- Be up to 2 gigabytes
- Store up to 32,7678 objects such as tables, queries, forms, and reports
- Have 64 characters in an object name
- Have 14-character passwords
- Support up to 255 concurrent users

Microsoft Access tables can

- Have up to 64 characters in each field name
- Have up to 255 fields
- Be one of 2048 concurrent open tables
- Be up to 2 gigabytes minus the space needed to store system objects
- Have 32 indexes

making *the grade*

1. When fields are listed in parentheses after the table name, how is the primary key identified?

2. T F   The Format attribute controls how data values are stored in the table.

3. What is the maximum number of characters a text field can store?

4. To enter the most common value of a field automatically you would set the _____ attribute.

5. T F   The Undo button on the Access toolbar can be used to undo 20 items when entering data in Datasheet View.

6. T F   Currency format is dependent on the regional settings of the computer.

SESSION 2.3 SUMMARY

To keep data accurate, it must be maintained. In Datasheet View the rows and columns of a table can be reorganized to make maintenance easier without impacting the underlying table structure or data. When sorting by multiple columns, the sort columns must be adjacent and in order of their importance (primary sort field first). Columns such as the primary key can be frozen so that they remain on the screen to identify records when scrolling to the right in a datasheet to ensure updates are being made to the correct record. Columns can be hidden when they are not relevant to the current operation.

Adding, deleting, and editing existing records can easily be accomplished in Datasheet View. A NewRecord indicator (*) displays in an empty row at the bottom of a table's datasheet. Click in the NewRecord row to enter new data using the Tab key to move between table columns. Updates made to table data are saved automatically when the cursor is moved to another record—the Save File button is not needed. The Microsoft Office Clipboard operates between Office products with storage for 24 items.

Find and Replace allows both a search criterion and a replace value to be specified. By clicking the Find Next button, each occurrence of the search value can be found and replaced with the new value. Wildcards such as * and ? can be used to search for specific patterns of data such as Ton? or Ton*.

The Undo feature operates differently in the various Access views. In the Design View where the table file is not updated until you leave the view, both Undo and Redo are available for 20 actions. In table Datasheet View, Undo is available for the last action and the last record update can be reversed from the Edit menu.

Database design is critical to the development of a stable database with valid data. The 90/10 rule states that 90 percent of the time should be spent designing the database structure so that only 10 percent of the time is spent maintaining it. The design process includes outlining the mission, determining the outputs, listing fields, assigning fields to tables, defining table relationships, and building a prototype. Once the database design is complete, the tables are built by defining their fields, field attributes, and relationships.

Visit www.mhhe.com/i-series/ to explore related topics.

MICROSOFT OFFICE SPECIALIST OBJECTIVES SUMMARY

- Enter, edit, and delete records—MOS AC03S-2-1
- Format datasheets—MOS AC03S-3-4
- Sort table data—MOS AC03S-3-5

making the grade *answers*

SESSION 2.1

1. Indicates the new record row.

2. Wildcards are used to set match values for searching text. * replaces any number of characters. ? replaces a single character. [] can be used to include alternative values such as [jf].

3. The Access table file is updated with changes made in a record when the pointer is moved to a new record.

4. The column order is important when sorting because the first field is primary and the second field is secondary—only used to break ties in the first value.

5. False.

6. False.

SESSION 2.2

1. Underline the primary key.

2. False.

3. 255.

4. default.

5. False.

6. True.

task reference *summary*

Task	Page #	Preferred Method
Finding specific data values	AC 2.6	• Click in the column that you would like to search • Click the **Find** button • Enter the Find What criteria using the data value that you would like to find. Remember that a question mark (?) can be used as a wildcard for one character and an asterisk (*) is a wildcard for multiple characters • Click the **Find Next** button. If multiple rows match the Find What criteria, you may need to repeat this step until the row you are searching for is found
Office Clipboard: collect items to paste	AC 2.14	• Display the Office Clipboard by selecting **Office Clipboard** from the **Edit** menu • Select the item to be copied • Click the **Copy** or **Cut** button in the Standard toolbar • Continue placing items on the Clipboard (up to 24) until you have collected everything that you need
Office Clipboard: paste collected items	AC 2.14	• Display the Office Clipboard if it is not already present. If the Office Clipboard option of the Edit menu is not available, you are in an application or view that does not support the Office Clipboard • Click or select the area where you want to place items • Do one of the following: • Select the **Paste All** button to paste the entire contents of the Office Clipboard or • Select a Clipboard item and choose **Paste** from its drop-down menu

task reference *summary*

Task	Page #	Preferred Method
Office Clipboard: remove items	AC 2.14	When the Clipboard is open • To clear one item, click the arrow next to the item you want to delete and then click **Delete** • To clear all Clipboard contents, click the **Clear All** button • Placing more than 24 items on the Clipboard will replace existing items beginning with the oldest item
Hiding datasheet columns	AC 2.16	• Open a table, query, or form in Datasheet View • Click the field selector of the column to be hidden • Click **Hide Columns** on the **Format** menu
To unhide a column	AC 2.16	• On the **Format** menu, click **Unhide Columns** • Select the names of the columns that you want to show from the Unhide Columns dialog box
Freezing and unfreezing datasheet columns	AC 2.17	• Open a table, query, or form in Datasheet View • Select the column(s) that you want to freeze or unfreeze • To freeze column(s), select **Freeze Columns** on the **Format** menu • To unfreeze column(s) select **Unfreeze All Columns** on the **Format** menu
Defining a Table field	AC 2.26	• Click **Tables** in the Options bar • Click the **Design View** button on the toolbar • Enter a field name • Select a data type • Define other field attributes as needed

TRUE/FALSE

1. A subtable displaying related data can be accessed by clicking the plus sign (+) in front of a record displayed in Datasheet View.

2. The format property of a field controls how values stored in the field will display to the user.

3. The table on the many side of a relationship is referred to as the parent or primary table.

4. Hiding a table field causes it to stay on the screen while the remaining columns scroll.

5. The Default Value property of a field causes a value to be automatically displayed for that field.

6. The mission of a database defines exactly what it will and will not accomplish.

7. Undo buffer is cleared by deleting the contents of the Clipboard.

FILL-IN

1. The _____ View of a table has more levels of undo than the _____ View.

2. Access has a maximum capacity of _____ open tables.

3. The _____ dialog box is used to enter criteria for searching a table.

4. The first sort field is the _____ sort.

5. A table column that does not scroll off the screen is said to be _____.

6. A _____ is a rapidly developed test copy of the database used to test design.

7. The _____ holds up to 24 Office items that can be pasted into any Office document.

MULTIPLE CHOICE

1. The maximum size for an Access database is
   a. 1 user.
   b. 2 gigabytes.
   c. 2,000,000 fields.
   d. all of the above.

2. A subdatasheet
   a. opens on top of a datasheet.
   b. displays data from another table.
   c. is activated by clicking a plus sign (+).
   d. does all of the above.

3. The _____ attribute of a field should be set to yes when the field cannot be left blank.
   a. Required
   b. No Blank
   c. Compulsory
   d. Mandatory

4. The data type of a field controls
   a. appropriate field names.
   b. the table a field belongs to.
   c. what type of data it can store.
   d. how the field's data values display.

5. In table design the underlined field of a table is the
   a. primary key.
   b. index.
   c. foreign key.
   d. table name.

review of concepts

REVIEW QUESTIONS

Each of the following topics should be addressed in one to three paragraphs.

1. Explain the meaning of the following:
   Product (*ProductID*, ProductDescription, ProductPrice).

2. Explain how at least two of the rules used to assign fields to tables are used.

3. What is the process of modeling tables with a many-to-many relationship?

4. Assume that you are designing a Products table for a candy manufacturer. The fields that you are considering are CandyType, CandyFilling, CandyCost, CandyPicture, QuantityOrdered, TotalYTDProduction. How would you determine what fields to include in the table? Is there a natural primary key for this table?

5. If you were to build a database to store information on your CD collection, what fields would you consider? How many tables? What would be the key field(s)? Why?

6. Explain how Undo works in Datasheet View while maintaining data.

7. Describe how to use wildcards in a Find and Replace operation.

CREATE THE QUESTION

For each of the following answers, create the question.

ANSWER	QUESTION
1. Things that you can do to improve the order of columns in Datasheet View	_____
2. Secondary sort field	_____
3. The entry in the Find What text box	_____
4. ?	_____
5. When the cursor is placed in another record	_____

FACT OR FICTION

For each of the following determine whether the statement is fact, fiction, or both and present your arguments for that conclusion.

1. An edit on a record can be undone after moving to another record and storing the edit from the second record.

2. Setting the Caption property of a field changes the label that displays with the field data without any further impact.

3. There are no problems with entering data into tables before all of the table relationships have been defined.

4. Records entered into a table are physically stored in the order that they were entered so there is no "insert" operation that places a record in a specific table location.

5. When building new tables with the New Table Wizard, you have complete control over all of the field properties.

1. Creating BBs Shoes Database

BBs Shoes is a family-owned shoe store specializing in athletic shoes. Roberto and Benita Lopez started the store to provide name-brand shoes at a discount price. They are dedicated to being a neighborhood resource, by providing needed shoes and jobs to the neighborhood. Benita has decided that a database would help track inventory. She has asked you to build it for them.

1. Start Access and open a new blank database. If a database is already open, use the **Toolbars** option of the **View** menu to open the **Task Pane**

2. Name the database **ac02BBsShoes.mdb**

3. Create the table shown in Figure 2.40 using Design View

4. Save the table as **Shoes**

5. Add the data in Figure 2.41

6. Although there are not enough data to make a Find truly operational, practice using Find with wildcards. Use Find to locate all inventory stored in aisle A. What Find What value did you use? How many did you find?

7. Enter three more records with data about your favorite shoes. Give each a unique stock number and a storage location of B1

8. Update the data as follows:
   - Change *Nike Tiemp 2000 D* to **Nike Tiempo 2000 D**
   - Change *Rio Zoom* to **Rio Zoom Hrdgrnd**
   - Use **Undo** to reverse the previous change. If you have already saved the update by moving to another record, use **Undo Saved Record** from the **Edit** menu

9. Delete the record for AR17208

10. Hide the StockNbr column, sort by descending price, and print the result. Close the table and save your changes

11. What forms and reports using these data can you think of to help Benita?

12. Are there other tables that could benefit this business? What would they track?

FIGURE 2.40

Shoes table design

Field Name	Data Type	Field Size	Notes
StockNbr	Text	7	Primary key
ShoeDescription	Text	30	
ShoePrice	Currency		
QtyOnHand	Number	Integer	
Location	Text	3	Aisle and shelf location

FIGURE 2.41

Shoes table data

StockNbr	ShoeDescription	ShoePrice	QtyOnHand	Location
AG87473	Adidas Gazelle	$59.95	78	B3
AR17208	Air Roma II	$69.95	15	B1
NT17165	Nike Tiemp 2000 D	$89.95	28	A2
NT17166	Nike Tiempo 2000 M	$84.95	45	C3
PC19435	Puma Cellerator	$149.95	20	A1
PS19439	Puma Sting	$74.95	36	C1
RK19387	Rio Zoom	$119.00	22	C2
*		$0.00	0	

Record: 1 of 7

2. Creating the Snow Rentals Database

Jagitt Jain is the proprietor of Snow Rentals, an Alberta, Canada, company that rents recreational equipment. As the name implies, Snow Rentals specializes in snow-related equipment with the bulk of its rentals involving downhill snow skis, cross-country snow skis, and snowboards. Jagitt has several store locations located near resort areas. Each location has a local supply of rental equipment and the ability to "borrow" from a central warehouse when demand for an item exceeds the local supply.

Jagitt is still using a paper-based checkout system to keep track of which store has "borrowed" from the central warehouse. Each warehouse item has a card (similar to an old library card) kept with the item when it is in the warehouse. To check an item out, the card is removed and the name of the borrower, date checked out, and return date are written on the card before it is filed with other checkout cards.

As the organization grows, this system is proving cumbersome and inadequate. Jagitt has to thumb through thousands of cards to determine what items have not been returned on time or to find out where to look for a lost item.

1. Start Access and open a new blank database. Name the database **ac02SnowRentals.mdb**

2. Create the **Store** and **Inventory** tables shown in Figure 2.42 using Design View

3. Enter the table data shown in Figure 2.43. Remember that StoreID and InventoryID are automatically generated

FIGURE 2.42

Store and Inventory table designs

Store Table			
Field Name	**Data Type**	**Field Size**	**Notes**
StoreID	AutoNumber		Key
StoreName	Text	25	
StoreManager	Text	25	
Phone	Text	13	

Inventory Table			
Field Name	**Data Type**	**Field Size**	**Notes**
InventoryID	AutoNumber		Key
InventoryClass	Text	25	
InventoryDescription	Text	25	
QtyInStock	Number	Integer	

4. Verify your data entry and make any needed changes

5. If your work is complete, exit Access; otherwise, continue to the next assignment

FIGURE 2.43

Store and Inventory table data

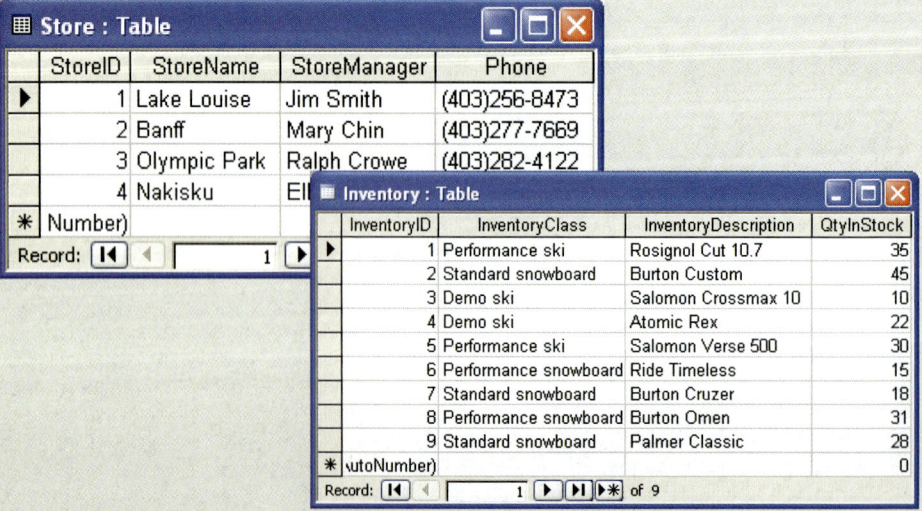

challenge!

1. HealthCare2Go Employee Tracking

HealthCare2Go is a temporary services agency providing short-term employees to the medical community. Temporary employees are scattered across the United States and travel to their temporary positions. Riki Lee is charged with tracking the availability of employees and needs help building an effective database.

1. Start Access and open a new blank database. If a database is already open, use the **Toolbars** option of the **View** menu to open the **Task Pane**

2. Name the database **ac02MedTemps.mdb**

3. Create the table shown in Figure 2.44 using Design View

4. Print the table design

5. Use the Office Clipboard to copy records from the **ac02TempEmployees.mdb** table into your Employee table

6. Use Find with wildcards to locate all RNs and LPNs. What Find What value did you use? How many did you find?

7. The JobClass field was too small and has truncated data. MedTe should be **MedTech**. Use Find and Replace to change the field values. Document how you accomplished this

8. Test field size by trying to change the JobClass for Cecilia Wong to **Operations Manager**. Document the result

9. Add the data in Figure 2.45. Make up the addresses and phone numbers using your city, state, zip code, and area code. Remember that EmployeeID is generated for you

10. Sort the table data by last and first names. Order and resize the columns appropriately. Print the result

FIGURE 2.44

Employee table design

Field Name	Data Type	Field Size	Notes
EmployeeID	AutoNumber		Key
LastName	Text	25	
FirstName	Text	25	
Address	Text	30	
City	Text	30	
State	Text	2	
Zip	Text	5	
Phone	Text	10	
JobClass	Text	10	

FIGURE 2.45

Employee table data

LastName	FirstName	Phone	JobClass
Andersen	Tom	314-404-0000	RN
Andersen	Sam	874-588-5234	LPN
Bartlen	Connie	874-588-5234	LPN
Anderson	Nancy	887-582-5835	MedTech
Callaway	Lois	879-502-3303	LPN
Carter	Mary Jane	306-588-9302	RN
Decett	Lana	113-563-8751	MedTech
Drennen	Leo	932-587-2193	RN
French	Jennifer	773-500-8370	MedTech
Hampton	Dan	425-557-5368	RN
Harris	Jerry	291-546-8297	LPN
Ricker	Ricky	128-532-7321	RN
Werner	Paul	761-598-9891	LPN
Waxman	Sue	412-593-3232	LPN

Record: 1 of 14 (Filtered)

2. Tracking Video Rentals

Video Extravaganza is a rural Ohio video store run by Vaughn and Linda Aimes. Inventory, customer lists, and checkouts are currently being maintained on Excel spreadsheets. Vaughn and Linda believe that an Access database will simplify their record keeping and reduce expenses caused by lost and misplaced inventory items. They have asked you to begin developing their database.

1. How would you go about designing a database for this organization?

2. Open Access, create a new blank database, and name it **ac02VideoExtravaganza.mdb**

3. Create the Movie table outlined in Figure 2.46

4. Print the design of the table

5. Open **ac02NewVideoReleases.mdb.** Use Copy and Paste to place all 94 records from the NewReleases table in the Movie table

6. Enter the data shown in Figure 2.47

7. Use Find with wildcards to locate Dramas in the Movie table. What Find value did you use? How many did you find?

8. Use Find and Replace to change Action Category values to **Action/Adventure** in the Movie table

9. Make Category the leftmost column and then sort the Movie table by Category. Save this layout update

10. Hide the ID field in the Movie table. Save this layout update

F I G U R E   2.46

Video Extravaganza Movie table design

Field Name	Data Type	Field Size	Notes
ID	AutoNumber	Long Integer	Key
StreetDate	Date/TIme		
Title	Text	40	
YearReleased	Text	4	
Rating	Text	5	
Actor	Text	30	
RentalAvailability	Text	25	
Category	Text	25	

F I G U R E   2.47

Video Extravaganza data

Title	YearReleased	Rating	Actor	RentalAvailability	Category
Basic Instinct	1992	R	Sharon Stone	VHS/DVD	Suspense
X2: X-Men United	2003	PG-13	Hugh Jackman (more)	VHS/DVD	Action/Fantasy
Bad Boys II	2003	R	Will Smith (more)	VHS/DVD	Action/Comedy
Chasing Papi	2003	PG	Roselyn Sanchez (more)	VHS/DVD	Comedy

e-business

1. SportBabies.com Product List

SportBabies.com is an online storefront selling replica sports uniforms for babies and toddlers. It carries products for all NFL, NHL, NBA, Major League Baseball, National League Baseball, and college teams. The uniforms are exact replicas of those currently worn on the field and come in standard baby and toddler sizes. Product manufacturers include Champion, Nike, Russell, and Wilson. Classic player gear is also available.

The current Web site is based on static HTML, which means that it must be manually maintained each time products and prices change. To automate this heavy maintenance project, a database is being created. The database will be maintained and generate updates to the Web site. You have been asked to build the ProductList database. You will be using NFL products for testing.

1. Start Access and open a new blank database. If a database is already open, use the **Toolbars** option of the **View** menu to open the **Task Pane**

2. Name the database **ac02SportBabies.mdb**

3. Create the table shown in Figure 2.48 in Design View

4. Add the data in Figure 2.49

5. Add records for three non-NFL players with a price of $30

6. Add yourself and a friend as NBA players with a price of $48

7. Make League, Team, and Player the first columns of the datasheet by hiding the ProductID column. Sort by League, Team, and Player and print the result

8. Print the table design

9. Use Find with wildcards to locate records for NFL and NBA players. Document the Find criteria

10. Sort the data by descending price. Make Price the first column and print

11. Document at least three business questions that could be answered using these data

FIGURE 2.48

ProductList table design

Field Name	Data Type	Field Size	Notes
ProductID	AutoNumber		Key
League	Text	3	
Team	Text	30	
Player	Text	25	
Price	Currency		

FIGURE 2.49

ProductList data

ProductList : Table

ProductID	League	Team	Player	Price
1	NFL	49ers	Rice	$29.99
2	NFL	Bears	Enis	$31.48
3	NFL	Bengals	Dillon	$24.52
4	NFL	Bengals	Warric	$28.92
5	NFL	Broncos	Davis	$32.45
6	NFL	Broncos	Greese	$35.32
7	NFL	Broncos	Price	$25.68
8	NFL	Cowboys	Sanders	$21.15
9	NFL	Cowboys	Galloway	$21.15
10	NFL	Cowboys	Smith	$20.44
11	NFL	Jets	Martin	$20.44
12	NFL	Jets	Johnson	$23.83
13	NHL	Avalanche	Foresburg	$34.88
14	NHL	Oilers	Gretzky	$185.99
15	NHL	Avalanche	Roy	$42.38
16	NBA	Bulls	Pfeifer	$25.00
17	NBA	Jazz	Audette	$25.00

Record: 20 of 22

2. Tracking Services for xXtreMeSportz

Casey Lewis, Evan Roach, and Wei Wong are extreme sports enthusiasts. They play hockey, skateboard, and snowboard. After talking to many of their friends the three decided to create a cooperative organization for extreme sports aficionados. The main goal of the co-op would be to act as a clearinghouse for equipment and events so that members would be able to purchase supplies, clothing, and event tickets at a bulk reduced rate.

After enlisting over 300 local members, the partners launched the www.xXtreMeSportz.com Web site to communicate their services and recruit additional members. Keeping the Web site updated has become too time-consuming so the partners have agreed to use an Access database to store their services. The Web site will be automatically updated from the database.

1. Open Access and create a new blank database named **ac02xXtreMeSportz.mdb**

2. Use Design View to create the Event table outlined in Figure 2.50

3. Print the table design

4. Add the data shown in Figure 2.51

5. Open **ac02Calendar.mdb**. Use Copy and Paste to place all 109 records from the Calendar table into the Event table of ac02xXtreMESportz.mdb

6. Verify your data entry and then use Find and Replace to change all occurrences of ASP WQS 6 in the Sponsor field to **ASP WQS 8**

7. Use Find and Replace with a **null** Find What value to set empty sponsor fields to **ASP WQS 8**

8. Make Sponsor the first column and add a descending sort by that field. Close and save

9. Close the database and exit Access if your work is complete

F I G U R E 2.50

Event table design

Field Name	Data Type	Field Size	Notes
EventID	AutoNumber		Key
Category	Text	30	
StartDate	Text	15	
EndDate	Text	15	
EventTitle	Text	50	
Venue	Text	50	
Sponsor	Text	20	
Contact	Hyperlink		

F I G U R E 2.51

Event table data

EventID	Category	StartDate	EndDate	Event Title	Venue	Sponsor	Contact
1	SURF	May-24	May-27	Local Motion Surf Into Summer	Honolulu,Oahu-Hawaii	ASP WQS 1	http://www.aspworldtour.com/
2	SURF	May-26	Jun-7	Quiksilver Pro	Tavarua/Namotu-Fiji	ASP WCT	http://www.aspworldtour.com/
3	SKATE	May-30	Jun-2	Mountain Dew National Championships	Cleveland, Ohio	Vans TC	http://www.vans.com/
4	BMX	May-31	Jun-3	CBF II Bikes, Boards and Blades	Wheatfield, NY		http://www.hsacentral.com/
5	IN-LINE	Jun-1	Jun-6	ASA Pro Tour	Cincinnati, OH	ASA	http://www.asaskate.com/
6	SURF	Jun-5	Jun-9	SMAS	Newport Beach,California-USA	SMAS	http://www.vanssmas.com/
7	BMX	Jun-6	Jun-9	Mervyn's Beach Bash	Hermosa Beach, CA		http://www.hsacentral.com/

Record: 1 of 7

1. Toy Purchase Statistics by Internet Research Inc.

Internet Research Inc. (IRI) is a statistical evaluation organization specializing in Internet commerce. The evaluations are based on many facets of commerce including product price, shipping costs, timely delivery, ease of Web site navigation, product quality, and return policies. The statistics generated by IRI are published on a Web site for consumers and used by Shopping Bots to rank and evaluate shopping requests entered by users.

You have been hired by IRI to maintain the statistical evaluations of toy sales sites. As a training exercise, you will gather data manually and use Access to evaluate the results. You will begin by researching toy prices and building an Access table to hold your findings. The goal is to familiarize you with the sites and tools you will be evaluating and provide an understanding of the underlying research methodologies.

1. Use a Shopping Bot such as www.mysimon.com or a search engine to find at least two sites that sell toys
   a. At your first site, determine the lowest priced Barbie (you can choose another popular toy with multiple models)
   b. Find the price for the same toy at the second site
   c. At the second site determine the highest priced Barbie
   d. Find the price for the same toy at the first site
   e. Perform the previous steps for a third toy of your choice

2. Start Access and open a new blank database. If a database is already open, use the **Toolbars** option of the **View** menu to open the **Task Pane**

3. Name the database **ac02IRI.mdb**

4. Create the table shown in Figure 2.52 in Design View

5. Print the table design

6. Input the data from your search, use a unique key value for each record, verify your data entry, and make any necessary edits

7. Further testing of the table uncovers a need for a ReviewDate field. Switch to table Design View and add it as the last table field with an appropriate data type and format

8. Test your update by adding review dates to all of the records

9. Sort the table data by ascending ToyName. Order the columns so that the sort field is first and adjust the column width to fit the data. Print the results

10. Sort the table data by ascending Web site. Order the columns appropriately. Print the results

FIGURE   2.52

Toys table design

Field Name	Data Type	Field Size	Notes
ToyID	Text	3	Key
WebSite	Hyperlink		
ToyName	Text	25	
ToyDescription	Text	50	
Price	Currency		

around the world

1. Getz International Travel Corporate Customers Database

Getz International Travel is the largest travel agency in the world. The organization consists of over 5,000 full-time employees working in offices in San Francisco, Los Angeles, Phoenix, Chicago, Detroit, Indianapolis, Orlando, London, Budapest, Warsaw, Taiwan, and Paris. Getz arranges every facet of travel for both domestic and international treks.

Schedules are happily arranged for individuals, small groups, and large groups of up to 300. Arrangements include airfare, tours, hotels, car rentals, and more.

The over 5,000 corporate customers are the backbone of the organization. Currently, all customers are kept in the same table. You have been assigned the task of creating a separate table for corporate customers because they are being assigned to a new division of the organization.

1. Start Access and open a new blank database. If a database is already open, use the **Toolbars** option of the **View** menu to open the **Task Pane**

2. Name the database **ac02Getz.mdb**

3. Create tblCustomers shown in Figure 2.53 in Design View. Make the lengths of text fields fit the data

4. Print the table design

5. Add the data in Figure 2.54.

6. Create a format for the CustomerID field that will cause the five digits to display with a dash after the first two digits (03-129)

7. Due to a data entry error, you need to use Find and Replace to change all of the area codes from 303 to 313

8. Add five local businesses to the table. Use your friends' names for primary and secondary contacts

9. Sort the table data by CompanyName. Order and resize the columns appropriately. Print the results

10. Sort the table by City within State. Order the columns appropriately. Print the results

11. Create a Find that will locate Colorado records. Document the Find What criteria

FIGURE 2.53

Corporate customers table design

	Field Name	Data Type	Description
🔑▶	CustomerID	Number	Customer identification number
	CompanyName	Text	Company Name
	Contact	Text	Contact person within company
	2ndContact	Text	Secondary Contact person
	Address	Text	Street address or Post Office Box
	City	Text	City
	State	Text	State (two character abbreviation)
	ZipCode	Text	Five-digit ZIP code
	PhoneNumber	Text	Telephone number
	FaxNumber	Text	Facsimile phone number
	CreditLimit	Number	Credit Limit

FIGURE 2.54

Corporate customers table data

CustomerID	Company	Contact	2ndContact	Address	City	State	ZipCode	PhoneNumber	Fax
1768	Alpine Construction Group	James Darling		805 W. 44th Ave.	Wheat Ridge	WI	20321	(103) 674-1753	
1873	Eye Wear Inc.	Kathleen Paduano		60605 US Hwy 285	Pine	CO	80637	(303) 674-2114	
2048	1st Bank	Marie Baal		3560 Evergreen Pkwy.	Evergreen	CO	80453	(303) 674-7809	
2718	Vision Land Consultants	Ramona Hyde		30960 Stagecoach Blv	Arvada	FL	30932	(803) 674-3025	
2892	Arvada Villa	Jim Rogers	Betty Truett	5453 West 57th Avenu	Arvada	CO	80004	(303) 422-3123	
3312	Block's Plumbing & Heating	Elliott Waterman	Sam Patterson	3121 West 80th Avenu	Thornton	CO	80131	(303) 428-5300	
4312	Integrative Physical Therapy	Sandra Dawson	Lynn Bryant	2200 South Federal	Denver	CO	80231	(303) 441-9882	
5132	Quest Academy	Jennifer Botts	Nancy Kind	3005 30th Street	Boulder	CO	80321	(303) 441-7887	
7312	Sportline	George Jenson	Angela Alston	6510 Wadsworth Blvd.	Arvada	OH	50004	(503) 422-1312	
20931	Sutton Attorneys	Bill Skewes		30752 Southview Dr.	Evergreen	CO	80439	(303) 674-7041	
0									

Record: I◄ ◄ 1 ► ►I ►* of 10

running project: tnt web page design

Create a New TnT Table

TnT is a custom Web page development company founded by Victoria (Tori) Salazar and Tonya O'Dowd. The background for this case was presented in Chapter 1. Go back and review it if necessary.

1. Use Windows to create a copy of ac01TnT.mdb and rename the copy **<yourname>TnT.mdb**. Replace ac02<yourname> with your last name and first name (e.g., WellsJim)

2. Start Access and open the <yourname>TnT.mdb database

3. Open **tblCustomers** in Datasheet View

4. Use Find and Replace to remove the parentheses () and the dash (-) from the cusPhone and cusFax fields

5. In Design View, add a format to each field that will display the deleted characters even though they are not stored in the field

6. Create a new table in Design View

   a. The first table field is custID with a Number data type and LongInteger field size because it will join to the custID field of tblCustomers carrying an AutoNumber data type

   b. The second table field is SiteNumber with a Number data type and Integer field size

   c. The third field is URL with a Hyperlink data type

   d. Set the combination of custID and SiteNumber as the primary key

   e. Close the Design View and save the table as **tblCustomerSites**

7. You will need to build a one-to-many relationship between these two tables, since each customer can have more than one site built by TnT

   a. Open the Relationships window by right-clicking in the database window and choosing **Relationships**

   b. Right-click in the Relationships window and choose **Show Table...**

   c. In the Show Table window click **Add** to add the tblCustomerSites (it is selected by default) table to the Relationships window

   d. In the Show Table window select **tblCustomer** and click **Add** to add it to the Relationships window

   e. Close the Show Table window

   f. In the Relationships window click the custID field in CustomerSites and drag to the cusID field in tblCustomers. The Edit Relationships window should open

   g. Click the check boxes as shown in Figure 2.55 and choose **Create**

   h. A one-to-many relationship should now display in the Relationships window

   i. Close the Relationships window, saving the relationship

8. Close CustomerSites

9. Open tblCustomers and review the data you entered in the subdatasheets

10. Print both tables and exit Access

FIGURE 2.55

Edit Relationships window settings

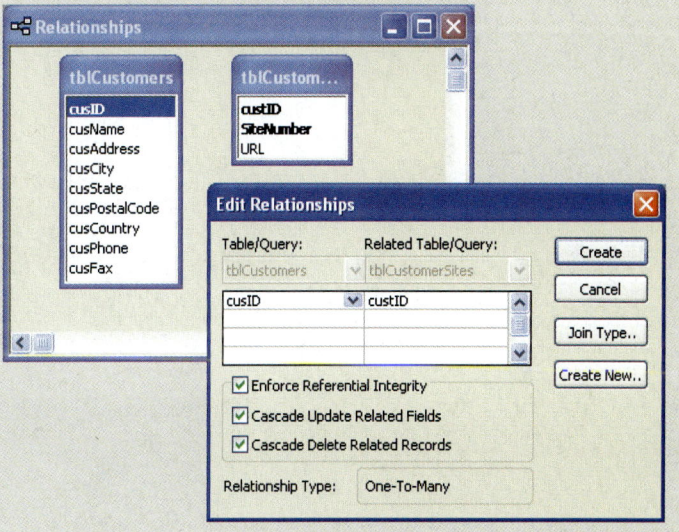

1. Evaluate Database Requirements

Yoko Yim is a small-business owner who would like to track personal data about her customers. Yoko provides various types of massage and personal training in clients' homes. The primary goal for the database is to be able to send follow-up thank-you messages to new customers and appropriate holiday greetings. Her customers are from many cultural and religious backgrounds. She would also like to know the last date a service was provided and what that service was. The business is run on a cash basis, so there is no need to create invoices.

Document your evaluation of Yoko's database needs. Describe how Yoko will be able to use the database to support her stated business needs. Create a new blank database named **ac02YimCustomers.mdb**. Use Design View to build the tables you designed.

2. Start a Database for Your Hobby

Assume that you are starting a database to store data about your hobby or pastime. Document the type of data that you would need to track. Use the design techniques outlined in the chapter to design tables for your database. Describe how you could use this database. Are there valid reasons to create a database? Not to create a database?

Create a new blank database named **ac02<your name>Hobby.mdb**. Use Design View to build the tables for your database. Populate at least one table with 10 or more records.

3

Introducing Queries, Filters, Forms, and Reports

did you know?

the *scientist Anders Celsius developed a measuring scale with freezing at 100 degrees and boiling at 0 degrees. Fellow scientists waited until Celsius died to reverse the scale.*

cooking *and salad oils with an additive developed by Penn State chemical engineers performed as well as commercial oils when used to lubricate machinery, such as cars and boats.*

the *first video game was Pong, introduced in 1972 by Noel Bushnell, who then created Atari.*

in *Rome, the world's first paved streets were laid out in 170 B.C. The new streets were popular as they were functional in all types of weather and were easier to keep clean, but they amplified the city's noise level.*

to *make a daguerreotype, an early photograph, required a 15-minute average exposure time.*

to *find out what percentage of computer data loss cases are due to human error, visit www.mhhe.com/i-series.*

Chapter Objectives

- Filter data in Datasheet View—MOS AC03S-3-6
- Create and run Select Queries—MOS AC03S-1-7
- Create and modify calculated fields and aggregate functions in Query Design View—MOS AC03S-3-1
- Construct and customize simple forms—MOS AC03S-1-9
- Create, customize, and print simple reports—MOS AC03S-1-10
- Modify form layout—MOS AC03S-3-2

KoryoKicks: Using Access to Evaluate Products and Markets

Missy and Micah need to make some tough business decisions. Their martial arts classes and products are selling very well. KoryoKicks is successful and, as is often the case with personal businesses that take off, the twins are unable to keep up with demand. They are considering:

- Limiting the number of classes offered to what they can personally teach
- Reducing the number of martial arts products they provide

- Moving the business into a storefront so they can hire additional help
- Finding a partner or partners to share the workload
- Selling the business

To evaluate the viability of these options, the twins need information about their business (see Figure 3.1). The only thing that they are sure of at this point is that current profits are not sufficient to support even a part-time employee. To decide how to proceed, they need to evaluate the additional

F I G U R E   3.1
Potential KoryoKicks queries and reports

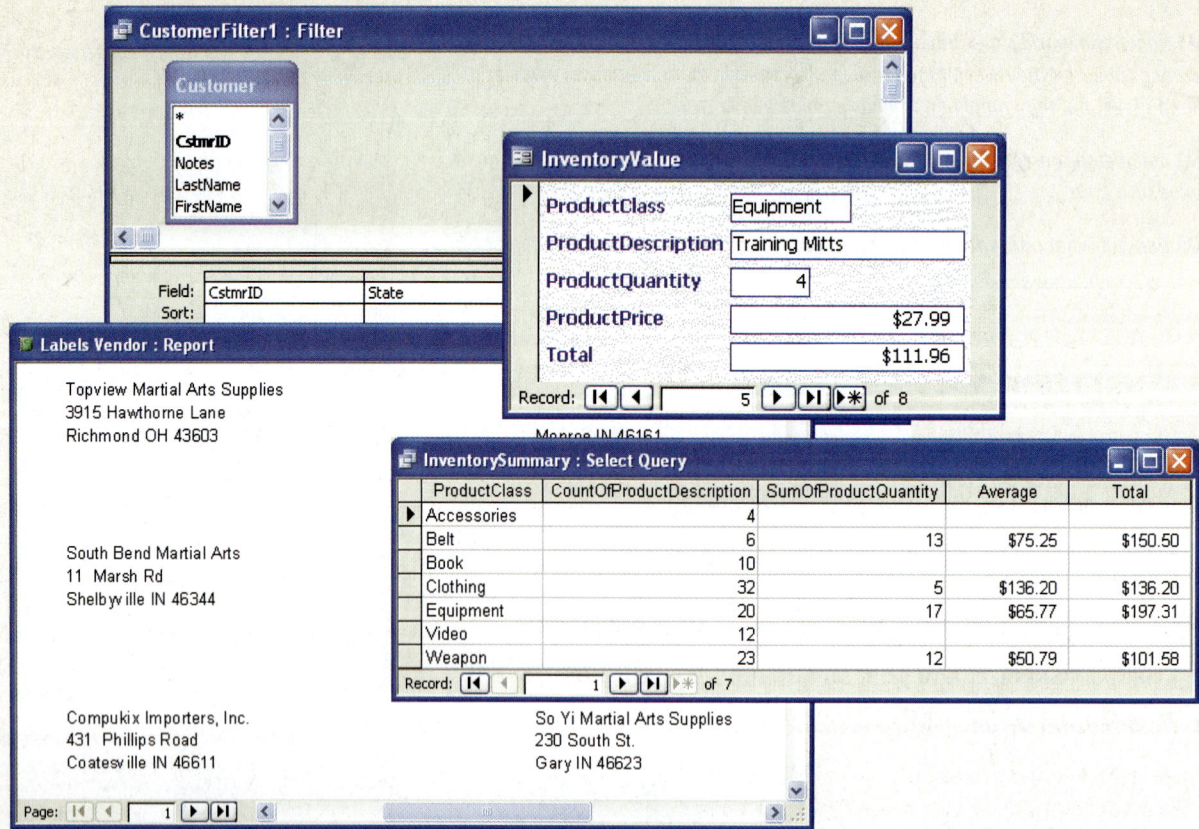

potential of their products and markets. Is the market sufficient to allow increased product and class sales? Can the existing suppliers support an increase in product sales? Have all customers paid their bills? Invoices are being sent out, but there is currently no way to track payments. It is possible that adding tracking and follow-up to the current system could significantly increase profits. Another way to increase profits is to cut costs. The twins would like to know if there are products that can be discontinued because they are unprofitable.

Although existing data are limited, the twins can see the potential of Access query and report fa-cilities to answer their business questions. Queries and reports can be used to organize and analyze their business data to help make decisions. While no amount of information can guarantee the result of a business decision, timely and effective information can significantly improve the likelihood of a positive outcome. Missy and Micah have asked you to guide them through the process of creating effective queries and reports for their business. They plan to use this information to help determine how to best proceed.

SESSION 3.1 SELECTING AND ORGANIZING DATA

Access provides an array of options for selecting and organizing data into useful information. This session evaluates the effectiveness of various filters and introduces select queries.

Selecting Data with Filters

Filters are used to restrict (limit) the rows of data displayed in the current datasheet so that a subset of the data can be manipulated. An ideal time to use filters is to maintain or print only some of the rows in a table. Missy and Micah are curious about how filters can be used with KoryoKicks data. They do not understand the functionality of the various types of filters and have asked you to show them.

Introducing Filters

There are four ways to apply filters to the datasheet. The first, *Filter By Selection*, returns records matching the datasheet selection. The second, *Filter By Form*, presents an empty version of the current datasheet where match values can be typed. *Filter For Input* accepts a value or expression to restrict the records. The *Advanced Filter/Sort* window presents a design grid used to build filter criteria. Regardless of the type of filter being applied, the goal is to display only records that meet specific criteria. Creating the criteria is slightly different for each type of filter. You will experience each type of filter using the KoryoKicks prototype database to gain an understanding of their utility.

Creating Filter by Selection Criteria

Filter By Selection is not only the most intuitive filtering tool, but also the most limited. All or part of a data value in any field can be selected to control which records will display. The selection is evaluated as described in Figure 3.2.

F I G U R E   3.2

Filter By Selection criteria

Selection	Action	City Field Example
Click in a field	The whole field value will be used to search that field for matches	Click in the value Berlin and only records for Berlin will be selected
Select an entire field	The whole field value will be used to search that field for matches	Select the value Berlin and only records for Berlin will be returned
Select the first character(s) of a field value	Records starting with the selected characters will be returned	Select the characters "Ber" and all records starting with Ber will be retrieved (i.e., Berlin, Berlington, Berton, etc.)
Select character(s) after the first character	Records that contain the selection anywhere will be returned	Select "er" from Berlin and all records containing er will be retrieved (i.e., Anderson, Berlin, Merlin, Waterberry, etc.)

---

task reference   Filter By Selection

- Open the table in Datasheet View

- Select the field and character(s) of the search criteria (see Figure 3.2)

- Click the **Filter By Selection** ⚡ toolbar button to return values matching the selection

  or

- Right-click and choose **Filter Excluding Selection** to filter the selection out of the data

- Evaluate the results of the filter

- Click **Remove Filter** 🔽 on the Access toolbar

Filtering the Customer table:

1. Open the **Customer** table of the **ac03KoryoKicks.mdb** database in Datasheet View

2. Click in the City cell containing the value **Coatesville**

3. Click the **Filter By Selection** ⚡ toolbar button (see Figure 3.3)

4. Click the **Remove Filter** 🔽 toolbar button

5. Select **on** in any City value

6. Click the **Filter By Selection** ⚡ toolbar button

7. Click the **Remove Filter** 🔽 toolbar button

8. Select **G** in any City value where it is the first character

9. Click the **Filter By Selection** ⚡ toolbar button

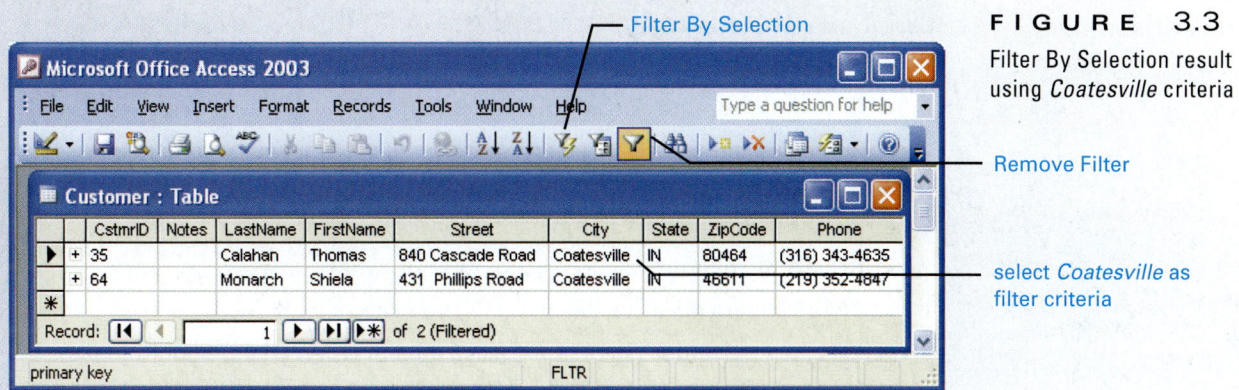

Filter By Selection

FIGURE   **3.3**

Filter By Selection result using *Coatesville* criteria

Remove Filter

select *Coatesville* as filter criteria

10. To demonstrate that filters are cumulative, select **IN** as the State value and click **Filter By Selection** again

   By combining two filters, you were able to retrieve Indiana cities that begin with the letter G

11. Click the **Remove Filter** toolbar button to remove all active filters

Filters also can be used to exclude the selection. Select a value and then right-click to bring up the pop-up menu. Select ***Filter Excluding Selection*** from the pop-up menu and all records containing that value will be excluded from the datasheet.

Excluding records from the Customer table:

1. Verify that the Customer table of the ac03KoryoKicks.mdb database is open in Datasheet View

2. Click in any **CO** State value

3. Right-click on the selection to bring up the pop-up menu

4. Select **Filter Excluding Selection**. The datasheet should not display Colorado records

5. Click the **Remove Filter** toolbar button to remove all active filters

Filters are cumulative, so a second filter can be applied to the result of the first filter. The results of a filter stay in effect until *Remove Filter* is selected or the datasheet is closed.

Creating Filter By Form Criteria

Clicking Filter By Form presents a blank datasheet containing two tabs where filter values can be selected from a drop-down list box or typed manually. Unlike Filter By Selection, Filter by Form accepts multiple criteria. Conditions entered in the Look for tab must all be true to retrieve a record. The Or tab allows alternate values to be entered for the same field.

Like many Access operations, Filter by Form has its own unique toolbar that is visible only in this view. Besides the Standard toolbar options such as Print, Cut, Copy, and Paste, there are also some unique toolbar options such as Open Filter and Save Filter. To leave the view, use the Close button on the Filter by Form toolbar.

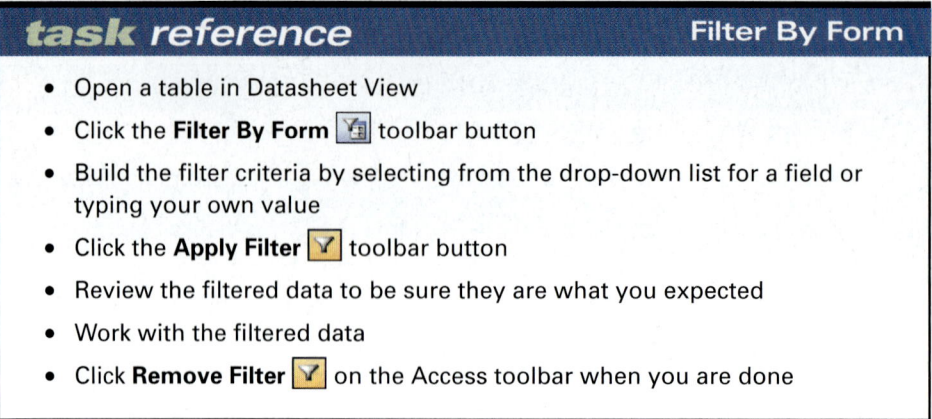

Filtering the Customer table with Filter by Form:

1. Verify that the Customer table of the ac03KoryoKicks.mdb database is open in Datasheet View

2. Click the **Filter By Form** button on the Access toolbar

3. Remove any existing criteria by selecting them and pressing **Delete**

4. You want to retrieve records for customer numbers greater than five from Indiana. To accomplish this, enter the criteria shown in Figure 3.4 and click **Apply Filter**

5. Review the records to be sure that the results are what you expected

F I G U R E   3.4

Filter By Form using compound criteria

Filter By Form toolbar

CstmrNmbr criteria

use this tab to enter multiple criteria for one field

filter results

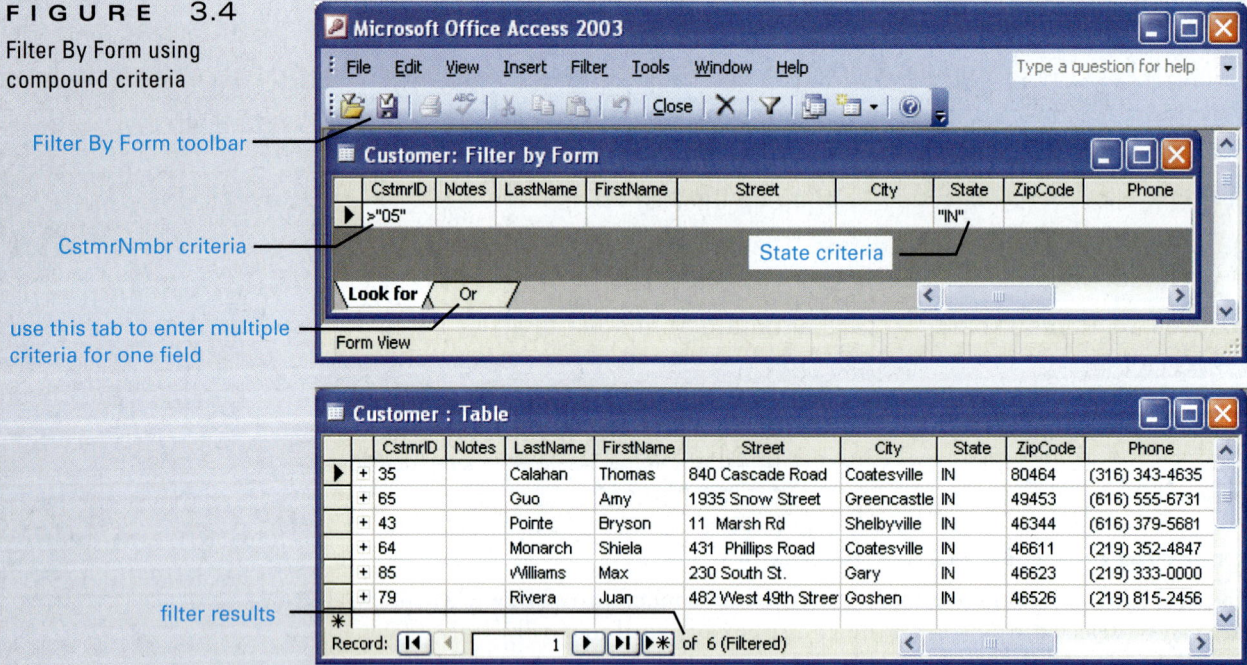

tip: *When sorting or filtering numbers stored in text fields, 0s are important. Leading 0s (005) are entered so that the numbers sort correctly. They also must be entered when filtering or the records returned will be inappropriate (5, 05, and 005 each returns a different result). You must match what is stored in the table*

6. Click the **Remove Filter** toolbar button to remove all active filters

When filtering, double quotes ("") are required around match values for fields containing text data. Access adds the double quotes for you if you forget. As you have just seen, Filter by Form uses relational operators (=, >, <, >=, <=, and <>). The equal condition is the default and does not need to be stated, as was demonstrated with the "IN" criterion for State. All other operators must precede the value in the criteria, as was demonstrated with the > "05" criterion for CstmrID. Criteria also can be entered using keywords including In, Like, and Between. More detail on building criteria will be presented in the next session.

Filtering the Customer table with an Or condition:

1. Verify that the Customer table of the ac03KoryoKicks.mdb database is open in Datasheet View

2. Click the **Filter By Form** button on the Access toolbar

3. Remove any existing criteria by selecting them and pressing **Delete**

4. You want to retrieve records for customers in Colorado, Indiana, or California. The Or tab will be used to enter each of the alternate state abbreviations. Enter **CO** in the State field of the Look for tab

5. Click the **Or** tab at the bottom of the window. Enter **IN** in the State field of the Or tab

FIGURE 3.5

Filter By Form using *Or* criteria

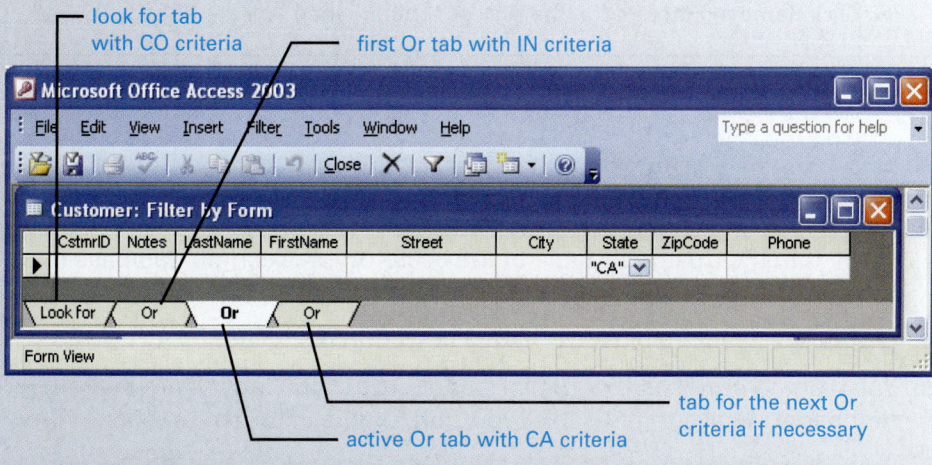

look for tab with CO criteria
first Or tab with IN criteria
tab for the next Or criteria if necessary
active Or tab with CA criteria

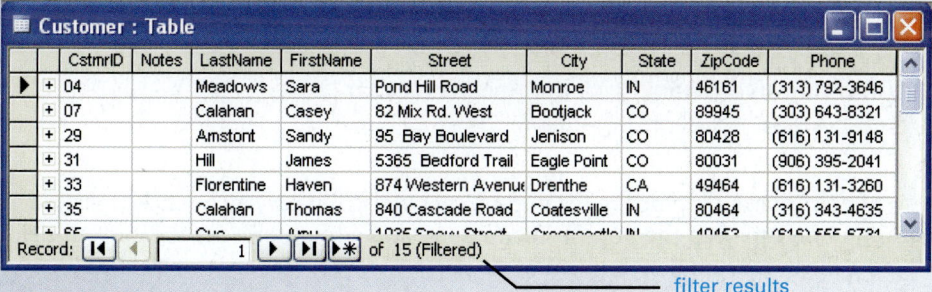

filter results

6. Click the second **Or** tab and enter **CA** in its State field

7. Click the **Apply Filter** toolbar button

8. Review the records to be sure that they match the filter criteria (see Figure 3.5)

9. Click the **Remove Filter** toolbar button to remove all active filters

Filter by Form also can be used to see the filter criteria created by other types of filters. Did you notice that when you first opened the Filter by Form grid, it contained the criteria from the last Filter by Selection filter that you applied?

Creating Filter for Input Criteria

Filter for Input allows filter criteria to be entered from the pop-up menu. Simply right-click in the field to be filtered and type your criteria in the Filter For text box. Filter for criteria can include combinations of identifiers, operators, wildcards, and values.

---

task reference   **Filter for Input**

- Open a table in Datasheet View

- Right-click the field to be filtered

- Type the filter criteria in the Filter For text box using wildcards, operators, and values

- Press **Enter** to activate the filter

- Review the filtered data to be sure they are what you expected

- Work with the filtered data

- Click **Remove Filter** [Y] on the Access toolbar when you are done

---

Filtering the Customer table with Filter For:

1. Verify that the Customer table of the ac03KoryoKicks.mdb database is open in Datasheet View

2. Right-click in any data value of the FirstName field

3. You want to select all records for people with "am" anywhere in their first name. To accomplish this type *am* in the Filter For text box

4. Press **Enter** to activate the filter (see Figure 3.6)

5. Evaluate the filter results

6. Click **Remove Filter** [Y] on the Access toolbar

After a criterion is typed in the pop-up menu, the Tab key can be clicked instead of pressing Enter to keep the pop-up menu open and add criteria for the current field. Because filters are cumulative, opening the pop-up window for another field will accept criteria to further filter data.

Creating Advanced Filter/Sort Criteria

The Advanced Filter/Sort grid allows criteria to be entered on multiple fields and sorted in one step. The grid is very similar to the Query by Example grid that will be covered in the next topic.

FIGURE 3.6

Filter For criteria and results

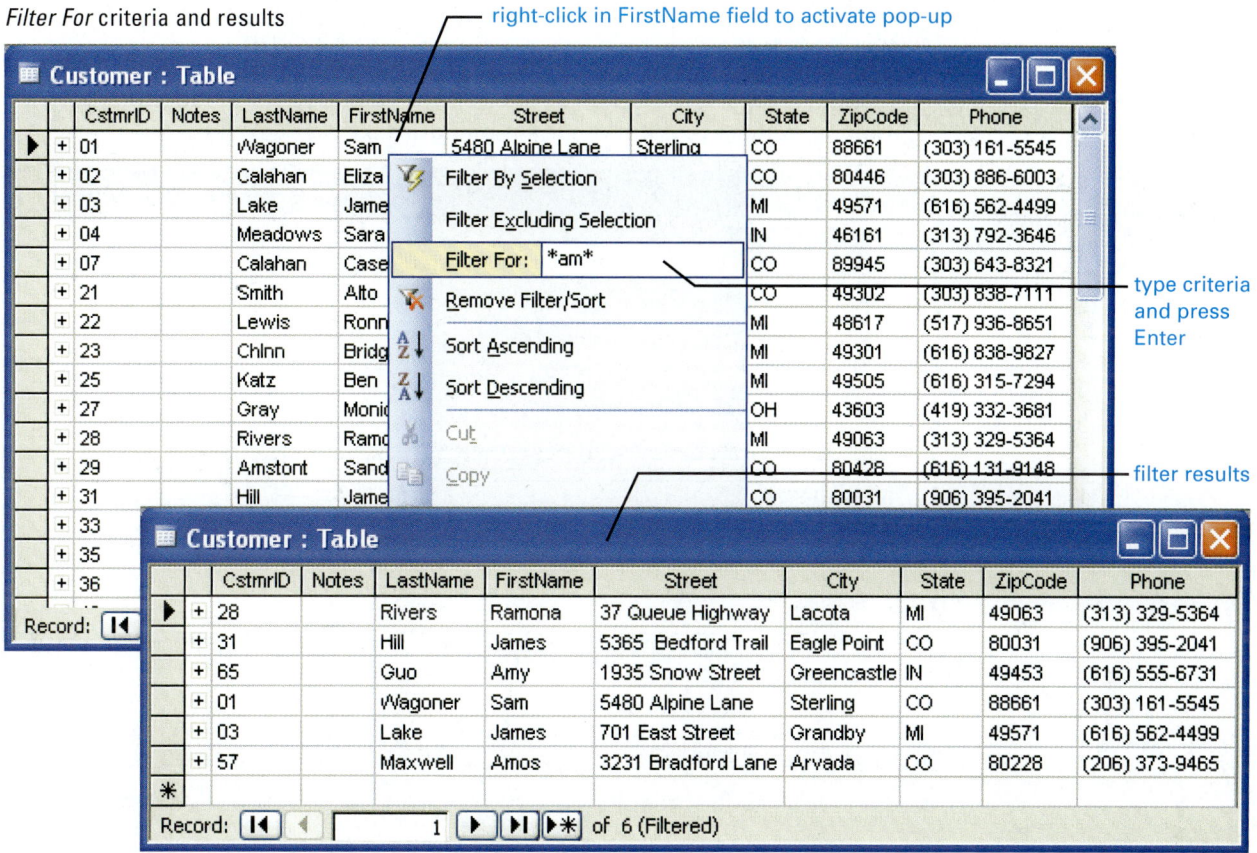

task reference　　　Advanced Filter/Sort

- Open a table in Datasheet View
- On the **Records** menu, point to **Filter**, and then click **Advanced Filter/Sort**
- Add criteria fields to the design grid
- Enter the filter and sort criteria
- Click the **Apply Filter** button on the toolbar
- Review the filtered data to be sure they are what you expected
- Work with the filtered data
- Click **Remove Filter** on the Access toolbar when you are done

Filtering the Customer table with Advanced Filter/Sort:

1. Verify that the Customer table of the ac03KoryoKicks.mdb database is open in Datasheet View
2. Click **Remove Filter** to remove any active filters

3. On the **Records** menu, point to **Filter**, and then click **Advanced Filter/Sort**

4. To select records for CstmrID over 5 and from both Colorado and Indiana, enter the criteria shown in Figure 3.7

FIGURE 3.7

Advanced Filter/Sort grid with criteria

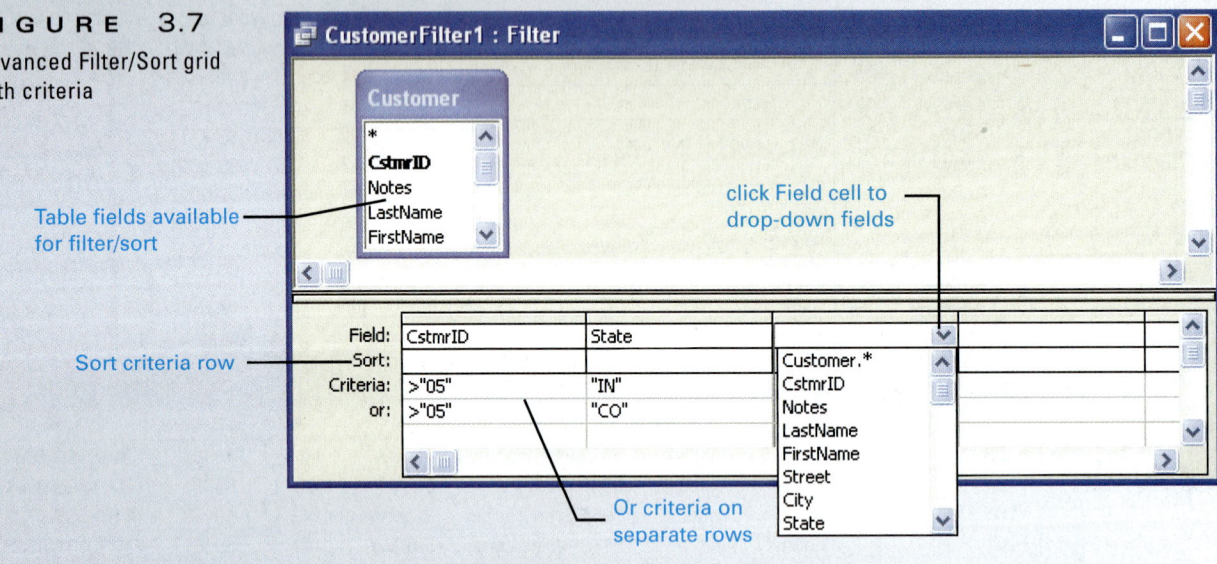

5. Click **Apply Filter** [Y]

6. Evaluate the filter results

7. Click **Remove Filter** [Y] on the Access toolbar

As you can easily see, the Advanced Filter/Sort is the most powerful and the most complex filtering tool. The type of filter used depends on the complexity of the filter criteria and the user's comfort with the filtering options.

Saving a Filter as a Query

Filters are not one of the Access database objects and so they cannot be stored. To remedy this situation, a filter can be saved with a table, form, or query object. In each case, a query, which is more powerful than a filter, is saved. A saved filter can be reapplied without reentering the criteria.

---

task reference   **Saving a Filter as a Query**

- Display the filter in either the Filter By Form window or the Advanced Filter/Sort window (recall that any filter can be displayed in these windows regardless of how it was created)

- Click the **Save As Query** [💾] button on the toolbar

- Type a name for the query and click **OK**

- The new query will appear with the other query objects in the Database Window

---

Limitations of Filters

While filters are valuable tools when selecting and organizing data, there are some significant limitations in what they can accomplish. The most obvious limitation of filtering data is that all table fields must display in the filtered result. There is no way to select specific fields or even change the order in which fields are displayed. It is true that you can manually hide fields and change column order, but that becomes tedious.

> **anotherword**   . . . on Filters
>
> Besides filtering data in Datasheet View, filters can be used to restrict data displayed in a form or a sub-datasheet. One filter can be associated with each form so that it activates when the form is opened. This is useful when multiple users share a database and each only wants access to his or her specific data

Finally, only one table can be filtered at a time—there is no join capability. Only one filter can be associated with a table or form; however, any number of filters can be saved as queries. The functions that are missing in filters are the strength of queries.

Selecting Data with Queries

Queries are used to view and analyze data in different ways. They are much more powerful than filters because they can retrieve data from multiple tables and perform calculations on the results. Stored queries also can be used to select records that will be displayed in a form or report.

Introducing Queries

Queries are commonly used to support the business decision-making process. For example, Missy and Micah could use a query to profile their customers so they can understand how to better market their products. They also could find out if there are any products that have never been purchased so they can discontinue them. In addition, a query could list customers who have not been billed so that invoices can be sent to them.

To answer such questions, the necessary data must be stored in one or more tables in the database. For example, the current KoryoKicks database could not provide much demographic information on who customers are because no data are stored about the customer's gender, age group, income, or other factors that are generally used to set advertising strategy.

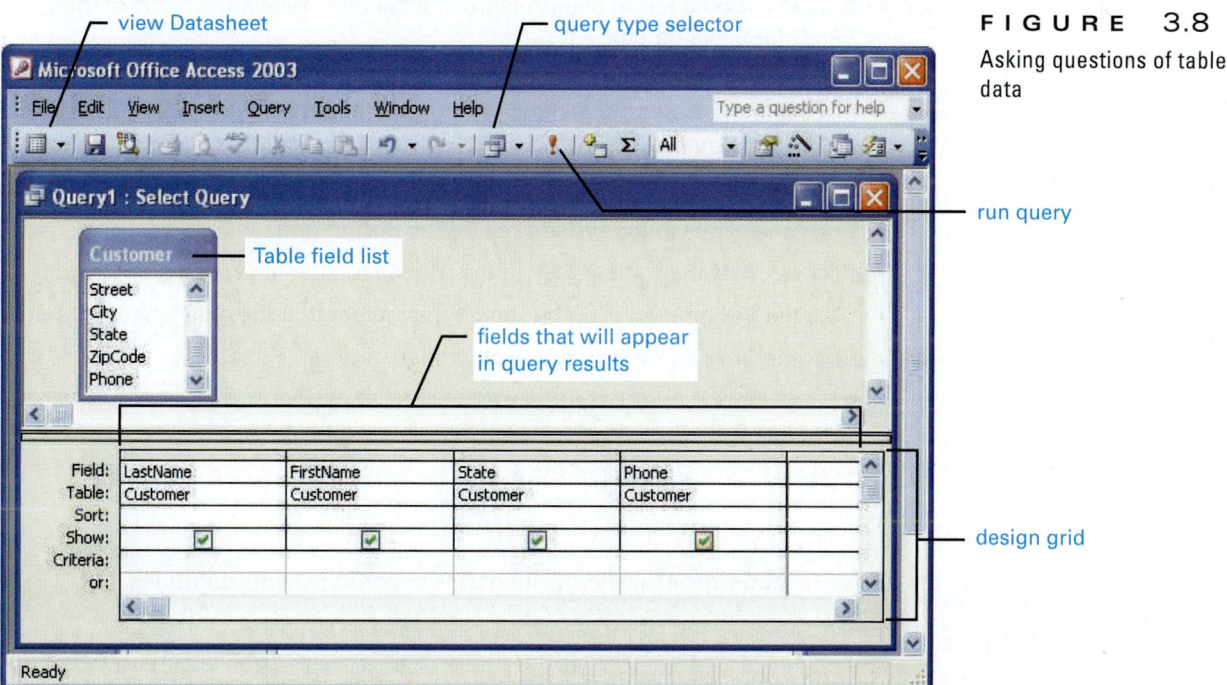

FIGURE 3.8

Asking questions of table data

The most common type of query is a Select Query. Select Queries retrieve data from one or more tables and display the results in Datasheet View. Once displayed, the records can be updated. Select Queries can

- Display selected rows of data
- Display selected columns of data
- Sort query results
- Calculate within records (e.g., calculate gross pay for each employee record)
- Group records and create subtotals (e.g., subtotal expenses for each department)
- Calculate totals such as sums, counts, and averages

You have already created a query using a Wizard. As with other Wizards, the Simple Query Wizard asks questions and produces a query based on your answers but does not provide a way to use the full scope of query capabilities. Informational queries are better developed in query Design View.

Specifying Simple Query Criteria

In query Design View a Query by Example (QBE) grid is used to enter question criteria. The *design grid* is used to provide examples of the information to be retrieved and Access will select all data matching the criteria. Since the most popular type of query is a Select Query, that is the QBE default.

One of the queries that the twins are interested in building is a phone list for customers. On the phone list, they want the customer's full name, state, and phone number. This is a select query that you will create in query Design View.

---

task reference　　　　　　　　**Create a Select Query**

- Select the **Queries** object from the Database Window
- Click **New** from the toolbar
- Select the **Design View** ✎ ▾ button from the New Query dialog box and click **OK**
- Double-click the name of each table that contains relevant data from the Show Table dialog box
- Double-click each table field that is to be contained in the query result to place it in the Field row of the design grid. The order of the columns is the order of the output
- Enter sort criteria in the Sort row of the design grid
- Enter selections in the Criteria row of the design grid
- Click the **Datasheet View** ▦ ▾ button on the toolbar to see the query results
- Click the **Design View** ✎ ▾ button on the toolbar to update the query criteria
- Click the **Save** 🖫 button to save the query criteria

Creating a Customer table query:

1. Close the Customer table of the ac03KoryoKicks.mdb database
2. Select the **Queries** object from the Database Window
3. Click **New** on the toolbar

4. Select **Design View** from the New Query dialog box and click **OK**

5. Double-click on the **Customer** table in the Show Table dialog box to add it to the design grid (see Figure 3.9)

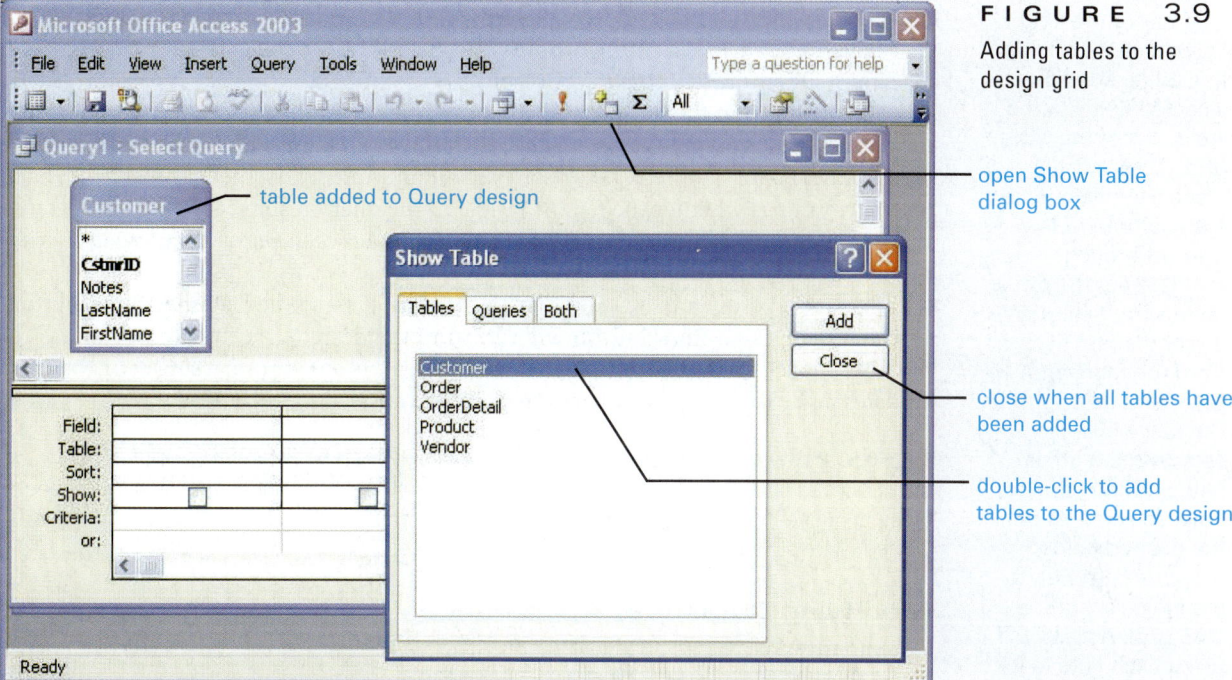

FIGURE 3.9

Adding tables to the design grid

open Show Table dialog box

table added to Query design

close when all tables have been added

double-click to add tables to the Query design

6. Click **Close** in the Show Table dialog box

7. Double-click the **LastName, FirstName, State**, and **Phone** fields from the Customer table field list, adding each to the Field row of the design grid

tip: *If you place an undesired field in the design grid by mistake, delete it by clicking the cursor on the bar above the field to select the column. When the column is selected, press the **Delete** key to remove the column from the grid*

If fields are selected in the wrong order, move a column by clicking the cursor on the bar above the field to select the column. When the column is selected, click and drag it to the desired location

8. Click the **Datasheet View** button to see the query results (see Figure 3.10)

9. Click the **Design View** button to return to the query Design View

10. Click the **Save File** button

11. Name the query **PhoneList**

The query Design Window contains the tables that will be queried and the design grid that is used to enter query criteria. The Title bar of the Design Window contains the query name and the type of query, or *Query1: Select Query* by default. The Query Type button on the toolbar also reflects the query type as well as allowing the selection of a different query type.

FIGURE 3.10

PhoneList query results

LastName	FirstName	State	Phone
Wagoner	Sam	CO	(303) 161-5545
Calahan	Eliza	CO	(303) 886-6003
Lake	James	MI	(616) 562-4499
Meadows	Sara	IN	(313) 792-3646
Calahan	Casey	CO	(303) 643-8321
Smith	Alto	CO	(303) 838-7111
Lewis	Ronnie	MI	(517) 936-8651
Chinn	Bridgett	MI	(616) 838-9827
Katz	Ben	MI	(616) 315-7294
Gray	Monica	OH	(419) 332-3681
Rivers	Ramona	MI	(313) 329-5364
Amstont	Sandy	CO	(616) 131-9148
Hill	James	CO	(906) 395-2041
Florentine	Haven	CA	(616) 131-3260
Calahan	Thomas	IN	(316) 343-4635

Record: 1 of 2

*another***way**
**. . . to Move Fields
to the QBE Grid**

Double-click on the
Title bar of the field
list to select all fields
in a table. Drag the
selected fields to the
Field row of the QBE
grid. Access will
place each field in its
own column of the
grid. To move
multiple fields from a
table simultaneously,
select the first field
from the table and
then hold down the
Ctrl key while
selecting the other
fields. When you
have selected all of
the desired fields,
drag the selection to
the Field row of the
QBE grid. Access will
place each field in its
own column in the
order that they
appear in the table

Each table in the Design Window displays the field list for that table. The first option of each table field list is the asterisk (*) wildcard (see Figure 3.11). To be included in the query results, the fields must be moved from the field list to the design grid. Clicking and dragging a field, double-clicking a field, or clicking in the Field row of the design grid and selecting from the drop-down list are alternative ways to move fields into the design grid. Placing the wildcard (*) in the design grid causes all fields from that table to be included in the output. The order of field columns in the design grid determines their order in the query results.

Each column in the design grid contains a field and the selection criteria for that field. Query criteria include *Sort, Show, Criteria,* and *Or. Sort* allows ascending or descending sorts on each field. If sorts are set on multiple fields, the leftmost is primary. *Show* determines whether the field is visible in the query results. *Criteria* is a selection value similar to that entered in a filter. The *Or* row allows the entry of alternative criteria for a field.

The query results can be viewed at any time by clicking the Datasheet View button. Clicking the Design View button will return to the design grid. It is important to remember that the datasheet displayed from a query is a temporary subset of the data. Updates made to data in the query datasheet are applied to the table data.

help yourself *Use the Type a Question combo box to improve your understanding of queries by typing* **select query**. *Review the contents of* About queries *including* About types of queries, About select and crosstab queries, *and* Create a select or crosstab query. *Close the Help window when you are finished*

Modifying Datasheet Appearance

As with the table datasheet, query results displayed in query Datasheet View can be formatted for better viewing. Columns can be hidden or reordered or have their width adjusted. Formats can be saved with the query or abandoned on exit.

The appearance of a datasheet can be modified for readability, or to visually distinguish it from other datasheets, using the Datasheet Formatting toolbar (see Figure 3.12). Turn on the toolbar by selecting *Formatting (Datasheet)* from the Toolbars option of the View menu. Formatting toolbar options apply to the entire datasheet—not just the selection.

FIGURE 3.11

Designing a query

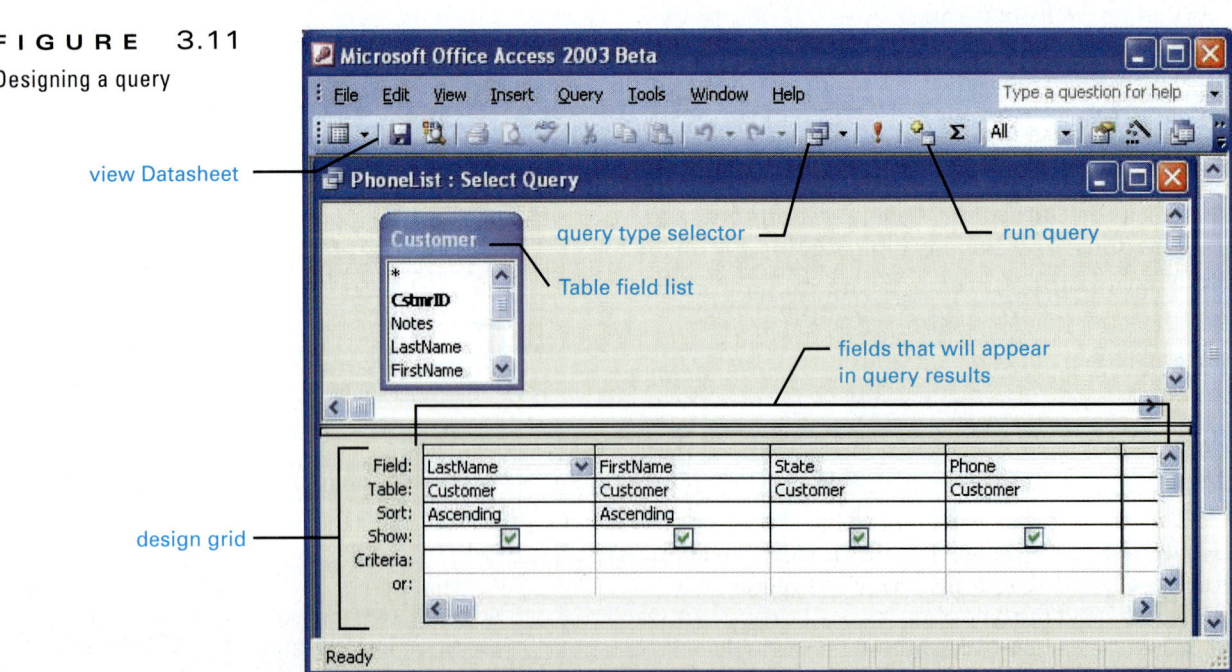

FIGURE 3.12
Datasheet formatting

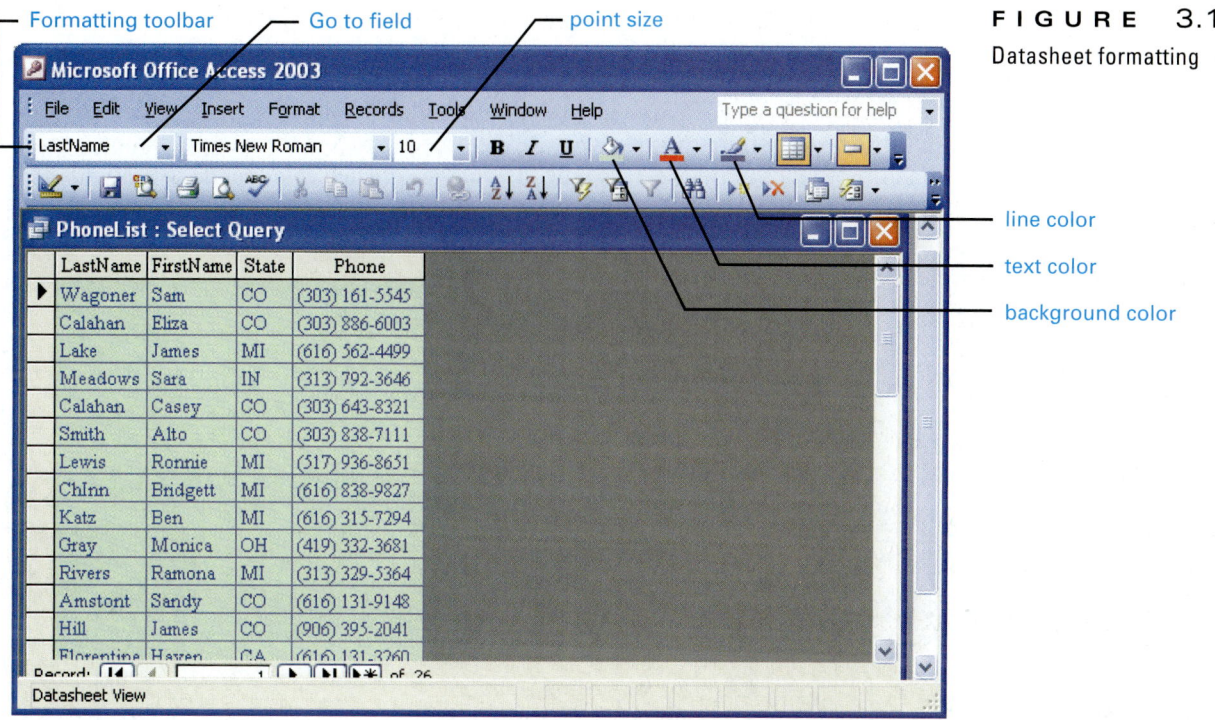

Figure 3.12 demonstrates Access's datasheet formatting capabilities. The point size (8 is the default), background color, text color, and line color have all been modified. The options were not selected for visual appeal but for ease of identification.

Formatting the Customer table query:

1. Verify that the PhoneList query of the ac03KoryoKicks.mdb database is open in Datasheet View

2. Activate the Formatting toolbar by selecting **Formatting (Datasheet)** from the **Toolbars** option of the **View** menu

3. Select **Phone** from the Go to Field box to place the cursor in the Phone field (see Figure 3.12)

4. Change the font to **Times New Roman** and the point size to **10**

5. Choose background, text, and line colors that you think look appealing

6. Click the **Print** button to print the results

7. Close the Datasheet Window without saving the formatting

Sorting Query Data

Sorting data is critical to making it simple to use. The current PhoneList query is in order by CstmrID, because it is the primary key of the source table. Most users would expect a phone list to be in order by LastName and FirstName so a phone number could be easily retrieved.

There are two ways to sort query results. The first is to use the Sort Ascending and Sort Descending buttons on the toolbar. This technique works exactly as presented in the discussion about sorting table datasheets. It is simple but has the drawback of not being stored as part of the query criteria. Each time the query is opened, the sort process must be applied.

Fortunately, the QBE grid has a sort row that allows the sort order for the query results to be part of the query. This sort will be stored as part of the query and therefore automatically will be applied each time the query is opened. The PhoneList should open sorted by LastName and FirstName, so you will add those criteria to the QBE grid.

Sorting the Customer table query:

1. Open the PhoneList query of the ac03KoryoKicks.mdb database in Design View

2. Verify that the field order is LastName and then FirstName so that LastName is the primary sort and FirstName is the secondary sort

3. Add Ascending to the Sort criteria of each field as shown in Figure 3.13

FIGURE 3.13

The PhoneList query with sort criteria

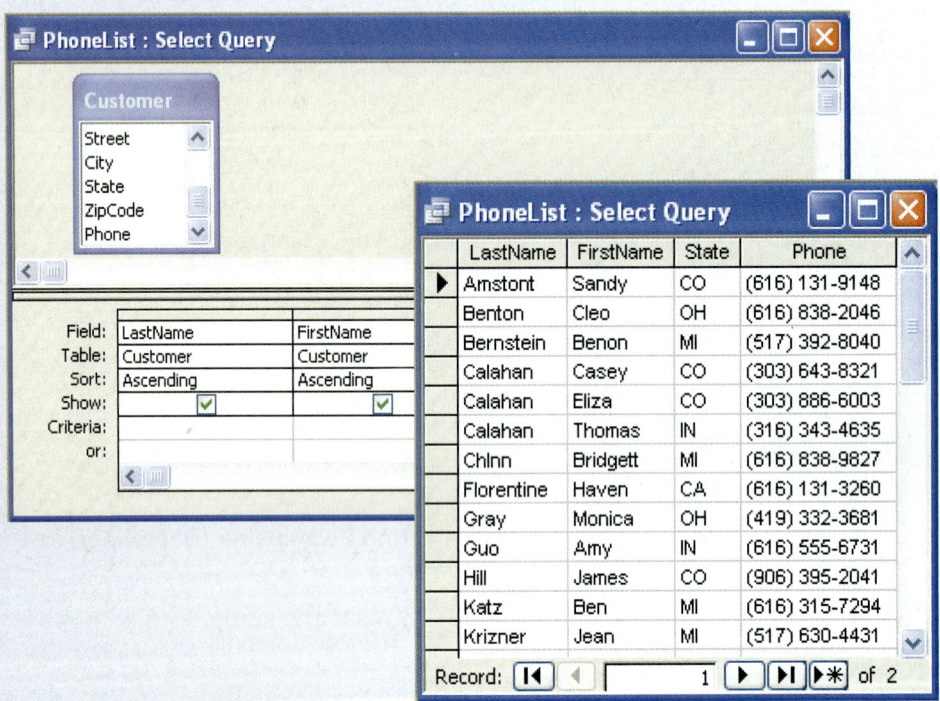

4. Click the **Datasheet View** button to see the query result

5. Click the **Design View** button to return to the query Design View

6. Click the **Save File** button to save the sort criteria with the query

7. Close the Query window

---

*another**way***

. . . to Run a Query

The instructions for viewing query results have used the Design View button, which automatically runs the query. The Run query button on the toolbar will accomplish the same task

making *the grade*

1. What happens when part of a field is selected and then Filter By Selection is applied?

2. T F   Filters restrict the columns that display for the filtered table.

3. How can you exclude a value from the results of a filter?

4. T F   Filters remain in effect until another filter is executed.

5. What is the purpose of Or in filters?

6. What is the benefit of saving a filter as a query?

SESSION 3.2 SELECTING AND CALCULATING WITH QUERIES

Queries are a powerful analytical tool that will allow complete control over which fields and records from a table or tables display. In this session power will be added to select queries by entering record selection criteria and performing simple calculations.

Selecting Records in Queries

Query record selection criteria are entered in the Criteria rows of the QBE grid using conditions. Conditions define how records will be selected and are placed in the field to which they will be applied. A typical condition uses a relational operator and a value, such as > 30000 in the Salary field, to tell Access which records to include in the query result. All records for which the condition is true will be incorporated into the query result.

Relational operators were briefly presented in the discussion on filters. Figure 3.14 gives a more complete presentation on the meaning of the various comparison operators.

FIGURE   3.14

Relational operators

Operator	Function	Example
=	Returns records that match the value exactly. It is optional because it is the Access default	"CA" #11/23/02#
>	Returns records with values greater than the condition value	> 30000 > "Collins"
>=	Returns records with values greater than or equal to the condition value	>= 30000 >= "Collins"
<	Returns records with values less than the condition value	< 45 < "Simes"
<=	Returns records with values less than or equal to the condition value	<= 89 <= "Sam"
<>	Returns records that are not equal to the condition value	<> 4 <> "Smith"
Between	Returns records with values between the two stated values. Both values are included in the result	Between 12 And 28 Between "e" And "k"
In	Returns records with values that match those in the condition list	In ("Jan", "Mar", "Sep") In (1998, 2001)
Like	Returns records with values that match the pattern stated with wildcards	Like "Pren*"

The KoryoKicks database for this chapter contains a Product table that holds data about the various martial arts products that Micah and Missy sell. Additional data are stored about the vendors that supply these products. These data are ideal for practicing selection queries and implementing calculations. Such queries can be used to evaluate the effectiveness of current offerings.

Selecting Product table records:

1. Open the ac03KoryoKicks.mdb database

2. Open the **Product** table and familiarize yourself with the data

3. Select the **Queries** object from the Database Window

4. Click **New** on the toolbar

5. Select **Design View** on the New Query dialog box and click **OK**

6. Double-click on the Product table in the Show Table dialog box to add it to the design grid

7. Click **Close** in the Show Table dialog box

8. You'll start by creating a current inventory list. Place ProductClass, ProductDescription, ProductPrice, and ProductQuantity in the Field row of the QBE grid

9. Click the **Datasheet View** button to see the query results

10. Return to **Design View**

11. This list is to display products currently in inventory. To accomplish this enter the criterion **>0** in the ProductQuantity column Criteria row

12. Click the **Datasheet View** button to see the query results (see Figure 3.15)

FIGURE   3.15

CurrentInventory query

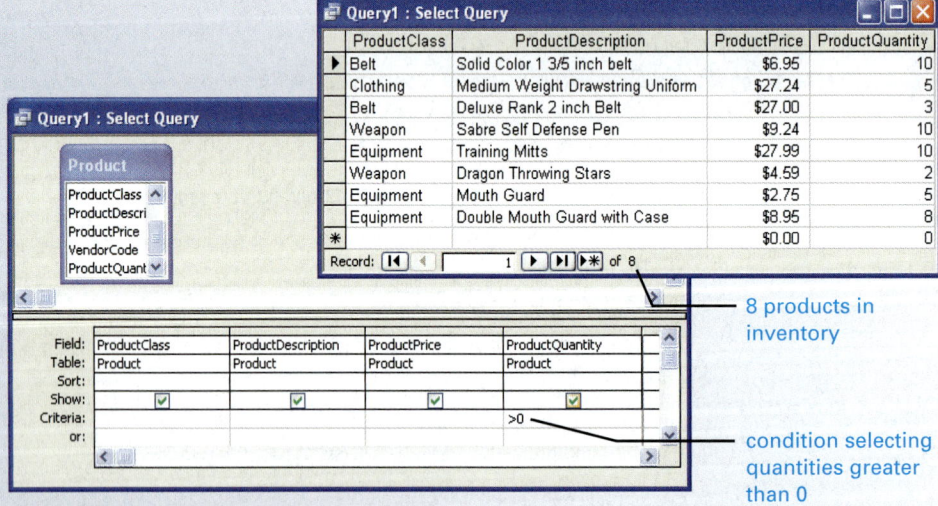

8 products in inventory

condition selecting quantities greater than 0

13. Save the query as **CurrentInventory**. The criteria will be saved and run weekly to generate a current list of products to order

The greater than (>) relational operator was used to state the condition in the previous example, but any of the other operators could have been applied. The operator is determined by the question that is being posed. There are currently several products

FIGURE   3.16

Data type delimiters

Data Type	Delimiter	Example
Number, Currency, AutoNumber	None	>5302.28
Text	Double quotes ("") delimit text match values	"Miller"
Date/Time	Pound signs (##) delimit date and time values	<#3/30/02#
Yes/No	Keywords True/False or Yes/No are used to select data in Yes/No fields	Yes

not carried in inventory but available for order. To retrieve items that could be ordered the criteria <=0 would be used. Although there should not be any negative quantity values in the table, it is a good idea to use <= rather than = to verify the lack of negative values. If you want to know what products are purchased from So Yi Martial Arts Supplies (SC), a criterion of SC in the VendorCode of the Product table would return that list. Remember that the equals (=) sign is optional when stating equality conditions.

When stating queries, delimiters are required for each match value. The data type of the field being matched determines the appropriate delimiter, as shown in Figure 3.16. Access QBE adds these delimiters to conditions entered without them.

Adding Calculations to Queries

When the KoryoKicks database was designed, the calculated fields were purposely not stored. One of the rules of normalization precludes storing calculated values because they can be re-created with current data each time a report or query is run.

Calculated Fields

To calculate a value for each row of data in a table, you must add a *calculated field* to the QBE grid. A calculated field holds a mathematical expression whose results will be displayed in the field. A typical expression contains database fields, constants, and mathematical operators. The database fields in an expression must be Number, Currency, or Date/Time data type. Access does not support mathematical operations on other data types. Constants must be numeric values such as 8238 or 0.36.

The mathematical operators are +, −, *, /, and ^. When several operators are used in a single formula, the algebraic order of precedence outlined in Figure 3.17 applies. If a formula contains operators with the same precedence— for example, if a formula contains both a multiplication and division operator—the operators are evaluated from left to right. To change the order of evaluation, enclose the part of the formula to be calculated first in parentheses.

FIGURE   3.17

Mathematical order of precedence

Order	Operation	
1	−	Negation (as in −1)
2	^	Exponentiation
3	*, /	Multiplication and division
4	+, −	Addition and subtraction

A calculated field can be entered directly into the Field row of a QBE grid, or the **Expression Builder** can be used to select the components of the calculation. Because the space in the QBE grid is fairly small, a large text box called a **Zoom box** can be opened to provide greater visibility for complicated expressions. Click in a Field cell of the QBE grid and then press Shift+F2 to open a Zoom box.

> ### *task* reference — Create an Expression Using Expression Builder
>
> - Click in the Field row of the QBE grid column that will display the calculation
> - Click the **Build** button in the query Design toolbar
> - Select expression elements and operators to create the desired calculation
> - Click **OK** to place the calculation in the QBE grid

The Product table contains data about the price and quantity on hand for each KoryoKicks product. The inventory value of each product was not stored but can be calculated when needed for queries and reports. Inventory value provides information needed to answer questions about the value of a company or where costs could be cut in the current system.

Creating an expression field with the Expression Builder:

1. Verify that the ac03KoryoKicks.mdb database is open

2. Select the **Queries** object from the Database Window

3. Double-click **Create query in Design View** to open the QBE grid and Show Table dialog box

4. Double-click on the **Product** table in the Show Table dialog box to add it to the design grid

5. Click **Close** in the Show Table dialog box

6. Place **ProductClass**, **ProductDescription**, **ProductQuantity**, and **ProductPrice** in the Field row of the QBE grid

7. Click in the empty Field row to the right of ProductPrice and activate the **Expression Builder**

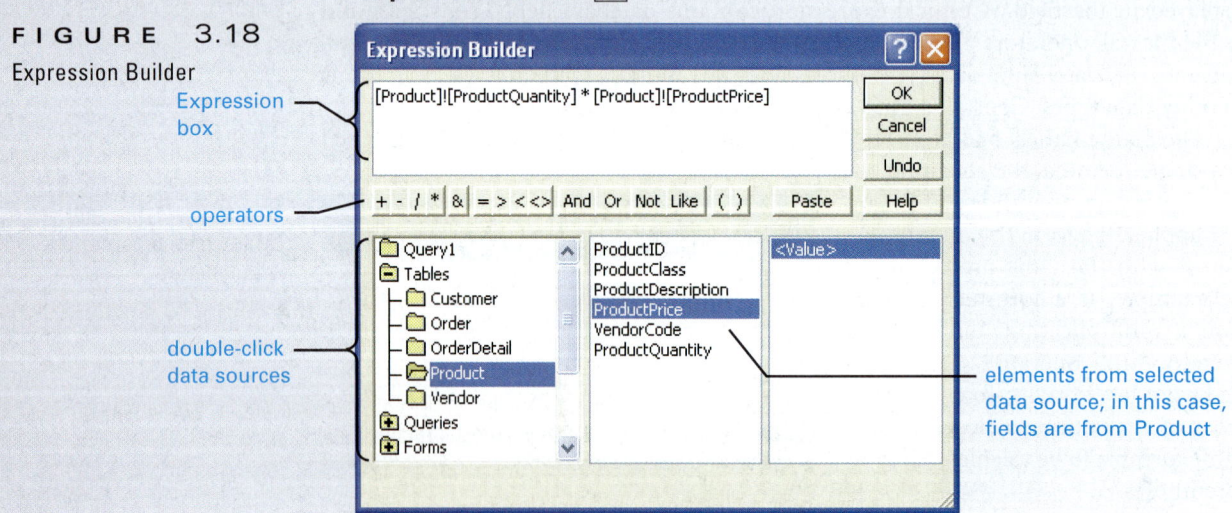

FIGURE 3.18

Expression Builder

- Expression box
- operators
- double-click data sources
- elements from selected data source; in this case, fields are from Product

8. Double-click **Tables**, then **Product** to list the fields that will be used in the calculation

9. Build the expression by double-clicking **ProductQuantity**, clicking the **multiplication** button, and then double-clicking **ProductPrice** (see Figure 3.18)

tip: *If you make a mistake, you can make edits directly in the Expression box. Notice that Access includes the table name with each field so that you can perform calculations involving multiple tables. Square brackets [] enclose table and field names*

10. Click **OK** to close the Expression Builder and place the expression in the QBE grid

11. Place **>0** in the Criteria row of ProductQuantity to select only in-stock items

FIGURE 3.19

Expression in the QBE grid

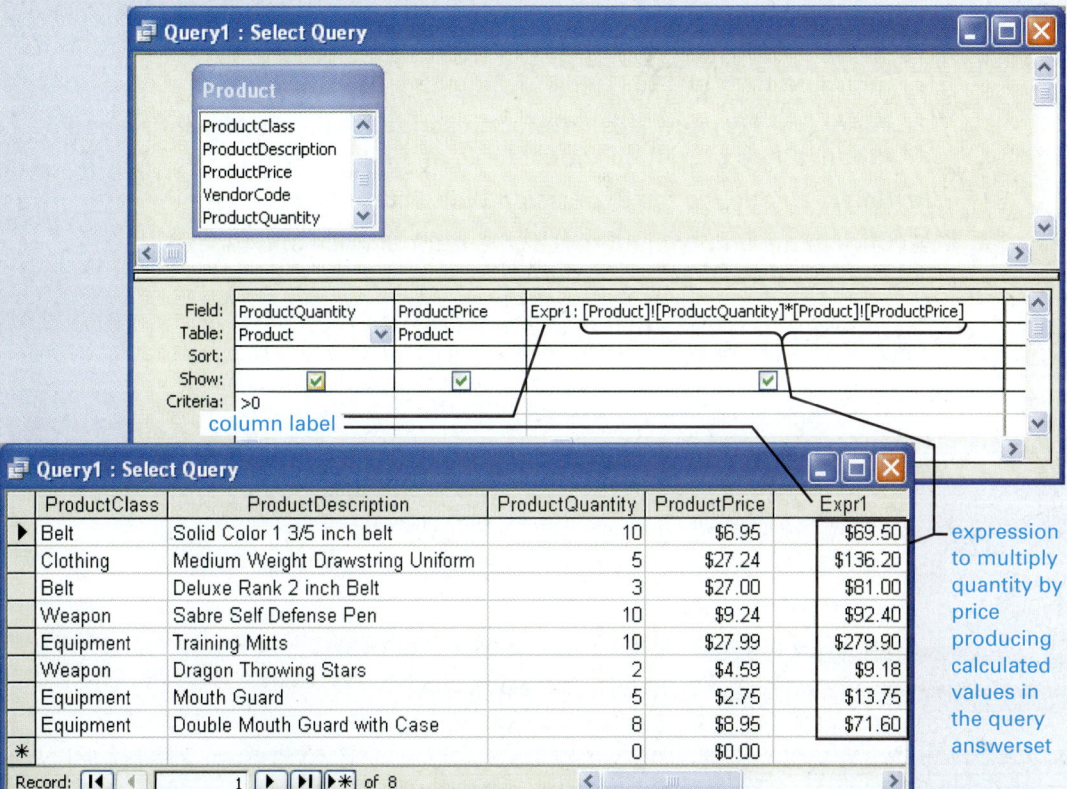

12. Click the **Datasheet View** button to see the query results (see Figure 3.19)

13. Return to **Design** View

Notice that the Expression Builder has a folder of functions. Functions are predefined calculations for common operations. Available functions include calculating the difference between two dates (DateDiff), determining a loan payment (Pmt), and averaging values (Avg). When using a predefined function, the appropriate calculation values must be provided in the correct order, a task that Expression Builder supports.

Notice also that the Expression Builder always places extra punctuation ([]!) in the expression. Access requires a field name that is used as the column heading for every column and provides one if you do not. Consider the following expression.

```
Expr1: [Product]![ProductQuantity]*[Product]![ProductPrice]
```

The colon (:) separates the column heading from the expression. The default column heading is Expr1 for the first expression, Expr2 for the second, and so on. If you provide a value to the left of the colon, it will be used. The exclamation point (!) is the delimiter or separator that differentiates between the table name and the field name. The table name is optional unless there are fields from different tables with the same name. For example, Product!VendorCode and Vendor!VendorCode need the table name to differentiate the two fields. The square brackets [] are only required when there are spaces in a field or table name, so VendorCode does not require them, but [Vendor Code] does. You may choose to eliminate the extra punctuation or leave it since it only impacts the readability of an expression, not the performance.

Creating an expression by typing:

1. Return to the previous query design

2. Verify that **ProductClass, ProductDescription, ProductQuantity,** and **ProductPrice** from the Product table are in the design grid

3. Select and delete the expression built with Expression Builder

4. Click in the empty Field row to the right of Price and type **Total:ProductQuantity*ProductPrice**

tip: *When field names are unique, the table name does not need to be included in the expression. The value to the left of the colon (:) is the column label. Square brackets [] are only required when field or table names contain spaces, but Access will add them*

FIGURE 3.20

Typed expression in QBE grid

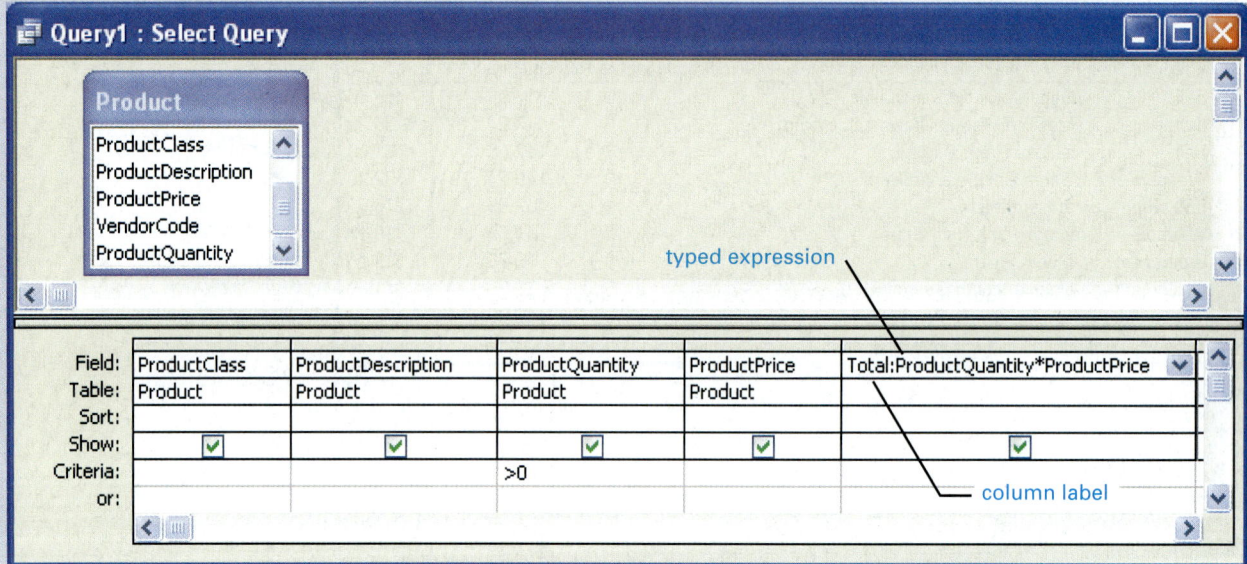

5. Click the **Datasheet View** 🔲 ▾ button to see the query results

6. Close the query and save it as **InventoryValue**

For short, well-defined calculations, typing in the expression is usually faster than using the Expression Builder and results in less expression punctuation. It is important to know when the punctuation must be included. To recap the earlier discussion:

- The colon (:) separates the column heading from the expression
- The exclamation point (!) separates a table name from its field name. The table name is only required if you are using multiple tables with identical field names
- The square brackets [] are required to enclose both field names and table names that contain spaces

FIGURE 3.21
Aggregate functions

Aggregate Function	Use	Data Types
Sum	Totals the field values for selected records	AutoNumber, Currency, Date/Time, and Number
Avg	Averages the field values for selected records	AutoNumber, Currency, Date/Time, and Number
Count	Counts the number of selected records	AutoNumber, Currency, Date/Time, Memo, Number, OLE Object, Text, and Yes/No
Max	Returns the highest field value	AutoNumber, Currency, Date/Time, Number, and Text
Min	Returns the lowest field value	AutoNumber, Currency, Date/Time, Number, and Text

Aggregate Operations

Aggregate operations are used to calculate summary data such as averages and sums. These operations make use of the predefined functions mentioned in the previous topic and are outlined in Figure 3.21. *Aggregate functions* can be applied to all of the data in a table or any subset specified by the query. Because only one aggregate function can be applied to a table column, multiple copies of the same field must be placed in the design grid to achieve multiple aggregate operations on one field.

Suppose that Missy and Micah need to evaluate their product mix and want to know how many products they carry (Count ProductDescription), the average number of items on hand (Avg ProductQuantity), the total number of products on hand (Sum ProductQuantity), the average inventory cost of a product (Avg ProductQuantity* ProductPrice), and the total inventory cost (Sum ProductQuantity*ProductPrice). Such information is valuable when determining the cost of adding new products or discontinuing existing products. The following steps produce this query.

Summarizing selected data with aggregate functions:

1. Verify that the ac03KoryoKicks.mdb database is open

2. Open a new query in Design View with **Product** as the table being queried

3. Create the QBE fields outlined in Figure 3.22

4. Click the **Totals** Σ button to insert the Total row into the QBE grid

5. In the Total row, select the aggregate function for each column, as shown in Figure 3.22

6. Click the **Datasheet View** button to see the query results

7. Double-click the column borders to resize them

8. Return to **Design View**

9. Change the Field row for ProductDescription to read **Nmbr of Product: ProductDescription** to customize the field heading

FIGURE   3.22

Aggregate functions assigned to each field

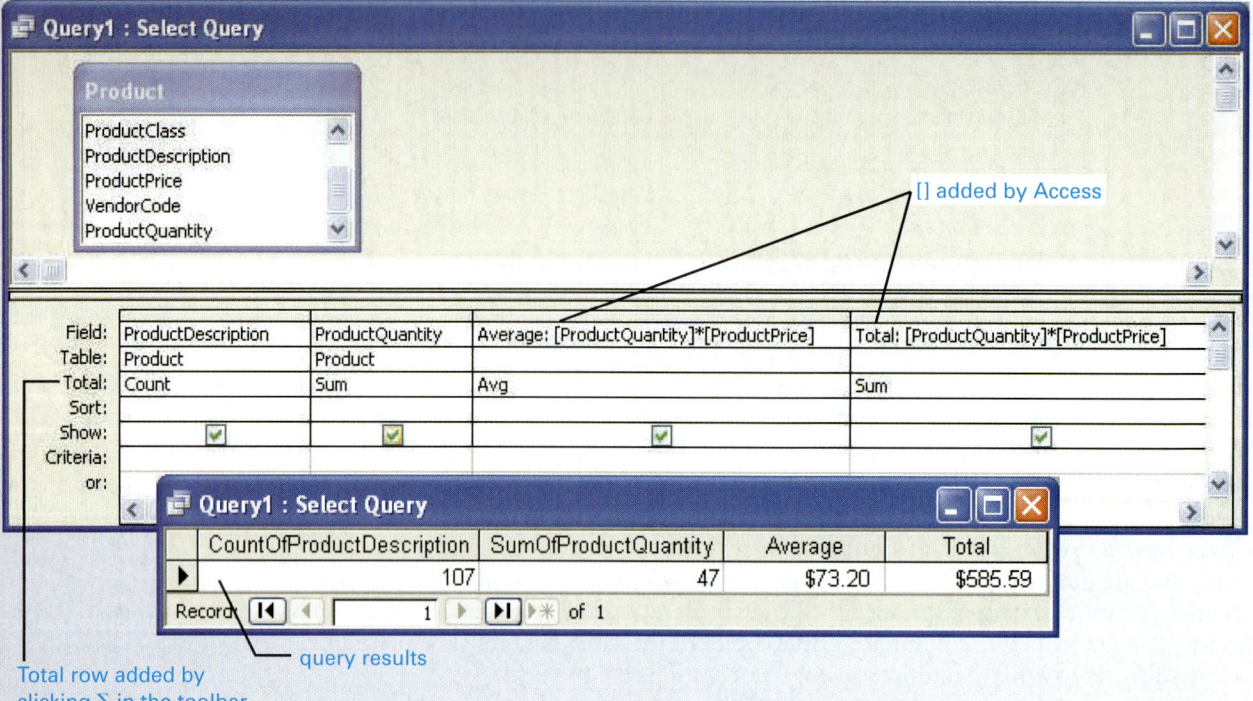

Total row added by clicking Σ in the toolbar

query results

10. Click the **Datasheet View** button to see the revised query results

11. Close the query and save it as **InventorySummary**

Notice that Access created a unique field heading for each column by combining the aggregate function with the field name. The default name can be overridden by providing your own column headings before the colon in the field name, as demonstrated in the previous steps.

Record Group Calculations

Another calculation requirement is to create subtotals for specific groups of records. Returning to the Product table, we could use record group calculations to determine statistics for each ProductClass. Record group calculations are accomplished using the *Group By* operator in the Total row of a query.

Summarizing grouped data:

1. Verify that the ac03KoryoKicks.mdb database is open

2. Open the **InventorySummary** query in Design View

3. To the right of the last field, add the field **ProductClass**, select the ProductClass column, and drag it until it is the leftmost column

4. Verify that the Total row of ProductClass is set to **Group By** since we want summaries for each vendor

FIGURE 3.23

Using Group By to summarize data by ProductClass

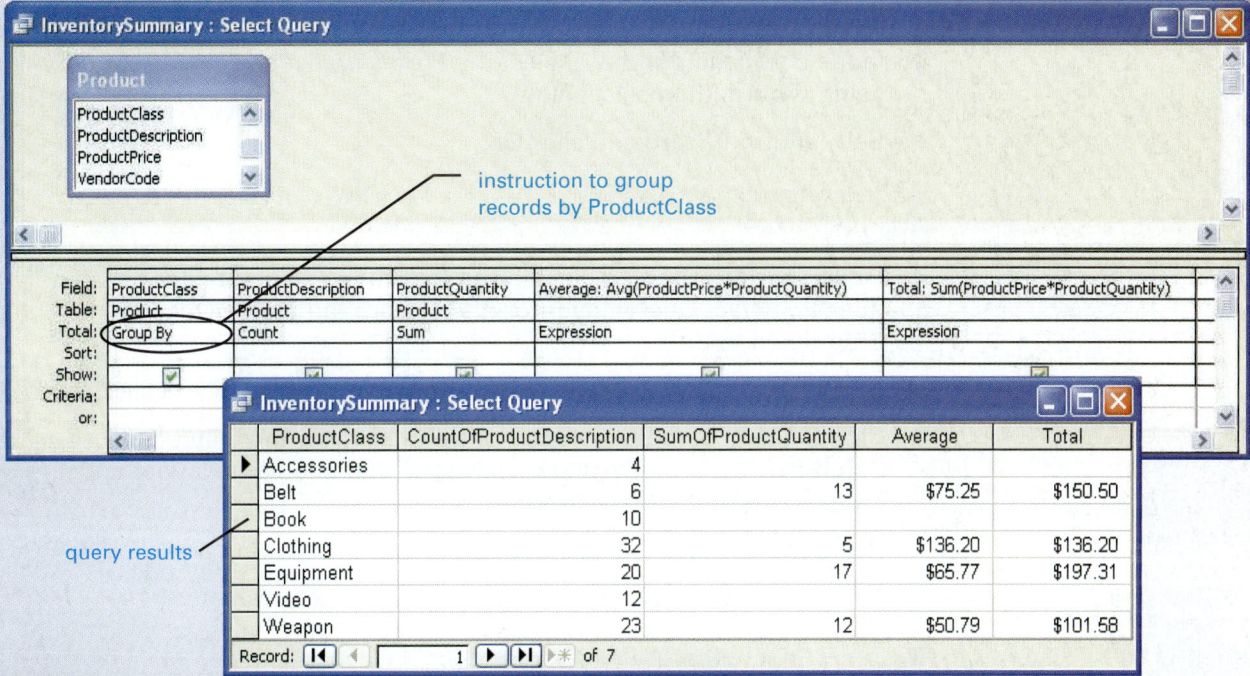

5. Click the **Datasheet View** button to see the query results

6. Double-click the column borders to resize them

7. Select **Save As** from the **File** menu and name the revised query
   ProductClassSummary

Once a query has been saved, it is listed as a Query object in the Database Window. Only the query specifications are saved, so the next time the query is run, all calculations will be computed based on the current table data. Running a saved query is as simple as double-clicking its name.

Creating and Using Forms

A form is an Access object like a query, meaning that its design is specified, saved, and then run against current data on demand. Access forms are used to organize and display data on the screen in a more effective format than Datasheet View. Typically, forms display only one record at a time.

Like queries, forms support multiple views: Design View, where the form layout and content can be altered; and *Form View*, where the data are displayed for maintenance, selection, printing, and other data update and analysis tasks.

Building a Simple Form

There are five types of AutoForm Wizards that work like the tabular and columnar forms explored in the first chapter. Each *AutoForm Wizard* will allow one table and a form layout to be specified, but nothing more. The **Form Wizard** allows fields to be selected from one or more tables and the display format to be specified, and then it creates the form based on that input. Finally a form can be created in Design View with control over fields, formats, and calculations. Let's start by creating a form based on the InventoryQuery built earlier in this session.

Using the Form Wizard:

1. Verify that the ac03KoryoKicks.mdb database is open

2. In the Database Window, select the **Forms** object and **Create form by using wizard**, then select **New**

3. Select **Form Wizard** and click **OK**

tip: *There is no need to select a table before entering the Form Wizard as you did with AutoForm*

4. Fields for this form can be selected from any existing tables and queries. Select **Query: InventoryValue** from the Tables/Queries drop-down list

5. Use the **>>** button to select all of the fields for the form and click **Next**

6. Click on each of the Layout options and preview the result. Select **Columnar** for this form and click **Next**. A sample of the layout appears on the left side of the dialog box

7. Preview all of the styles and then select **Sumi Painting** and click **Next**

8. Name your form **InventoryValue** and then click **Finish**

F I G U R E   3.24

Completed form displaying the Training Mitts record

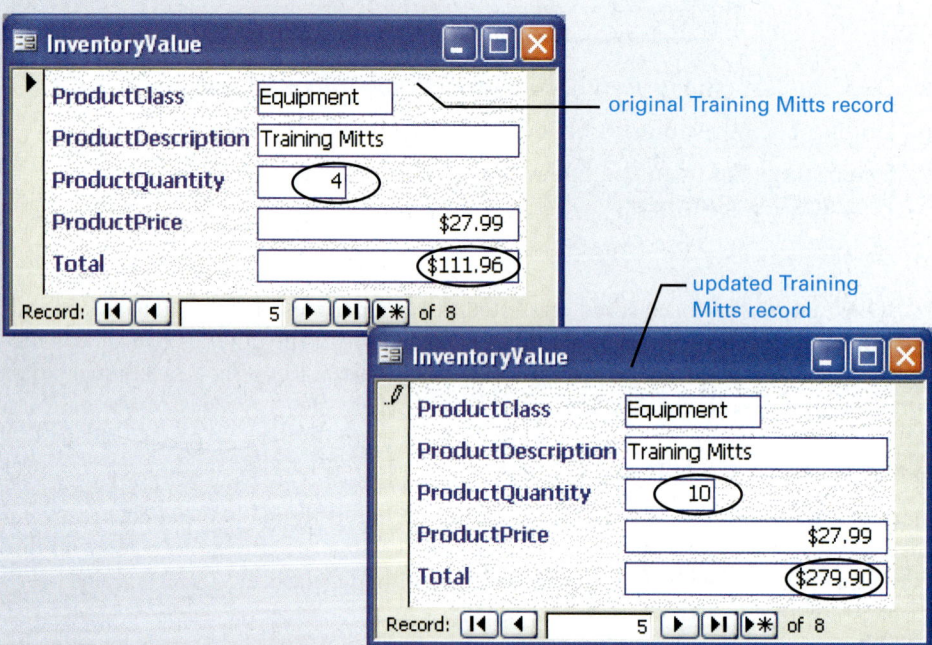

9. Use the navigation bar to move through the data to the **Training Mitts** record

10. Notice that the Training Mitts Total value is $111.96. Change the Quantity to **10**, move to the next record, and then back to the Training Mitts record. Notice that the Total has also updated

11. Click the **Print Preview** button to see how your forms would print if you clicked the **Print** button. The Print option of the File menu contains options for printing only the current record or a range of records

As was just demonstrated, forms can be used to maintain the data in a database. Calculated fields (expressions) display in the form but cannot be updated. Calculation values are automatically updated when edits made to the expression fields are saved (when you move to another row of data).

Finding, editing, and deleting data are accomplished with the same techniques used in table Datasheet View. The same Sort, Filter, Find, New Record, and Delete buttons appear on the toolbar. Sorts can be applied to change the presentation order. Filters allow a subset of the data to be manipulated and Find will find records that meet a criterion. As when editing data in the datasheet, deletes cannot be undone.

Customizing a Form

Forms created with the Wizard can be modified in Design View. Developers frequently create the first cut of a form with the Wizard and customize to achieve the desired result.

task reference — **Modify the Format of a Form**

- Open the form in Design View
- Click the **AutoFormat** button in the Form Design toolbar
- Select from the same formats that were available in the Wizard

Changing the AutoFormat of the InventoryValue form:

1. Open the **InventoryValue** form in Design View
2. Select the **AutoFormat** button from the Form Design toolbar
3. Select the format that appeals to you
4. Click the **Options** button. You can choose portions of the format to apply. Click each option to see the impact
5. Click the **Form View** button to see the full impact
6. Move back and forth between Design View and Form View until you get the effect you desire
7. Close the form saving your changes

A word of caution: when using forms that do not display all of the fields of a table, users can update only the displayed fields, which can cause problems with finding and entering the data later on.

Producing Reports

Reports are used to effectively format and print data from tables and queries. All aspects of a report can be customized, including formatting and graphics.

The Report Wizards

The AutoReport Wizard was introduced in Chapter 1 to provide an overview of what the report object does. Like tables, queries, and forms, the report object stores the criteria for creating a report.

FIGURE   3.25

InventoryValue form in
Design View

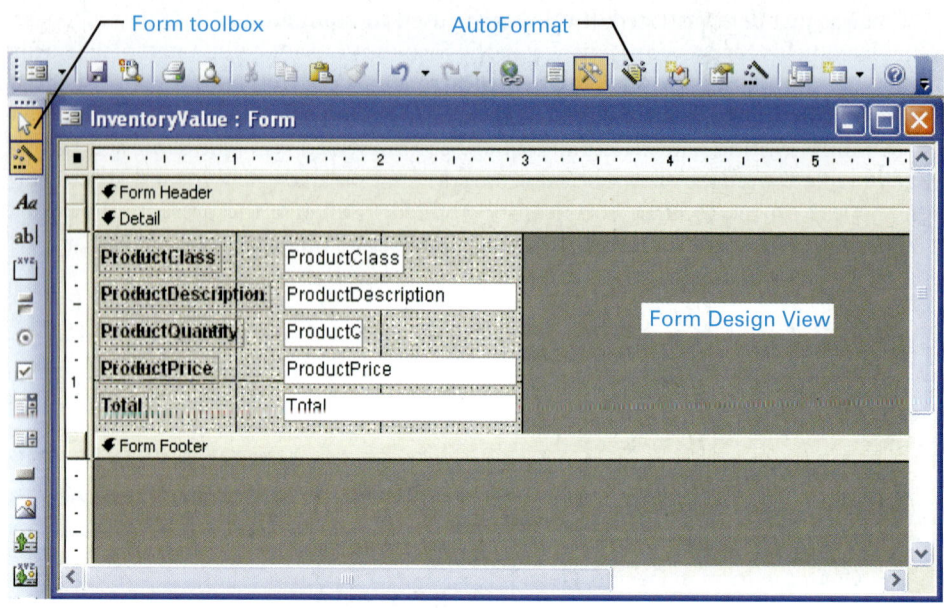

When a report opens, the saved report criteria are run against current data. Data displayed in a report can be drawn directly from a table, a group of related tables, or a query. Expressions can be used to calculate values for every record, subtotals for groups of records, or report totals. Charts and graphics also can be added.

The AutoReport Wizard presented in Chapter 1 is the most restrictive way to create a report. It allows you to select only one table or query as the data source and uses a default layout. The Report Wizard is very similar to the Form Wizard. It will allow you to choose fields from multiple tables and queries, control the order of those fields, define calculations, and select a report layout.

Using the Report Wizard:

1. Verify that the ac03KoryoKicks.mdb database is open

2. In the Database Window select the **Reports** object, then double-click **Create report by using wizard** (the fastest way to start the Report Wizard)

3. Fields for this query can be selected from any existing tables and queries. Select **Query: InventoryValue** from the Tables/Queries drop-down list

4. Use the **>>** button to select all of the fields for the form and click **Next**

5. Grouping will create subtotals. This report needs to be grouped by ProductClass. Select **ProductClass** from the list of available fields and click the **>** selection button to group by ProductClass and then click **Next** (see Figure 3.26)

6. Select **ProductDescription** from the first sort list to cause the records to be sorted by ProductDescription within ProductClass. Click on **Summary Options** to add summary calculations

7. For the ProductPrice field, click on **Avg** to calculate average price by class (the group you set). For the Total field, click on both **Sum** and **Avg** to calculate both the total inventory value by category and the average inventory value by category. Click **OK** in the Summary Options dialog box and then **Next** in the Report Wizard dialog box (see Figure 3.27)

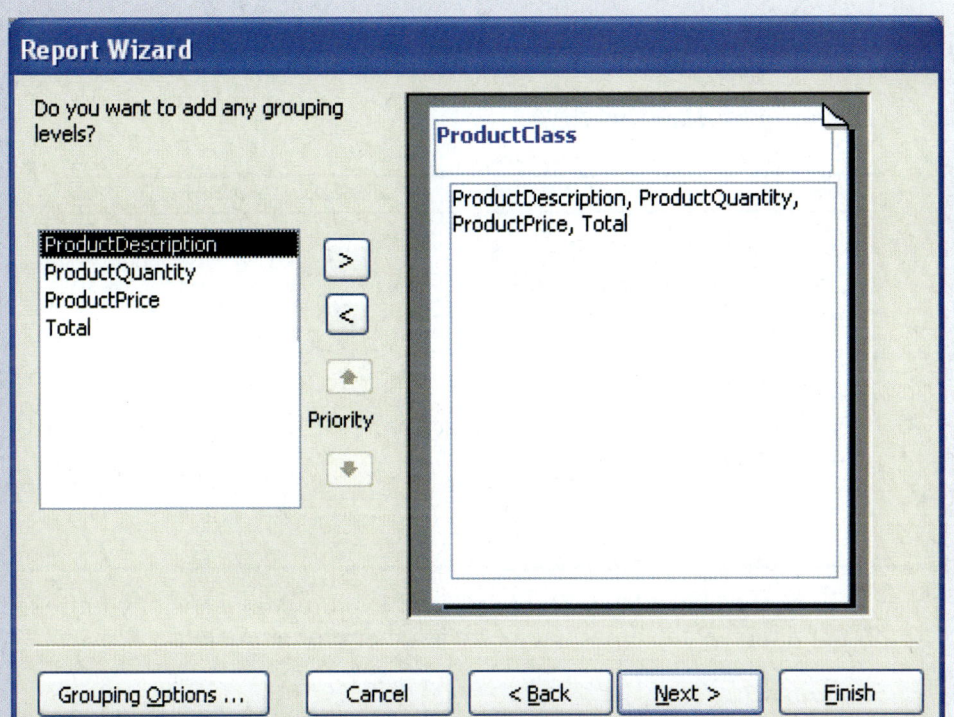

FIGURE 3.26

ProductClass added as a group to the form

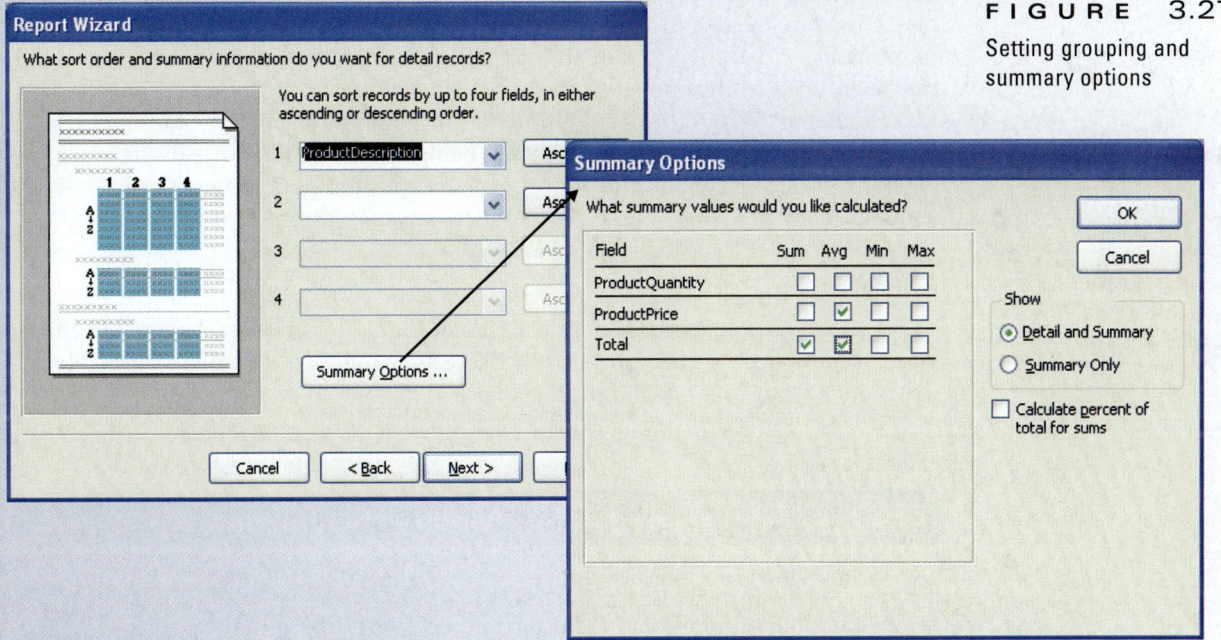

FIGURE 3.27

Setting grouping and summary options

8. Explore the various sort layouts by clicking each and reviewing the sample. Select **Stepped** and click **Next**

9. Explore the styles by clicking each and reviewing the sample. Select **Corporate** and press **Next**

10. Name the report **InventoryValueByClass**, verify that **Preview the report** is selected, and click **Finish** (see Figure 3.28)

FIGURE 3.28

Completed
InventoryValueByClass
report

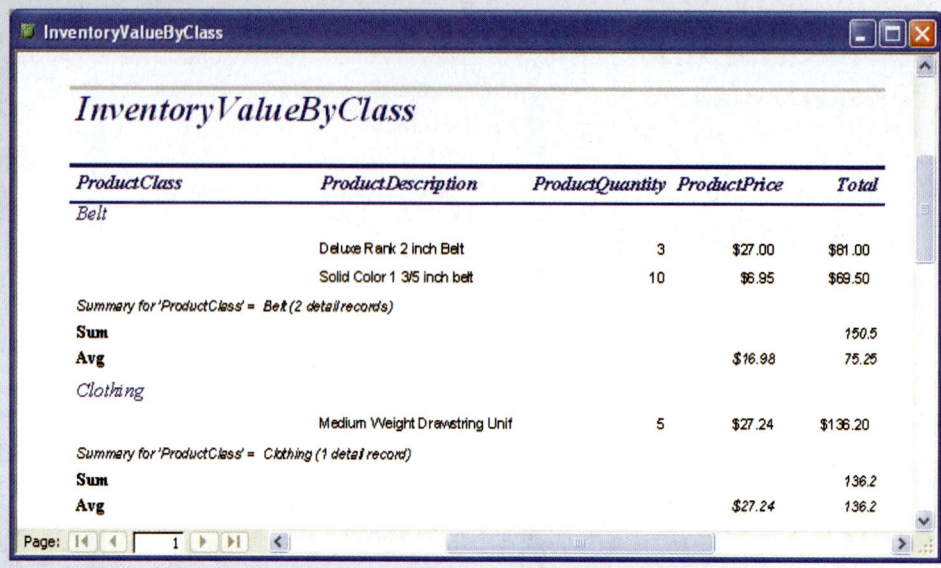

11. Your report will display in Print Preview. Explore the pages of your report and review the criteria to correlate them to the results

Grouping records is an important concept. Reports without grouping cannot contain subtotals. When records are grouped, the group value (ProductClass in our example) is used to create a header that appears above the records of that group. A group footer is also created to contain any summary statistics for the group. Up to 10 fields can be grouped with summary statistics for any or all of the 10.

The Report Wizard displays option buttons to Show Detail and Summary records or Summary Only records as the report is being built. Detail reports display each row from the selected input, like the report just created. Summary reports display only the summary statistics, for example, the ProductClass footer from the previous report.

Formatting Reports

To format reports, it is necessary to use Design View. The simplest change is to choose another AutoFormat. This process is the same as changing the AutoFormat of a form.

---

task reference   **Modify the Format of a Report**

- Open the report in Design View
- Click the **AutoFormat** button in the Report Design toolbar
- Select from the same formats that were available in the Wizard

Changing the AutoFormat of the InventoryValueByClass report:

1. Open the **InventoryValueByClass** report in Design View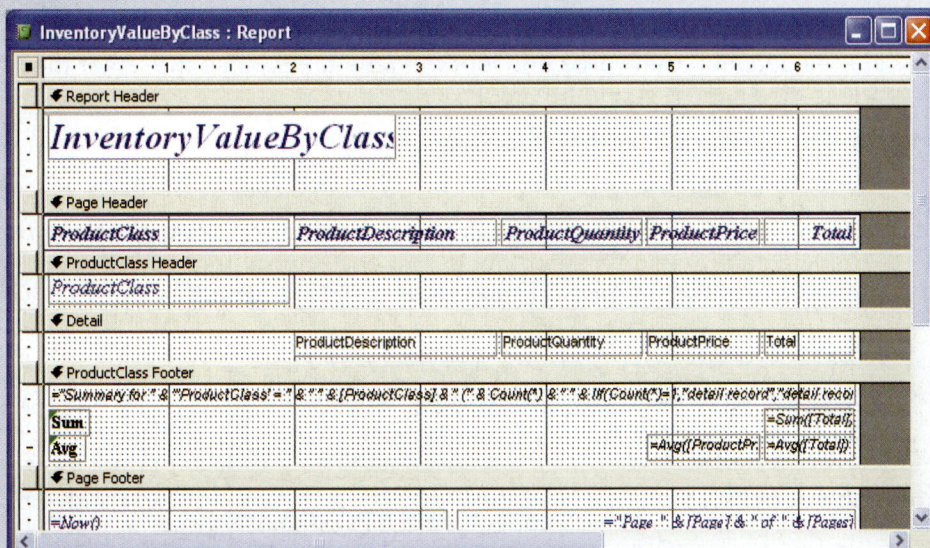

2. Select the **AutoFormat** button from the Form Design toolbar

3. Preview the available formats (they are the same as those presented in the Wizard) and select the format that appeals to you

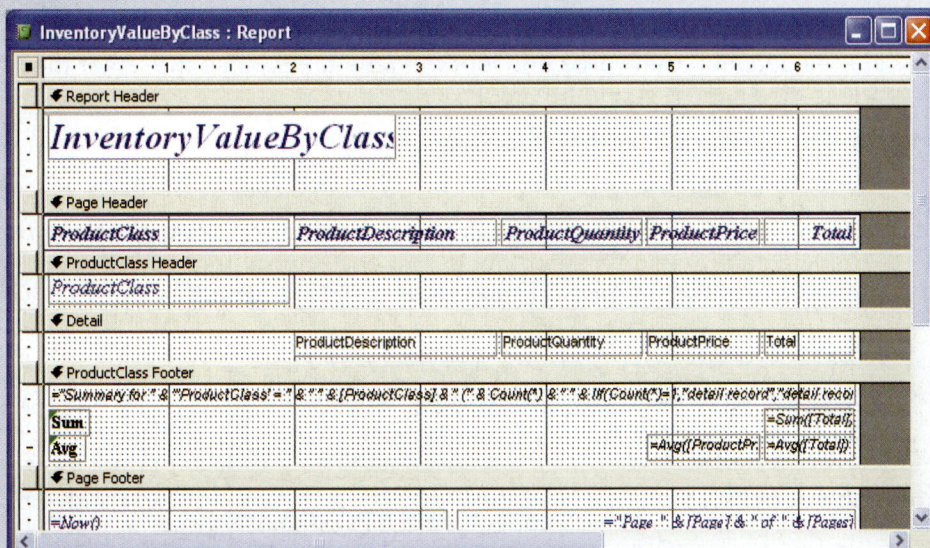

FIGURE 3.29

InventoryValueByClass report in Design View

4. Click the **Options** button. You can choose portions of the format to apply. Click each option to see the impact

5. The **Customize** button allows you to save your custom format. Click **OK**

6. Click the **Form View** button to see the full impact

7. Move back and forth between Design View and Form View until you get the effect you desire

8. Return to **Corporate** style

9. Save your changes

Access forms and reports consist of objects called controls. Each control performs a specific task. For example, a label displays text; a text box displays the value of a field and accepts input from the user. In Design View, you can see that each field is composed of two controls: a label that holds the field's caption and a text box that will display the field's value.

All of the objects displayed on a form or report can be modified. Modifications include altering the labels, moving labels and text boxes, and adding new objects. To add objects, use the toolbox containing Controls and the Control Wizards.

Adding descriptive column names is accomplished by editing the labels on the form or report. To edit a label, select it and click an insertion point. Once the text is changed, the label may need to be resized to properly display the complete content. The InventoryByClass report should be updated with labels that better describe the data.

Changing the labels of the InventoryValueByClass report:

1. Open the **InventoryValueByClass** report in Print Preview . Page through the report and notice that the report title would look better with spaces and that the complete ProductDescription does not always display (Black V-neck Elastic Waist unif)

2. Change to **Design View** ![icon]

3. In the Report Header, select the title (InventoryValueByClass). Insert spaces between the words and lengthen the text box so that all of the title is displayed (see Figure 3.30)

4. Use **Print Preview** ![icon] to evaluate your changes

5. Return to **Design View**

6. Add spaces to the ProductClass, ProductDescription, ProductPrice, and ProductQuantity Page header labels. Use the Formatting Form/Report toolbar to right-align the Product Price and Total headings

FIGURE 3.30

Labels and corresponding text boxes selected

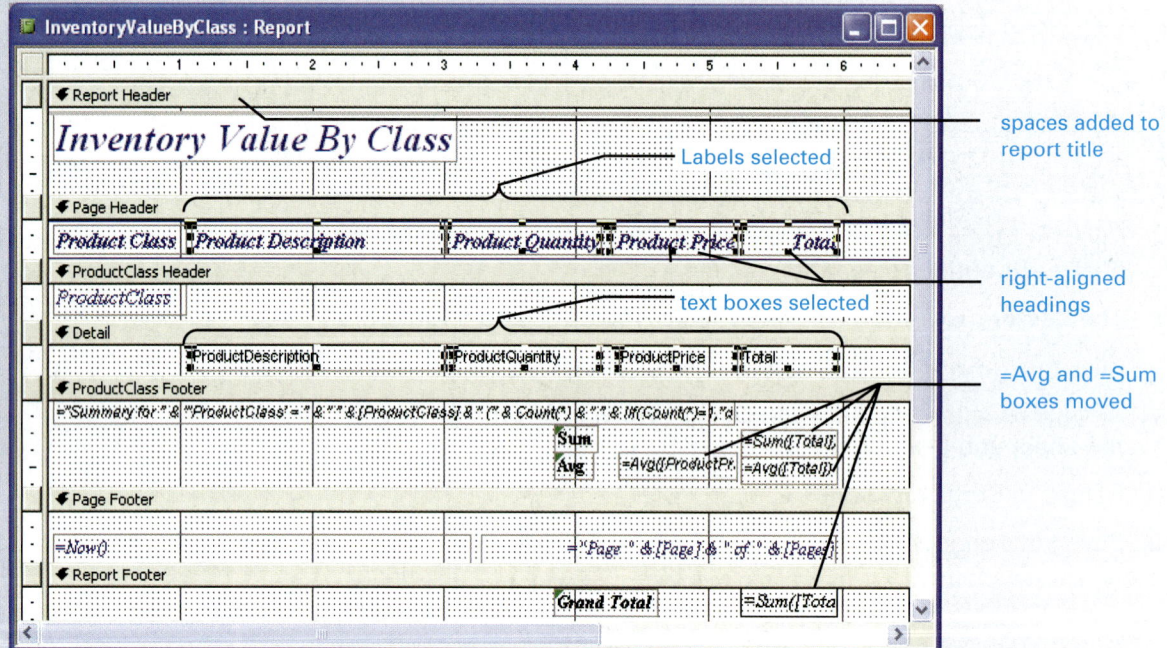

7. Click the **Product Class** text box in the Product Class Header and drag the right border to the left reducing its width by about 1/3. Adjust the ProductClass label to match

8. Move to **Print Preview** and verify that all ProductClass data display correctly. Make any necessary adjustments in **Design View**

9. Click the **Product Description** label in the Page Header and then hold down the Shift key while clicking the **ProductDescription** text box in the Detail section. With both the label and text box selected, drag the left border to the left increasing their width by about 1/3

10. With both the ProductDescription label and text box still selected, drag them to the left so that they are 2 dots away from ProductClass

11. Use the same techniques to move the remaining columns to the left and adjust their widths

12. In the Product Class Footer move the =Avg and =Sum boxes to align with the ProductPrice and Total columns. Similarly adjust the controls in the Report Footer

13. Click the Save button to save your changes and preview the report (see Figure 3.31)

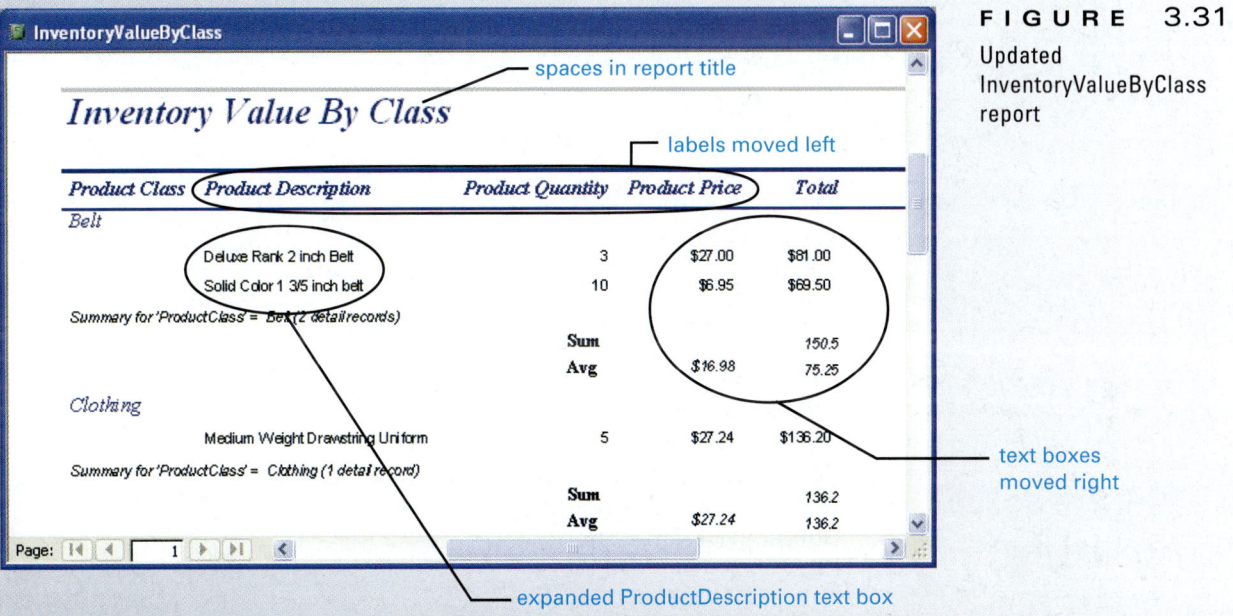

FIGURE 3.31

Updated InventoryValueByClass report

Notice that in Design View, the report title is placed in the Report Header section of the design, causing it to appear once at the beginning of the report. The labels for a field appear in the page header section, causing them to appear once at the top of each page of the report. The text boxes that will display the values of a field appear in the Detail section of the report, which repeats for each value.

Producing Mailing Labels

Producing mailing labels is a common business task made easy by Access. The Report Wizard has options to format labels for standard business forms (available from office supply stores).

Making mailing labels for KoryoKicks vendors:

1. Verify that the ac03KoryoKicks.mdb database is open

2. In the Database Window, click the **Reports** object and then **New**

3. Select the **Label Wizard** and **Vendor** as the data source and click **OK**

4. The next step selects the type of mailing label. We will use **Avery**, **J8162**, a popular label type, and click **Next** (see Figure 3.32)

5. Select Arial **10** point as the label font and click **Next**

FIGURE **3.32**

Selecting label type and font

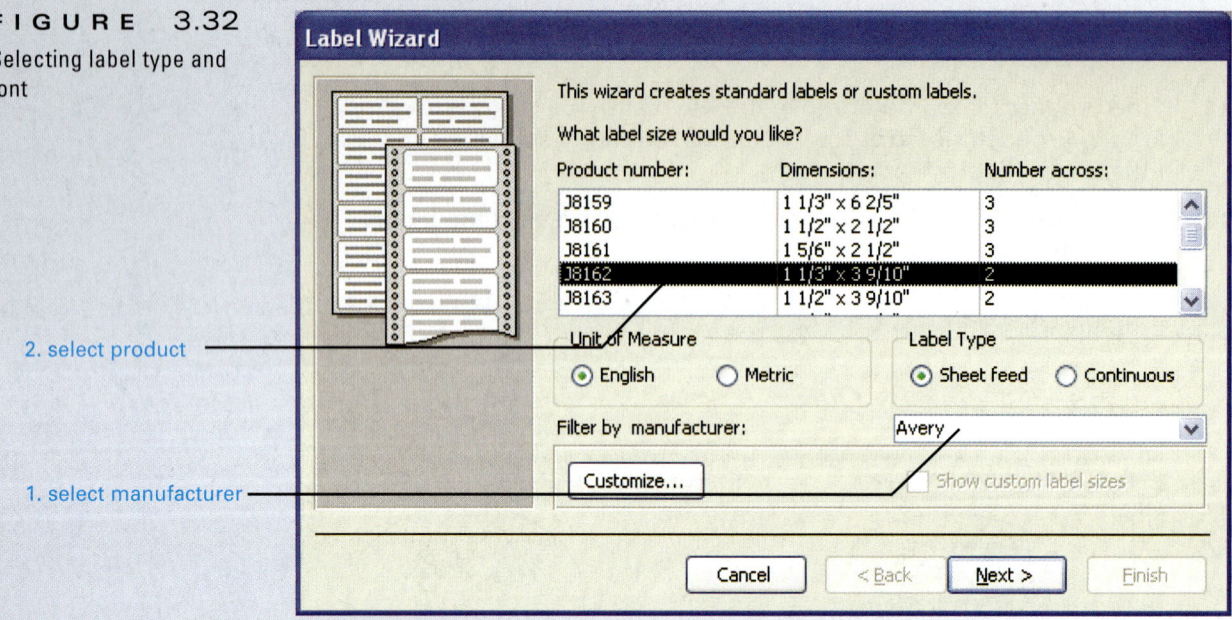

2. select product

1. select manufacturer

6. Build the label content as follows:
   a. Double-click **Name** and press **Enter**
   b. Double-click **Address** and press **Enter**
   c. Double-click **City** and type a comma and a space
   d. Double-click **State** and type a space
   e. Double-click **Zip Code**
   f. Click **Next**

FIGURE **3.33**

Formatting the mailing label

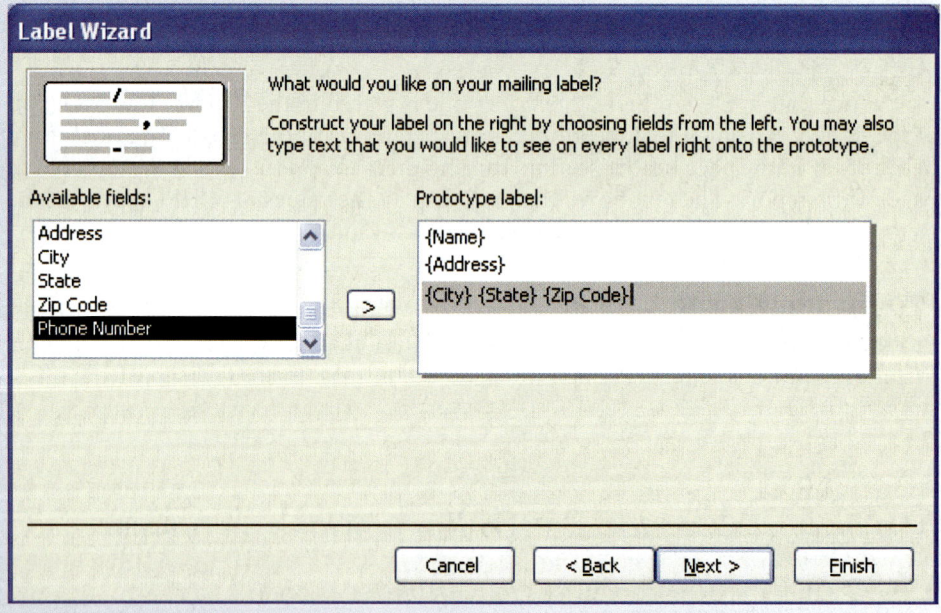

7. Sort the labels by **ZipCode** and press **Next**

8. Name the report **LabelsVendor** and click **Finish** (see Figure 3.34)

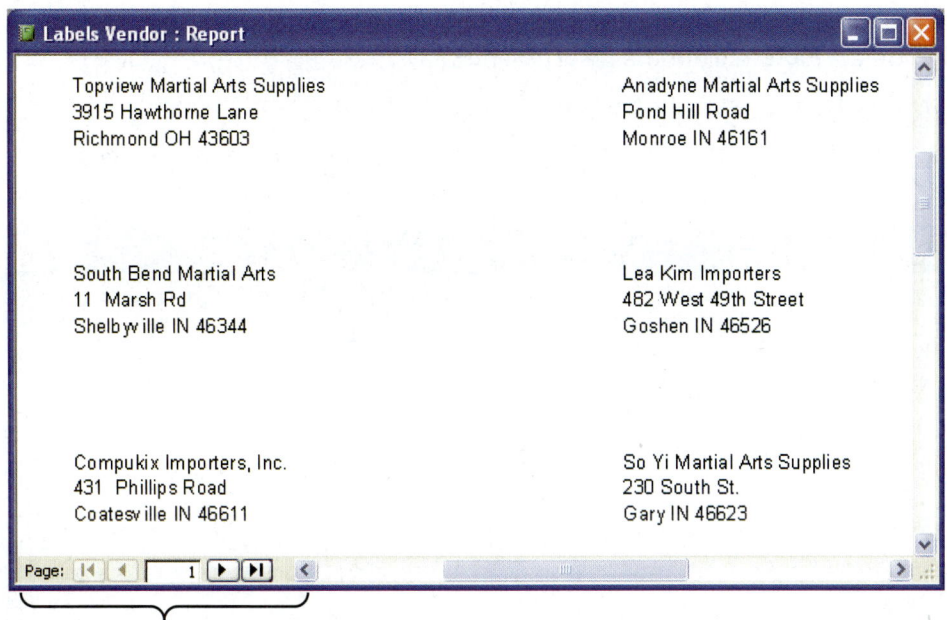

FIGURE 3.34

Mailing labels in Print Preview

Adding Graphics to Reports and Forms

Although graphics do not usually add to the functionality of a report or form, they do improve visual appeal. They also can promote brand identity or distinguish one type of form or report from another. Graphics are added to reports and forms with the same technique, so only a form example is provided.

help yourself *Use the Type a Question combo box to enhance your understanding of how to adjust form and report controls by typing* **move or resize controls**. *Review the contents of* About customizing a control and Resize a control, *and* Move one or more controls to a new position. *Close the Help window when you are finished*

---

task reference   Add a Graphic to a Report or Form

- Open the report or form in Design View

- Select the section that is to display the graphic

- Select **Picture** from the **Insert** menu

- Navigate to the folder containing the image and change the file type selector to the image file type

- Select the file and click **OK**

- Move and size the image as needed

Adding a graphic to InventoryValueByClass:

1. Verify that the ac03KoryoKicks.mdb database is open

2. Open **InventoryValueByClass** in Design View

3. Click the Report Header (you must click the report or form section where you want the graphic to appear)

4. Select **Picture** from the **Insert** menu

5. Change the Files of type setting to **.gif**

6. Select the **ac03KoryoKicksLogo.gif** file from the Chapter 3 data files list and click **OK**

FIGURE **3.35**

Selecting a picture

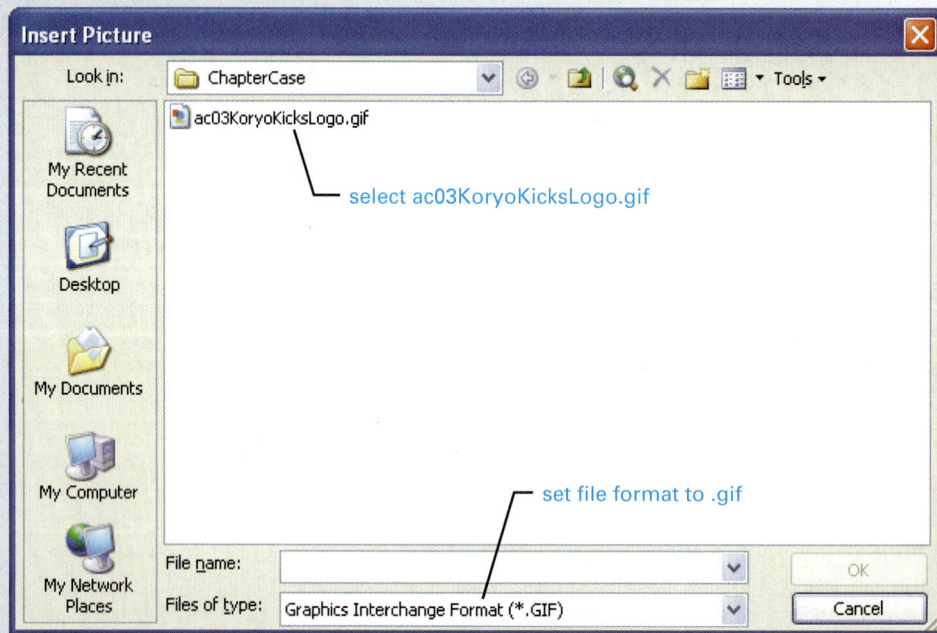

7. The image loads over the report title. Select the report title and drag it to the right of the image until all of the text displays and it is aligned with the bottom of the image

8. Use Print Preview to see the result (see Figure 3.36)

9. Save changes to the report and close Access

SESSION 3.2

making the grade

1. When would you use a form? A report?

2. T F   Forms cannot display data from a query.

3. What is the difference between the > and the >> buttons used to select fields in Access queries?

4. Why and how would you add an expression to a query?

5. What is the difference between a field label and a field text box in the Design View of reports and forms?

6. Describe grouping in reports.

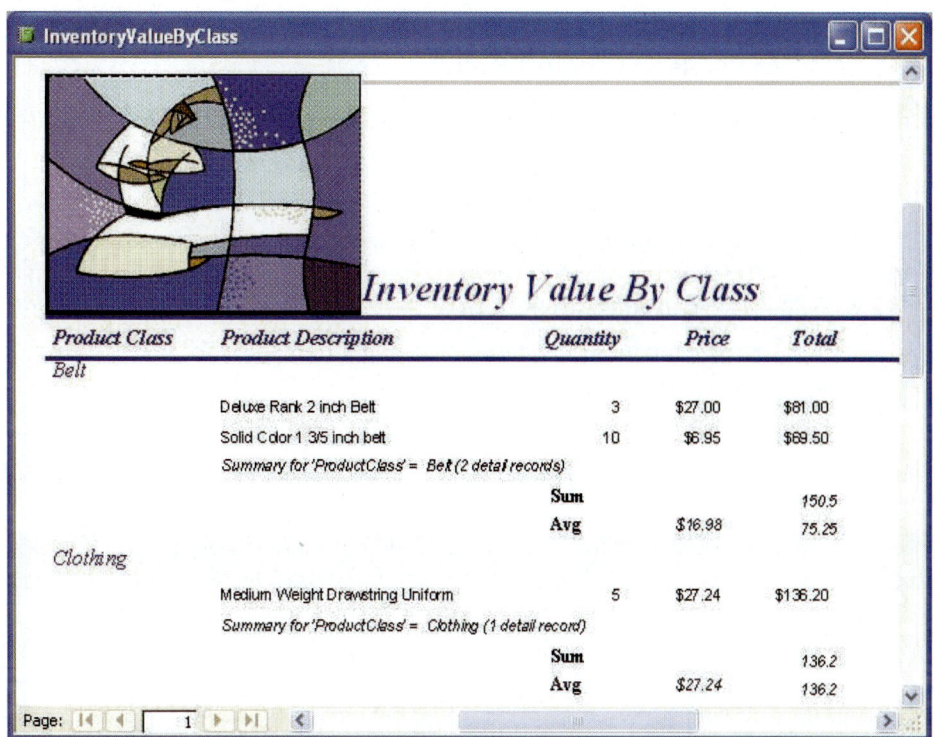

F I G U R E   3.36

Form with image in the Report Header section

SESSION 3.3 SUMMARY

Access provides an array of options for selecting and organizing data into useful information. The strength of relational databases lies in the simplicity and flexibility of the analytical tools provided.

Filters are used to restrict rows of data to work with a subset of a table. The simplest filter is Filter By Selection, which allows the selection of all or part of a datasheet value and then retrieves records that match the selection. Filter By Form, Filter For Input, and Advanced Filter/Sort are other filtering tools. Each filtering tool has a different interface and provides progressively more functionality. Filter Excluding Selection allows the selected value to be excluded from the filter return set. Filters are cumulative and remain in effect until specifically removed. Filters must be saved as a query to be reusable.

Select Queries are a more powerful data analysis tool that can retrieve and organize data from multiple tables. With queries, both columns and rows can be selected and sorted. Calculated fields can compute based on data in detail records or summarize data based on defined groups. Query criteria are built in a Query By Example (QBE) grid. Relational operators are used to state the conditions to retrieve records. Query results can be formatted for better viewing by changing the column width and adjusting the font.

Forms can be used to display and maintain data from multiple tables and queries. Find, sort, edit, delete, and filter operations work in forms in exactly the same way that they do in datasheets. Deleted records cannot be retrieved.

Reports are used to format printed output based on table data. Data from multiple tables and queries can be grouped, sorted, and summarized before printing. The print can include only detail records, detail and summary records, or only the summary records.

Forms and reports are similar in Design View. Each section of a form or report has a specific function, such as to format the detail record. Graphics can be added to forms and reports from the Insert menu.

MICROSOFT OFFICE SPECIALIST OBJECTIVES SUMMARY

- Creating Select Queries using the Simple Query Wizard—MOS AC03S-1-7
- Adding a calculated field to queries in query Design View—MOS AC03S-3-1
- Creating forms using the Form Wizard—MOS AC03S-1-8
- Modifying specific form controls (e.g., text boxes, labels, bound controls)— MOS AC03S-1-9
- Creating reports—MOS AC03S-1-10
- Using aggregate functions in queries (e.g., Avg, Count)—MOS AC03S-3-1
- Aligning and spacing controls—MOS AC03S-3-2
- Filtering records by form and by selection—MOS AC03S-3-6

making the grade *answers*

SESSION 3.1

1. If the selection is at the beginning of a field, records that begin with the selected values will be retrieved. If the selection is in the middle of a field, records with the selected characters anywhere in their value will be selected.

2. False. Filtering restricts the rows.

3. Select the value to be excluded, right-click on it, and choose Filter Excluding Selection.

4. False. Filters are cumulative until the Remove Filter instruction is executed.

5. The Or tab in Filter By Form and the Or row in the Advanced Filter/Sort both allow you to enter multiple criteria for the same field.

6. The first benefit is that you can execute the filter again without re-creating the criteria. Secondly, the saved filter could be used as the basis for creating forms, reports, or a more complex query.

SESSION 3.2

1. A Form object is used to create a custom format for input and display of data from tables or queries. A report is used to design printed output from tables and queries.

2. False. The Form Wizard allows you to select fields from multiple tables or queries.

3. Both buttons are used to select fields. The > button selects the current field, while the >> button selects all available fields.

4. Expressions are used to calculate values that are not stored in tables such as gross pay. An expression is entered in the Field row of the QBE grid to create a calculated field.

5. Labels and text boxes are the controls that make up forms and reports. The label contains the heading or descriptive text for the field, while the text box holds the field value from each record.

6. Setting the Grouping in a report is the same as setting the Group By option in a query. Both allow you to select a field or fields that will control summary statistics. For example, to create an inventory report by department, you would want totals for each department, so department would be the group field.

task reference *summary*

Task	Page #	Preferred Method
Filter By Selection	AC 3.4	• Open the table in Datasheet View • Select the field and character(s) of the search criteria (see Figure 3.2) • Click the **Filter By Selection** ⟦icon⟧ toolbar button to return values matching the selection or • Right-click and choose **Filter Excluding Selection** to filter the selection out of the data • Evaluate the results of the filter • Click **Remove Filter** ⟦icon⟧ on the Access toolbar
Filter By Form	AC 3.6	• Open a table in Datasheet View • Click the **Filter By Form** ⟦icon⟧ toolbar button • Build the filter criteria by selecting from the drop-down list for a field or typing your own value • Click the **Apply Filter** ⟦icon⟧ toolbar button • Review the filtered data to be sure they are what you expected • Work with the filtered data • Click **Remove Filter** ⟦icon⟧ on the Access toolbar when you are done
Filter For Input	AC 3.8	• Open a table in Datasheet View • Right-click the field to be filtered • Type the filter criteria in the Filter For text box using wildcards, operators, and values • Press **Enter** to activate the filter • Review the filtered data to be sure they are what you expected • Work with the filtered data • Click **Remove Filter** ⟦icon⟧ on the Access toolbar when you are done
Advanced Filter/Sort	AC 3.9	• Open a table in Datasheet View • On the **Records** menu, point to **Filter** and then click **Advanced Filter/Sort** • Add criteria fields to the design grid • Enter the filter and sort criteria • Click the **Apply Filter** ⟦icon⟧ button on the toolbar • Review the filtered data to be sure they are what you expected • Work with the filtered data • Click **Remove Filter** ⟦icon⟧ on the Access toolbar when you are done
Saving a filter as a query	AC 3.10	• Display the filter in either the Filter By Form window or the Advanced Filter/Sort window (recall that any filter can be displayed in these windows regardless of how it was created) • Click the **Save As Query** ⟦icon⟧ button on the toolbar • Type a name for the query and click **OK** • The new query will appear with the other query objects in the Database Window
Create a Select Query	AC 3.12	• Select the **Queries** object from the Database Window • Verify that **Create query in Design View** is selected • Click **New** on the toolbar • Select the **Design View** ⟦icon⟧ button from the New Query dialog box and click **OK** • Double-click the name of each table that contains relevant data from the Show Table dialog box • Double-click each table field that is to be contained in the query result to place it in the Field row of the design grid. The order of the columns is the order of the output • Enter sort criteria in the Sort row of the design grid • Enter selections in the Criteria row of the design grid • Click the **Datasheet View** ⟦icon⟧ button on the toolbar to see the query results • Click the **Design View** ⟦icon⟧ button on the toolbar to update the query criteria • Click the **Save** ⟦icon⟧ button to save the query criteria

task reference summary

Task	Page #	Preferred Method
Create an expression using Expression Builder	AC 3.20	• Click in the Field row of the QBE grid column that will display the calculation • Click the **Build** button in the Query Design toolbar • Select expression elements and operators to create the desired calculation • Click **OK** to place the calculation in the QBE grid
Modify the format of a form	AC 3.27	• Open the form in Design View • Click the **AutoFormat** button in the Form Design toolbar • Select from the same formats that were available in the Wizard
Modify the format of a report	AC 3.30	• Open the report in Design View • Click the **AutoFormat** button in the Report Design toolbar • Select from the same formats that were available in the Wizard
Add a graphic to a report or form	AC 3.35	• Open the report or form in Design View • Select the section that is to display the graphic • Select **Picture** from the Insert menu • Navigate to the folder containing the image and change the file type selector to the image file type • Select the file and click **OK** • Move and size the image as needed

TRUE/FALSE

1. Relational operators include $+$, $-$, $*$, and $/$.

2. An aggregate function with no Group By returns a value for every detail record.

3. Only bitmaps (.bmp) format images can be displayed in Access forms and reports.

4. Each section of a form or report is used to define a different output component. For example, the header appears once at the beginning of a form or report.

5. Summary reports display only statistical or summarized data and suppress the detail line prints.

6. To add a calculation to a query, an expression containing the calculation *must* be typed directly into the query grid.

FILL-IN

1. Graphics are placed in a form or report using the _____ menu.

2. The title of a report that appears only on the first page is placed in the _____ section of the design.

3. A field from a table or query is composed of a _____ control and a _____ control when displayed on a form.

4. When using Wizards _____ determines the background and text color applied.

5. The Form Wizard allows you to select from a list of fields in a table or query. The field list displayed is determined by _____.

6. To create a query that calculates total expenses by department, you would _____ on the Department field.

7. The format for the output of each record in a report is defined in the _____ section.

MULTIPLE CHOICE

1. Which of the following relational operators could be used to retrieve a contiguous range of values defined by an upper and lower limit in a query?
   a. Between
   b. In
   c. Like
   d. all of the above

2. Which of the following presents a blank datasheet containing all the fields of a table for the entry of filter criteria?
   a. Filter by Selection
   b. Filter for Input
   c. Filter by Form
   d. all of the above

3. A filter can be saved as a
   a. filter.
   b. form.
   c. table.
   d. query.

4. What views are supported for the query object?
   a. Design and Report
   b. Datasheet and Design
   c. Datasheet and Report
   d. Form and Datasheet

5. Which of the following is not a control used to design a form?
   a. label
   b. image
   c. expression
   d. text Box

review of concepts

REVIEW QUESTIONS

Each of the following topics should be addressed in one to three paragraphs.

1. Discuss what you would need to do to create mailing labels for the dog owners in the Clients table of the Westside Vet Clinic database.

2. Discuss the difference between detail and summary reports and when you would use each.

3. How do you decide to what groups to apply summary statistics in a grouped report?

4. In a table containing a record for each class a student has taken this semester, how would you calculate the student's GPA? The record consists of the student ID, class ID, class credits, and a score representing the letter grade (0 = F, 1 = D, 2 = C, 3 = B, 4 = A).

5. Discuss the methods that could be used to return a contiguous range of values in a query.

6. Describe how many rows will result from using an aggregate function in a query.

CREATE THE QUESTION

For each of the following answers, create the question.

ANSWER	QUESTION
1. It doesn't have to be stated in query criteria because it is the default	_____
2. They can only operate on all fields of one table	_____
3. The only way to retrieve such a record is to restore it from a backup made prior to the update	_____
4. Double-clicking a field in the field list, clicking and dragging a field from the field list, and selecting from a drop-down list box are all ways to do this	_____
5. Doing this will cause all of the fields of a table to be displayed in the output without placing each field in the QBE grid	_____
6. Because you can select from fields in all of the tables in the database, operators, and Access functions to create an expression	_____
7. These are only required in an expression when the field name or table name contains spaces	_____

FACT OR FICTION

For each of the following, determine whether the statement is fact, fiction, or both and present your arguments for that conclusion.

1. In the expression Extended Total:Quantity*Price, the colon (:) is optional.

2. Aggregate functions can only be applied to the entire contents of a table or query.

3. The query, form, and report objects of a database store only specifications that can be used to re-create the object, not data.

4. The Form Wizard is one of the five types of AutoForms.

5. The Count aggregate function can be used on nonnumeric data.

1. Creating Filters, Forms, Queries, and Reports for Curbside Recycling

Curbside Recycling was introduced as a Hands-on Project in Chapter 1; review the organization's background if needed. You have added the CustomerRecords table to Curbside's database prototype. The Customers table holds static customer information such as name, address, and phone. The CustomerRecords table holds data about each recyclable pickup. Enough test data have been added to each table to test filtering, queries, reports, and forms.

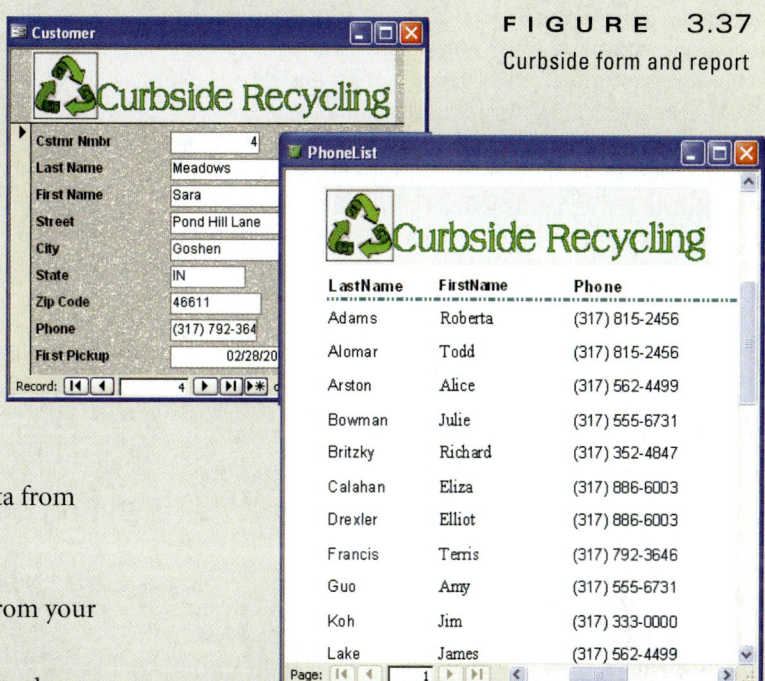

FIGURE 3.37
Curbside form and report

1. Make sure that you have access to the data from your data disk

2. Start Access and open the **ac03CurbsideRecycling.mdb** database from your Chapter 3 files

3. Use a filter to select records for customers who had their first pickup in October of 2002

   a. Document the filtering method you used. (*Hint:* Two Filter by Selection filters are required; only one Filter by Form filter is required.)

   b. Sort the filtered data by service date and print the result

4. Use a filter to

   a. Select all customers who live on a street that has "hill" anywhere in the street address

   b. Save the filter as a query named **HillCustomers**

5. Create a form (see Figure 3.37) to be used to enter new customers and update existing customers. The columnar form should

   a. Contain all of the Customer table data

   b. Use the SandStone AutoFormat

   c. Display the logo in ac03Curbside.tif (located with the Chapter 3 data files) in the Form Header

   d. Use spaces and complete words in the field labels (e.g., CstmrNmbr changes to Customer Number)

   e. Print the form displaying the record for Alice Arston

   f. Save the form as **Customer**

6. Create a report named **PhoneList** to be used as a customer phone list. The report should

   a. Contain only the fields LastName, FirstName, and Phone

   b. Be sorted by the full customer name

   c. Use the Casual AutoFormat

   d. Display the logo in **ac03Curbside.gif** (located with the Chapter 3 data files) in the Report Header. Select and delete the default title

   e. Have the column widths narrowed to better fit the data (see Figure 3.37)

7. Use a query on CustomerRecords to determine the total and average weights of Paper and other products each customer has had picked up

   a. Print the query results

   b. Save the query as **CstmrWeights**

8. Create a detailed report with summary records displaying the Average and Total of Paper and Other weights from the CustomerRecords table. Save the report as **CstmrWeights**

9. If your work is complete, exit Access; otherwise, continue to the next assignment

2. Evaluating Data in the BestBakery Database

Montgomery (Monty) Best started the Best Bakery and Catering Company 30 years ago in Orlando, Florida. The organization has been very successful with several bakeries throughout the Orlando area. Best products are marketed through grocery stores, delis, and event catering. Catering is available for any event from a small gathering of 8 to a banquet for 700.

Monty is frequently asked to share the recipes that have led to his success. While there are many specialty recipes that Monty is not willing to share, many commonly prepared dishes can easily be scaled down for home use. Monty has begun developing a database of the recipes he is willing to share. The goal is to create kiosks in grocery stores and delis where customers can browse and print their personal favorites.

1. Start Access and open **ac03BestBakery.mdb**

2. Open the **Recipes** table in Datasheet View

3. Locate the record for Italian Meatballs and notice that the Category is Mead. Use a filter to locate any other Mead records. Document the filter used and then change all Mead Categories to **Meat**. Print the filtered data. Save the filter as a query named **MeadUpdates**

4. Use a filter to select all Bread recipes. Save the filter as a query named **BreadRecipes**

5. Create a form (see Figure 3.38) to be used to enter new recipe data and update existing data. The form should
   a. Use the **Columnar** layout and **Ricepaper** style
   b. Contain all table fields
   c. Include the **ac03Food.jpg** graphic sized and placed as shown in Figure 3.38
   d. Have spaces in the field labels
   e. Print the form displaying the Irish Spaghetti record
   f. Save the form as **RecipeUpdate**

6. Create a query using the RecipeKeywords and NumberofServings fields to retrieve all chocolate recipes that will serve 24 or more people. Name the query **ChocolateLarge**

7. Create a query that counts the number of recipes in each Category. Name the query **RecipeCount**

8. Create a detailed report with all Recipes table fields and no calculations. Group the records by **Category** and sort by **RecipeName**. Include the **ac03Food.jpg** graphic. Adjust the image size and put spaces in the headings. Name the report **Recipes**

9. If your work is complete, exit Access; otherwise, continue to the next assignment

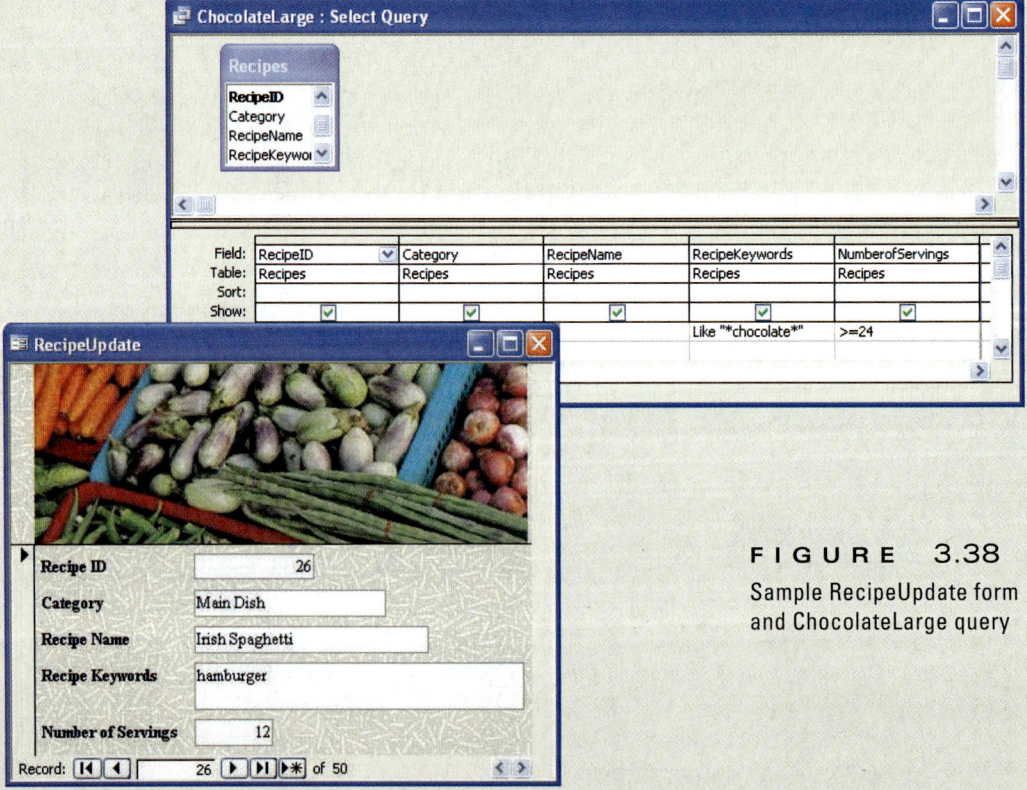

FIGURE 3.38

Sample RecipeUpdate form and ChocolateLarge query

1. Tracking Employees at Little White School House

Little White School House was introduced as a Challenge project in Chapter 1; review the organization's background if needed. You are in the process of converting the existing spreadsheets into database tables. You have cleaned up some of the data, but the transition is not going well because the spreadsheet data have not been normalized. Samuel Mink is anxious to see the reporting capabilities of Access before paying for a complete conversion. You have successfully converted a subset of the spreadsheet containing student data into a table called Students in the ac03lwsh.mdb. The StdntID is an AutoNumber field because the school has only used names in the past.

1. If you did not complete this assignment in Chapter 1, open **ac03Lwsh.mdb** and skip to step 2. If you completed this assignment in Chapter 1, retrieve your **ac01LittleWhiteSchoolHouse** database. Import the Students table from ac03Lwsh.mdb

   a. Use the **Import** option of **Get External Data** from the **File** menu

   b. Select **ac03Lwsh.mdb** and click **Import**

   c. Select the **Students** table and click **OK**

2. Review the Students table data to become familiar with them. Notice that the student's name needs to be broken up into two fields

3. Use a filter to select only students from Pine

   a. Print the result

   b. Save the filter as a query named **Pine**

4. Create a form that can be used to enter new students and update existing student records. The form should

   a. Use columnar format

   b. Use the Expedition AutoFormat

   c. Display the logo in **ac03Lwsh.gif** (located with the Chapter 3 data files) in the Form Header

   d. Print the form displaying the record for Ricky Maus

   e. Save the form as **Students**

5. Create a query that counts the number of students on each bus. The query should display one row per bus. Save the query as **BusCount**

6. Create a report that lists students grouped by their teacher. The report should

   a. Display all fields

   b. Sort by student name

   c. Use Landscape orientation

   d. Use Bold AutoFormat

   e. Display the logo in **ac03Lwsh.tif** (located with the Chapter 3 data files) in the Form Header

7. Be saved as **StudentsByTeacher**

8. Close the database and exit Access if your work is complete

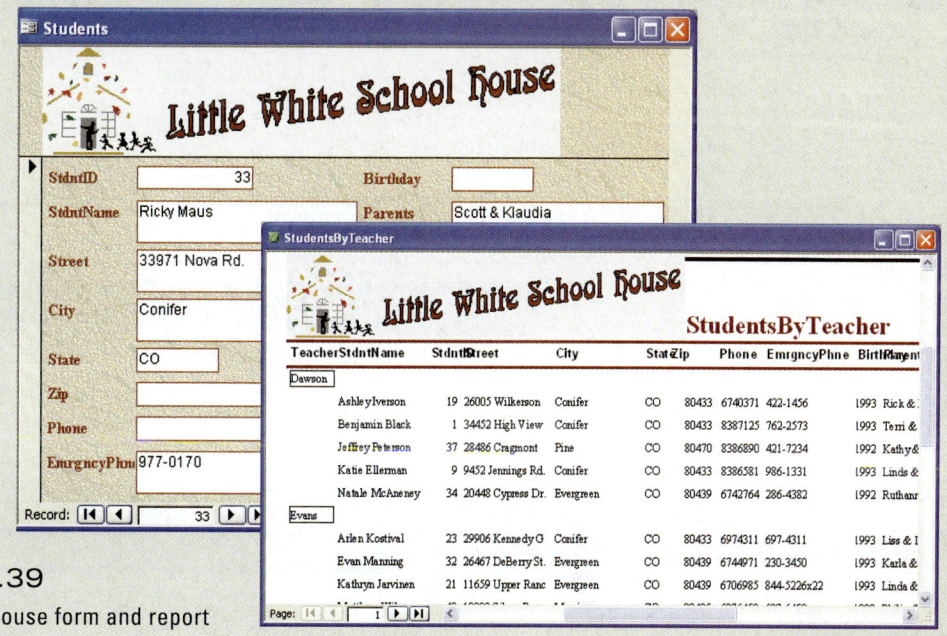

FIGURE 3.39

Little White School House form and report

2. Tracking Software Inventory and Vendors

The ac03Software.mdb database contains data about the software inventory of a small retailer and the vendors that sell each software product.

1. Start Access and open **ac03Software.mdb**

2. Use Design View to create a new query based on the tblSoftware table. Include the **Name**, **Category**, **Quantity**, and **Price**. Select products that have fewer than 10 copies on hand and therefore need to be reordered. Name the query **ReorderList**

3. Create a new query in Design View based on the Products table that includes the **Name**, **Category**, **Quantity**, **Price**, and a calculated field named **Total** that multiplies Quantity by Price. Sort by Name and save the query as **InventoryValue**

4. Create a new query in Design View based on the tblSoftware table that counts the number of software products in each category, averages the quantity, averages the inventory cost of each product, and sums the inventory cost of each product (see Figure 3.40). Add custom headings to each column and name the query **InventoryValueSummary**

5. Use the InventoryValueSummary query to create a new query that returns one calculated row for all data. Delete the Category column. Name the query **InventorySummary**

6. Create a **Columnar** report based on the InventoryValue query. Include all query fields, group by Category, sort by Name, sum the Total field, use **block** layout, and use the **Corporate** style

   a. Adjust the title to include spaces

   b. Adjust column widths as needed

   c. Include the graphic ac03Software.gif in the report header and reposition the title to the bottom-right corner of the image

   d. Name the report **InventoryValue**

7. Create a columnar form for tblSoftware. Include all fields and use the **Sumi Painting** style. Use the form to update the Tax Wizard record. Change Quantity to **8** and verify that the Total also changed. Name the form **tblSoftware**. Print the form displaying this record

8. Use the Vendor table to create **Avery J8162** mailing labels. Sort by ZipCode. Name the report **LabelsVendor**

9. If your work is complete, exit Access; otherwise, continue to the next assignment

F I G U R E   3.40

InventoryValueSummary query

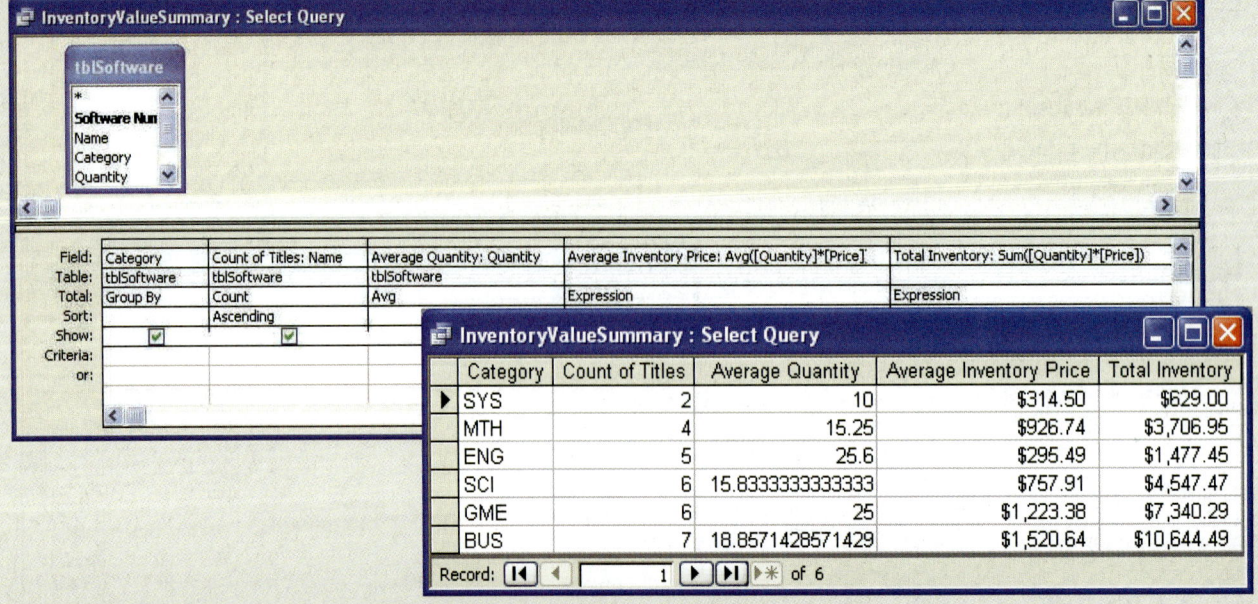

e-business

1. ScaleClassics.com Product Lists

Ricardo (Rico) Juarez runs a body shop that specializes in restoring classic cars. Rico owns three classics and began collecting scale models when his wife put her foot down and said no to building more garage space for his cars.

Although Rico frequently used the Internet and e-mail, he had never considered starting an e-business. The Scale Classics Web site began as a technology class project for Rico's son Marcel. Marcel created a basic text and graphics informational site. Rico liked the site, but wanted a complex site dedicated to the serious collector. He envisioned a storefront, auction house, and collector's forums and had been unable to find such a site in his online searches. Rico hired a local consultant to build the site, found a processing house to manage orders and payments, and began shipping scale models from the body shop.

The storefront is largely for American classic cars, which come in 1/18, 1/24, 1/43, and 1/64 scale. Popular foreign cars are also available. Rico has hired you to maintain the Product List and product analysis, which is in Access.

1. Retrieve the **ac03Cars.mdb** database

2. Review the **Catalog** table data to become familiar with them

3. Use Find and Replace to correct the spelling of Chevrolet

4. Use a filter to select any record with "coupe" in the model name
   a. Print the result
   b. Save the filter as a query named **Coupe**

5. Create a form that can be used to enter new classics and update existing records. The form should
   a. Use columnar format
   b. Use the SandStone AutoFormat
   c. Display the logo in **ac03ClassicCars.gif** (located with the Chapter 3 data files) in the Form Header

d. Print the form displaying the record for the Dodge 1957 Pick-Up

e. Save the form as **Cars**

6. Create a query to select the models that cost less than $35. The query should display all of the table fields and sort the result from the highest to the lowest price. Save the query as **LT35**

7. Create a report listing classic cars grouped by their make. The report should
   a. Display all fields
   b. Sort by the model
   c. Calculate the average price for each make
   d. Use Align Left 2 layout
   e. Use the Formal AutoFormat
   f. Display the logo in **ac03ClassicCars.gif** (located with the Chapter 3 data files) in the Form Header
   g. Be saved as **CarsByModel**
   h. Adjust the titles and headings to match Figure 3.41

8. Close the database and exit Access if your work is complete

FIGURE 3.41

Scale Classics form and report

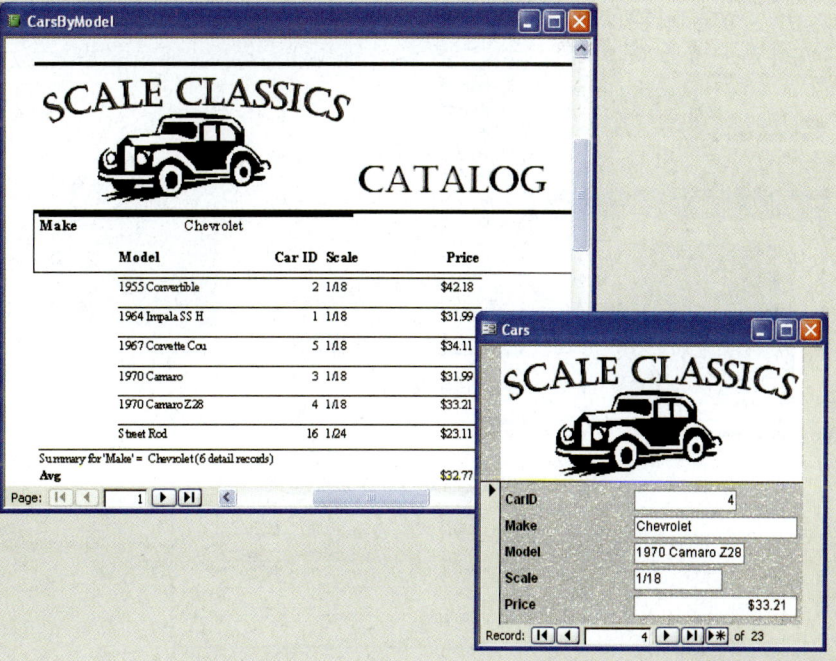

2. Tracking Enrollment at Governor's University

Governor's University is a consortium of 28 colleges and universities. The consortium was formed to allow students to take courses from any member and have them apply toward a degree. The goal is to offer the best curriculum at all 28 locations so that students have the widest possible choice and do not lose credits by moving or changing degree plans. To accomplish this, registration, enrollment, counseling, and all student services are available from the Web. A new Access database for course listings that will drive interactive Web pages is being tested. You will create queries, a form, and a report on this database to help test it.

1. Open Access and open **ac03GovernorsUniversity.mdb**

2. Open the **Courses** table and review the contents. Close the table

3. Create a query that will select all courses taught by a professor named Lewis. Include all fields in the result. Sort by Department, CourseNumber, and Section. Name the query **LewisClasses**

4. Create a query listing the Department, CourseNumber, Section, Title, Instructor, and Seats Remaining. Seats Remaining is calculated by subtracting Enr from Seat. Name the query **AvailableSeats**

5. Use a filter to find any record with the word Study in the course title. Save the filter as a query named **IndependentStudy**

6. Low enrollment courses are often canceled. Create a query listing the Department, CourseNumber, Section, Title, Instructor, and Enr of all non-Independent Study courses with eight or fewer students enrolled. Name the query **LowEnrollment**

7. Create a form that can be used to enter and update data. The form should
   a. Use columnar format
   b. Use the **SandStone** AutoFormat
   c. Display **ac03Study.gif** in the Detail section of the form
   d. Print the form displaying the record for BIOL 1021 section 1
   e. Save the form as **Classes**

8. Create a query listing with Department, CourseNumber, Section, Title, Enr, and Seats Remaining (Seats − Enr). Use this query to create a report. The report should
   a. Include all of the query fields
   b. Group by Department
   c. Sort by CourseNumber and Section
   d. Use **Align Left 2** layout and **Corporate** style
   e. Sum Enrollment and Seats Remaining
   f. Display **ac03Study.gif** in the Form Header
   g. Be saved as **DeptStats**
   h. Have titles and heading adjusted as shown in Figure 3.42

9. Close the database and exit Access if your work is complete

FIGURE 3.42

Governor's University form and report

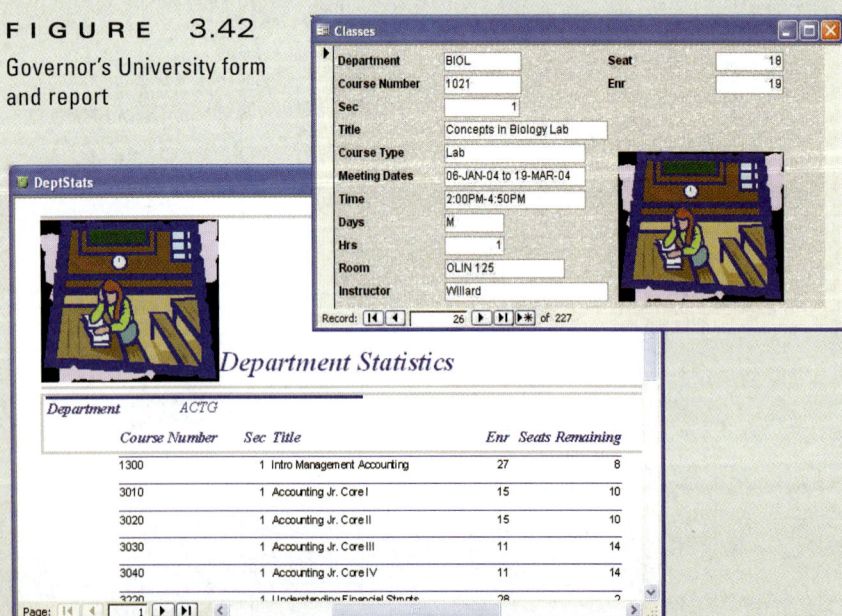

on the web

1. Toy Purchase Statistics by Internet Research Inc.

Internet Research Inc. (IRI) is a statistical evaluation organization specializing in Internet commerce that was introduced in Chapter 2. You have been asked to maintain statistical information on the various Web sites selling toys. The statistics are used to rank the sites and aid Shopping Bots in their searches for products. As a training exercise you have been manually retrieving price comparison information. You still need to retrieve a few more pieces of data and then you will be ready to create reports with groups and calculations to evaluate what you have gathered.

1. Use a Shopping Bot like www.mysimon.com or a search engine to find at least two sites that sell popular toys (www.eToys.com and www.ToysRUs.com are good sites, but there are many others). Select a video or computer game that you would like to purchase for a relative or friend

    a. Determine the price of the game at the first site
    b. Find the price for the same game at the second site
    c. Repeat this process for another game

2. Add your new research to the data that already exist in the ac03IRI.mdb database Toys table

3. Use a filter to select only Barbie items. There should be 22 rows in this answerset

    a. Print the result
    b. Save the filter as a query named **Barbie**

4. Create a form that can be used to enter new toy data and update existing Toys records. The form should

    a. Use columnar format
    b. Use the Expedition AutoFormat
    c. Display the logo in **ac03IRI.jpg** in the Form Header
    d. Include spaces in the field labels
    e. Print the form displaying one of the computer game records
    f. Save the form as **Toys**

5. Create a query that counts the number of prices for each Web site. The query should display one row per Web site. Save the query as **SiteCount**

6. Create a report that lists ToyName grouped by Web site. The report should

    a. Display all fields except ToyID (see Figure 3.43)
    b. Sum all of the prices for a Web site
    c. Sort by ToyName
    d. Use the Align Left 1 Layout
    e. Use the Corporate AutoFormat
    f. Display the logo in **ac03IRI.jpg** (located with the Chapter 3 data files) in the Form Header
    g. Be saved as **SiteTotals**

7. Close the database and exit Access if your work is complete

FIGURE   3.43

IRI Report

hands-on projects

around the world

1. Tracking the World's Population

Brandon Pryor is a middle school geography and civics teacher who is trying to make faraway places seem real to his students. Each of his students has an e-mail pen pal in another country and has researched his or her lineage and reported on one of the countries of his or her ancestors.

His classes participate in a Web forum by posting daily weather conditions and events. The name of each participating school has been entered on a sheet of paper and placed into a lottery box. Every day, the class draws a school from the lottery box and then spends time reviewing the information recorded by those students.

The next project is geared toward helping students understand the size of other cities in the world. Mr. Pryor has created an Access database of world populations for the students to analyze. You are assisting Mr. Pryor and his students in this process.

1. Open the **Cities** table of the **ac03Populations.mdb** database

2. Mr. Pryor's students are in Denver, Colorado, so the first task is to find out how many people live there. Use Filter by Form to determine the population of Denver and print the results. Save as a query named **Denver**

3. Now that you know how large Denver is, use separate filters to determine what cities around the world are the same size, larger, and smaller. Save each filter as a query and print each result

4. Use a query with an aggregate function to determine the smallest city in the table. Display only the population. Print the results and save the query as **SmallestPopulation**

5. Now use a query to determine the largest city. Print the results of and save the query as **LargestPopulation**

6. Create a form for entering and maintaining the population data. The form must
   a. Use Columnar layout
   b. Use the Sumi Painting style
   c. Contain **ac03Globe.gif** in the header
   d. In Design View, adjust the size and position of the text boxes as needed
   e. Save the form as **PopulationUpdate**

7. Average the city population in each country to determine which country has the largest cities. Create a report containing the city, country, and population
   a. Group the data by country
   b. Sort by city name and average the population. Display summary rows only
   c. Use **Block** layout and Corporate AutoFormat
   d. Add the Clip Art used in the form
   e. Update the title as shown in Figure 3.44
   f. Save the report as **AvgPopulation**

8. Close the database and Access if your work is complete

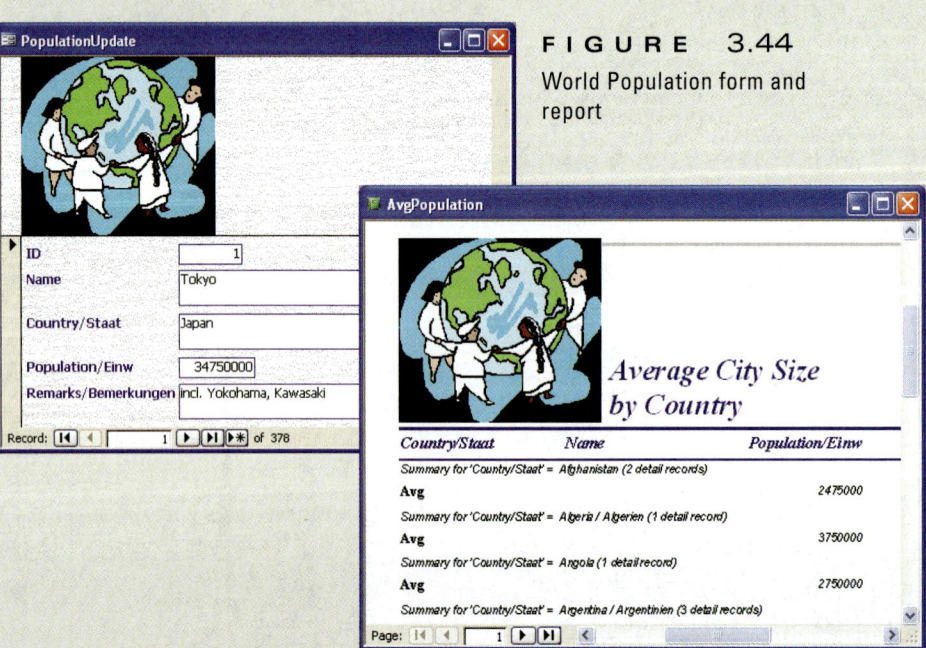

FIGURE 3.44

World Population form and report

running project: tnt web design

Querying TnT Customer Data

The TnT database now consists of two related tables. The tblCustomers table holds the static data about the organization's customers. The CustomerSites table contains the URLs for the sites TnT has built. The CustomerSites table has a Lookup field for the customer name so that you do not have to remember CustomerID values when entering data. Tori is very pleased with the progress that you are making on the TnT database. She has asked for a copy of the database so that she can begin exploring its design and content.

1. Start Access and open the **ac03TnT.mdb** database
2. Use a filter to select non-United States records from tblCustomers. Print the result and save the filter as a query named **OutsideUSA**
3. Create a columnar form that can be used to enter and update customer data. The form should
   a. Include all customer data
   b. Use a columnar format
   c. Use the Sumi Painting style
   d. Save the form as **CustomerUpdate**
   e. Display the logo from the file **ac03TnT.gif** in the Form Header

f. Change the cusID label to read **Customer ID**
g. Remove cus from the remaining labels
h. Print the form with the record for Ross & Homer

4. Create a query that lists the customer name and address (excluding other fields) by country, state, and city. Print the result. Save the query as **CityList**
5. Tori wants a phone list for U.S. customers. Create a phone list report named **PhoneListByState** that
   a. Includes the state, customer name, and phone information only
   b. Groups by state and sorts by customer name
   c. Uses the **Corporate** style
   d. Displays the logo from the file **ac03TnT.gif** in the Report Header
   e. Has spaces in the title and cus removed from the column headings
6. Create mailing labels with the following attributes:
   a. Use Avery C2163 labels
   b. Contain the customer's full name and address with each field on a new line
   c. Use 12-point Garamond font
   d. Change the text color to dark blue
   e. Sort by Postal Code
   f. Print one page of labels
   g. Save the report as **CustomerLabels**
7. Close the database and exit Access if your work is complete

FIGURE   3.45

CustomerUpdate form and CityList query

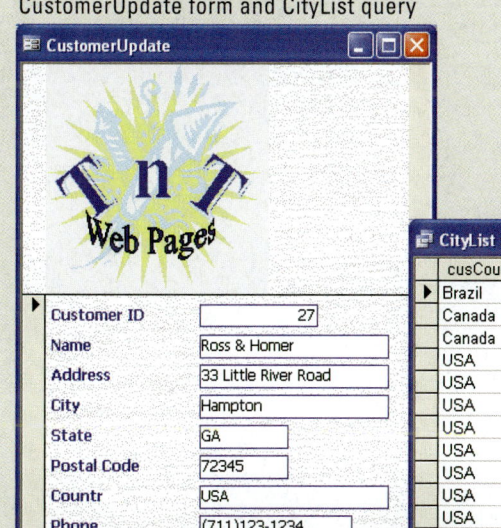

cusCountry	cusState	cusCity	cusName	cusAddress	cusPostalCode
Brazil		São Paulo	Comércio Mineiro	Av. Dos Lusíadas, 23	05432-043
Canada	BC	Vancouver	Bacchus Wine Cellars	1900 Oak St.	V3F 2K1
Canada	Québec	Montréal	Mère Paillarde	43 rue St. Laurent	H1J 1C3
USA	AK	Layfield	Cash & Carry	45 Medigas Rd	12345
USA	AL	Trenton	Bakertime Mobile	759 East 31 Ave	22345
USA	AZ	Sandy Row	Harper & Ronick	288 Landsdowne	32345
USA	CA	Creston	MMB Holdings	4090 Lethbridge	42345
USA	CA	El Rio	Silver Cloud	111 Rand Avenue	42345
USA	CO	Stoney Bluff	Summit Supply	Ridgeway Connector	80217
USA	CT	Nicola	DesJardins	808 Seymour	52345
USA	FL	Riverside	Omega Distributions	32 Merrit Ave	62345
USA	GA	Hampton	Ross & Homer	33 Little River Road	72345
USA	KY	Southgate	Dalhousie Inc.	2233 Southgate Avenue	82345
USA	LA	Ashcroft	Whitley	588 Tulin Drive	92345

CustomerUpdate form:

Customer ID: 27
Name: Ross & Homer
Address: 33 Little River Road
City: Hampton
State: GA
Postal Code: 72345
Countr: USA
Phone: (711)123-1234
Fax: (711)123-1235

Record: 27 of 32

CityList : Select Query — Record: 1 of 32

1. Evaluate Courses at Your School

Create an Access database that could be useful for your school. For example, you could track people who have been contacted as potential students, enrollment, student athletes, alumni, financial donors, student activities, or the like. The database you develop should contain data that can be grouped and used to create subtotals. Document the purpose of your database being sure to include a description of how it can be used. Include a form that can be used to maintain all fields in a table. Create at least one report with grouping, a sum, and an average. Create at least one simple Select Query and at least one query with a calculation. Call the database **ac03MySchool.mdb**.

2. Start a Database for Your Hobby

If you started a database for your hobby in Chapter 2, you can enhance it; otherwise, assume that you are starting a database to store data about your hobby or pastime. Document the type of data that you would need to track and how the database will be used. Name the database **ac03<yourname>Hobby.mdb**. Include a form that can be used to maintain all fields in a table. Create at least one report with grouping, a sum, and an average. Create at least one simple Select Query and at least one query with a calculation.

4 Compound Queries and Database Utilities

did you know?

an *ostrich's eye is bigger than its brain.*

Maine *is the only U.S. state that borders only one other state.*

in *the world of dolls, Midge Hadley was Barbie's best friend in the 1960s.*

the *U.S. Congress passed a law in 1832 requiring all American citizens to spend one day each year fasting and praying.*

Antarctica *is the only continent without any reptiles or snakes.*

to *find out the first product to have a bar code on its package, visit* www.mhhe.com/i-series.

Chapter Objectives

- Build, run, and save compound queries using In, Like, Between, And, and Or

- Understand and use Crosstab Queries—MOS AC03S-1-7

- Modify Access table definitions by adding fields, deleting fields, and changing field properties—MOS AC03S-1-3 and MOS AC03S-1-4

- Add an input mask to a field—MOS AC03S-1-4

- Create Lookup fields—MOS AC03S-1-3

- Schedule and execute database backups—MOS AC03S-4-5

- Repair damaged databases—MOS AC03S-4-6

chapter case

KoryoKicks: Analyzing Data with Crosstab Queries

Missy and Micah have found the Select Queries you and they created very useful. They now know that sales volumes are greater than previously believed and that only a handful of customers have not paid their bills. They were able to calculate the average monthly income and expense for KoryoKicks and to project future income and expenses. KoryoKicks is continuing to grow and the twins are no closer to making a decision about how to handle the volume and money issues. Simple Select Queries are nice (see Figure 4.1), but they don't provide the analytical power needed to understand the purchasing behavior of their customers. It is important to chart the current purchasing behavior of customers to accurately project future purchases.

To understand who buys their products and in what quantities, Missy and Micah need to learn to create queries using multiple conditions. Using multiple conditions, data retrieved can be restricted using several values or a combination of values from multiple fields. For example, they would like to analyze sales from the last quarter and compare them to the previous quarter. That would require selecting records in three-month groups.

Missy and Micah would also like to cross-tabulate KoryoKicks data to see the relationship between two values simultaneously (see Figure 4.2). Crosstab Queries will allow the twins to analyze sales by month and state in one table. Sales data can also be simultaneously evaluated by both date and product.

Databases are critical to the operation of the organization using them. When data are lost, the ability to bill customers, order products, and support the business decision-making process also is lost. An important aspect of using a database is to know how to properly back up and restore tables

FIGURE 4.1

First quarter KoryoKicks sales

OrderID	CstmrID	OrderDate	QuantityOrdered	ProductDescription
41	Calahan	01-Jan-2004	2	Solid Color 1 3/5 inch belt
41	Calahan	01-Jan-2004	5	Bo Case
41	Calahan	01-Jan-2004	10	Chest Protector
41	Calahan	01-Jan-2004	8	Rank Belt 2 1/2 inches
41	Calahan	01-Jan-2004	10	Wushu Kung Fu Dragon Head Kwandao
41	Calahan	01-Jan-2004	28	Simplified Tai Chi
42	Calahan	15-Jan-2004	10	Satin Kick-boxing Shorts
37	Wagoner	15-Jan-2004	1	Knife Techniques
42	Calahan	15-Jan-2004	5	Nothern Shaolin
42	Calahan	15-Jan-2004	5	Training Mitts
42	Calahan	15-Jan-2004	35	Shaolin Long Fist Kung Fu
42	Calahan	15-Jan-2004	10	Chen Style Tai Chi Chuan
37	Wagoner	15-Jan-2004	3	Deluxe Rank 2 inch Belt
37	Wagoner	15-Jan-2004	1	Maple Bo

Record: 1 of 112

AC 4.2

ProductByStateCrosstab : Crosstab Query

ProductDescription	Total Of QuantityOrdered	CA	CO	IN	MI	OH
1001 Street Fighting Secrets	5		3		2	
3-sword set with stand	163	15	36	69	37	6
A Woman's QiGong Guide	10					10
Ancient Chinese Weapons	14	2	10		2	
Bag Gloves	17		15		2	
Balisong Butterfly Knive	10				10	
Bamboo Dragon Fighting Fan	5			1	4	
Bamboo Short Staff	16		6		10	
Black oak 3-section staff	33		22	1		10
Black V-neck Elastic Waist Uniform	6				6	
Bo Case	5		5			
Bruce Lee t-shirt	129		35	75	14	5
Chen Style Tai Chi Chuan	11		10		1	
Chest Protector	26		21		5	
Chrome Sais	5		5			
Closed-chin Head Gear	17			15		2

Record: 1 of 74

FIGURE 4.2
KoryoKicks sales by product and state

or entire databases. Tables should be backed up before major update operations such as changing table design. Such backups protect against possible data loss. Scheduled backups should be conducted regularly to protect against data loss caused by unforeseen events such as a hardware failure. Backups reduce the likelihood of lost data and thereby protect the organization's ability to continue doing business.

SESSION 4.1 USING QUERIES TO ANALYZE DATA

Queries are the central tool in the database arsenal providing the ability to perform complex analysis on table data. Besides creating analytical information to support the decision-making process, queries allow appropriate data to be retrieved before creating formal reports. Queries also can be used to calculate totals or select data for forms when a user's view is restricted to a subset of the data. In the previous chapter, simple queries were used to retrieve rows and columns of data based on one condition. Most of the time, you will need to use multiple conditions when retrieving data.

CHAPTER OUTLINE

Specifying Complex Query Criteria

Compound queries specify multiple conditions for data retrieval. The conditions can be as simple as using a list of values or as complicated as connecting a series of expressions and controlling their order of evaluation.

Selecting Records with In, Between, and Like

Using the Between, In, and Like conditional operators was briefly introduced in the previous chapter but warrants further exploration. Each of these operators allows a specific group of match values to be stated for a table field. Between provides an upper and lower selection limit. All values between those limits will be selected, including the limits. So a condition of Between 12 And 14 will retrieve records with values of 12, 13, and 14.

The twins want to retrieve sales information for the first quarter of 2004 so that they can compare it to the current quarter. You will create the first quarter query using an existing query.

Selecting Customer table records with Between:

1. Verify that the ac04KoryoKicks.mdb database is open

2. Select the **Queries** object in the Database Window

3. Double-click **Create query in Design View** (this is a faster way to initiate a Design View query)

4. Click the **Queries** tab of the Show Table dialog box

5. Add **CustomerOrdersJoin** to the query design grid and choose **Close** in the Show Table dialog box

6. Add all of the fields to the design grid

tip: *Double-click in the Title bar of CustomerOrdersJoin, click on the selected fields, and then drag them to the field row of the first query grid column*

7. Enter the condition **Between #1/1/2004# And #3/31/2004#** in the Criteria row of the OrderDate field to retrieve first quarter data

tip: *You do not have to enter the #s around the date values. Access will insert them*

8. Add an ascending sort to the OrderDate field

FIGURE 4.3

Selecting first quarter sales data

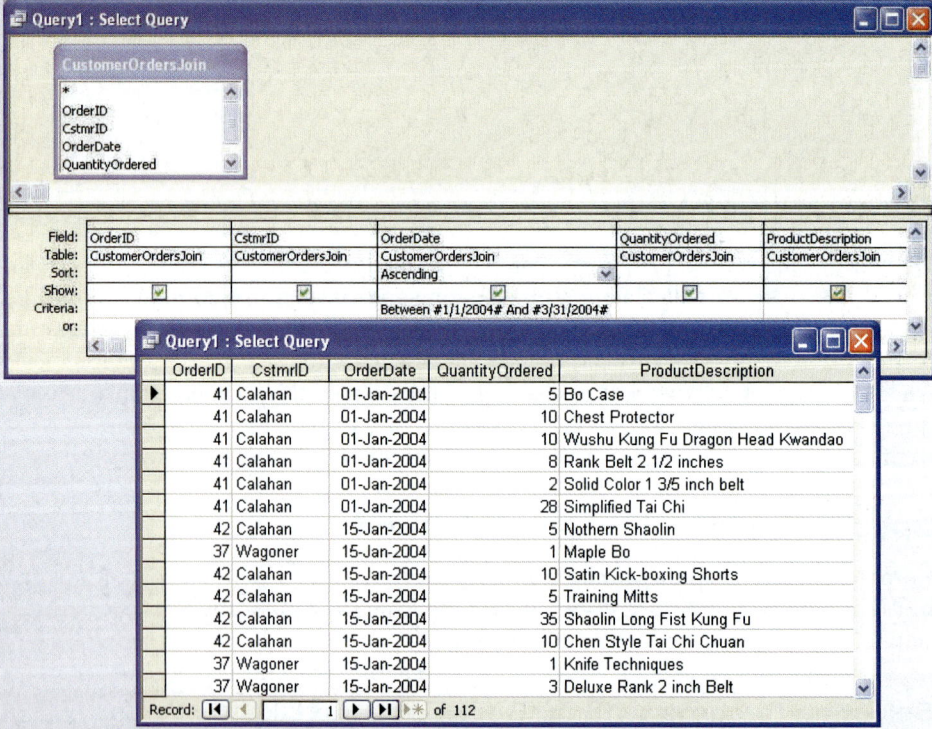

9. Run the query

10. Save the query as **FirstQuarter2004**

As was just demonstrated, an existing query can be used as the data source for other queries. In this case, the original query joined the data from three tables and then a new query was built to select first quarter data from the results of the join query.

The In operator allows a list of match values to be specified. This is effective when the match values are not logically grouped. For example In ("CA","CO","IN") would retrieve records for California, Colorado, and Indiana. The parentheses are a required part of the condition syntax for the In condition. Double quotes are a required delimiter when entering match values for Text data type fields. Suppose the twins need a list of customers that live in Coatesville, Greencastle, and Monroe, Indiana.

Selecting Customer table records with In:

1. Close any open windows except the Database Window in ac04KoryoKicks.mdb

2. Select the **Queries** object in the Database Window

3. Double-click on **Create query in Design View**

4. Add the **Customer** table to the query design and **Close** the Show Table dialog box

5. Put all of the fields except CstmrID and Notes in the design grid

6. Enter the criteria **In ("Coatesville","Greencastle","Monroe")** in the City field

7. Because all of the cities are in Indiana, it is not necessary to display the State field. Click the Show check box for State off

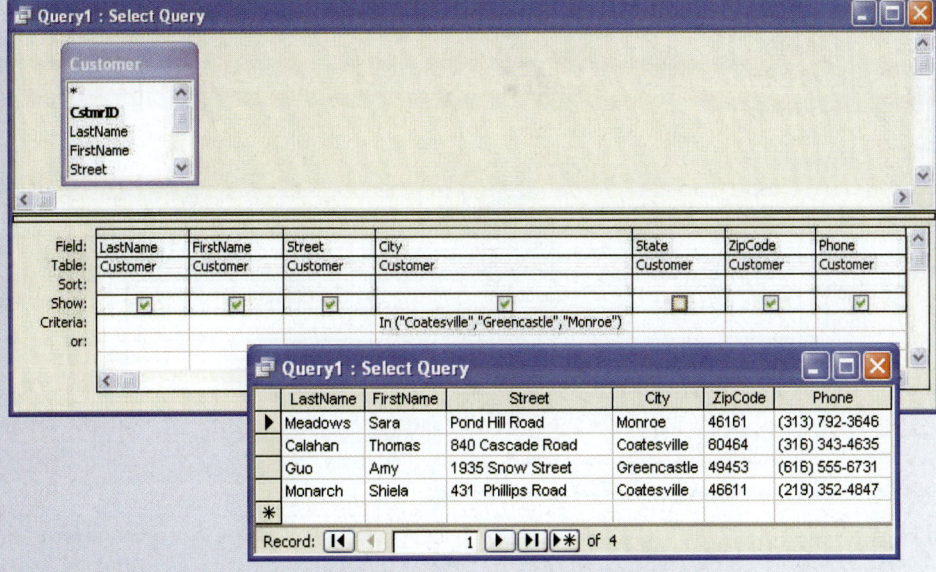

FIGURE 4.4

Customers from Coatesville, Greencastle, and Monroe

8. Run the query

9. Save the query as **INCustomers**

Each field in the QBE grid has a Show check box. When the check box is checked, values for that field will be displayed in the query results. When the check box is unchecked, the field will not display in the query results.

help yourself: *Use the Type a Question combo box to improve your understanding of Like query conditions by typing* **wildcards**. *Review the contents of* Like Operator *and* About using wildcard. *Close the Help window when you are finished*

The Like operator allows a pattern to be matched using wildcards. Wildcards are designed to be used with Text fields and can provide haphazard results with other data types. Recall that the wildcards are ? to replace one character, * to replace multiple characters, and # to replace one numeral.

Let's assume that the twins need to talk to a customer, but can't remember the full name or that customer's city. They believe that the city name starts with or contains *grand*. You could use the condition *Like "*grand*"* to retrieve all records with the word "grand" anywhere in the city.

Selecting Customer table records with Like:

1. Verify that the ac04KoryoKicks.mdb database is open
2. Select the **Queries** object from the Database Window
3. Double-click **Create query in Design View** to open the QBE grid and Show Table dialog box
4. Double-click on the **Customer** table in the Show Table dialog box to add it to the design grid
5. Click **Close** in the Show Table dialog box
6. Place **LastName**, **FirstName**, and **City** in the Field row of the QBE grid

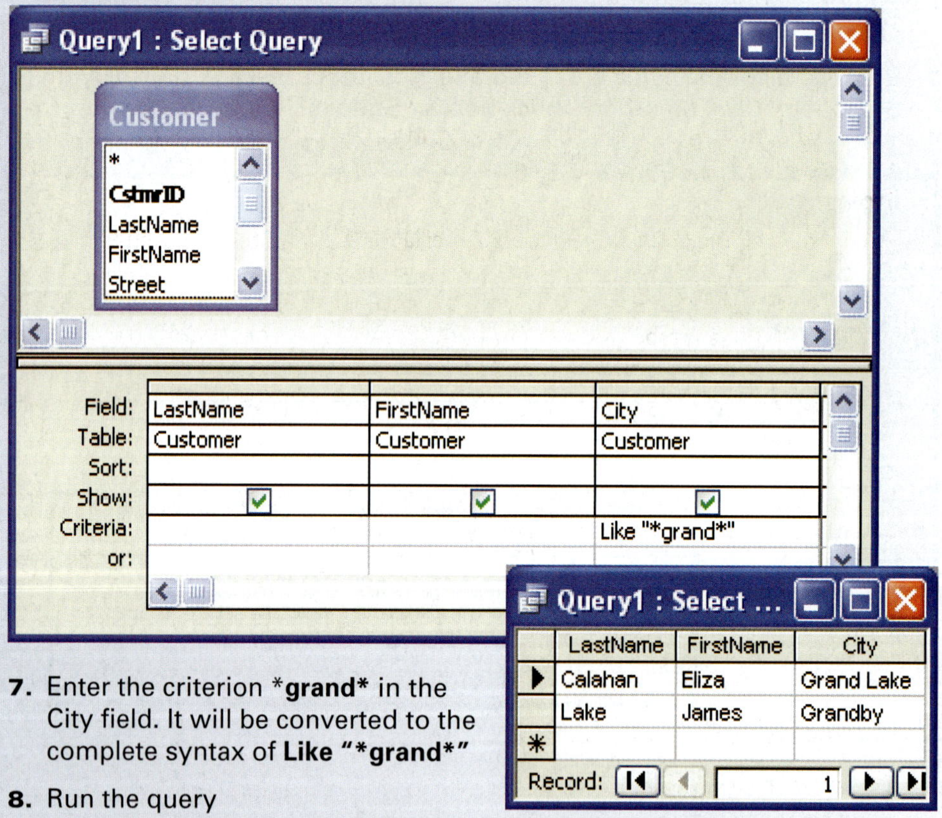

FIGURE 4.5

Customer records for cities containing *grand*

7. Enter the criterion *grand* in the City field. It will be converted to the complete syntax of **Like "*grand*"**
8. Run the query
9. Save the query as **GrandCitys**

In addition to selecting values that are In, Between, and Like, users often need to apply multiple selection criteria in a query. For example, to retrieve female employees who make less than $15 per hour would require a criterion for selecting records by gen-

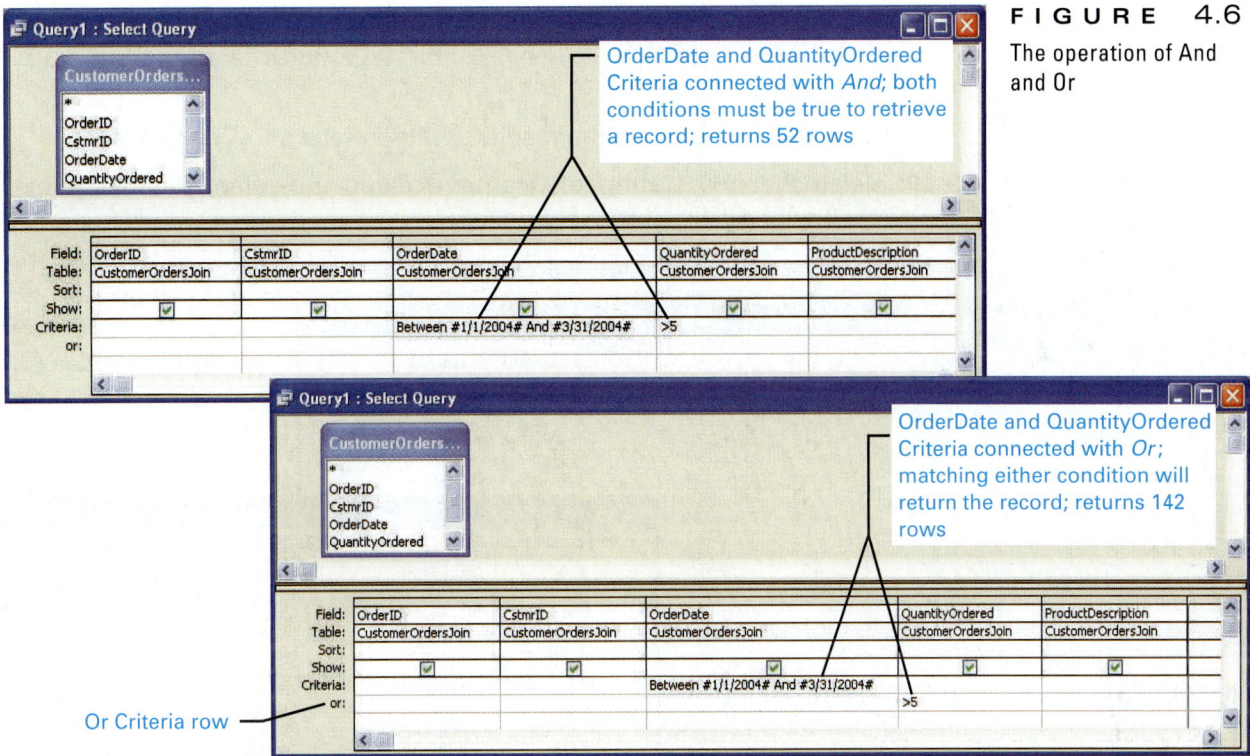

FIGURE **4.6**

The operation of And and Or

der and a criterion for selecting records by hourly rate. The next section discusses how to place these conditions in the query design grid.

Using Logical Operators

Logical operators are used to join multiple criteria for selecting records. Conditions can be joined with **And** or **Or**. Use *And* to join two or more conditions when all of the conditions must be true to retrieve the record. Use *Or* to join two or more conditions when any of the conditions can be true to retrieve the record.

When using the QBE grid, conditions placed in the same row are connected with And, while those places in separate rows are connected with Or. Take a look at the conditions demonstrated in Figure 4.6.

Selecting Customer table records with compound criteria:

1. Verify that the ac04KoryoKicks.mdb database is open

2. Select the **Queries** object in the Database Window

3. Double-click **Create query in Design View**

4. Click the **Queries** tab of the Show Table dialog box

5. Add **CustomerOrdersJoin** to the query design grid and choose **Close** in the Show Table dialog box

6. Add all of the fields to the design grid

7. Enter the condition **Between #1/1/2004# And #3/31/2004#** in the OrderDate field's Criteria row to retrieve first quarter data (see Figure 4.6)

8. In the same Criteria row enter **>5** in the QuantityOrdered column (see Figure 4.6)

9. Run the query to view the results and then return to Design View

10. Delete the >5 condition for QuantityOrdered and enter **>5** in the Or row of QuantityOrdered (see Figure 4.6)

11. Run the query (see Figure 4.7)

FIGURE 4.7

Results of And and Or compound queries

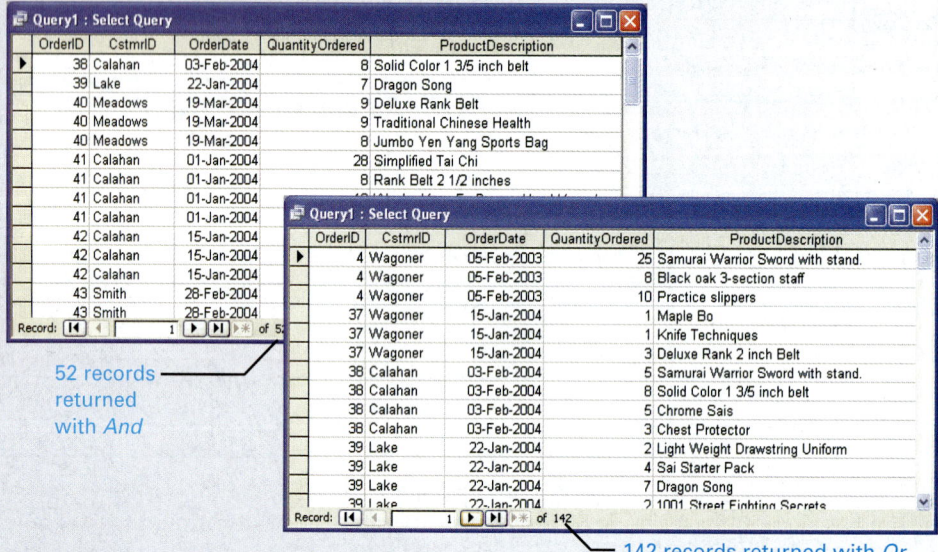

52 records returned with *And*

142 records returned with *Or*

12. Save the query as **HighVolume**

As was just demonstrated, compound conditions connected with And retrieve fewer records because both conditions must be true to return a row. Connecting conditions with Or retrieves more records because only one of the conditions has to be true to return the row. It is important to correctly use And and Or to retrieve valid query results.

Using the Not Operator

The *Not* logical operator negates a condition to select nonmatching values. Not can be placed in front of any condition created with any of the other operators ($=$, $>$, $<$, $>=$, $<=$, $<>$). For example, the condition *Not > 10* would retrieve records where the value of that field is less than or equal to 10.

Selecting Customer table records with Not:

1. Verify that the ac04KoryoKicks.mdb database is open

2. Select the **Queries** object from the Database Window

3. Click the **InCustomers** query and then click the **Design View** button to open the design

4. Place **Not** in front of the In condition (see Figure 4.8)

5. Run the query

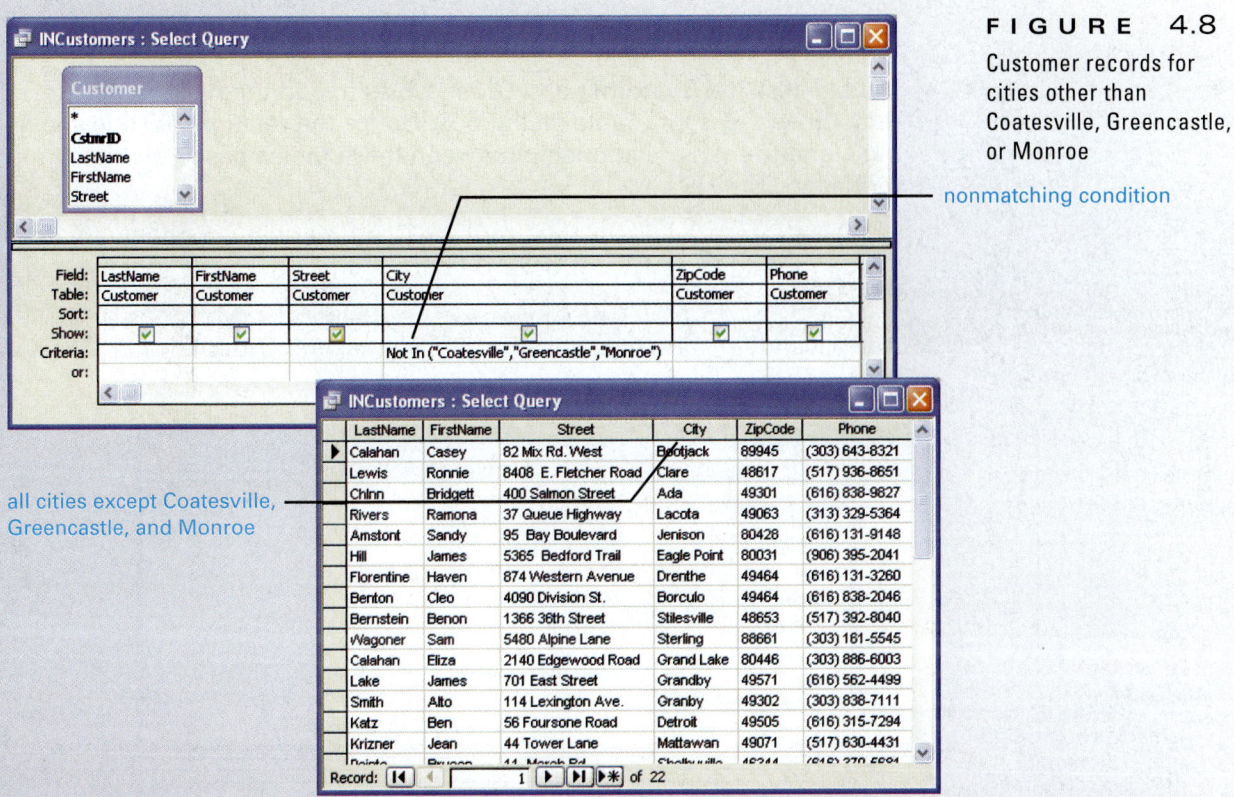

6. Use the **Save As** option of the **File** menu to save the query as **NotInCustomers** and close the query window

The previous example also demonstrated how to modify an existing query and save the modification with a new name. It is often easier to use this technique than it would be to create a new query from scratch.

Joining Two Tables with a Query

Database users should be able to retrieve any data regardless of where they are stored. Multitable queries merge the data from two or more tables into one query result. The process of retrieving data from two or more tables is referred to as joining. To join tables, they must share a common column of data that can be used to match rows from one table to related rows in the second table. When the relationships between tables have been properly designed and built (covered in Chapter 6), it is just as easy to build a query to retrieve data from multiple tables as it is to build a query based on a single table.

The twins would like to review orders placed by their customers. They believe that most customers have multiple orders, but the twins have nothing to support this view. You will create a list of customers with their orders that can be reviewed to validate or disprove this belief.

Joining the Order and Customer tables in a query:

1. Verify that the **ac04KoryoKicks.mdb** database is open

2. Select the **Queries** object from the Database Window

3. Double-click the **Create Query in Design View**

4. Double-click the **Customer** and **Order** tables to add them to the design grid. Close the Show Table dialog box. Notice the relationship line showing a one-to-many relationship between these tables based on the common field CstmrID

5. Add LastName and FirstName from the Customer table to the query design grid. Add OrderID and OrderDate from the Order table to the query design grid

6. Add ascending sorts to LastName, FirstName, and OrderID

7. Run the query

FIGURE 4.9

Query using the Customer and Order tables

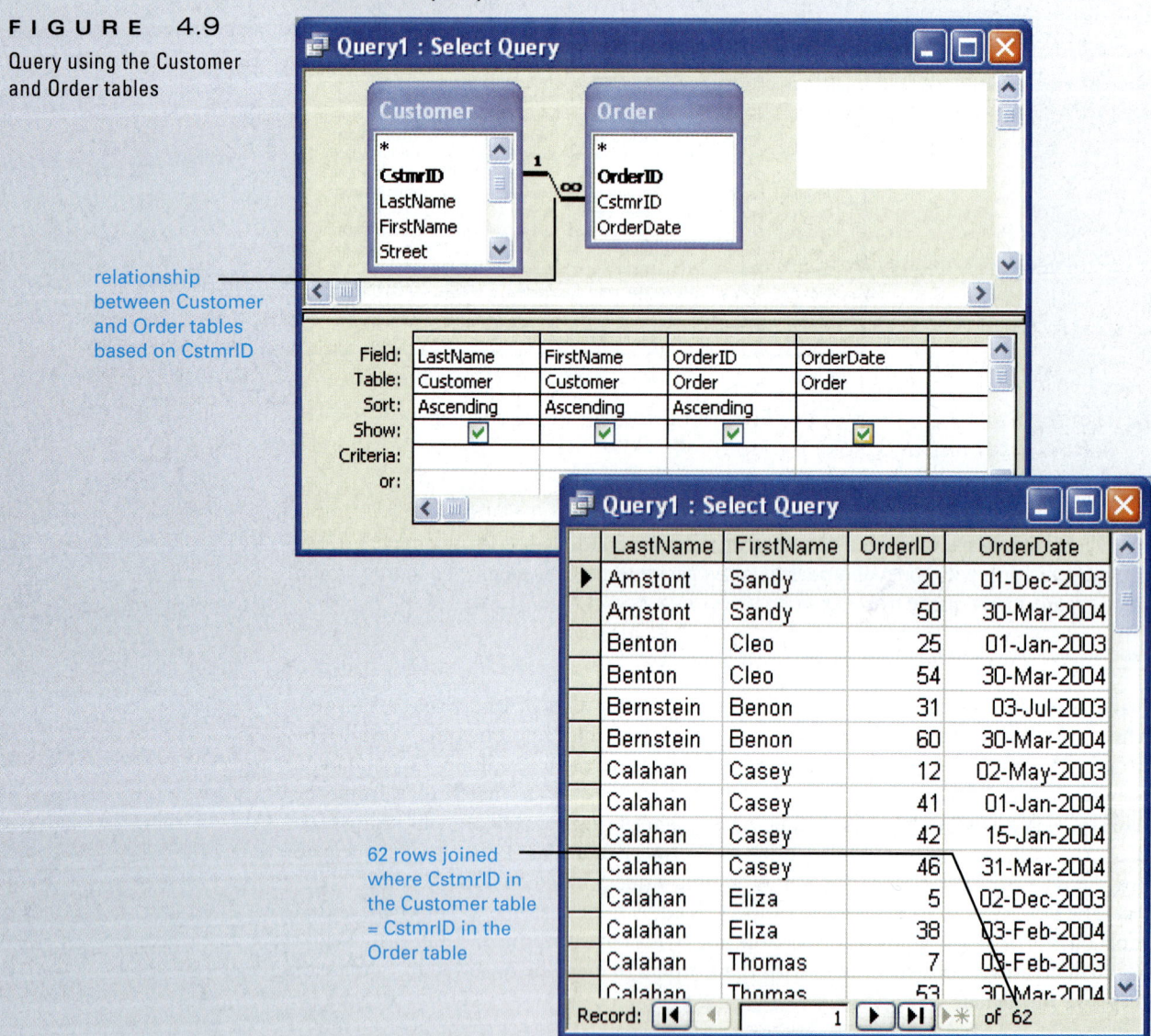

relationship between Customer and Order tables based on CstmrID

62 rows joined where CstmrID in the Customer table = CstmrID in the Order table

8. Close and save the query as **CustomerOrderList**

Missy and Micah would like a list of their products that are in inventory and the customers who have purchased those products. These data are stored in two tables:

Customer and Product. The relationships have already been built, so these data can be retrieved by including all tables in the relationship in the query. If you do not include all of the tables that make up the relationship, the result will be a Cartesian product where each row of the first table is joined with each row of the second table.

Creating a Cartesian product:

1. Verify that the **ac04KoryoKicks.mdb** database is open

2. Select the **Queries** object from the Database Window

3. Double-click the **Create Query in Design View**

4. Double-click the **Customer** table in the Show Table dialog box

5. Double-click the **Product** table in the Show Table dialog box. Notice that no relationship lines show between the Customer and Product tables

6. Close the Show Table dialog box

7. Double-click LastName and FirstName from the Customer table. Double-click ProductClass and ProductDescription from the Product table

8. Run the query and observe the resulting Cartesian product

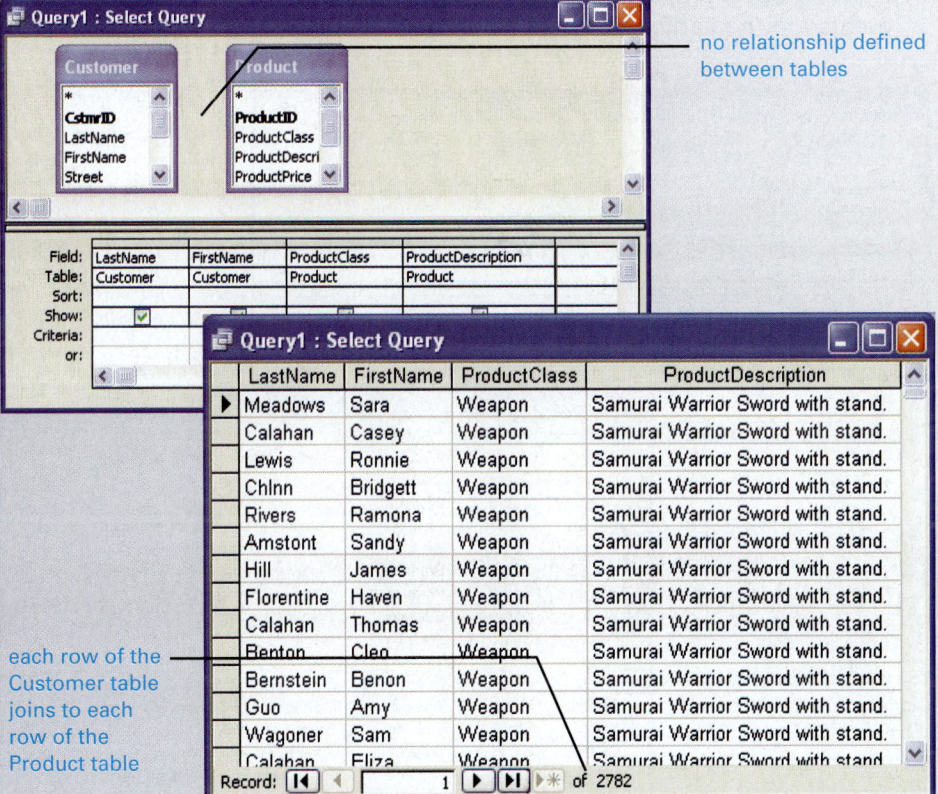

FIGURE 4.10

Tables joined without a defined relationship create a Cartesian product

9. Close the query naming it **CartesianProduct**

The query just viewed created a Cartesian product because the relationships between the tables involved were not defined so every row of the first table was joined with every row of the second table. This is not usually the desired result. Remember that Missy and Micah wanted to know what products each customer ordered. The CartesianProduct query does not provide this information. To produce the desired output, you must include all of the tables that make up the relationship, whether or not any fields from those tables will be displayed. You will repair the query by adding the Order and OrderDetail tables that create the relationship between the Customer and Product tables.

Repairing a Cartesian product:

1. Verify that the **ac04KoryoKicks.mdb** database is open

2. Select the **Queries** object from the Database Window and open CartesianProduct in Design View

3. Click **File** and then **Save As**. Name the query **CustomerProducts**

4. Click the **Show Table** button on the toolbar. Add the **Order** and **OrderDetail** tables to the design grid and then close the Show Table dialog box

5. Use the Product table Title bar to drag it to the right of Order and OrderDetails. Observe the relationships

6. Run the query and note the difference from the Cartesian product created in the earlier steps

FIGURE 4.11

CustomerProducts query

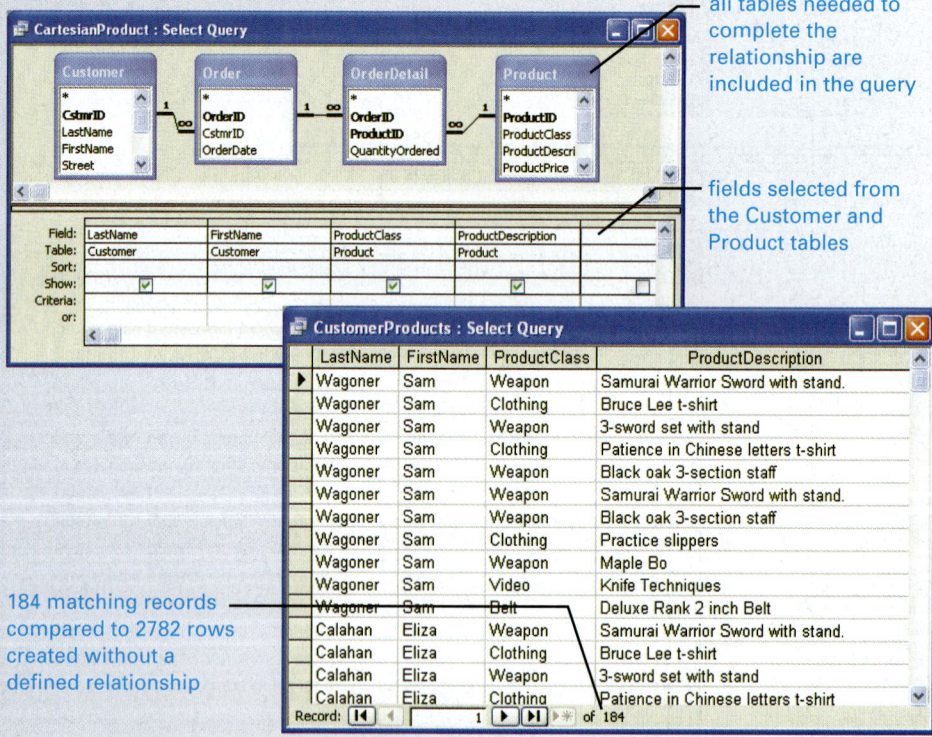

all tables needed to complete the relationship are included in the query

fields selected from the Customer and Product tables

184 matching records compared to 2782 rows created without a defined relationship

7. Close the query, saving your changes

This query will allow the twins to analyze the products that have been purchased by each customer. Any tables from the database can be used to create the desired query output as long as Access has a way to establish a relationship between the tables being used. Be sure to verify relationships and query output before using the results to make business decisions.

Analyzing Data Using Crosstab Queries

Select Queries retrieve specified data and create groups and calculations based on those data. Using this methodology, data can only be grouped vertically to create sums, averages, and other calculations. *Crosstab Queries* are used to calculate and organize data for easier analysis of more complex problems. Crosstab Queries perform calculations such as sum, average, or count and then group them by two types of information—one down the left side of the datasheet and another across the top.

Crosstab Queries can be created using the Crosstab Query Wizard or in Query Design View. Which field will be used as the column heading (across the top of the datasheet) and which field will be used as the row heading (down the left side of the datasheet) must be specified to let Access know how to group the data. The available aggregate functions include Sum, Avg, Count, Min, and Max.

KoryoKicks sells multiple products. Missy and Micah want to know which product sells best in each state. This query will list KoryoKicks products down the left side and states across the top. The Sum function will total each product by state. Since the Crosstab Query Wizard is the easiest way to create a Crosstab Query, you will start there.

---

task reference — Creating a Crosstab Query

- Click the **Queries** object in the Database Window, select **Create query by using wizard**, and then click **New**

- Select **Crosstab Query Wizard** from the New Query dialog box and then click **OK**

- Follow the Wizard's instructions to choose the data source, row heading, column heading, and aggregate functions for the query

- Name the query and then view the results

Analyzing sales with a Crosstab Query:

1. Verify that the ac04KoryoKicks.mdb database is open
2. Select the **Queries** object from the Database Window
3. Double-click the **CustomerStateJoin** query and review the result. Notice that many of the products have multiple rows for each state. The Crosstab Query will sum these into one value for each product and state
4. Close the CustomerStateJoin window
5. Click **New** to open the New Query dialog box
6. In the New Query dialog box, click **Crosstab Query Wizard** and select **OK**
7. Click the **Queries** option button and then select the **CustomerStateJoin** query and click **Next** (see Figure 4.12)
8. Select **ProductDescription** as the row heading and click **Next**
9. Select **State** as the column heading and then click **Next**

FIGURE 4.12

Selecting a query for the crosstab data source

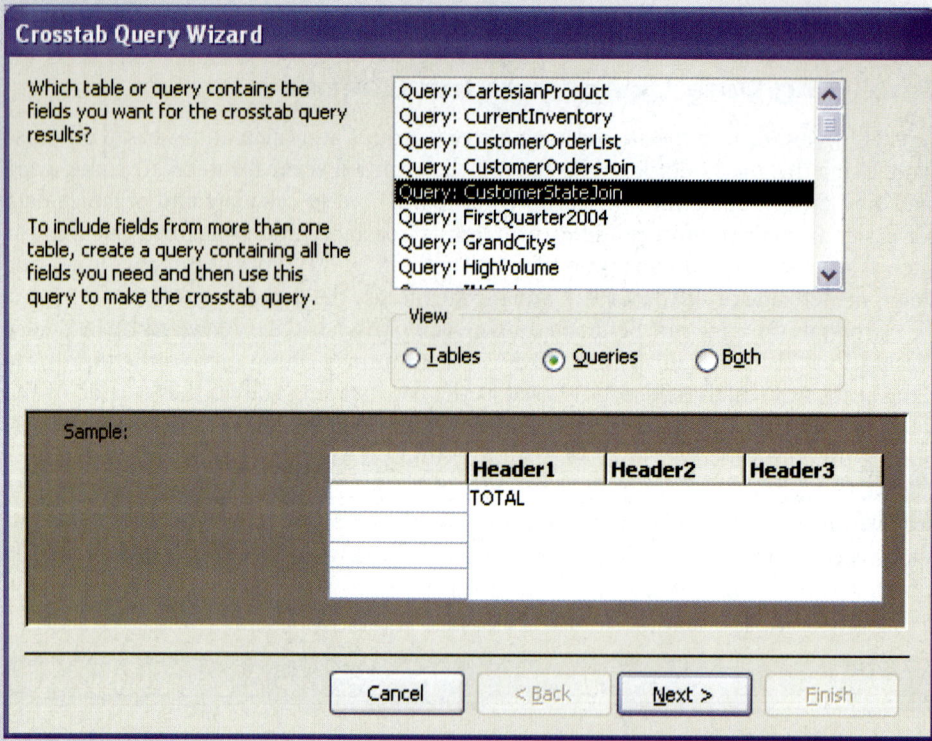

10. Select **QuantityOrdered** as the field and **Sum** as the function and then click **Next**

11. Name the query **ProductByStateCrosstab** and click **Finish**

FIGURE 4.13

Crosstab results

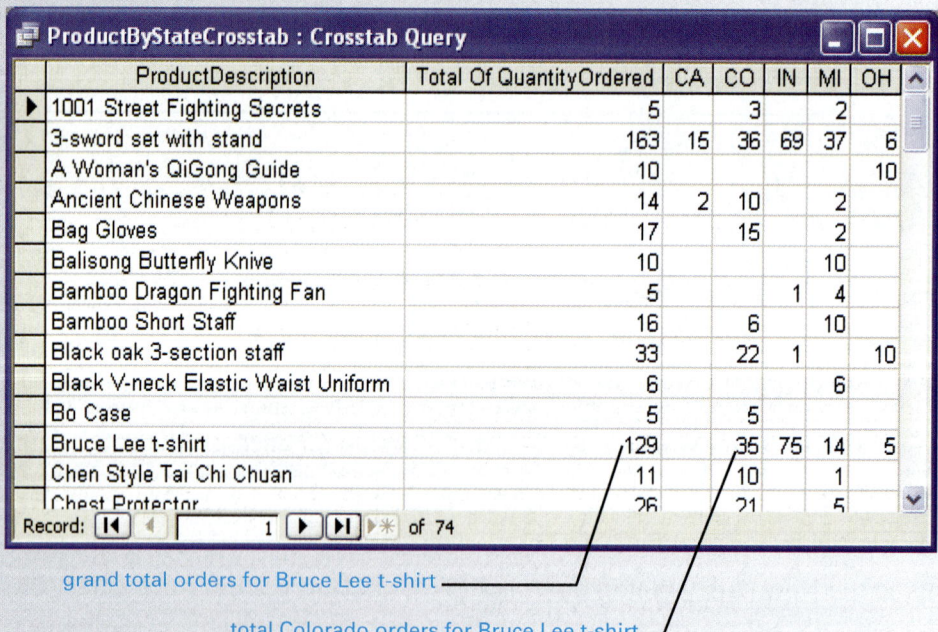

12. Change to Design View (see Figure 4.14) to see the QBE grid for this query

13. Close the query

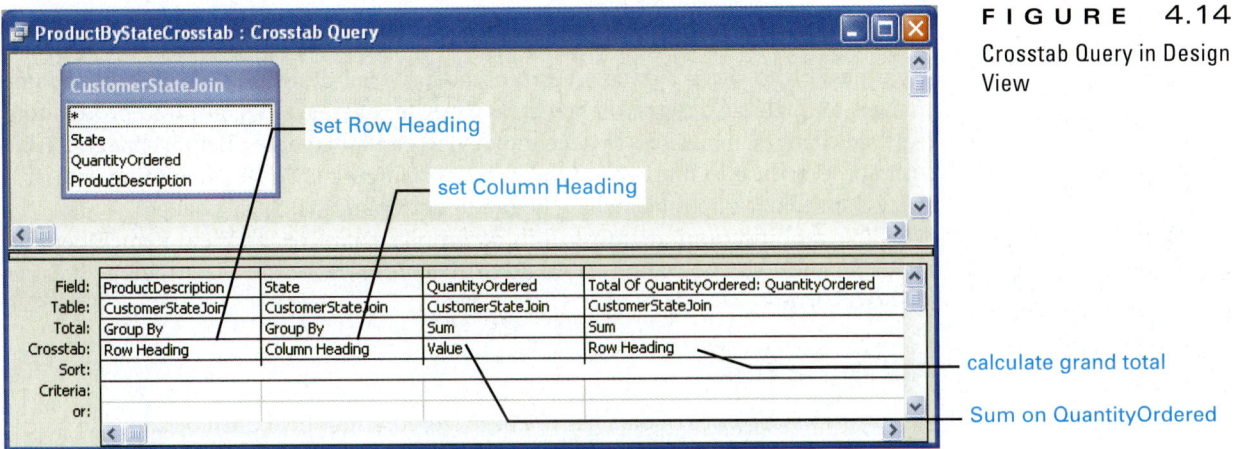

FIGURE 4.14
Crosstab Query in Design View

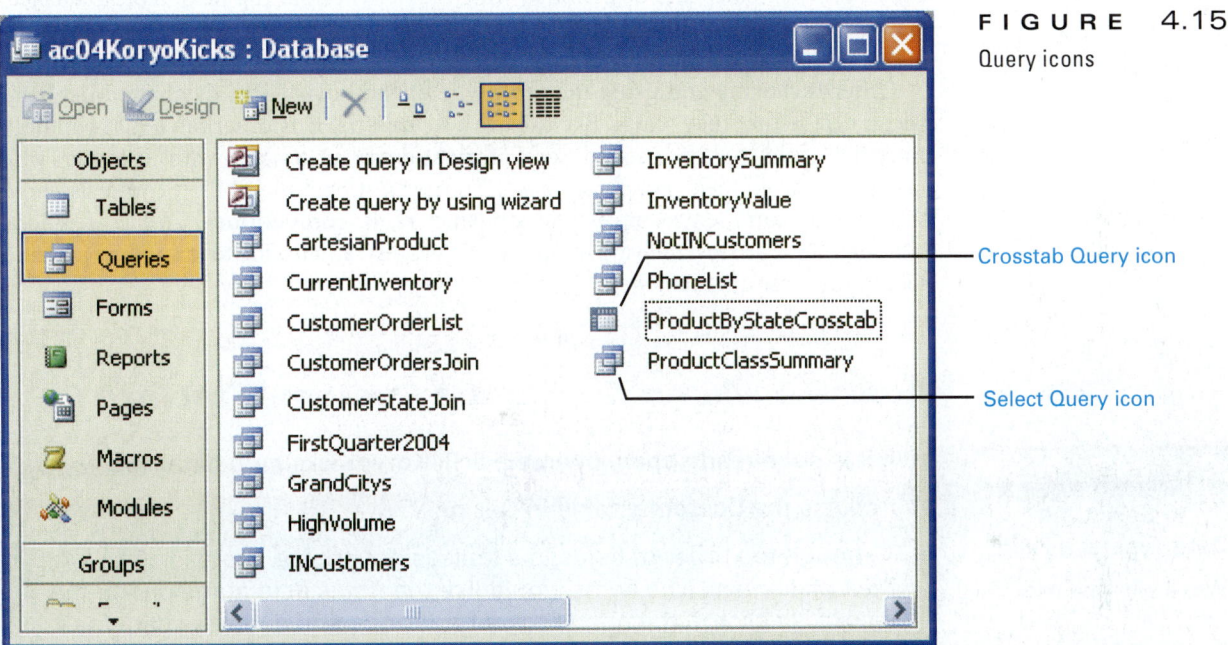

FIGURE 4.15
Query icons

This query will allow the twins to analyze the sales of each of their products by state. Notice that Access uses different icons for each type of query in the Database Window. Figure 4.15 shows Select and Crosstab Query icons.

As you add other types of queries to the database, more icons will display. The icons are representative of the query operation being performed.

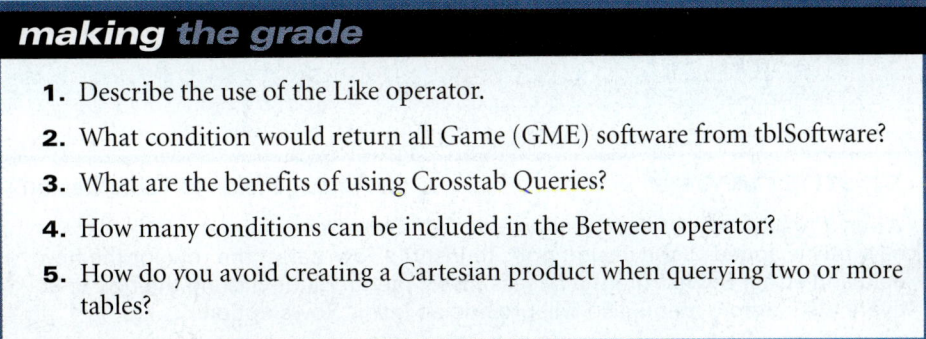

making the grade

1. Describe the use of the Like operator.

2. What condition would return all Game (GME) software from tblSoftware?

3. What are the benefits of using Crosstab Queries?

4. How many conditions can be included in the Between operator?

5. How do you avoid creating a Cartesian product when querying two or more tables?

SESSION 4.1

ACCESS

SESSION 4.2 MODIFYING TABLE DEFINITIONS

Regardless of how well a database prototype has been designed, it is likely that some changes to the table design will be necessary. After databases are put into production, required changes in business and technology necessitate updates. Before changing table design, it is critical to understand the impacts changes may have on existing data. It is always best to back up the database before undertaking structural changes.

Table modifications are most easily accomplished in Design View. Remember that the Undo and Redo operations store up to 20 actions in Design View, making it easier to correct errors.

Adding a Field

When a necessary piece of data has not been stored, a new field must be added to an existing table. Determining which table should hold the new field requires revisiting the design process. Once it is determined which table will hold the field, table Datasheet View can be used to add the new column using steps that are similar to those used when building a new table.

After reviewing and using the prototype of the KoryoKicks database, Missy and Micah decide that they would like to have a field in the Customer table that will hold notes. This field could be used to store information about contacts with customers who have not received their merchandise or who have not paid their bill. It could also hold notes about comments concerning students' rank, competitions, and preferences. Although there are several ways to provide this ability, you decide to try adding a Memo field to the Customer table.

Adding a Memo field to the Customer table:

1. If it is not already open, open the ac04KoryoKicks.mdb database

2. Activate the **Customer** table in Design View

3. Although the order of fields in a table is not critical, there is often logic in their placement. The twins would like the notes field at the end of the record, so click in the empty row after Phone and enter the data for a field named **Notes** with a **Memo** data type

4. No other fields are required for the table to be functional, but we will add a dummy field to be deleted in the next series of steps

5. Click on the **Notes** field that you just added, then select the **Rows** option of the **Insert** menu to add a new field between Phone and Notes

6. Type **Dummy** as the Field Name and leave the default Text data type

7. Click the **Datasheet View** [icon] button on the Access toolbar to view the results (see Figure 4.16). You will be prompted to save your changes. Answer **Yes**

---

*another***way**

. . . to Select the Data Type of a Field

When working with table designs, it can be time consuming to move from typing to selecting with the mouse. Access allows you to keep your hands on the keyboard. For example, when entering a new table field, type the Field Name and then press Tab to move to the data type. Type the first character of the data type (m for memo, n for number, and so on). Access will complete the entry and you can Tab to the next field

---

*another***word**   **. . . on Adding Fields to Table Design**

When it makes sense to add a new table field between existing table fields, a new row is added to the design grid. To insert a row, select the row for the new field and select **Rows** from the Access **Insert** menu. Right-clicking the row to activate the shortcut menu also will provide an Insert Rows option

Notes and Dummy fields added to Customer table

	CstmrID	LastName	FirstName	Street	City	State	ZipCode	Phone	Dummy	Notes
+	01	Wagoner	Sam	5480 Alpine Lane	Sterling	CO	88661	(303) 161-5545		
+	02	Calahan	Eliza	2140 Edgewood Road	Grand Lake	CO	80446	(303) 886-6003		
+	03	Lake	James	701 East Street	Grandby	MI	49571	(616) 562-4499		
+	04	Meadows	Sara	Pond Hill Road	Monroe	IN	46161	(313) 792-3646		
+	07	Calahan	Casey	82 Mix Rd. West	Bootjack	CO	89945	(303) 643-8321		
+	21	Smith	Alto	114 Lexington Ave.	Granby	CO	49302	(303) 838-7111		
+	22	Lewis	Ronnie	8408 E. Fletcher Road	Clare	MI	48617	(517) 936-8651		
+	23	Chinn	Bridgett	400 Salmon Street	Ada	MI	49301	(616) 838-9827		
+	25	Katz	Ben	56 Foursone Road	Detroit	MI	49505	(616) 315-7294		
+	27	Gray	Monica	3915 Hawthorne Lane	Richmond	OH	43603	(419) 332-3681		
+	28	Rivers	Ramona	37 Queue Highway	Lacota	MI	49063	(313) 329-5364		
+	29	Amstont	Sandy	95 Bay Boulevard	Jenison	CO	80428	(616) 131-9148		
+	31	Hill	James	5365 Bedford Trail	Eagle Point	CO	80031	(906) 395-2041		
+	33	Florentine	Haven	874 Western Avenue	Drenthe	CA	49464	(616) 131-3260		
+	35	Calahan	Thomas	840 Cascade Road	Coatesville	IN	80464	(316) 343-4635		
+	36	Benton	Cleo	4090 Division St.	Borculo	OH	49464	(616) 838-2046		
+	43	Pointe	Bryson	11 Marsh Rd	Shelbyville	IN	46344	(616) 379-5681		

Record: 1 of 26

It is essential to make design changes like adding a field as early in the life of a table as possible. When an empty field is added, it can be overwhelming to gather and enter the new data for the existing records.

Deleting a Field

Deleting a field from a table is as simple as deleting a record from a table, but the repercussions are much more involved. Deleting a field in a database that already contains data deletes all of the values held in the field. Delete operations can be undone as long as Design View is active but become permanent after changing views.

Deleting a field from the Customer table:

1. If it is not already open, open the ac04KoryoKicks.mdb database

2. Activate the **Customer** table in Design View

3. Select the **Dummy** field using the record selector

4. Press the **Delete** key on your keyboard and answer **Yes** to the prompt

5. Use the **Undo** ↺ ▾ button to undo the delete

6. Use the **Redo** ↻ ▾ button to delete the Dummy field again

7. Change to Datasheet View to review the results. Save the table design changes when prompted

The delete operation on the Dummy field is permanent because you changed views. As a precaution against destroying valuable data, it is strongly recommended that you back up tables in production databases before deleting fields from the table design.

Moving a Field

The order of fields in a table is not important to its overall functionality, so they can move without impacting data functionality. The field order set by the table definition is the default column order that displays when viewing data. Typically, the leftmost field(s) represents the table's primary key and other fields are in order by how they are used.

Moving a field in the Customer table:

1. If it is not already open, open the ac04KoryoKicks.mdb database

2. Activate the **Customer** table in Design View

3. Select the **Notes** field by clicking its record indicator

4. Click and drag to move the Notes field between CustomerID and LastName

tip: *During the drag process, a line across the record indicator and data grid represents where the field will be dropped. If you missed on the first drag attempt, repeat steps 3 and 4 until Notes is positioned properly*

5. Change to **Datasheet View** to review the results. Save the table design changes when prompted

6. Change back to **Design View** and restore Notes to its original position of the last field in the table

7. Close the Customer table, saving your changes

All database objects allow you to control the order of the fields displayed, thereby overriding the field order of the table design.

Changing Field Attributes

Of all the table design updates, changing field properties is the most likely to destroy needed data and/or invalidate other database objects. Changing the Field Name can produce invalid results in objects that refer to fields by name, including Queries, Forms, Reports, and Modules. Making a field smaller will truncate existing data if they exceed the new size. Altering the data type causes Access to perform a conversion from the original type to the new type that can result in loss of data. A message will display when Access detects conversion errors so the user can choose to cancel or continue the process. Access does not detect all conversion errors. Making fields larger or changing other field attributes has little impact on the validity of the database.

help yourself: *Use the Type a Question combo box to improve your under-standing of how to update a field's data type by typing* **change field type**. *Review the contents of About changing a field's data type. Close the Help window when you are finished*

Changing field properties in the Product table:

1. If it is not already open, open the ac04KoryoKicks.mdb database

2. Activate the **Product** table in Design View

3. Select the **ProductDescription** field. When entering the Products data, the twins discovered that the ProductDescription field was not long enough for a full product description. They would like it expanded to 50 characters

4. Change the Field Size from 40 to **50**

5. Click the **Save** 🖫 button on the Access toolbar to save your work

After making changes to table field attributes that might impact the validity of data held in the tables, it is recommended that the table be thoroughly tested and its data validated before placing it in production.

Building Lookup Fields

A *Lookup field* is a tool to ease data entry. Rather than requiring users to remember important values that identify customers, orders, or vendors, a Lookup field displays the list of possible values. Missy and Micah are having difficulty entering product vendors because they don't remember the VendorCode. They have asked for a Lookup field that will access valid VendorCodes in the Vendor table and reduce errors. The Lookup field will allow them to select from a list of vendors rather than type a VendorCode.

---

task reference   Creating a Lookup Field

- Remove any existing table relationships based on the Lookup fields. The most likely relationship is one-to-many where the child (many sides of the relationship) table will look up the key value of the parent table (one side of the relationship)

- Open the child table and change the Data Type of the foreign key field to Lookup Wizard

- Follow the Lookup Wizard instructions

Setting a Lookup field for vendors in the Product table:

1. If it is not already open, open the **ac04KoryoKicks.mdb** database

2. Activate the **Product** table in Design View

tip: *Lookup fields must be built between tables that do not already have a defined relationship. There is no defined relationship between the Product and Vendor tables*

3. Select the Data Type of VendorCode and change it to **Lookup Wizard**

4. The Lookup Wizard will prompt you through the rest of the process (see Figure 4.17). In the first Lookup Wizard screen, select **I want the lookup column to look up the values in a table or query** and then click **Next**

5. In the second Wizard screen choose the **Vendor** table as the source of your Lookup data and click **Next**

6. In the third Wizard screen select the **VendorCode** and **Name** fields using the field selector button (>) as shown in Figure 4.18. VendorCode must be selected because it is the shared column between the tables identifying the foreign key. Name is the identifying field that the twins can use to lookup the VendorCode. Click **Next**

7. The next Wizard screen allows you to sort by up to three fields. Sort by **Name** and click **Next**

8. In the next Wizard screen, verify that **Hide key column** is checked so that VendorCode does not display. Double-click on the right border of the Name field selector and adjust the column width to match the width of the data and click **Next**

FIGURE 4.17

Lookup Wizard opening screen

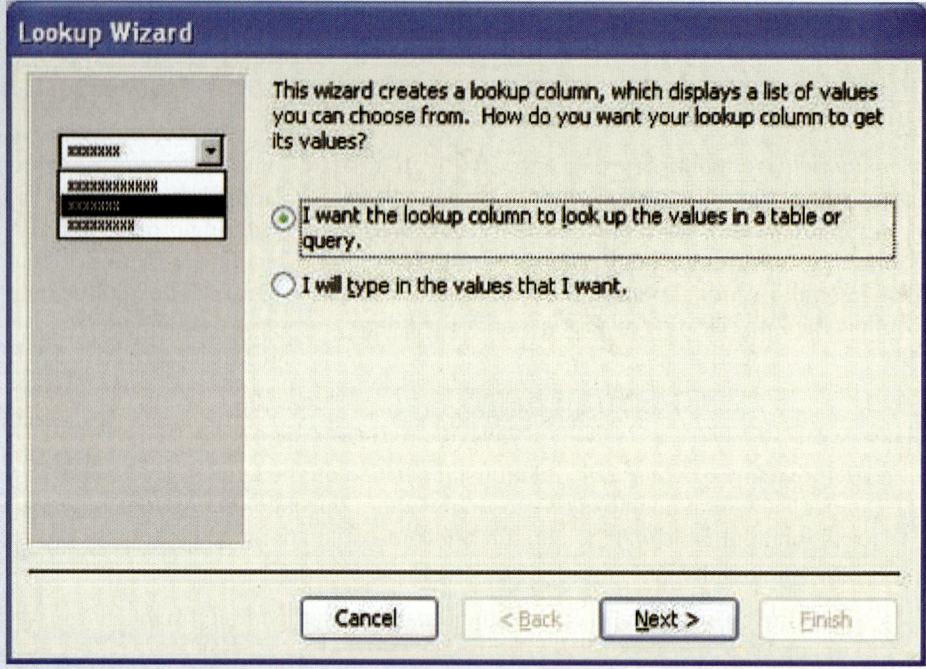

FIGURE 4.18

The third Lookup Wizard screen

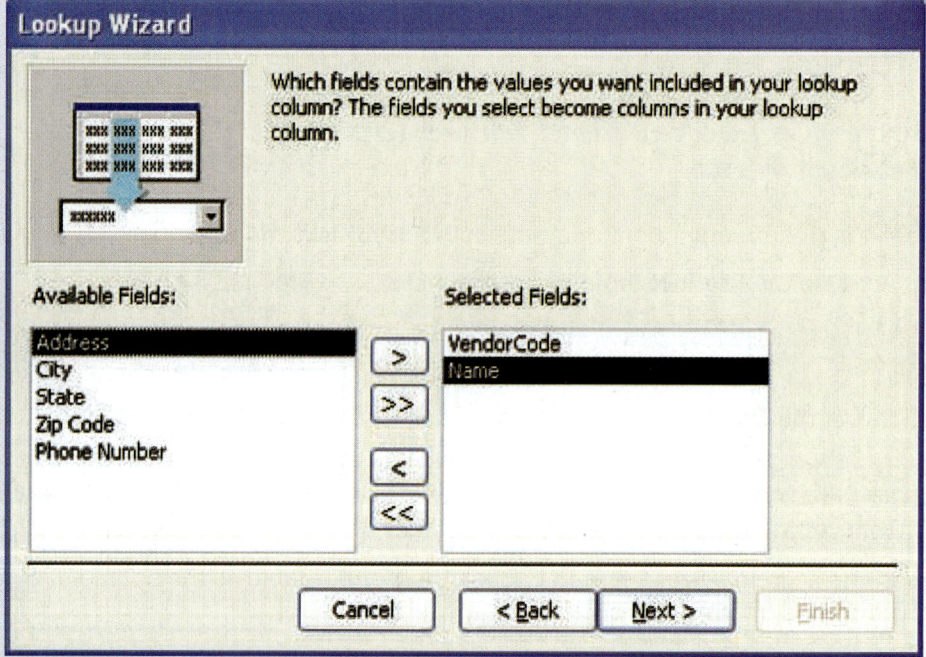

9. The final Wizard screen asks you to name the Lookup column. The default, VendorCode, is fine, so just click **Finish**. You will be prompted to save the table changes; choose **Yes**

10. Change to Datasheet View. The VendorCode field will now display the vendor's name, but store VendorCode (see Figure 4.19). When you enter a new record, a list of valid vendor names will be presented

11. Change the Vendor for product 9 to **Topview Martial Arts Supplies** using the Lookup field

12. Close the Product table

FIGURE 4.19

The Product table with VendorCode Lookup field

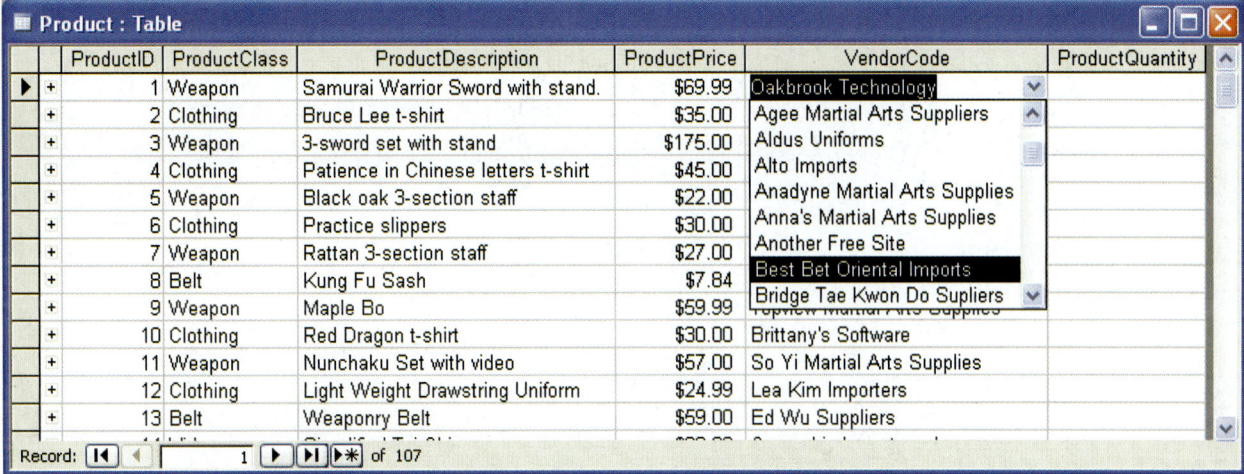

With the Lookup field set, each new product added to the Product table will automatically list the valid vendors from the Vendor table. You can also create Lookup lists that contain a fixed set of values. Lookup lists should only be used when the values are limited and don't change. For example, a Lookup list of salutations (Mr., Mrs., Ms.) would be appropriate.

Creating Input Masks

Field templates or *input masks* improve data entry for Text, Date, Number, and Currency field types. The input mask provides a pattern of input for the user to follow. For example, a 10-character Text field to store phone numbers would allow the user to enter any character from the keyboard and would not force the user to enter all 10 characters. Applying an Input Mask property would present the user with a template like (_____)_____-_____ and require that all 10 digits of the phone number be entered.

A string of characters is entered into the Input Mask property to tell Access what to display to the user as a template and what to accept as valid input. The syntax used to enter the mask is outlined in Figure 4.20. Literal values in the string, like the ( ) in the phone number example, are entered where you want them to appear. To use one of the mask characters like the # sign, precede it with a backslash (\#).

---

task reference   Creating an Input Mask

- Open a table in Design View

- Select the field for which you want to define an input mask

- From the General tab select the **Input Mask** property and either

- Click the **Build** 🪄 button and follow the Input Mask Wizard instructions (Text and Date fields only)

  or

- Type the input mask definition (Numeric and Currency masks must be entered manually)

FIGURE 4.20

Input mask definition characters

Character	Description
0	Required digit (0–9); no plus (+) or minus (−) sign
9	Optional digit; no plus (+) or minus (−) sign
#	Optional digit; plus (+) or minus (−) sign allowed
L	Required letter (A–Z)
?	Optional letter (A–Z)
A	Required letter or digit
a	Optional letter or digit
&	Required character or space
C	Optional character or space
.,:;-/	Placeholders and separators
<	Causes all characters that follow to be converted to lowercase
>	Causes all characters that follow to be converted to uppercase
!	Causes input mask to display from right to left
\	Used to display any of the characters in this table as a literal
Password	Creates a password entry text box with all entries displayed as *

Setting an input mask for the OrderDate field:

1. If it is not already open, open the ac04KoryoKicks.mdb database

2. Open the **Order** table in Design View

3. Click in the **OrderDate** field

4. In the General tab click the **Input Mask** text box and evaluate the existing input mask. Click the ellipsis to initiate the Input Mask Wizard (see Figure 4.21)

5. Select the **Medium Date** format and click **Next**

6. Review the input mask created and the placeholder characters. Without updating them, click **Next,** and then click **Finish**

7. Switch to Datasheet View, saving your changes (see Figure 4.22)

8. Enter a new record for Ronnie Lewis using today's date (i.e., 28-May-04). Notice that the template displayed by the input mask is replaced by the Format display when entry is complete

9. Try entering a day of 41 in Sheila Monarch's record. You will receive an error

10. Close the Order table

F I G U R E　4.21

Input Mask Wizard

F I G U R E　4.22

Input Mask created by the Wizard

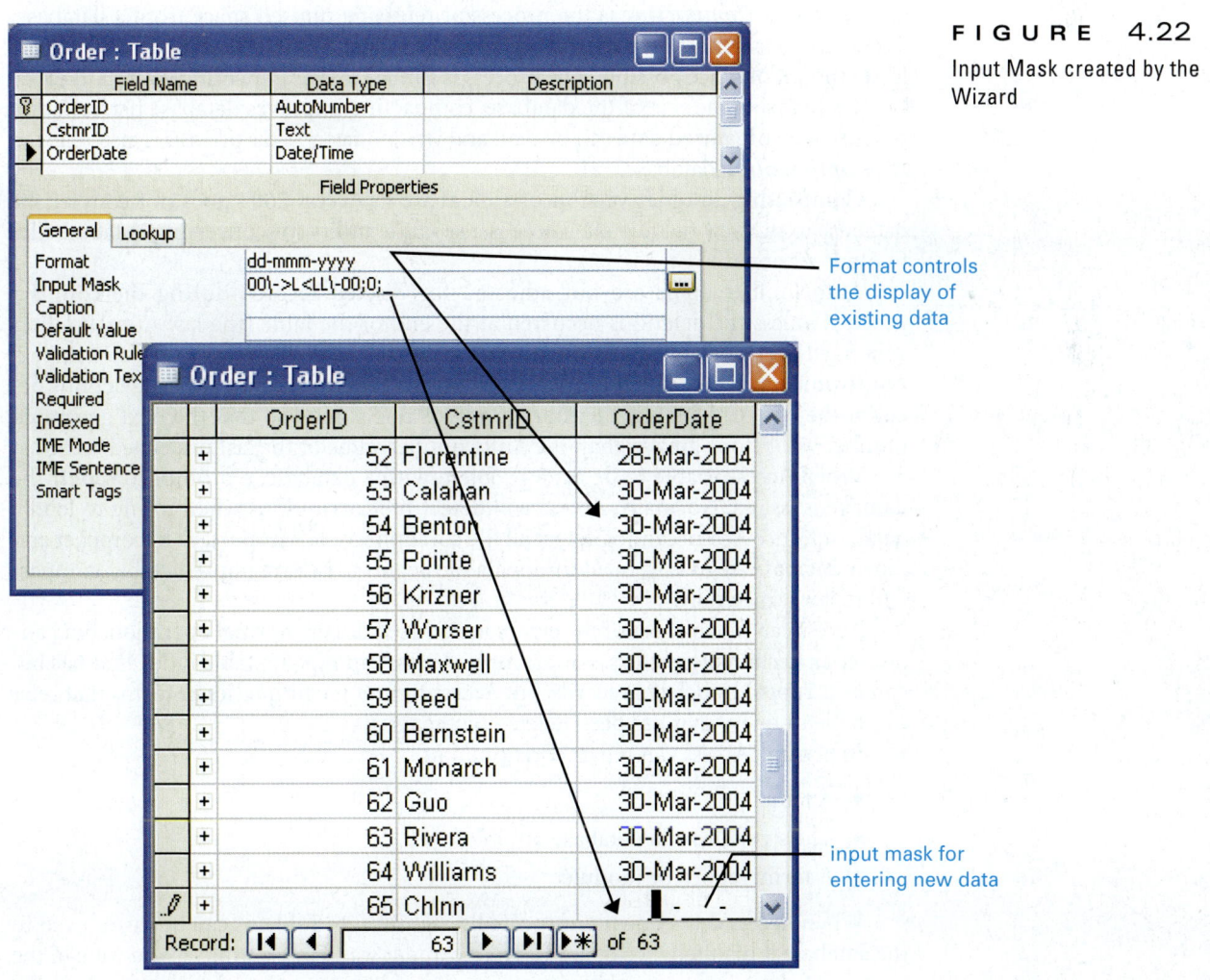

Format controls the display of existing data

input mask for entering new data

---

anotherword   . . . on Input Masks and Formats

At first glance, input masks and formats are similar field properties, but really
serve different purposes. A Format property controls how the data display to the
user, but does not control how they are entered or stored. To control how data
are entered, use an input mask. An input mask ensures that the data match the
format and values you define. When both properties are defined for a field,
Microsoft Access uses the input mask when you are adding or editing data and
the format when data are displayed. It is important that the results of these settings don't conflict

---

The Input Mask Wizard supplies a list of standard input masks such as the
Medium Date mask demonstrated in the steps. These masks provide a template for data
entry and perform simple data validation tasks like testing for the entry of a valid
month. When these masks are not sufficient, a custom mask is built using the definition
characters outlined in Figure 4.20.

Compacting and Repairing a Database

As an Access database is used, it becomes larger. Each data item and database object
added increases the file size. Deleting data records and database objects does not release
the space that was occupied by that object.

Access combines the processes of compacting and repairing a database into a single operation. *Compacting* is the process of releasing unused space from a database.
Access compacts the database by reorganizing all database objects so that they take the
least amount of space possible. The process is similar to defragmenting your hard drive.
Besides reducing the size of the database, compacting improves database performance
because well-organized data can be read and written faster. This process is also referred
to as *optimizing* a database.

Compacting an older version of a database in Access 2003 does not convert the
database to the new file format. There is a separate utility for converting database files
to other versions.

AutoNumber fields are not adjusted for deleted records during the compact
process, unless the deletions occurred at the end of the table (the last AutoNumbers
generated). So deletion of any record that is not the last table record does not impact
AutoNumbers. Such deleted numbers will not be generated again. When deletions occur at the end of the table, the AutoNumber value is reset so that the next generated
number will be one greater than the AutoNumber value of the last undeleted record.

When Access is able to detect a problem with a database, a prompt to *repair* the
damage is issued. Normally, Access will detect file corruptions when trying to load a
database. Since Access cannot detect all file corruptions, it is important to compact and
repair databases regularly. In addition, if a file begins to behave unpredictably, compact
and repair it manually.

Access can repair most of the errors introduced during normal operation, but cannot repair certain user errors. For example, Access can repair a table index that has become corrupted by deleted records, but Access cannot repair queries or forms that refer
to a table or query that has been deleted by the user.

In general, Access can repair corruption in

- A table
- The structure of a database or table
- A form, report, or module

When Access shuts down unexpectedly, significant problems can be introduced to
the database if maintenance operations were under way. For example, if you were in the
process of changing a record but Access was unable to complete the process, the table

or tables involved become corrupted. To remedy this situation, when Access restarts, it creates a copy of the file that was open when the shutdown occurred. The copy is named filename_Backup.mdb, where filename is the name of the database file that was open during the crash. Access then attempts to compact and repair the original file.

---

task reference   **Compact and Repair the Open Database**

- If the open database begins to behave erratically, on the **Tools** menu, point to **Database Utilities**, and then click **Compact and Repair Database**

Compacting and repairing the KoryoKicks database:

1. Verify that the ac04KoryoKicks.mdb database is open

2. On the **Tools** menu, point to **Database Utilities**, and then click **Compact and Repair Database**

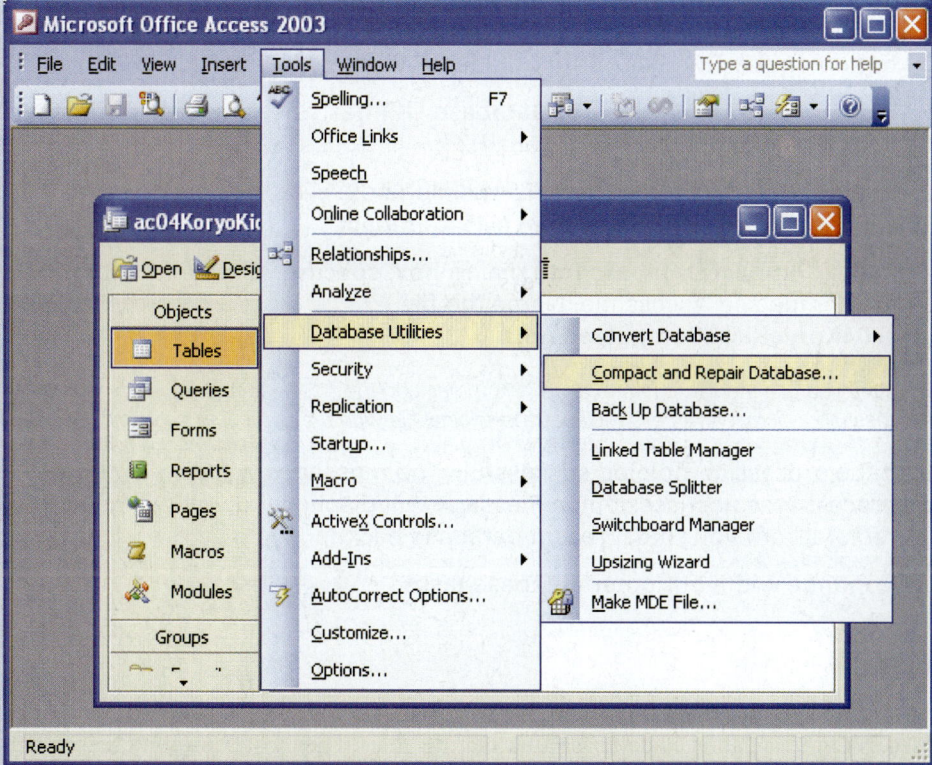

FIGURE 4.23

Manually compact and repair the open database

3. If the process completed successfully, no messages will display. If the process was unsuccessful, a message will display and you will need to restore from your most recent database backup

4. Close ac04KoryoKicks.mdb

Compact and repair can also be used on a database that is not open. This method has the advantage of allowing the compacted database to be stored in another file, maintaining both the original and the compacted file.

task reference	Compact and Repair an Unopened Database

- Access must be running with no open database
- On the **Tools** menu, point to **Database Utilities**, and then click **Compact and Repair Database**
- In the **Database to Compact From** dialog box, specify the Access file you want to compact, and then click **Compact**
- In the **Compact Database Into** dialog box, specify a name, drive, and folder for the compacted Access file
- Click **Save**

Compacting and repairing the unopened KoryoKicks database:

1. Verify that Access is running with no open databases. If the ac04KoryoKicks.mdb or another database is still open, click the Close button on the Title bar of the Database Window to close it

2. On the **Tools** menu, point to **Database Utilities**, and then click **Compact and Repair Database** (see Figure 4.24)

3. In the **Database to Compact From** dialog box, click on **ac04KoryoKicks.mdb**, and then click **Compact**

4. In the **Compact Database Into** dialog box, specify a drive and folder for the compacted Access file. Name the file **ac04KoryoKicksCompacted.mdb**

tip: *If you use the same name, drive, and folder, and the Access database is compacted successfully, Microsoft Access replaces the original file with the compacted version*

5. If the process completed successfully, no messages will display. If the process was unsuccessful, a message will display and you will need to restore from your most recent database backup

6. Continue with your other database tasks

Compacting into another file is one way to create copies of a database that can be used to restore a damaged database after maintenance. The most common use is to create a current snapshot of the database just before performing tasks that could result in invalid data. For example, a query to adjust the pay rate of all employees could destroy the entire contents of the table if it contained an error. Creating a snapshot just before running the query will allow you to return to the prequery condition without much effort.

You also can create backups of individual database objects such as a table, query, or form by creating a blank database and then importing the backup objects from the original database. If only one table of the database could be damaged by the planned maintenance, this method would allow only that table to be backed up and restored. Restoring the damaged table is as simple as importing the backup copy.

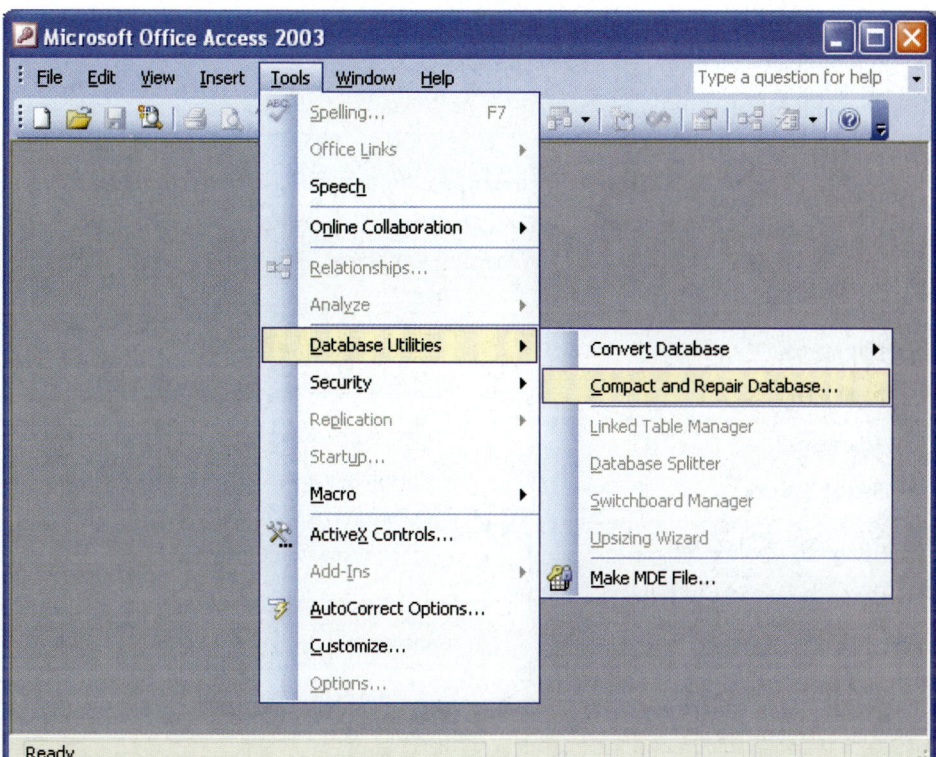

Compact and repair an unopened database

Compacting a Database Automatically

Since corrupted databases can lead to loss of data, queries, forms, and reports, it is important to compact and repair Access files regularly. Several generations of backup also should be maintained so that an unrepairable database can be restored to an earlier version. The most common user errors that cause database corruption are turning off the computer without closing Access or removing the disk (usually the A: or other removable disk) that Access is using before closing Access. Obviously avoiding these mistakes reduces the likelihood of database corruption.

Access automatically checks a file when it is being opened and will repair it if needed. You will not be prompted to compact the database if it is not performing optimally. Access also can be set to compact and repair the open Access file each time it is closed.

---

task reference   Setting Automatic Compact and Repair

- Open the Access database that you want to compact automatically
- On the **Tools** menu, click **Options**
- Click the **General** tab
- Select the **Compact on Close** check box

Setting the Automatic Compact and Repair option for KoryoKicks:

1. Open the ac04KoryoKicks.mdb database so that its Compact on Close property can be set

2. On the **Tools** menu, click **Options**

3. Click the **General** tab

FIGURE 4.25

Automatically compact and repair databases

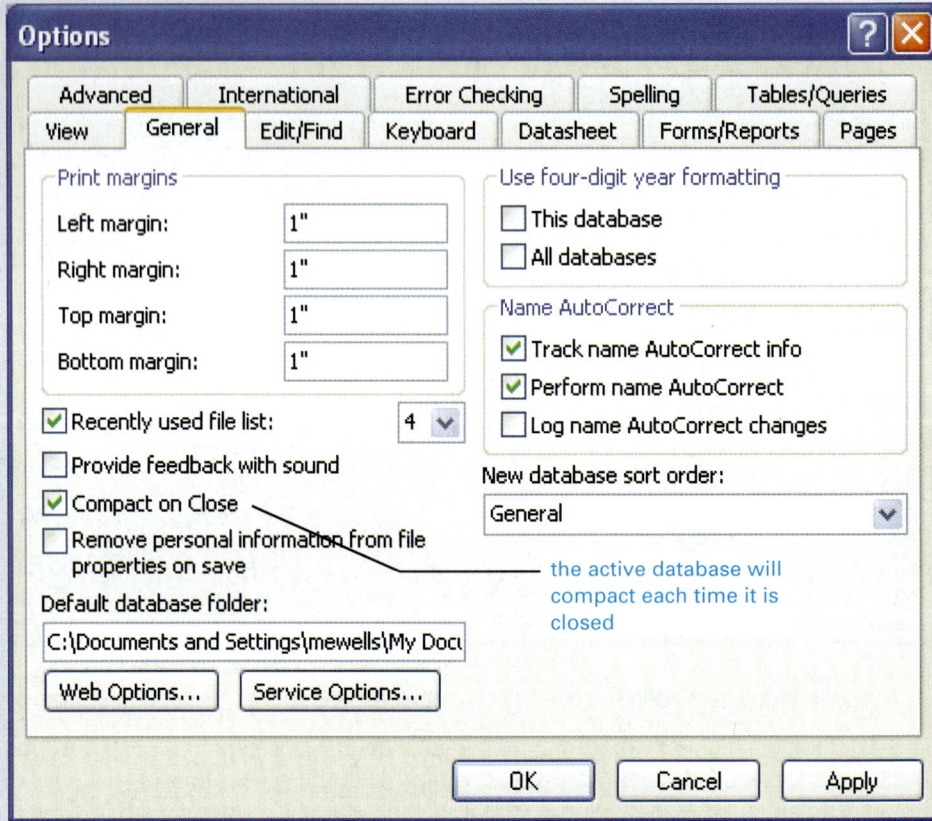

4. Click the **Compact on Close** option and click **OK**

5. ac04KoryoKicks.mdb will now compact and repair each time it is closed

tip: *You can stop the compact and repair process by pressing Ctrl+ Break or Esc*

It is important to note that ***Compact on Close*** is a property of the database, not a property of Access. As such it must be set for each database for which you want to automate this process.

Automatically Repairing Office Programs

The same problems that can cause databases to corrupt also can damage Microsoft Office programs. All Office products later than 2000 offer a ***Detect and Repair*** facility that will notify the user when this happens and reinstall the affected software.

task *reference*	Setting Detect and Repair for Microsoft Office

- On the **Help** menu, click **Detect and Repair**
- To restore the program shortcuts to the Windows **Start** menu, make sure the **Restore my shortcuts while repairing** check box is selected (see Figure 4.26)
- Click **Start**

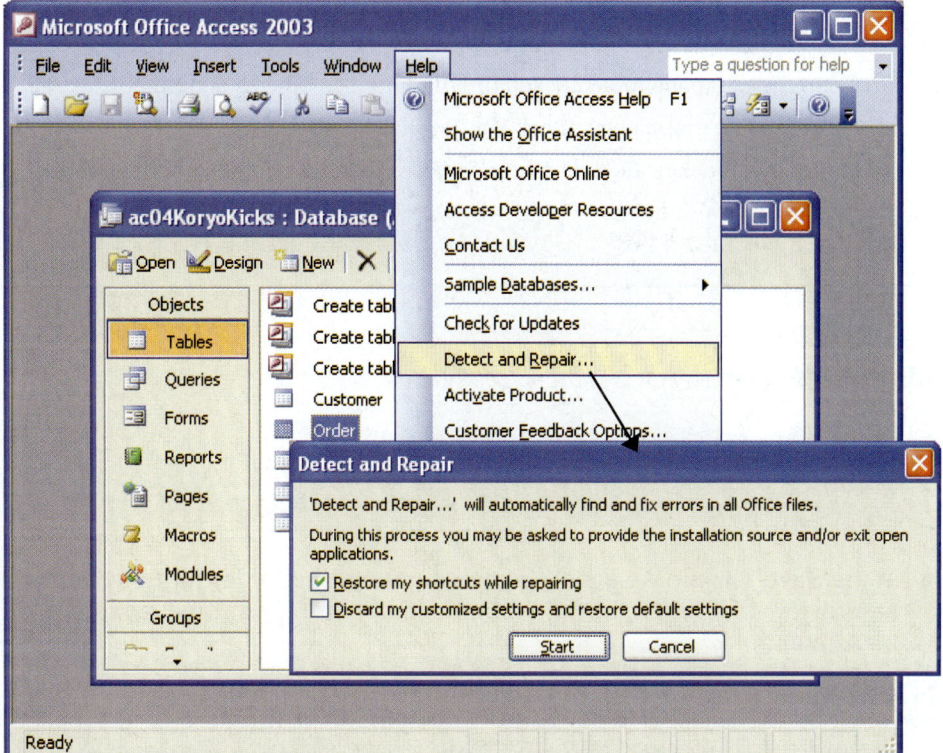

FIGURE 4.26
Microsoft Office Detect and Repair

This procedure detects and repairs problems such as missing files and registry settings associated with all installed Microsoft Office programs. It will not repair personal files such as spreadsheets or documents. If the Detect and Repair command does not fix the problem, you might need to reinstall Microsoft Office.

Backing Up and Restoring a Database

Database backups are critical in organizations that rely on data for their operation. Besides creating backups before performing tasks that could destroy data, it is important to have regularly scheduled backups to protect against other types of loss.

Remember that data are valuable and should be protected against unforeseen events. The volume of updates to data determines how often database backups are needed. Any changes made to the database since the last backup will need to be reapplied to make it current. The question you need to ask yourself is "How much maintenance am I willing to repeat?" Weekly backups are the most common, but daily backups are not at all unusual for critical data with a high maintenance volume.

It is important to note that documentation also must be maintained for backups to be effective. You must know what updates have been made to your database since the last backup so that these can be reapplied.

Catastrophes such as floods, fires, and other acts of nature are not frequent but also should be considered when creating a backup plan. The simplest way to protect against such devastating problems is to store backups at an offsite location. This can be as simple as taking a copy of the backup home or sending it to another company site.

Backups of individual database objects can be accomplished using Copy and Paste to create a duplicate object in the database. Manual backups of the entire open database can be completed using the Back Up Database option of the File menu.

task reference	Database Backup with Access

- Open the database to be backed up. All database objects should be closed
- From the **File** menu select **Back Up Database**
- In the Save Backup As dialog box, indicate the drive, folder, and filename for the backup
- Click **Save**

Using Access to back up KoryoKicks:

1. Verify that ac04KoryoKicks.mdb is open

2. Close and save any open objects

3. On the **File** menu, click **Back Up Database**

4. In the Save Backup As dialog box, navigate to the folder for this chapter and review the default backup name (a combination of the filename and backup date)

FIGURE 4.27

Microsoft Access Save Backup As dialog box

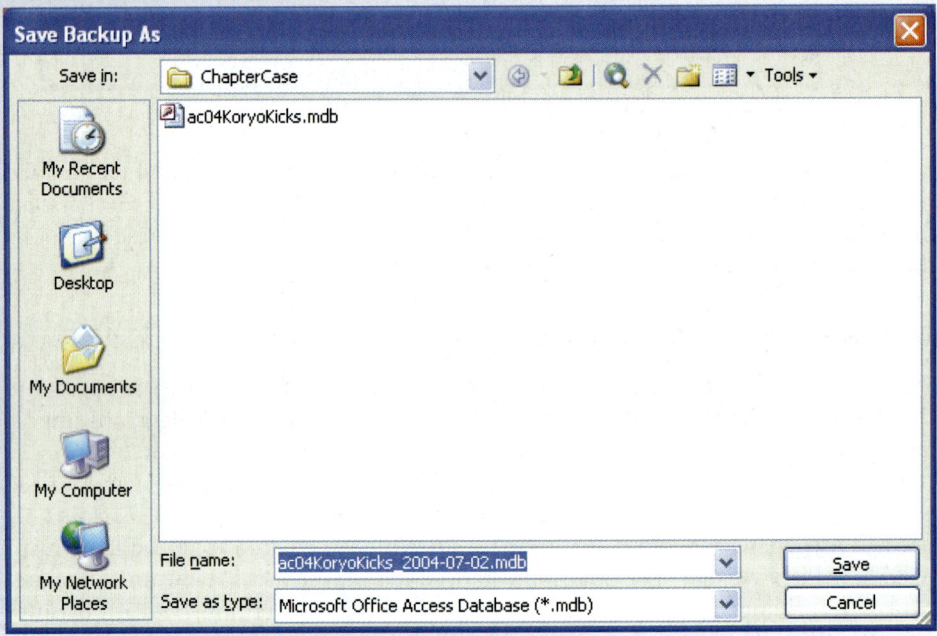

5. Click **Save**

To restore individual database objects from an Access backup, import them into the active database using the File menu. To restore the entire database, use Windows Explorer to delete the active database and then copy the backup to the active folder and rename it.

The demonstrated backup method requires the user to control the backup schedule, name, and process. For critical databases, it is advisable to use software tools such as Microsoft Windows XP Professional Backup and Recovery Tools. Such tools are designed to complete backups of multiple files on a scheduled basis, are optimized for restoring all or part of a particular backup, and can back up to multiple disks, CDs, and/or networked drives.

Converting Databases

Access cannot update database designs created in earlier versions of the product. When a database that was created in an earlier version of Access is opened, a notice that the database must be converted before making changes is issued (see Figure 4.28). The Enable the database option will open the database without converting it. Enabled databases allow users to view and change data and run existing forms, queries, and reports but not change the design of database objects. Since the database format has not been converted, the database will still function in the earlier version of Access.

If the database will be used only in the current version of Access, better database performance is achieved by converting it. If, however, there is still a need to use the database in an older version of Access, enable it in the current version by opening it without converting it. In this case, modifications to the design of database objects must be made in the original Access version. Once the database is open, it can still be converted using the Tools menu, as demonstrated in Figure 4.29.

Sometimes different parts of the same organization are using different Access versions, resulting in a need for multiple versions of the same database. Files created in the current version of Access can be converted to the file format of previous Access versions back to Access 97. Bear in mind that converting to a previous Access version will cause the database to lose all of the functionality that is specific to newer versions of Access.

FIGURE   4.28

Conversion notification

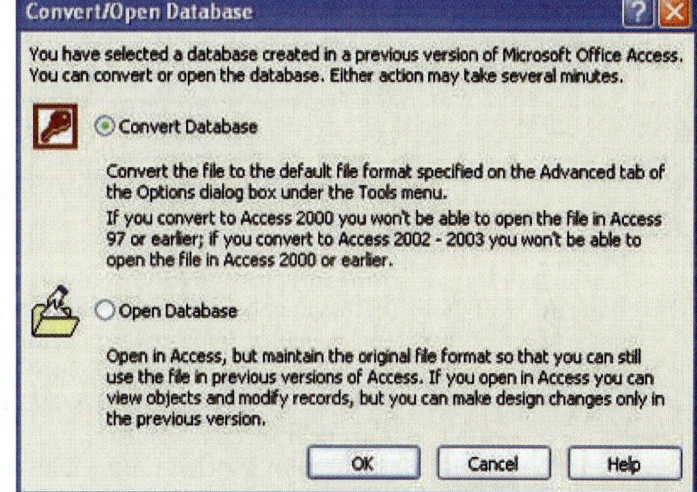

FIGURE   4.29

Converting an open database to an older or newer Access version

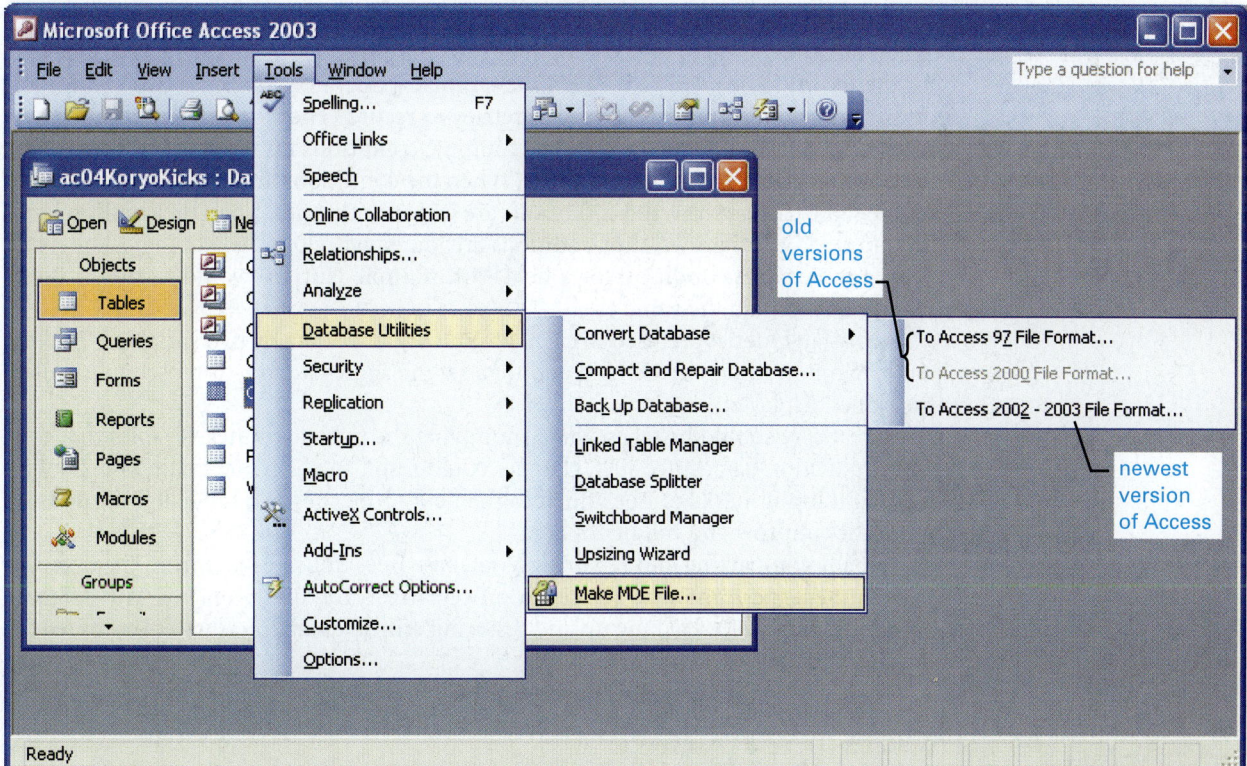

Knowing how and when to convert databases means that you can work on the same database with different versions of Access, making your work more portable.

making the grade

1. Why should you back up a database?

2. How do you decide when to convert a database to a newer version of Access?

3. What happens when you delete a field from a table structure?

4. What is the purpose of Detect and Repair?

5. What are some possible conversion issues when changing a field from single to integer?

SESSION 4.3 SUMMARY

Effective analysis of the data held in a relational database often requires creating queries with complex conditions. Multiple criteria can be applied to one field using the In, Between, and Like conditional operators. The In operator is used to submit a list of match values. The Between operator supplies an upper and lower limit for values that will be retrieved. All records with values between the upper and lower limit—including the limit values—will be retrieved. The Like operator is used to submit a pattern match for a field selection value.

Pattern matches for the Like operator make use of wildcards to state the criteria. The * wildcard is used to represent any number of characters, the ? wildcard is used to represent a single character, and the # wildcard is used to represent a single numeral. The Like operator is designed to work with Text fields and provides haphazard results with other field types.

The And and Or operators provide another way to enter compound conditions. When the And logical operator combines two conditions, both conditions must be true for the record to be retrieved. When the Or logical operator combines two conditions, one or both conditions can be true to retrieve a record. The words And and Or can be entered into Criteria for a field to state multiple conditions for that field or they can be used to join criteria for multiple fields. When the conditions are in different fields and on the same Criteria row, the conditions are joined with And. When the conditions are on different Criteria rows, the conditions are joined with Or. The Not logical operator is used to negate a condition for a field. For example Not =6 would retrieve records that do not contain the value 6.

Crosstab Queries are used to calculate and organize data by two variables. The row and column headings are defined and then set the aggregate function used to calculate the values displayed.

Great care should be taken when modifying the field attributes of tables that contain production data, since such changes could result in permanent data loss. Lookup fields and input masks can be added to the field properties of a table definition. Both properties improve the validity of data.

Finally compacting and repairing a database frees unused space from the database to optimize its performance. The repair process fixes structural problems with database objects. A strategy for backing up and restoring critical databases is necessary to reduce the risk of data loss.

Visit www.mhhe.com/i-series/ to explore related topics.

MICROSOFT OFFICE SPECIALIST
OBJECTIVES SUMMARY

- Creating Lookup fields—MOS AC03S-1-3
- Changing field types—MOS AC03S-1-3
- Changing field properties to display input masks—MOS AC03S-1-4
- Modifying field properties for tables in Table Design View—MOS AC03S-1-4
- Creating Crosstab Queries—MOS AC03S-1-7
- Back up a database—MOS AC03S-4-5
- Using Compact and Repair—MOS AC03S-4-6

making the grade *answers*

SESSION 4.1

1. The Like operator allows you to use wildcards to set a pattern that retrieved data must match. The question mark (?) wildcard replaces one character. The asterisk (*) wildcard replaces a group of characters. The pound sign (#) replaces one numeral. The Like operator is designed to work on Text fields.

2. Placing GME in the Criteria row of the Category field would produce the desired results.

3. Crosstab Queries allow you to perform aggregate functions using two controlling fields represented by the row and column header.

4. The Between operator has two arguments: an upper and lower limit. These arguments specify a range of values to be retrieved that can be any size.

5. A Cartesian product results when the relationship between tables is not defined in the query. To avoid this situation, place all tables involved in the relationship in the query, whether or not their fields will be included in the output.

SESSION 4.2

1. Databases need to be backed up to protect against data loss. Data loss can occur due to user errors like shutting off the computer without properly exiting Access, or computer errors like a drive failure.

2. A database should not be converted if there is still a need to use it in the older version of Access. Convert it if it won't be used in the older version.

3. All data stored in that field are also deleted.

4. Detect and Repair will detect problems with Office software and initiate the steps to repair the problem.

5. Integers store whole numbers that are smaller than Single formats and cannot keep decimals. Loss of any decimal values is certain. There is also a potential for loss of Single values that are larger than Integer format supports.

task reference summary

Task	Page #	Preferred Method
Creating a Crosstab Query	AC 4.13	• Click the **Queries** object in the Database Window, select **Create query by using wizard**, and then click **New** • Select **Crosstab Query Wizard** from the New Query dialog box and then click **OK** • Follow the Wizard's instructions to choose the data source, row heading, column heading, and aggregate functions for the query • Name the query and then view the results
Creating a Lookup field	AC 4.19	• Verify the relationship between the table that will have the Lookup field and the table where the field is being looked up. The most likely relationship is one-to-many, where the child (many sides of the relationship) table will look up the key value of the parent table (one side of the relationship) • Open the child table and change the data type to **Lookup Wizard** • Follow the Lookup Wizard instructions
Creating an input mask	AC 4.21	• Open a table in Design View • Select the field for which you want to define an input mask • From the General tab select the **Input Mask** property and either • Click the **Build** button and follow the Input Mask Wizard instructions (Text and Date fields only) or • Type the input mask definition (Numeric and Currency masks must be entered manually)
Compact and repair the open database	AC 4.25	• On the **Tools menu**, point to **Database Utilities**, and then click **Compact and Repair Database**
Compact and repair an unopened database	AC 4.26	• Access must be running with no open database • On the **Tools** menu, point to **Database Utilities**, and then click **Compact and Repair Database** • In the **Database to Compact From** dialog box, specify the Access file you want to compact, and then click **Compact** • In the **Compact Database Into** dialog box, specify a name, drive, and folder for the compacted Access file • **Click** Save
Setting Automatic Compact and Repair	AC 4.27	• Open the Access database that you want to compact automatically • On the **Tools** menu, click **Options** • Click the **General** tab • Select the **Compact on Close** check box
Setting Detect and Repair for Microsoft Office	AC 4.28	• On the **Help** menu, click **Detect and Repair** • To restore the program shortcuts to the Windows **Start** menu, make sure the **Restore my shortcuts while repairing** check box is selected • Click **Start**
Database backup with Access	AC 4.30	• Open the database to be backed up. All database objects should be closed • From the **File** menu select **Back Up Database** • In the Save Backup As dialog box, indicate the drive, folder, and filename for the backup • Click **Save**

TRUE/FALSE

1. Input masks control how data are displayed to the user after they are entered.

2. When a field is deleted from a table structure, the data it contained are stored in a backup table.

3. The Between operator selects values between an upper and lower limit, including the stated limits.

4. Double quotes are used to enclose selection values for Text data fields.

5. When both conditions need to be true to select records, the conditions are connected with *And*.

6. Crosstab Queries can only Sum data.

FILL-IN

1. The _____ operator would be used to select records containing the values Life, Love, and Death.

2. The value that appears across the top of a Crosstab Query is the _____.

3. The condition that would be used to select values Smith and Smyth is _____.

4. The oldest version of Access to which a current database can be converted is _____.

5. Compact on Close is a property of _____.

6. A _____ field retrieves valid values for a field from a related table.

7. In Datasheet View, data from related tables can be displayed in a _____ by clicking the plus sign before a record.

MULTIPLE CHOICE

1. The * wildcard is used to
   a. match any number of values in a numeric field.
   b. match values between stated limits.
   c. match any number of values in a Text field.
   d. all of the above.

2. The In operator
   a. uses a comma to separate match values.
   b. requires text values to be enclosed in double quotes.
   c. lists multiple values for selection.
   d. all of the above.

3. The condition *Not >= 20* could also be stated
   a. < 20.
   b. >= 20.
   c. Like *20.
   d. none of the above.

4. Tables and databases should be backed up
   a. before major design changes.
   b. on a scheduled basis.
   c. to reduce the risk of data loss.
   d. all of the above.

5. Changing a field's _____ property is one of the design updates that is most likely to destroy data.
   a. Size
   b. Data Type
   c. Default Value
   d. Lookup

review of concepts

REVIEW QUESTIONS

Each of the following topics should be addressed in one to three paragraphs.

1. What should you do if your database begins to behave erratically?

2. When should a snapshot backup be created?

3. What criteria would select records where the JobDescription is manager and the Salary is over 35000?

4. Why would you compact a database into another file?

5. How are Select Queries and Crosstab Queries the same?

6. When is the Table Design View Undo buffer cleared?

7. What are some possible conversion issues when changing a field from single to integer data type? Refer to Help Yourself on page 18 for the Number data type specifications.

CREATE THE QUESTION

For each of the following answers, create the question.

ANSWER	QUESTION
1. Like "C?ndy?"	_____
2. Clicking this allows a field to be used for selection criteria, but does not display in the result	_____
3. Between 7 And 9	_____
4. ?	_____
5. Shutting off your computer without closing Access properly	_____
6. &	_____
7. Both conditions must be true to retrieve records	_____

FACT OR FICTION

For each of the following, determine whether the statement is fact, fiction, or both and present your arguments for that conclusion.

1. It is not necessary to compact and repair a database each time it is used.

2. Not > 10 is the only way to enter this condition.

3. Like "5/##/01" will match all May values in a Date field.

4. Creating copies of databases using Windows Copy is an effective way to back up databases.

5. You should always convert databases to the newest version of Access.

6. AutoNumber fields are always reset when the database is compacted.

7. Changes made to a table's design have no impact on data already stored in the table.

8. Input masks improve data entry by displaying a template for user entry and restricting the type of data accepted in each input position.

practice

1. Merrill Middle School Software Tracking

Merrill Middle School maintains an inventory of its software in an Access database. To date no analysis of the data has been completed. There is no centralized purchasing and no one knows just exactly how much software they have, where it is stored, or what it cost. You have been asked to prepare some queries to help determine what policies should be set about software purchases.

1. Start Access and open the **ac04Merrill.mdb** database
2. Open the Software table and review the data to become familiar with them
3. Create a query in Design View that selects the English software that has been purchased from Learnit Software (LS)
   a. Enter **ENG** in the Criteria row of Category
   b. Enter **LS** in the Criteria row of Vendor (entering an And condition)
   c. Save the query as **LearnIt** (see Figure 4.30)
4. The administration has decided to begin by checking software that is valued at over $500. Since you believe that the bulk of software expense is in the business area, you will create a query for business software valued at over $500
   a. Open a new query in Design View
   b. Add the InventoryValue query to the query design grid and add all of its fields to the Field row of the query
   c. Place **BUS** and **>500** in the Criteria row of the appropriate columns to create an And condition
   d. Run the query
   e. Save the query as **BusOver500**
5. Since the school purchases up to five evaluation copies of each software title, you need to look at software in the other (nonbusiness) categories where there are more than five copies
   a. Open a new query in Design View
   b. Add the InventoryValue query to the query design grid and add all of its fields to the Field row of the query
   c. Place **ENG**, **MTH**, **SYS**, and **SCI** in separate rows of the Category column to create Or conditions
   d. **>5** needs to be entered in each of the corresponding Quantity rows to create an And condition for each Category value
   e. Run the query
   f. Save the query as **NonBus1**
6. There are often multiple ways to accomplish the same task. Here is a second and more efficient way to create the previous query
   a. Open a new query in Design View
   b. Add the InventoryValue query to the query design grid and place all of its fields in the Field row of the query
   c. Place **Not Bus** in the Criteria row of Category (see Figure 4.31)
   d. Place **>5** in the Criteria row of Quantity (creating an And condition with Not Bus)
   e. Run the query. The results should be the same as the previous query
   f. Save the query as **NonBus2**
7. Close the database and Access if you have competed your work

FIGURE 4.30

English software from Learnit

Software Number	Name	Category	Quantity	Price	VendorCode
1693	Kid-Writer	ENG	22	$29.95	LS
5950	Easy English	ENG	10	$29.95	LS
			10	$0.00	

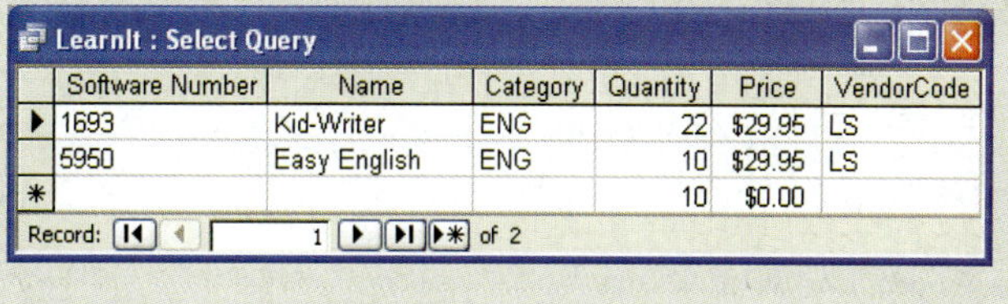

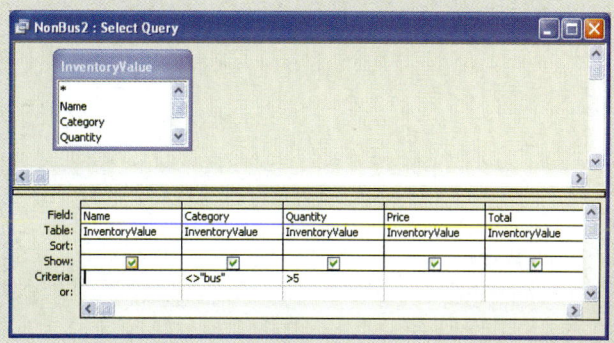

FIGURE 4.31

NonBus2 query

2. Using a Database for Sports Recruiting

Jon Zuccereli is the soccer coach at a small college in the eastern United States. Soccer is a new sport at the school and Jon is the third coach in three years. He believes that he must recruit and retain quality players to survive as a coach. Last year he was able to successfully recruit several players, and both the male and female teams have won more games than they have lost.

This year Jon has developed an Access database to improve his recruiting efforts. He has attended large tournaments across the United States and obtained data files used to track the entrants. The raw data files were imported into his database so that he had a list of all potential recruits. To be considered for admission, students must have a minimum GPA of 3.5. He has researched the players and eliminated all players who are not academically eligible from his database. You will help Jon evaluate the remaining players.

1. Start Access and open **ac04Recruiting.mdb**

2. Open the **Players** table in Datasheet View and review the data

3. Create a query in Design View that selects potential recruits from Michigan, Illinois, and Wisconsin for Jon's next recruiting trip. Include all table fields. Order the output by gender, last name, and first name. Place the sort columns to the left of the other columns. Name the query **NextTrip**

4. Jon saw a player at a midwestern tournament that he is particularly interested in recruiting. Her first name is Caitlin, but Jon is not sure whether it is spelled with a *C* or a *K*. Create a query using wildcards that will help Jon contact this person. Name the query **CaitlinSearch**

5. Jon would like to know how many candidates he has in each state by gender to help him decide where to recruit first. Create a Crosstab Query with Gender in the column headings and State in the row headings. Count ID. Name the query **GenderStateCrosstab** (see Figure 4.32)

6. Jon is paying existing team members to contact potential recruits. He needs several lists for this project. Each list should include the recruit's full name and address

   a. Create a list of female recruits from Michigan. Name the query **MichiganWomen**

   b. Create a list of male recruits from Michigan. Name the query **MichiganMen**

   c. Create a list of female recruits from Oklahoma. Name the query **OklahomaWomen**

7. Set this database to automatically compact and repair

8. If your work is complete, exit Access; otherwise, continue to the next assignment

FIGURE 4.32

GenderStateCrosstab

GenderStateCro...

State	Total Of ID	F	M
CO	1		1
IA	145	69	76
IL	5	3	2
IN	1	1	
MI	312	128	184
MN	1		1
MO	2	1	1
NE	136	52	84
OH	1	1	
OK	266	139	127
WI	22	3	19

Record: 1

challenge!

1. More Queries for Curbside Recycling

Curbside Recycling maintains a database of customers and their recyclable pickups. You have been asked to create some queries to help evaluate their business.

1. Start Access and open **ac04CurbsideRecycling.mdb**

2. Create a query in Design View that joins the Customer table to the Customer Records table. All fields from both tables should be included. Name the query **CustomerDetails**.

3. Run CustomerDetails to observe the resulting 53 records

4. Curbside is considering implementing a minimum pickup weight to improve its profit margin. Management would like to know how many customers have less than 10 pounds of each type of recyclable

   a. Open a new query in Design View using the CustomerDetails query. Include the name, street, address, and weight fields

   b. Add the criteria that will cause the query to retrieve records with less than 10 pounds in both recyclable categories

   c. Save the query as **LowVolumeBothCat**

   d. Alter LowVolumeBothCat to retrieve records with less than 10 pounds in either recyclable category. Save the query as **LowVolumeEitherCat**

5. Curbside employees are concerned about the impacts of repeatedly lifting the recyclables. You have been asked to determine how much each employee lifts per day

   a. Create a query called **TotalWeight** that lists the **CustID, SrvcDate, EmployeeID, WeightPaper, WeightOther**, and **TotalWeight:WeightPaper+WeightOther**

   b. Run the TotalWeight query to observe the result

   c. Use TotalWeight to create a new Crosstab Query with SrvcDate as the row headings and EmployeeID as the column heading. Sum TotalWeight. Save the query as **SumTotalWeightCrosstab** (see Figure 4.33)

   d. Run the SumTotalWeightCrosstab to observe the result

   e. Edit the SumTotalWeightCrosstab in Design View to find the Max value of TotalWeight. Use the **Save As** option of the **File** menu to save the modified query as **MaxTotalWeightCrosstab** (see Figure 4.34)

6. Close the database and Access if you have completed your work

FIGURE 4.33

SumTotalWeightCrosstab

SrvcDate	Total Of TotalWeight	218	382
10/15/2002	13		13
11/22/2002	46	46	
10/14/2003	33	20	13
10/15/2003	422	60	362
11/4/2003	20	20	
11/7/2003	242	148	94
11/14/2003	20	20	
11/15/2003	116		116
11/22/2003	1310	762	548
12/4/2003	286	91	195

Record: 1 of 10

FIGURE 4.34

MaxTotalWeightCrosstab

SrvcDate	Total Of TotalWeight	218	382
10/15/2002	13		13
11/22/2002	23	23	
10/14/2003	20	20	13
10/15/2003	117	20	117
11/4/2003	20	20	
11/7/2003	55	22	55
11/14/2003	20	20	
11/15/2003	58		58
11/22/2003	202	95	202
12/4/2003	39	34	39

Record: 1 of 10

2. Analyzing Texas Lacrosse Data

In Texas, like the rest of the United States, Lacrosse is growing in popularity. A new competitive league is being formed for players with the best skills. A Microsoft Access database table has been loaded with sample data from the three oldest age groups (under 30, under 19, and under 16). You will test the database by creating some useful queries.

1. Start Access and open **ac04Lacrosse.mdb**. Open the **Roster** table and review its contents

2. Coaches for each gender and age group need to be provided with lists of players who can be contacted to join their team. Each list should include full name, address, and phone number

   a. Create a list of potential under-30 players. Order the list by gender, last name, and first name. Name the query **U30**

   b. Create a list of potential male under-19 players. Order the list by last name and first name. Name the query **MU19**

   c. Create a list of potential female under-16 players. Order the list by last name and first name. Name the query **FU16**

3. Use the In operator to create a query that will retrieve potential players from **Irving**, **Ft Worth**, and **Dallas**. Include each person's full name, address, phone number, and gender. Order the output by gender, last name, and first name. Name the query **Area3Players**

4. To help determine the number of coaches and teams necessary, count the number of players grouped by gender and age group. Make gender the column heading and age group the row heading. Name the crosstab **AgeGenderSummary** (see Figure 4.35)

5. Create an input mask for the phone number field. The input display for entering new values should be ____-____-____. All 10 digits are required

6. Set this database to compact and repair automatically

7. If your work is complete, exit Access; otherwise, continue to the next assignment

FIGURE 4.35

AgeGenderSummary query

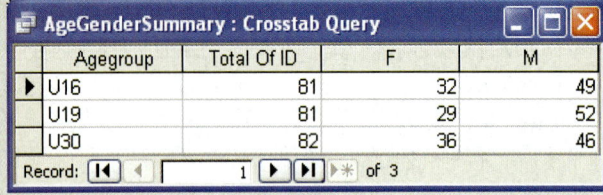

Agegroup	Total Of ID	F	M
U16	81	32	49
U19	81	29	52
U30	82	36	46

1. Tracking Photographs for SportsPix

SportsPix is a digital photography operation that specializes in taking pictures of youth sports teams. Ray Damask and Grace Bishop began photographing sports teams when their nephew was playing soccer at the local YMCA. They shoot individual and team pictures for baseball, softball, soccer, football, volleyball, tennis, and martial arts. Three other photographers pitch in during peak demand periods. On a busy day, they can shoot hundreds of children with their teams, resulting in over 10,000 customers in a year.

Tracking customer receipts is easy since all packages are paid for when the photographs are shot. Customers can preview their pictures on the Web and submit an order for the shots that they want included in their package. The biggest problem is keeping effective records on who is in each photograph, to which team they belong, when the photograph was shot, and where the photograph was shot. You have developed a prototype of a Photographs table that you believe will help Ray and Grace. You have selected some test data from the information that they provided and entered it into the table. Perform the following tests to ensure the effectiveness of this solution.

FIGURE 4.36

FilmID query and DateTimeCrosstab Query

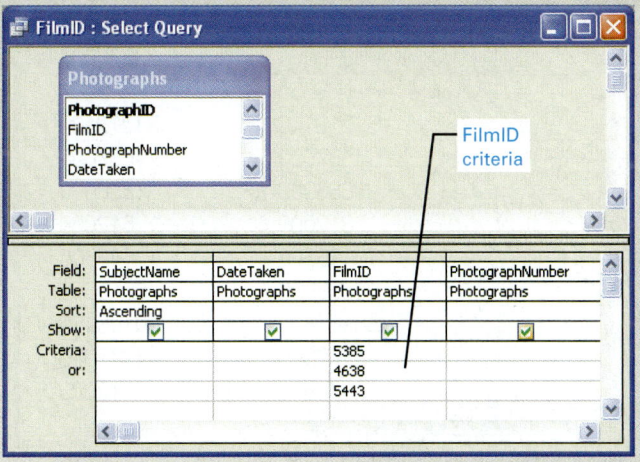

1. Make sure that you have access to the data from your data disk

2. Start Access and open the **ac04SportsPix.mdb** database from your Chapter 4 files

3. Open the **Photographs** table and add records for yourself and two of your friends. You should all be on the same team and have had your pictures taken at the same time and at the same location. Use Film ID **5443** and PhotographerID **1**

4. Create a query that will select all fields for photographs and the photographer's name from 8/14/2003 at 9 AM. Use Team as the primary sort and Subject Name as the secondary sort. Print the results and save the query as **DateTime**

5. Create a query that contains the Subject Name, Date, Film ID, and Photo #. Select records with Film ID values **5385**, **4638**, and **5443**. Sort the query datasheet by Subject Name and print the result (see Figure 4.36). Save the query as **FilmID**. Print the query datasheet

6. Create a query that lists the **Photographer's Name**, **Subject Name**, **Team**, and **Date Taken** where David Hough and Katharine O'Hara were the photographers. Name the query **PhotographersSubjects**

7. Create a query using the Like operator to select players from teams with *long* in the team name. Name the query **LongTeams**

8. Set the database to automatically compact and repair

9. Create a Crosstab Query to document the number of subjects photographed by date and time. Make Date the row header and Time the column header. Use the Count function on Subject Name (see Figure 3.36). Save the query as **DateTimeCrosstab**

10. If your work is complete, exit Access; otherwise, continue to the next assignment

2. Analyzing United States Crops

The United States Department of Agriculture provides access to National Agricultural Statistics from its Web site at www.usda.gov. The available statistics include all crops raised in the United States from 1970 through 2001. Over 99,000 records have been downloaded from this site representing crop production for 1999 through 2001. The downloaded Excel files were edited and then imported into the Crops table. You will be analyzing this data.

1. Open Access and open **ac04USDA.mdb**

2. Open the **Crops** table and review the contents. Close the table

3. Create a query that will select records with the word *red* anywhere in the Practice field. Include all fields in the result. Name the query **RedCrops**

4. Select records from Illinois, Indiana, Ohio, and Michigan. Include all fields in the result. Name the query **InIlOhMiData**

5. Create a query that will select records with the word *dry* anywhere in the Practice field. Include all fields in the result. Name the query **DryCrops**

6. Create a Crosstab Query with State as the row heading and Year as the column heading. Sum the Production value (see Figure 4.37). Name the query **ProductionByStateAndYear**

7. Create a Crosstab Query that reports total Idaho production with Year as the column heading and County as the row heading. Name the query **IdahoCountiesProduction**

8. The data downloaded from the Web site contained formatting errors that caused blanks in the County field. Create a query to retrieve all fields of records with a blank value in County. (*Hint: Null* is the match value for blank fields.) Name the query **BadData**

9. Set this database to automatically compact and repair

10. Close the database and exit Access if your work is complete

FIGURE 4.37

IdahoCountiesProduction Crosstab Query

County	Total Of Production	2000	2001
	42096000		42096000
Ada	4027400	102000	3925400
Bannock	6593000		6593000
Bear Lake	1215000		1215000
Benewah	5615000		5615000
Bingham	68241800		68241800
Blaine	3226000		3226000
Bonner	8000		8000
Bonneville	31212100		31212100
Boundary	4537000		4537000
Butte	3686000		3686000
Camas	812000		812000
Canyon	18915300	371800	18543500
Caribou	16053000		16053000
Cassia	50467600	301200	50166400
Clark	4472000		4472000
Clearwater	2540600	28600	2512000

Record: |◀ ◀ 1 ▶ ▶| ▶* of 51

1. Toy Purchase Statistics by Internet Research Inc.

Internet Research Inc. (IRI) is a statistical evaluation organization specializing in Internet commerce that was introduced in Chapter 2. You are gathering data from the Internet on Web sites that sell toys and using Access to evaluate them.

1. Use a Shopping Bot like www.mysimon.com or a search engine to find at least two sites selling popular toys (www.eToys.com and www.ToysRUs.com are good sites, but there are many others). Select and compare bicycle prices

    a. Determine the price of a model of bike at the first site

    b. Find the price for the same model at the second site

    c. Repeat this process for another bike

2. Add your new research to the data that already exist in the ac04IRI.mdb database Toys table with ToyIDs **500–503**

tip: *If you did this exercise in Chapter 3, use your updated copy of the database renamed ac04IRI.mdb*

3. Sometimes you want to convert data in a table to display with different row and column headings. This can be accomplished with a Crosstab Query

4. Create a new Crosstab Query with the Wizard

    a. Use the **Toys** table as the data source

    b. Make ToyName the row headings and Web site the column headings

    c. Display Price in the cells using the Sum function (since there is only one record per toy/Web site combination, the aggregate function will not do anything, but you must select one anyway)

    d. Click off the check box to include row sums so there is no Total column in the result

    e. Run the query. Your results should resemble those shown in Figure 4.38

    f. Save the Query as **PriceByToyAndSite**. Use the Report Wizard to create a report based on this query. Name the report **Crosstab Report**

5. Create a query in Design View that finds all products with Barbie in the ToyName. Sort the results by ToyName and Price. Save the query as **BarbieProducts**

6. Modify the query from step 5 to retrieve Barbie products that cost under $25. Save the query as **BarbieLT25**

7. Create a query to select toys without *Barbie* in the name at a price of less than $40.00. Name the query **LowPriceNotBarbie**

8. Set this database to automatically compact and repair

9. Close the database and exit Access if your work is complete

F I G U R E 4.38

PriceByToyAndSite Crosstab Query

ToyName	www_etoys_com	www_toysrus_com
Barbie Airplane	$58.99	$59.99
Barbie Family House	$49.28	$58.92
bike1		
bike2		
Celebration Barbie	$37.99	$36.99
Cool Blading Barbie	$22.50	$22.12
Cool Clips Barbie	$15.28	$15.87
Ferrari Barbie	$42.28	$39.99
Game Boy Army Men	$29.95	$32.99
Game Boy Asteroids	$23.32	$24.87
Game Boy Mario Golf	$31.15	$31.99
Game Boy Perfect Dark	$32.50	$59.99
Generation Girl Barbie	$21.64	$21.88
Princess Bride Barbie	$23.38	$22.99

Record: 1 of 17

around the world

1. Tracking the World's Population

Brandon Pryor's middle school class is still working on ways to evaluate the population of the world's largest cities. The students have a pretty good idea of how large these cities are compared to their hometown, but now they need to understand how the cities are related to each other.

1. Open the **Cities** table of the **ac04Populations.mdb** database

tip: *If you did this exercise in Chapter 3, use your up-dated copy of the database renamed to ac04Populations.mdb*

2. Create a query in Design View that will select all records with Korea in the country name. Sort the results by City and save the query as **Korea**

3. Create a query that will select cities with popula-tions between 15 and 35 million. Sort by descend-ing population and name the query **35M**

4. The class is looking for a Middle East city but can-not remember the full name. They believe that it starts with al. Write a query that will help them find the correct city. Save the query as **MiddleEast**

5. Create a query that will select cities in South America (Argentina, Bolivia, Brazil, Chile, Ecuador, Peru, and Venezuela). Sort the results by Country and then City (see Figure 4.39). Save the query as **SouthAmerica**

tip: *The countries have both English and German names displayed, so you will need to match for both or use wildcards*

6. Modify the previous query to select only ABC Powers (Argentina, Brazil, and Chile). ABC Powers are the nations striving to maintain peace in South and Central America. The alliance was formed to protect against aggressive policies of the United States prior to World War II. Save the query as **ABCPowers**

7. Create a query that will select all cities in North America. Sort the result from largest to smallest city. Save the query as **NorthAmerica**

8. With the world's largest population, China also has the greatest number of large cities. Create a query that will select all cities in China and order them by decreasing population. Save the query as **China**

9. Since the database contains the German names for countries as well as the English names, the stu-dents decide to see how large the cities in Germany are. Create a query that will display German cities sorted by ascending population. Save the query as **Germany**

10. Set this database to automatically com-pact and repair

11. Close the database and Access if your work is complete

FIGURE 4.39

SouthAmerica Query

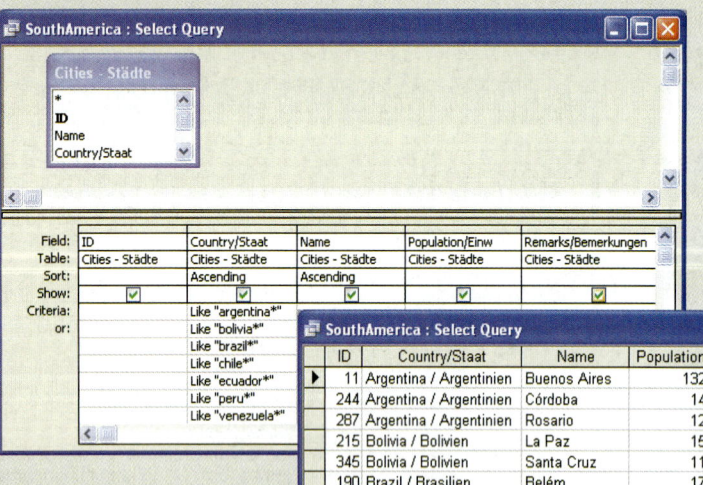

running project: tnt web design

More Analysis of TnT Table Data

The TnT database now consists of three related tables. The tblCustomers table holds the static data about the organization's customers. The CustomerSites table contains the URLs for the sites TnT has built. The CustomerSites table has a Lookup field for the customer name so that you do not have to remember CustomerID values when entering data. TnT's employees are listed in the Employees table. CustomerSites is related to both the Customers table and the Employees table. The employee listed in the CustomerSites table is the one who managed the Web site development project.

1. Start Access and open the **ac04TnT.mdb** database
2. Open each table and review the data
3. Create a query based on the Employees table that will list all of the employees who are either programmers or scripters. Order the data by JobClass, LastName, and FirstName. Save the query as **ContentDevelopers**
4. Modify the previous query to select programmers and scripters who live in Washington (WA) (see Figure 4.40). Save the query as **WAContentDevelopers**

5. There is an employee that you know as Jim, but you are not sure how he has been entered into the database. It could be Jim, Jimmy, or James. Create a query to search for this person. Save the query as **JimSearch**
6. The first six employees of TnT are the project managers. The site table lists the company, the URL, and the employee number of the project manager. Tori wants a table that outlines what companies each project manager has worked with. Create a Crosstab Query using the **CustomerSites** table that displays company name (CustID) as the row header, employee number as the column header, and counts the site number (so that it just displays that number). Do not display a totals column. Save the query as **ProjectManagersCrosstab**
7. Create a report with the previous query as the data source. Display the logo from ac04Tnt.tif in the report header. Save the report as **ProjectManagers**
8. Create a query using data from both Employees and CustomerSites tables. Include **LastName** and **FirstName** from Employees and **CustID** and **URI** from CustomerSites. Name the query **EmployeeSites**. Order the output by Employee Name
9. Set this database up to automatically compact on exit. Document the steps used to accomplish this

FIGURE 4.40

WAContentDevelopers Query

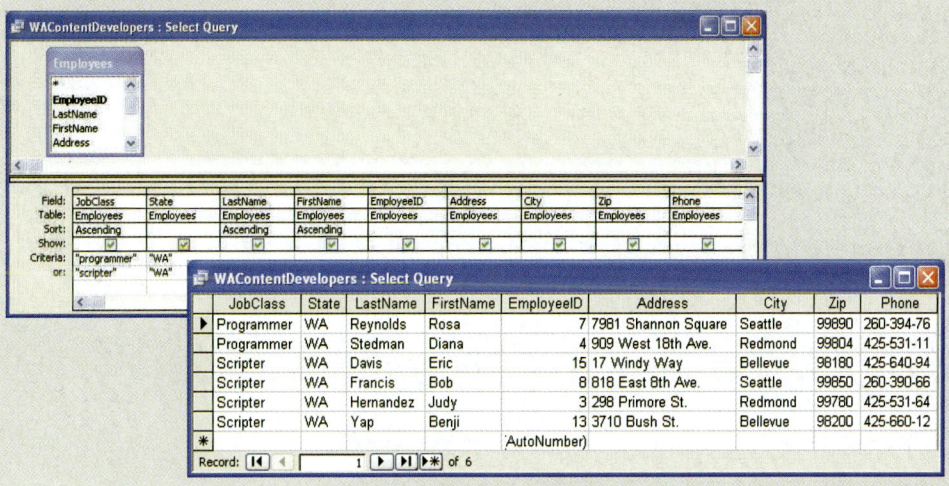

1. Tracking Travel Routes

In many countries public transportation is created by ride sharing rather than the buses, trains, trams, and vans used in the United States. Assume you are in a country where ride sharing is the norm and have decided to start a business that will coordinate ride-sharing activities. You will develop an Access database named **ac04Travel.mdb** to facilitate ride sharing.

The database will need to store information about drivers willing to accept riders such as the number of available seats, trip point of origin, destination, departure date, departure time, and so on. You will also need to store data on riders. Spend time designing this database and then develop the tables. Use destinations in South America or Africa to test your database. Add at least 10 routes with a minimum of two customers each. Build at least one multicondition query such as two or more seats available to a particular destination. Build a Crosstab Query that totals the number of rides available by destination and date.

2. Start a Database Charitable Organization

Design and develop a Microsoft Access database for a small charitable organization such as a local food bank or small church. The database should be named **ac04Charities.mdb** and include data to track services and clients. Include enough data to effectively create queries such as those demonstrated in the chapter. Be sure to document how your database will be used and include at least one query with multiple selection criteria and a Crosstab Query.

reference 1

Access *File Finder*

Location in Chapter	Data File to Use
CHAPTER 1	
Session 1.1	
Opening the Customer database	ac01Customers.mdb
Session 1.2	
Opening the Customer table	ac01Customers.mdb
Hands-on Projects	
Practice Exercise 1	ac01CurbsideRecycling.mdb
Practice Exercise 2	ac01LalierConstruction.mdb
E-Business Exercise 2	ac01DelroyTravel
Around the World Exercise 1	ac01AGC.mdb
Running Project	ac01TnT.mdb
CHAPTER 2	
Session 2.1	
Reorganizing datasheet columns	ac02Customers.mdb
Session 2.2	
Building the Orders table	ac02KoryoKicks.mdb
Populating the Order table	ac02KoryoKicks2.mdb
Hands-on Projects	
Challenge Exercise 2	ac02NewVideoReleases.mdb
E-Business Exercise 2	ac02Calendar.mdb
Running Project	ac01TnT.mdb copied and renamed to AC02<yourname>TnT.mdb
CHAPTER 3	
Session 3.1	
Filtering the Customer table	ac03KoryoKicks.mdb
Session 3.2	
Selecting Software table records	ac03KoryoKicks.mdb
Adding a Graphic to InventoryValueByClass	ac03KoryoKicksLogo.gif

REF 1.1

REFERENCE

Location in Chapter	Data File to Use
Hands-on Projects	
Practice Exercise 1	ac03CurbsideRecycling.mdb ac03Curbside.tif
Practice Exercise 2	ac03BestBakery.mdb ac03Food.jpg
Challenge Exercise 1	ac01LittleWhiteSchoolHouse.mdb or ac03Lwsh.mdb ac03Lwsh.tif
Challenge Exercise 2	ac03Software.mdb ac03Software.gif
E-Business Exercise 1	ac03Cars.mdb ac03ClassicCars.tif
E-Business Exercise 2	ac03GovernorsUniversity.mdb ac03Study.gif
On the Web Exercise 1	ac03IRI.mdb ac03IRI.tif
Around the World Exercise 1	ac03Populations.mdb ac03Globe.gif
Running Project	ac03TnT.mdb ac03TnT.tif
CHAPTER 4	
Session 4.1	
Selecting Customer table records with Between	ac04KoryoKicks.mdb
Session 4.2	
Adding a Memo field to the Customer table	ac04KoryoKicks.mdb
Hands-on Projects	
Practice Exercise 1	ac04Merrill.mdb
Practice Exercise 2	ac04Recruiting.mdb
Challenge Exercise 1	ac04CurbsideRecycling.mdb
Challenge Exercise 2	ac04Lacrosse.mdb
E-Business Exercise 1	ac04SportsPix.mdb
E-Business Exercise 2	ac04USDA.mdb
On the Web Exercise 1	ac04IRI.mdb
Around the World Exercise 1	ac04Populations.mdb
Running Project	ac04TnT.mdb Ac04TnT.tif

reference 2

Microsoft Office Specialist Objective	Task	Session Location	End-of-Chapter Location
CHAPTER 1	**Understanding Relational Databases**		
AC03S-1-1	Starting Access and opening a blank database	1.1	AC 1.35
AC03S-1-2	Using the Create Table Wizard	1.2	AC 1.35
AC03S-1-7	Querying the Customer table	1.2	AC 1.35
AC03S-1-7	Sorting the query results	1.2	AC 1.35
AC03S-1-8	Using AutoForm	1.2	AC 1.35
AC03S-2-2	Opening the Customer table	1.2	AC 1.35
AC03S-4-3	Printing the Customer table's design	1.2	AC 1.35
AC03S-4-3	Printing Forms with data	1.2	AC 1.35
CHAPTER 2	**Maintaining Your Database**		
AC03S-2-1	Finding and replacing values in the Customer table	2.1	AC 2.36
AC03S-2-1	Using wildcards to find Customer table data	2.1	AC 2.36
AC03S-2-1	Adding New Records to the Customer table	2.1	AC 2.36
AC03S-2-1	Deleting a record from the Customer table	2.1	AC 2.36
AC03S-2-1	Using the Office Clipboard with the Customer table	2.1	AC 2.36
AC03S-2-1	Populating the Order table	2.2	AC 2.36
AC03S-3-4	Sorting the Customer table	2.1	AC 2.36
AC03S-3-4	Hiding and unhiding columns of the Customer table	2.1	AC 2.36
AC03S-3-4	Freezing and unfreezing columns of the Customer table	2.1	AC 2.36
AC03S-3-5	Reorganizing datasheet columns	2.1	AC 2.36

Microsoft Office Specialist Objective	Task	Session Location	End-of-Chapter Location
AC03S-3-5	Sorting the Customer table	2.1	AC 2.36
CHAPTER 3	**Introducing Queries, Filters, Forms and Reports**		
AC03S-1-7	Creating a Customer table query	3.1	AC 3.38
AC03S-1-7	Formatting the Customer table query	3.1	AC 3.38
AC03S-1-7	Sorting the Customer table query	3.1	AC 3.38
AC03S-1-7	Selecting Software table records	3.2	AC 3.38
AC03S-1-7	Creating an expression field with the Expression Builder	3.2	AC 3.38
AC03S-1-7	Summarizing grouped data	3.2	AC 3.38
AC03S-1-8	Using the Form Wizard	3.2	AC 3.38
AC03S-1-9	Changing the AutoFormat of the InventoryValue form	3.2	AC 3.38
AC03S-1-10	Using the Report Wizard	3.2	AC 3.38
AC03S-1-10	Changing the AutoFormat of the InventoryValueByClass report	3.2	AC 3.38
AC03S-1-10	Changing the labels of the InventoryValueByClass report	3.2	AC 3.38
AC03S-1-10	Making mailing labels for software venders	3.2	AC 3.38
AC03S-1-10	Adding a graphic to InventoryValueByClass	3.2	AC 3.38
AC03S-3-1	Creating an expression field with the Expression Builder	3.2	AC 3.38
AC03S-3-1	Creating an expression by typing	3.2	AC 3.38
AC03S-3-1	Summarizing selected data with aggregate functions	3.2	AC 3.38
AC03S-3-1	Summarizing grouped data	3.2	AC 3.38
AC03S-3-2	Changing the AutoFormat of the InventoryValue form	3.2	AC 3.38
AC03S-3-6	Filtering the Customer table	3.1	AC 3.38
AC03S-3-6	Excluding records from the Customer table	3.1	AC 3.38
AC03S-3-6	Filtering the Customer table with Filter by Form	3.1	AC 3.38
AC03S-3-6	Filtering the Customer table with an Or condition	3.1	AC 3.38

Microsoft Office Specialist Objective	Task	Session Location	End-of-Chapter Location
AC03S-3-6	Filtering the Customer table with Filter For	3.1	AC 3.38
AC03S-3-6	Filtering the Customer table with Advanced Filter/Sort	3.1	AC 3.38
CHAPTER 4	**Compound Queries and Database Utilities**		
AC03S-1-3	Setting a lookup field for vendors in the Product table	4.2	AC 4.33
AC03S-1-3	Adding a Memo field to the Customer table	4.2	AC 4.33
AC03S-1-4	Deleting a field from the Customer table	4.2	AC 4.33
AC03S-1-4	Moving a field in the Customer table	4.2	AC 4.33
AC03S-1-4	Changing field properties in the Product table	4.2	AC 4.33
AC03S-1-4	Setting an input mask for the OrderData field	4.2	AC 4.33
AC03S-1-7	Selecting Customer table records with Between	4.1	AC 4.33
AC03S-1-7	Selecting Customer table records with In	4.1	AC 4.33
AC03S-1-7	Selecting Customer table records with Like	4.1	AC 4.33
AC03S-1-7	Selecting Customer table records with compound criteria	4.1	AC 4.33
AC03S-1-7	Selecting Customer table records with Not	4.1	AC 4.33
AC03S-1-7	Joining the Order and Customer tables in a query	4.1	AC 4.33
AC03S-1-7	Create a Cartesian product	4.1	AC 4.33
AC03S-1-7	Repairing a Cartesian product	4.1	AC 4.33
AC03S-1-7	Analyzing sales with a Crosstab Query	4.1	AC 4.33
AC03S-4-5	Using Access to backup KoryoKicks	4.2	AC 4.33
AC03S-4-6	Compacting and repairing the KoryoKicks database	4.2	AC 4.33
AC03S-4-6	Compacting and repairing the unopened KoryoKicks database	4.2	AC 4.33
AC03S-4-6	Setting the Automatic Compact and Repair option for KoryoKicks	4.2	AC 4.33

reference 3

Task	Page #	Preferred Method
Opening an Access object	AC 1.19	• Click the type of object that you would like to open in the Database Window's Objects bar • Select the object that you would like to open • Click the **Open** button
Activating Access Wizards	AC 1.24	• Click the object (Queries, Forms, Reports) whose Wizard you would like to access in the Database Window's Objects bar • Click **New** in the Database Window's toolbar • The available Wizards will be listed • Select the Wizard and respond to its questions
Getting help	AC 1.32	• Click in the Type a Question drop-down text box in the Access menu • Type in keywords relevant to your topic. Full sentences are not necessary and do not improve the performance of the search • Press **Enter** • Select from the topics provided or adjust the keywords and search again
Finding specific data values	AC 2.6	• Click in the column that you would like to search • Click the **Find** button • Enter the Find What criteria using the data value that you would like to find. Remember that a question mark (?) can be used as a wildcard for one character and an asterisk (*) is a wildcard for multiple characters • Click the **Find Next** button. If multiple rows match the Find What criteria, you may need to repeat this step until the row you are searching for is found
Office Clipboard: collect items to paste	AC 2.14	• Display the Office Clipboard by selecting **Office Clipboard** from the **Edit** menu • Select the item to be copied • Click the **Copy** or **Cut** button in the Standard toolbar • Continue placing items on the Clipboard (up to 24) until you have collected everything that you need
Office Clipboard: paste collected items	AC 2.14	• Display the Office Clipboard if it is not already present. If the Office Clipboard option of the Edit menu is not available, you are in an application or view that does not support the Office Clipboard • Click or select the area where you want to place items • Do one of the following: • Select the **Paste All** button to paste the entire contents of the Office Clipboard or • Select a Clipboard item and choose **Paste** from its drop-down menu
Office Clipboard: remove items	AC 2.14	When the Clipboard is open • To clear one item, click the arrow next to the item you want to delete and then click **Delete** • To clear all Clipboard contents, click the **Clear All** button • Placing more than 24 items on the Clipboard will replace existing items beginning with the oldest item

REF 3.1

REFERENCE

Task	Page #	Preferred Method
Hiding datasheet columns	AC 2.16	• Open a table, query, or form in Datasheet View • Click the field selector of the column to be hidden • Click **Hide Columns** on the **Format** menu
To unhide a column	AC 2.16	• On the **Format** menu, click **Unhide Columns** • Select the names of the columns that you want to show from the Unhide Columns dialog box
Freezing and unfreezing datasheet columns	AC 2.17	• Open a table, query, or form in Datasheet View • Select the column(s) that you want to freeze or unfreeze • To freeze column(s), select **Freeze Columns** on the **Format** menu • To unfreeze column(s) select **Unfreeze All Columns** on the **Format** menu
Defining a Table field	AC 2.26	• Click **Tables** in the Options bar • Click the **Design View** button on the toolbar • Enter a field name • Select a data type • Define other field attributes as needed
Filter By Selection	AC 3.4	• Open the table in Datasheet View • Select the field and character(s) of the search criteria (see Figure 3.2) • Click the **Filter By Selection** toolbar button to return values matching the selection or • Right-click and choose **Filter Excluding Selection** to filter the selection out of the data • Evaluate the results of the filter • Click **Remove Filter** on the Access toolbar
Filter By Form	AC 3.6	• Open a table in Datasheet View • Click the **Filter By Form** toolbar button • Build the filter criteria by selecting from the drop-down list for a field or typing your own value • Click the **Filter** toolbar button • Review the filtered data to be sure they are what you expected • Work with the filtered data • Click **Remove Filter** on the Access toolbar when you are done
Filter For Input	AC 3.8	• Open a table in Datasheet View • Right-click the field to be filtered • Type the filter criteria in the Filter For text box using wildcards, operators, and values • Press **Enter** to activate the filter • Review the filtered data to be sure they are what you expected • Work with the filtered data • Click **Remove Filter** on the Access toolbar when you are done
Advanced Filter/Sort	AC 3.9	• Open a table in Datasheet View • On the **Records** menu, point to **Filter**, and then click **Advanced Filter/Sort** • Add criteria fields to the design grid • Enter the filter and sort criteria • Click the **Apply Filter** button on the toolbar • Review the filtered data to be sure they are what you expected • Work with the filtered data • Click **Remove Filter** on the Access toolbar when you are done
Saving a filter as a query	AC 3.10	• Display the filter in either the Filter By Form window or the Advanced Filter/Sort window (recall that any filter can be displayed in these windows regardless of how it was created) • Click the **Save As Query** button on the toolbar

Task	Page #	Preferred Method
		• Type a name for the query and click **OK**
		• The new query will appear with the other query objects in the Database Window
Create a Select Query	AC 3.12	• Select the **Queries** object from the Database Window
		• Verify that **Create query in Design View** is selected
		• Click **New** on the toolbar
		• Select the **Design View** button from the New Query dialog box and click **OK**
		• Double-click the name of each table that contains relevant data from the Show Table dialog box
		• Double-click each table field that is to be contained in the query result to place it in the Field row of the design grid. The order of the columns is the order of the output
		• Enter sort criteria in the Sort row of the design grid
		• Enter selections in the Criteria row of the design grid
		• Click the **Datasheet View** button on the toolbar to see the query results
		• Click the **Design View** button on the toolbar to update the query criteria
		• Click the **Save** button to save the query criteria
Create an expression using Expression Builder	AC 3.20	• Click in the Field row of the QBE grid column that will display the calculation
		• Click the **Build** button in the query design toolbar
		• Select expression elements and operators to create the desired calculation
		• Click **OK** to place the calculation in the QBE grid
Modify the format of a form	AC 3.27	• Open the form in Design View
		• Click the **AutoFormat** button in the Form Design toolbar
		• Select from the same formats that were available in the Wizard
Modify the format of a report	AC 3.30	• Open the report in Design View
		• Click the **AutoFormat** button in the Report Design toolbar
		• Select from the same formats that were available in the Wizard
Add a graphic to a report or form	AC 3.35	• Open the report or form in Design View
		• Select the section that is to display the graphic
		• Select **Picture** from the Insert menu
		• Navigate to the folder containing the image and change the file type selector to the image file type
		• Select the file and click **OK**
		• Move and size the image as needed
Creating a Crosstab Query	AC 4.13	• Click the **Queries** object in the Database Window, select **Create query by using wizard**, and then click **New**
		• Select **Crosstab Query Wizard** from the New Query dialog box and then click **OK**
		• Follow the Wizard's instructions to choose the data source, row heading, column heading, and aggregate functions for the query
		• Name the query and then view the results
Creating a Lookup field	AC 4.14	• Verify the relationship between the table that will have the Lookup field and the table where the field is being looked up. The most likely relationship is one-to-many, where the child (many sides of the relationship) table will look up the key value of the parent table (one side of the relationship)
		• Open the child table and change the data type to **Lookup Wizard**
		• Follow the Lookup Wizard instructions

Task	Page #	Preferred Method
Creating an input mask	AC 4.21	• Open a table in Design View • Select the field for which you want to define an input mask • From the General tab select the **Input Mask** property and either • Click the **Build** button and follow the Input Mask Wizard instructions (Text and Date fields only) or • Type the input mask definition (Numeric and Currency masks must be entered manually)
Compact and repair the open database	AC 4.25	• On the **Tools** menu, point to **Database Utilities**, and then click **Compact and Repair Database**
Compact and repair an unopened database	AC 4.26	• Access must be running with no open database • On the **Tools** menu, point to **Database Utilities**, and then click **Compact and Repair Database** • In the **Database to Compact From** dialog box, specify the Access file you want to compact, and then click **Compact** • In the **Compact Database Into** dialog box, specify a name, drive, and folder for the compacted Access file • **Click** Save
Setting Automatic Compact and Repair	AC 4.27	• Open the Access database that you want to compact automatically • On the **Tools** menu, click **Options** • Click the **General** tab • Select the **Compact on Close** check box
Setting Detect and Repair for Microsoft Office	AC 4.28	• On the **Help** menu, click **Detect and Repair** • To restore the program shortcuts to the Windows **Start** menu, make sure the **Restore my shortcuts while repairing** check box is selected • Click **Start**
Database backup with Access	AC 4.30	• Open the database to be backed up. All database objects should be closed • From the **File** menu select **Back Up Database** • In the Save Backup As dialog box, indicate the drive, folder, and filename for the backup • Click **Save**

glossary

Access Window: The main window of the Microsoft Access user interface. Other windows display inside it.

Action queries: Queries that update the data in a database in some fashion; for example, to delete a group of records that meet a criterion, update a group of records, add records to an existing table, or add records to a new table.

Active Server Page: A Web page designed to display up-to-date read-only data. The data are selected by the server and displayed in a table format. Opening or refreshing an ASP file from a Web browser causes the page to be dynamically created from current values and sent to the browser.

Advanced Filter/Sort: The most comprehensive filtering method that presents a grid of the table being filtered and allows you to enter record selection criteria.

Aggregate function: Access predefined calculations used to summarize groups of data (e.g., Sum and Avg).

Alternate keys: A table field that could have been assigned as the primary key but was not.

And: The logical operator that combines two conditions that must both be true to retrieve a record.

Between: The relational operator used to select records whose values fall between the stated upper and lower bounds; for example, between 14 and 18.

Calculated field: A field of a query that contains an expression.

Candidate key: Each table field that could be defined as the primary.

Caption: The table field property that determines what displays as the label for the field in Datasheet and other views.

Client/server databases: DBMSs that are designed to support multiple users in a networked environment.

Compact on Close: The database option that causes a database to automatically compact each time it is closed.

Compacting: The process of removing excess space from a database.

Composite key: The result of multiple attributes being combined for the primary key.

Condition: The method of entering selection criteria using operators such as >, <, >=, <=, and <>.

Crosstab Queries: Queries that are used to analyze data by grouping data and calculating values for each group.

Crosstab Query: A query format that allows data to be tabulated by two variables: a row header and a column header.

Data access language (DAL): RDBMS language for rapidly retrieving and organizing stored data. SQL is the standard.

Data access pages: Web pages that allow a Web browser to be used to view and update table data via a live connection to the data in your database.

Data definition language (DDL): The language provided by RDBMS for structuring the data tables and their relationships.

Data integrity: A term used to describe the reliability of data.

Data redundancy: Storing the same data such as a customer's last name multiple times. Redundant data increase the likelihood that data will not be updated properly in all locations and so reduce data integrity.

Data Type: The table field property that determines what type of data it can store and how much storage space it will require.

Data validation rules: Rules that verify data entered are within appropriate bounds. For example, Gender should contain only M for male or F for female.

Data value: The intersection of a table row and column containing data pertaining to one attribute of one entity.

Database: A file that organizes Access objects (tables, queries, forms, reports, and so on) that are related to each other.

Database management system (DBMS): The software used to store data, maintain those data, and provide easy access to stored data.

Database Window: The window displaying an open Access file.

Datasheet View: The default grid layout used to display Access table data.

Default Value: The table field property that determines the value that will automatically be loaded for the field in a new record. The user can overtype the default value.

Design grid: The form used to specify fields and criteria in a query.

Design View: The view of an object that is used to change the structure of the object.

Detect and Repair: A facility to detect and repair problems with Office software.

Domain: All valid entries for one table attribute (column).

Entity: A person, place, object, idea, or event about which data are being collected.

Expression Builder: A tool for building expressions by selecting fields from tables, operators, and other calculation components.

Field: A table column representing a unique property of an entity such as LastName, BirthDate, or Quantity; it can also be referred to as an attribute.

Field list: The listing of fields for a table used to select fields to be included in a query.

Field Name: The attribute of a table field that identifies it and is used to refer to it in queries, forms, reports, and modules.

Field selector: The button containing the field name that can be used to select an entire column of a datasheet.

Field Size: The table field property that determines the maximum value that the field can store, how much space is required to store it, and how fast it can be processed.

Filter by Form: A method of filtering or selecting records using an empty version of the current datasheet where you can type match values.

Filter by Selection: The simplest type of filter, which selects records that match the datasheet value you have selected.

Filter Excluding Selection: A method of selecting records that do not meet the stated criteria.

Filter for Input: A filter initiated from the pop-up menu that provides a text box for entering record selection criteria.

Foreign key: The value used to match the attributes from one table to those in another table.

Form: A user-friendly way to view and update data on a computer screen.

Form View: The view used to manipulate data in a form.

Form Wizard: An Access Wizard that walks you through the process of building a form by selecting fields from multiple tables and queries.

Format: The field property of a table definition that controls how data display to the user after they have been entered.

Freezing columns: Keeping the leftmost columns of a datasheet on the screen when scrolling through columns to the right. The leftmost columns would scroll off of the screen if they were not frozen.

Group by: Option used to set a field or fields that will be used to calculate subtotals.

Groups bar: A bar in the Access Database window to allow users to group database objects for easier manipulation.

In: The relational operator used to select records whose values match those listed; for example, In ("CO", "IN", "CA").

Index: Used to speed data access and sorting by allowing direct access to a specific value. Works like the index of a book.

Indexed: The field property of a table definition that determines whether or not this field indexes the table.

Input mask: The table field property used to create a template displayed to the user for data entry and controlling the data that can be entered.

Joining: The process of using a foreign key from one table to link to the data in another table.

Like: The relational operator used to select records using wild cards (*, ?, #).

Lookup field: A tool to ease data entry by listing valid values from a related table. Lookup fields are created using a Wizard in table Design View.

Macros: Used to automate repetitive database tasks using a series of *actions;* a self-contained instruction or command.

Many-to-many: A table relationship that exists when one row in the first table matches with multiple rows in the second table and one row in the second table matches with multiple rows in the first table. Many-to-many relationships can't be directly modeled in relational databases but are broken into multiple one-to-many relationships. (abbreviated M:N or $\infty:\infty$)

Module: A collection of Visual Basic statements and procedures that are organized and stored together to be accessed as a unit.

Not: The logical operator that negates the condition that it precedes.

Object: Virtually anything—traditional data, a moving image, people talking, a photograph, narrative, text, music, or any combination.

Objects bar: A bar displaying icons in the Access Database window for each of the objects that can be created for a database.

One-to-many: The table relationship that exists when one row of the first table matches to multiple rows in the second table. (abbreviated 1:M or 1:∞)

One-to-one: The table relationship that exists when one row of the first table matches to one and only one row of the second table and both tables have the same primary key. (abbreviated 1:1)

Optimizing: A series of performance-enhancing operations that will result in a more efficient database.

Or: The logical operator that combines two conditions when either one or both of the conditions can be true to retrieve a record.

Parameter query: A query that prompts the user for criteria that will be used in selecting data from the database.

Personal databases: Systems like Microsoft Access that work best in single-user environments.

Primary key: A table field or fields that uniquely and minimally identify an entity.

Primary sort: The first field that is used to order rows of data.

Query: Questions that are posed to a relational database using structured query language (SQL).

Record: One row in a relation (table) representing the unique data for one entity (person, place, object, idea, or event); also referred to as a tuple.

Record selector: The buttons to the left of records in Datasheet View used to select a row.

Relational database: A collection of data relations defined using related tables.

Relational database management systems (RDBMS): A type of DBMS that stores data in interrelated tables. Tables are related by sharing a common field.

Relational operator: The operators (>, <, >=, <=, <>) used to set conditions in queries.

Repair: The process of fixing errors in the structure of database objects.

Report: RDBMS object used to format data for printing.

Required: The table field property that determines whether or not the user must enter a value in this field.

Secondary sort: The second field that is used to order rows of data.

Select Queries: The most common type of query used to retrieve (select) data from one or more tables.

Sort Ascending: Toolbar button used to cause an ascending sort based on the selected column(s).

Sort Descending: Toolbar button used to cause a descending sort based on the selected column(s).

Static HTML: Web pages used to publish a snapshot of the data, which have to be manually updated.

Structured Query Language (SQL): The language used to pose questions or queries to a relational database, which has been standardized by the American National Standards Institute (ANSI).

Subdatasheet: A small datasheet that presents over the main datasheet to display related data. Activated by clicking the plus (+) sign on the main datasheet.

Table: Rows and columns used to store data in a relational database management system.

Validation: The table field property that contains the rule or rules that govern what data are acceptable for that field of a table.

Wizards: Provide the user with step-by-step instructions on common tasks such as creating simple queries, forms, and reports.

Zoom box: An enlarged area for entering long expressions activated by pressing Ctrl+F2.

index